A History of Music in the British Isles

Volume 1

Other books from The Letterworth Press
by Laurence Bristow-Smith

The second volume of
A History of Music in the British Isles:
Empire and Afterwards

and

Harold Nicolson: Half-an-Eye on History

A History of Music in the British Isles

Volume 1

From Monks to Merchants

Laurence Bristow-Smith

The Letterworth Press

Published in Switzerland by the Letterworth Press
http://www.TheLetterworthPress.org

Printed by Ingram Spark

ISBN 978-2-9700654-6-3

1 3 5 7 9 8 6 4 2

To

Peter Winnington

editor and friend for forty years

Contents

Acknowledgements

First and foremost, I want to pay tribute to Peter Winnington for his tireless editing of the text and his tolerance of my erratic and often idiosyncratic typing. My wife Jennifer suffered repeated exposure to the works of obscure composers in the name of research and then had to listen to me working out my ideas. A number of those ideas had their origins in musical conversations with my friend Adrian Abbott, sometimes in the pubs of Victoria and Marylebone, sometimes in hotel bars as far away as Athens and Ankara. Nigel Gibson gave invaluable help about the technical aspects of Church of England doctrine and terminology. Elizabeth Bates kindly allowed me to borrow her fascinating collection of papers relating to her father, Cuthbert Bates, and the Tudor Singers. Stan Calder read great chunks of manuscript and claimed to have enjoyed it. Brian Smith at the Shetland Museum was very helpful tracking down information about John Glass. Stephen Pern and Damian Leeson also read and commented on some of the early chapters. And there have, of course, been many other people who have given assistance along the way, helping me find references or recordings or just pointing me in the right direction.

Extracts from *Music and Monarchy* by David Starkey, published by BBC Books, are reproduced by permission of The Random House Group Ltd.

Quotations from J. J. Scarisbrick's *Henry VIII* are reproduced by permission of Yale University Press.

Lawrence & Wishart kindly gave permission to use quotations from Ernst Meyer's *History of English Chamber Music.*

The University of Illinois Press gave permission to use the extracts from *Women Making Music: The Western Tradition, 1150–1950* by Jane Bowers and Judith Tick.

The quotation from Jeffrey Howard Denton's *English Royal Chapels 1100–1300* is reproduced by permission of Manchester University Press.

Dr Tim Rishton kindly allowed me to quote from his article 'William Smethergell, Organist' published in the *Musical Times.*

David Whitwell kindly gave me permission to quote from his essays.

I am grateful to Isobel Preece and CORO for permission to quote from the CD-liner notes to The Sixteen, *Robert Carver*, CORO COR16051.

Hyperion Records generously gave permission to quote from Davitt Moroney's CD-liner notes to *William Byrd, the Complete Keyboard Music*, Hyperion, CDA66551/7; and from Andrew Carwood's notes to *William Byrd, Assumpta est Maria*, The Cardinall's Musick, Hyperion, CDA 67675.

Simon O'Dwyer and Maria Cullen O'Dwyer kindly gave permission for me to quote from the Ancient Music Ireland website.

The Guardian gave permission to quote from Vanessa Thorpe's 2011 article on *The Tempest*.

Cambridge University Press gave permission to use a short quotation from Ernest Newman's *Life of Richard Wagner*.

Preface to Volume 1 of *A History of Music in the British Isles*

These two volumes – *From Monks to Merchants* and *Empire and Afterwards* – tell the story of music in the British Isles and how we got to where we are today.

I have spent much of my life living outside Britain, in places as distant and diverse as Norway, Italy, Morocco, Taiwan and China; so that when, in 2011, I finally stopped travelling and returned to Britain with the firm intention of staying here for good, I felt the need to reconnect with my own culture. For me, the obvious way to do this was through music, for while words have been my discipline, music has been my passion – ever since, as a twelve-year-old, I played trombone in the Kent Youth Orchestra. I became addicted to Radio 3. From our home in Kirkcudbright in South-West Scotland, my wife Jennifer and I drove across to concerts at the Sage in Gateshead and down to Hereford and Gloucester for the Three Choirs Festival. When in London, I went to the Proms, the Barbican and the Wigmore Hall. I read books on Tallis, Purcell and Handel, on Stanford, Elgar and Bax, on Finzi, Britten and Tippett. Then I decided that what I really needed was a narrative history of British musical life that would fit all the pieces together. I could not find one. The nearest thing was Percy Young's *History of British Music,* published in 1967; but even that was not quite what I was looking for.

I wanted a broad narrative that told the story of music in Britain – the composers and their lives, their music and the way it evolved over the centuries – and also set that story against the background of social, political, technical and technological change. I wanted a book that could be useful to the musically-minded and musically-informed, and would also appeal to lay readers, those who love music but do not play it and cannot face a succession of musical examples on the page.

So I have written the book I wanted to read. Researching and writing has taken five years. There has been a vast amount of material to be absorbed – books, internet sources, CD-liner notes, lectures, radio programmes. I have listened to a vast amount of music. The demands of space have required a rigorous selection process, and even then the narrative has stretched to two volumes. There is much that, under other circumstances, I would have liked to examine in more depth and at greater length. I have mentioned as many as I could of those works that seem to me to have had a significant impact on the development of music in Britain, or that the reader may hear on the radio or find on a concert programme. Where I offer any kind of detailed description or assessment of a work, it means (with, I think, only one exception) that I have listened to the piece – often more than once. Where that has not been possible, I have drawn on contemporary criticism or on whatever critical consensus has built up over the years.

All the selections, omissions, judgements, and any errors of fact or interpretation are mine.

Writing anything about the British Isles is complicated from the beginning by questions of terminology. I am well aware – as Norman Davies points out in his study, *The Isles* – that 'Great Britain' refers to the island that includes modern-day England, Scotland and Wales; that Ireland is Ireland; and that together they form the British Isles. Technically, therefore, the adjective 'British' refers only to Great Britain. Simply for stylistic reasons – to avoid repeatedly saying 'of the British Isles' and 'in the British Isles' – I have used 'Britain' and 'British' to refer to the whole of the British Isles. Where there is a distinction to be drawn between Great Britain and Ireland, I hope it will be clear in the text.

These niceties are further complicated by the inexcusable habit of many writers, commentators and politicians of saying 'English' when they mean 'British' or even 'of the United Kingdom'. I hope any problems that arise are clarified by the context or by my comments.

Different types and styles of music have to be described and classified in one way or another. Broadly speaking, there is the 'classical' tradition and the 'popular' tradition – with 'light' music coming somewhere in between. The classical tradition includes, and was for a long time dominated by, church music. Over the years, the terms 'serious' and 'art' music have also come to be used, usually in relation to secular classical music. The 'popular' tradition was for many centuries synonymous with the 'folk' tradition, but, with the passing of time, it began to subdivide to include glees and the whole range of songs and dances that are evidently not part of the classical tradition – from the music of the pleasure gardens and the music halls to songs from stage musicals and films, to jazz and dance-band music, right down to the pop and rock of the late-twentieth century. Such categories are helpful to the critic or the historian who is trying to generalise or draw meaning from a broad spectrum of musical and cultural activity, but they should not be seen as in any sense rigid. Some incidental music for the theatre, for example, clearly derives from and belongs to the classical tradition, whereas some of it is closer to light or even popular music; and different commentators will draw the dividing line in different places. Music is too flexible an art, too open to interpretation, for classification to be inflexible. Once more, I hope that context will clarify any issues that arise.

I have concentrated on the classical tradition, but not to the exclusion of folk and popular music, which remain essential parts of the story. In part, this is simply because, up until the beginning of the nineteenth century, the classical tradition was far better documented. More important, however, is the fact that only in the latter part of the eighteenth century did social change stimulate the democratisation of music. Once that process was under way, popular music became more varied and diverse and began to exercise an ever-greater cultural influence in all areas of the British Isles. Popular music, therefore, features more strongly in Volume Two.

In the arts, each new generation builds on or reacts against the work and achievements of its predecessors. A book such as this, which spans the centuries, must pay attention to the nature of that progression and set the music of each age in its longer-term context. I have used terms such as 'conservative' and 'progressive', 'forward looking' and 'backward looking' in order to position individual works and the styles of individual composers in relation to what had gone before or what was going on elsewhere in the musical world at the time. These terms should be taken as descriptive rather than judgemental.

I chose the title, 'A History of Music in the British Isles', both to avoid being drawn into the debate about what constitutes British music or a British composer, and because it seems to me that non-British factors have been fundamental from the beginning. The majority of the composers whose lives and works are considered in this study were born, lived and worked in Britain. Some – Handel, Carl Friedrich Abel, Johann Christian Bach – were born in Germany but spent most of their working lives in Britain. Percy Grainger was born in Australia and, although he lived to be seventy-nine, spent only thirteen years living in Britain. Others – William Vincent

Wallace, Cecil Sharp, A. L. Lloyd – spent considerable parts of their lives working in Australia. The story could not be told without including them. Nor could it be told without considering the role of composers such as Mendelssohn, Grieg, Dvořák and Sibelius, who only visited but nonetheless exercised considerable influence on British tastes and British music. And the same must be said of the many American singers, entertainers and composers who became popular in Britain during the twentieth century: Fred Astaire, Ginger Rogers, Bing Crosby, Doris Day, Cole Porter, Rodgers and Hart, Bill Haley, Bob Dylan.

To some, the idea of writing a history of music of a particular country or region may seem odd or even offensive. I have actually been told that this book will stimulate chauvinism; that it runs counter to the spirit of music, which should transcend national boundaries and national consciousness. Obviously, I do not agree. The British Isles and the nations that grew up within them have their own cultures. Their music is their own; and their response to music is their own. I am not offering any social or political message, nor yet indulging in any special pleading. I am simply telling a story.

Laurence Bristow-Smith
Glenholme, Kirkcudbright
2017

1 Very Early Music

In 2003, archaeologists working on the site of a new housing estate at Greystones in County Wicklow uncovered six pipes carved from yew wood. They were all different lengths and had no holes or perforations, but they clearly formed a set and had clearly been attached to something, though that something had not survived. Experiments showed that, when blown, the three least-damaged pipes produced the notes of E flat, A flat and F natural; and experts now think that the Wicklow Pipes, as they have become known, may have formed a set of panpipes or part of a very early pipe-organ. The remains have been dated to *c.*2000 BC, making them the oldest wooden instrument ever discovered. So we know that even then the inhabitants of the British Isles were capable of making and playing relatively sophisticated musical instruments.[1]

This should not come as a surprise. Music is a human universal. No culture has yet been discovered which did not have some form of music, produced by the human voice or by those specialised tools which we now call instruments. Chinese mythology holds that music, and much else, originated with Huang Di, the Yellow Emperor, who is supposed to have ruled for a hundred years from 2697 to 2597 BC. Huang Di sent Ling Lun, a scholar and court official, into the western mountains with orders to cut bamboo pipes that would imitate the call of the Fenghuang, a strange, immortal bird, believed to be the bringer of classical harmony. The Emperor then cast five bells to ring in tune with the flutes in the hope that their music would spread harmony throughout his domain. In Mesopotamia, between 2500 and 2000 BC, the Sumerians were not only playing music but developing the first form of musical notation. Ancient Greece was full of music: it featured at weddings and funerals, during religious ceremonies and on important political occasions; it was an essential accompaniment to the reciting of poetry and to theatrical productions. Percussion, wind and stringed instruments were common to all these cultures, and in each case music seems to have fulfilled a broadly similar function within society. It was heard at official and formal social occasions and it accompanied artistic performances of various kinds. In both China and Ancient Greece, we have evidence of folk songs as well as more formal music – in China, they were considered sufficiently important to be performed at the Emperor's court – and of love songs, which were sung or recited to music. But, as far as one can judge from the available evidence, the use of music as a vehicle for the expression of individual emotions or a personal point of view seems to have been very much a secondary function. Music's principal purpose was to serve society.

The Wicklow Pipes belonged to the people of the Early Bronze Age, which is usually dated between *c.*2300 and 1500 BC. They herded livestock and could work gold, but we can only guess how music fitted into their society. With the people of the Middle and Late Bronze Age we are on slightly firmer ground. We know at least that they were capable of casting and welding bronze instruments of great beauty and sophistication. Ireland offers much archaeological evidence – presumably because the population there was neither reorganised under Roman occupation, nor displaced by Anglo-Saxon invasion and settlement. Simon O'Dwyer, who has spent many years researching ancient Irish instruments, has shown how certain kinds of Bronze Age horn, originating about 1500 BC, remained in use until about 700 BC. Over such a long period, their design and method of manufacture would presumably have evolved, but, taken as a whole, O'Dwyer sees them as representing 'the largest surviving family of pre-Renaissance musical instruments in Europe.'[2]

One hundred and four such horns have survived, and there are reports of another ten that were discovered and have since gone missing.[3] They come in widely differing shapes and sizes. Many of the smaller examples, like the one found at the bottom of a well in Battle in East Sussex at the beginning of the nineteenth century, have a simple, curved shape, not unlike the traditional idea of a hunting horn. Some were end-blown in what we would regard as the normal manner; others were sounded through an aperture at the side. There is no direct evidence, but it is a fair assumption that such instruments would have been used in war, for tribal celebrations, and for ritual ceremonies.

The first inhabitants of the British Isles whose musical life we can reconstruct – albeit to a limited extent – are the Iron Age Celtic peoples who swept in waves across Europe and across what is today called the English Channel, between the ninth and first centuries BC. They were warlike, tribal peoples, given to coalescing into loose federations or kingdoms.

They had their tribal leaders, warlords and kings, but their religious and cultural life was controlled by their priests, the Druids. Some European Druids were literate in Greek, Latin and even Etruscan, but the Druids of the British Isles, whether literate or not, apparently banned writing in order to keep the mysteries of their race and religion to themselves.[4] As a result, the few written records that are available come from non-Celtic sources, and are condescending, disdainful or simply hostile. In 54 BC, when Cicero suggested that one could not expect to find anyone in Britain educated in music or the arts,[5] his opinion simply reflected the prevailing attitude towards a people that the Romans regarded as barbarians. He had never been to Britain and was basing his views on letters from other, equally prejudiced, Roman correspondents, including Julius Caesar.

The Celts were undoubtedly a musical people, but the precise nature of their music is a matter for speculation. Polybius, the Greek historian who lived from *c.*200 to 118 BC, suggests that at the Battle of Telamon in 225 BC, the Romans were 'terrified by the excellent order of the Celtic host and the dreadful noise, for there were innumerable horn-blowers and trumpeters, and ... the entire army was shouting its war-cries at the same time.'[6] That was in Italy, but horns and trumpets were evidently important to the Celts of the British Isles, too.

The Celts who reached Britain and Ireland about 500 BC quickly established the dominance of their civilisation. The existing proto-Celtic, Bronze Age population was either swept aside or assimilated, but there was some cultural continuity, and it appears to have included musical instruments. Again, Ireland provides most of the evidence, including a number of instruments which are impressive in both size and technical complexity. In 1837, four pipes made of yew wood and held together by copper rivets were found in a bog near Killyfaddy in County Tyrone. They date from *c.*300 BC and probably fitted together to form a wooden horn, or *trompa*, approaching three metres in length, bound with bronze and perhaps fitted with a bronze bell.[7] Four *trompa* were discovered in 1794 at the famous site of Navan Fort (Old Irish *Emain Macha*) in County Armagh, which spans both the Bronze Age and Celtic periods. Three have since disappeared, but the one that survives – the Loughnashade *trompa* – is spectacular. Dating from the first century BC, it consists of two curved bronze tubes which fit together to form a two-metre-long horn with a flat, decorated, bronze disk round the bell. The bronze has been so delicately worked – to a thickness of half a millimetre – that the instrument weighs only one kilo. The two sections were probably fitted together to form an S-shaped instrument which could be held upright above the head of the player or marching warrior. Reproductions of the Loughnashade *trompa* have been found to produce an E flat harmonic series and 'a powerful (shockwave) tone … which is further amplified and projected by the circular plate creating a blast of powerful sound … very out of proportion to the size of the tube … very valuable to *trompa* players leading an advancing army into battle.'[8]

One particular variety of *trompa* that has attracted much attention is the carynx (also spelled *carnyx*). This consists of a number of bronze sections which, when assembled, reach up to three metres in length and are topped by an elaborately fashioned boar's head. That it was held upright and played vertically is known from an illustration on the famous Gundestrup Cauldron, which was found in north-eastern Jutland at the end of the nineteenth century and has been dated to between 300 and 200 bc. One panel of the cauldron shows Celtic warriors undergoing some kind of initiation ceremony while a group of carynx players provides musical accompaniment. One of the first carynxes to be discovered was unearthed at Deskford in Banffshire, in north-eastern Scotland, in 1816. It has been dated to between 80 and 300 AD and the site evidently had some kind of ritual significance, again suggesting that the instrument was used in religious or votive ceremonies, perhaps before battle. Only nine other carynxes have survived; no fewer than five of them (four with boars' heads and one in the form of a serpent), were found together in the Limousin in 2004, appearing to confirm the implication of the Gundestrup Cauldron that carynxes were often played together. The noise, to judge from modern reconstructions, would have been booming, raucous, and very loud.

Besides horns (which probably attract a disproportionate amount of attention because, being made of metal, a good number have survived) the Celts had a range of other instruments. They had flutes – meaning, in this context, tube-shaped, end-blown instruments, more like recorders or whistles than the modern transverse-blown flute – made of wood or bone and perhaps of terracotta. They also had a range of drums and other percussion. The bodhrán is much favoured these days by Irish folk musicians. Its simplicity – a skin stretched over a circular wooden frame with two crossed struts strengthening the structure and acting as a grip for the player – suggests a long history, although the name does not appear before the seventeenth century. A similar instrument, the crowdy-crawn found in Cornwall, may indicate a shared Celtic origin, but drums of similar construction have a wide currency throughout the Mediterranean Basin and the Middle East. There was also a percussion instrument called a crotal – a hollow, pear-shaped, bronze casting with a ring at the top. Crotals, or something like them, were found in many early civilisations. Most of the examples from the British Isles were discovered in a single, late-Bronze-Age hoard in County Offaly in central Ireland. With a piece of metal or a pebble trapped inside, crotals may have been shaken like maracas as rhythmical accompaniment, or they may have been attached to a belt or harness so that they sounded during dancing in the manner of Morris bells.

Away from a martial or formal ceremonial context, however, the most important instrument in Celtic culture – at least until the arrival of the harp some centuries later – was undoubtedly the lyre. Lyres or something like them are known to have existed in Mesopotamia as far back as 2500 BC, and they were, of course, widely used in Ancient Greece, but they clearly have a long history in the British Isles as well. In 2012, archaeologists excavating a Celtic site at High Pasture Cave, near Torrin in the southern part of Skye, discovered what appears to be part of the bridge of a lyre, dating back to *c.*300 BC – which makes it the oldest stringed instrument ever discovered in Western Europe.[9] The Celtic lyre came in different shapes and quite probably evolved over the centuries; it had different names – the crotta or chrotta or cruit; and they were all plucked or strummed, not played with a bow (although a bowed variety, the crwth, did evolve in Wales in the tenth or eleventh century).[10] A striking statue of a seated Celtic figure with a seven-stringed lyre, discovered in central Brittany and dating from the second century BC – the so-called Lyre de Paule – gives a good idea what one looked like. So, too, do images on coins from the mid-first century BC unearthed in Sussex, although these appear to have fewer strings.

The Greek historian Diodorus Siculus wrote his *Bibliotheca historia* about the time the Sussex coins were minted. Having given a description of Britain, he goes on to describe the Celts of Gaul. They

> have sharp wits and are not without cleverness at learning. Among them are also to be found lyric poets whom they call Bards. These men sing to the accompaniment of instruments which are like lyres, and their songs may be either of praise or of obloquy. Philosophers, as we may call them, and men learned in religious affairs are unusually honoured among them and are called by them Druids. The Gauls likewise make use of diviners,

> accounting them worthy of high approbation, and these men foretell the future by means of the flight or cries of birds and of the slaughter of sacred animals.[11]

Four centuries later, the Roman historian, Ammianus Marcellinus, again describing the Celts in Gaul, wrote that

> Throughout these regions, men gradually grew civilised and the study of the liberal arts flourished, initiated by the Bards, the Euhages and the Druids. Now, the Bards sang to the sweet strains of the lyre the valorous deeds of famous men composed in heroic verse, but the Euhages, investigating the sublime, attempted to explain the secret laws of nature. The Druids, being loftier than the rest in intellect, and bound together in fraternal organisations, as the authority of Pythagoras determined, were elevated by their investigation of obscure and profound subjects, and scorning all things human, pronounced the soul immortal.[12]

Both writers indicate that the bards sang their poetry to the music of the lyre; and both indicate a close association, which was later to become a conflation of roles, between Druids, *euhages* (defined in French as a Celtic prophet and student of astronomy and divination) and bards.

It is impossible to draw any definite conclusions from this, but we can speculate that what we see here is a very early glimpse of that shadowy, undefined relationship between music, poetry, nature, mysticism and religion which has risen to the surface at various stages in the history of British music. It is there in the music of the great Tudor masters, in Purcell, in the music of the Celtic Revival, in early-twentieth-century English pastoral, in some predominantly Celtic folk and folk-rock music, even in some of the symphonic rock of the 1970s. It manifests itself as a sense of transcendental longing, of yearning, which, while not unique to British music, is certainly a recurrent characteristic, and may perhaps have its distant origins in the role of music in early Celtic society.

2 Romans, Druids, and Bards

During the four hundred years between Diodorus and Ammianus, a large part of Britain was invaded and occupied by the Romans. Ireland was uninvaded, unoccupied and – despite trading and diplomatic contacts based on fort settlements, such as Drumanagh on the east coast – largely unaffected by Rome. North of the line of Hadrian's Wall, in what later became Scotland and Northumberland, Pictish tribes skirmished with the Romans or traded with them, but remained largely uninfluenced by Roman culture.[1] South of Hadrian's Wall, the years of conquest were violent and divisive. Initially, the number of Romans living in the occupied portion of Britain was comparatively small, but the occupation lasted three hundred years and gradually, as the country was pacified, their numbers grew. Roman families established themselves as landowners and farmers. There was intermarriage with the local population, and many Celts working in the towns or on Roman estates became assimilated, living an essentially Roman way of life. By the fourth century AD, Roman Britain was stable and prosperous. A rich and landed elite had built themselves large country villas with elaborate furnishings, underfloor heating, mosaic floors, and painted walls. They enjoyed a standard of living and a quality of life which was probably not seen again until the time of Tudor squires or Georgian country gentry. It is hard to imagine that music did not play a significant part in their lives.

No doubt when Julius Caesar's forces raided the south-east shores of what is now England in 55 and 54 BC, and when the Emperor Claudius' invasion fleet landed in 43 AD, there was much braying of trumpets and horns – the Roman cavalry trumpet was often made of wood, covered with leather. No doubt Roman families living comfortably on their estates in Luguvalium or Vectis sang love songs to the accompaniment of the lyre – during the British rebellion of 61 AD, Boudicca, referring to the Emperor Nero's favourite pastime, stigmatised Roman troops as 'slaves to an inferior lyre-player.'[2] No doubt music provided the background to much of Roman social life: to performances at the amphitheatre in Castra Deva, to the taking of waters at Aquae Sulis, to dancing on summer evenings in country villas. No doubt there were marching songs as the soldiers tramped the length of Hadrian's Wall during the day, and drinking songs when they huddled round log fires in the milecastles at night. At Bridgeness on the Firth of Forth, at the eastern end of the Antonine Wall, a carved stone was discovered depicting, among other things, a group of Roman figures taking part in a ceremony of sacrifice, while one of them plays a set of mouth-blown double pipes, the *tibia*, which are known to have been associated with such rituals. In 1961, archaeologists at Silchester in Hampshire uncovered a small statue of a girl holding what appears to be a reed-blown flute or pipe with projecting stops.[3] The evidence for music is there, but the fact remains that in practical terms the Roman presence left no musical legacy at all.

In one respect, this may seem surprising, for it was the Romans who brought Christianity to Britain; and Christianity has been the greatest single influence on the western musical tradition. According to Origen, the early Christian theologian, Christianity had already reached Britain by the end of the second century AD. At first, it was a minority cult and still suffered occasional bouts of persecution – it was *c.*209 AD when St Alban, a former legionary, was martyred for sheltering a fugitive priest. In 313 AD, the Emperor Constantine promised toleration for Christians and then, in 391 AD, Theodosius declared Christianity to be the sole, official religion of the Roman Empire. Christianity grew in influence and popularity across Roman Britain, although never to the complete exclusion of pagan cults. We know that bishops were appointed and that theologians argued, and we must assume, despite a lack of written or archaeological evidence, that hymns of some kind were sung and that liturgical music of some kind was heard during services. When the Emperor Honorius withdrew imperial support from Britain in 410 AD, it marked a political but not necessarily a social watershed; so, in the absence of evidence to the contrary, we can assume that Roman Christianity with its attendant rites and music continued to be practised – including by the shadowy figure of King Arthur – until it was disrupted and pushed aside by the waves of pagan, Germanic tribes that swept across the North Sea.

Although the Romans left no direct musical legacy, two aspects of the Roman period did have a long-term impact on the musical future of the British Isles. Before it was effectively buried under a landslide of pagan Germanic invaders, the Christian Church of Roman Britain had begun to spread its influence beyond the area actually controlled by Rome. St Ninian began the process at the beginning of the fifth century, establishing the first Christian community beyond the northern border of Roman Britain at what is now Whithorn in Wigtownshire. Ninian's community did not survive, but St Patrick was more successful. Born to a Roman Christian family, probably somewhere near to Carlisle and the western end of Hadrian's Wall, and probably towards the end of the fourth century AD, Patrick is credited with converting the Irish. In fact, there were already Christians in Ireland in the fourth century, apparently coexisting with druidic cults, but St Patrick's arrival, probably in the 530s, seems to have speeded up the process of conversion, and by the seventh century Ireland was, officially at least, a wholly Christian island. It was St Columba, arriving from Ireland and settling on Iona in 593, who brought Christianity back to mainland Britain and began converting the Celts of the north, including the enigmatic Picts. Emissaries from Iona gradually spread their faith through the fragmented, tribal kingdoms of what is now Scotland. And it was from Iona, at the request of King Oswald, that St Aidan travelled to Lindisfarne to lead the conversion of Northumbria in the seventh century. The northern tribes and the Scandinavian-held islands to the north and west held out longer, but by the tenth century the whole of the north of Britain could be said to be Christian.

This strand of Christianity, which for convenience we may call the Celtic Church,[4] thus spread its influence over more than half the land area of the British Isles. Shaped in lands that had not known Roman occupation – lands where Rome was culturally as well as geographically distant – and cut off from the rest of Christian Europe by Germanic invaders, it developed independently over more than two hundred years. It evolved its own traditions, its own organisational structures, its own variations in the liturgy and, of course, its own music and its own way of using music during worship. Evidence is thin, and within the Celtic lands themselves there would undoubtedly have been variations, but nevertheless there clearly was a so-called Celtic rite, accompanied by a Celtic chant. It had largely disappeared by the twelfth century – overtaken by the standard Gregorian chant of the Roman rite – although one example survives in a fourteenth-century manuscript known as the Inchcolm Antiphoner.[5] From this and other sources, certain features of the Celtic chant, such as the use of alliteration and the repetition of melody to fit couplets, have been tentatively identified. Yet the real musical importance of the Celtic Church may well have been broader in that it created a sense, even an expectation, of musical distinctness which echoes down the long tradition of Celtic-influenced church and classical music.

A second and potentially more important legacy of the Roman period stems from the suppression of the Druids in 60 AD. The Romans, as polytheists themselves and out of political expediency, were traditionally tolerant where matters of religion were concerned. That tolerance did not extend to the Druids, partly because their rites and observances included ritual murder and human sacrifice, but also because it was the Druids who had inspired resistance and rebellion on the part of the native Celts. Eventually, they were driven back to their stronghold and the centre of their faith on the Isle of Anglesey. Suetonius Paulinus led his army across the Menai Straits in a fleet of specially constructed transports. The Druids were slaughtered; their sacred groves cut down and burned; and their power, at least in Roman Britain, destroyed. Druids continued to exist and function north of Hadrian's Wall and across the sea in Ireland, but their power was fatally weakened and, as far as one can tell, they and their belief systems were simply overtaken by the spread of Christianity.

With the end of druidical power and the emergence of Christianity, the figure of the bard appears to gain new importance in Celtic secular society. Much of the evidence for this period derives from myth and tradition, and what documentary evidence there is comes from manuscripts that date from several centuries after the events they describe. Nevertheless, it is possible to reconstruct a situation in which, detached from their previous religious function with the Druids, the bards attached themselves to political leaders. The image of the Irish bard sitting beneath the throne of the High King and singing songs of the wisdom and valour in battle of his lord may not be too far from the truth. We know that Taliesin, the great bard of the early sixth century, was in the service of Urien, King of Rheged (which corresponds roughly to modern Cumbria). In what is one of the oldest surviving pieces of vernacular literature in Europe, Taliesin not only extols the virtues of his lord, but also shows the extent to which the bard was dependent on his patron.

> Urien of Echwyd, most liberal of Christian men
> Much do you give to men in this world....
> Happy the Christian bards, so long as you live,
> Sovereign supreme, ruler all highest
> The stranger's refuge, strong champion in battle ...
> I shall have no delight
> If my lips praise not Urien.

So the bard was employed not only for his skill as a poet and musician; he was also a public relations man, a booster of the royal reputation and the royal ego – a role musicians have continued to play across the centuries.

Yet, at the same time, the role of bard was more than just political. It was the bard now who acted as the guardian of race, or tribal, memory. The inhabitants of the British Isles – both the Celts and, when they arrived, the Anglo-Saxons – maintained a tradition of preserving long and detailed genealogies of their royal and noble families which is not in evidence to the same degree elsewhere in Europe. It was a tradition that was certainly more developed among the Celts than among later arrivals, and may well have had Celtic origins: certainly the largest and most detailed corpus of ancient genealogy is to be found in Ireland. Until they began to be written down in the tenth and eleventh centuries, these genealogies, like the wealth of Irish mythological tales that have come down to us, survived by being sung. The story of *The Battle of Magh Tuireadh*, for example, exists in a sixteenth-century manuscript, but the text is believed to be a twelfth-century compilation of material first written down in the ninth century. The story tells of the mythological origins of the Irish people: a contest for possession of Ireland between the Tuatha Dé Danann and the Fir-Bolgs. At one point in the story, the Dagda, High King of the Tuatha Dé Danann, pursues his stolen harp into the enemy's camp. He regains possession of his instrument and plays the three strains of music which all harpers must have at their command – the Strain of Lament, the Strain of Laughter, and the Lullaby. His enemies naturally cry, laugh, and then fall asleep, allowing him to escape. Such tales must surely have been sung or chanted to the accompaniment of a harp or lyre.

In many of these early Irish stories, music is portrayed as having magical powers. This is, of course, a useful narrative device, but it also contributes to the idea of the musician as a figure of power and control. Later, this connection was developed to associate the figure of the bard with wisdom – often hidden, riddling or gnomic wisdom – and with the gift of prophecy. *The Book of Taliesin* survives in an early fourteenth-century manuscript, containing fifty-six poems – some probably by Taliesin himself; others dating from the tenth century. They cover a range of subjects. There are songs in praise of Urien and other great men, songs in praise of mead and ale, elegies for dead heroes, and Christian hymns, but also a solid core of works of prophecy, philosophy and mystical wisdom. The central figure is often the bard himself – his power, his truth-telling, his ability to assume different identities, and the mystical sources of his wisdom. The poems frequently take the form of lists of roles or guises that the poet has assumed, and of things he has experienced: lists which the audience or, later, the reader was clearly expected to understand or interpret in the light of esoteric knowledge to which modern readers no longer have access.[6]

> I am a bard to be praised. The unskilful
> May he be possessed by the ravens and eagles and birds of wrath.

Avagddu came to him with his equal
When the bands of four men feed between two plains.
Abiding in heaven was he, my desire,
Against the eagle, against the fear of the unskilful.
I am a bard, and I am a harper,
I am a piper, and I am a crowder.
Of seven score musicians the very great enchanter.[7]

The music of the bards was never written down and is impossible to reconstruct (though attempts have been made), but we can still see its distant legacy in the concept of the eisteddfod. In 517 AD, in what is now South Wales, Taliesin himself is thought to have directed an Eisteddfod; it was perhaps a sort of extended master-class run by senior bards in order pass knowledge and practice on to the next generation. Another took place at Conway in North Wales in 540 AD. No more are recorded until the twelfth century when there were at least four (in *c.*1100, 1107, 1135 and 1176), although that does not mean that others did not take place. The tradition surfaced again in the fifteenth century and, with occasional breaks and revivals, has persisted until the present day, when the annual National Eisteddfod of Wales attracts 5,000 participants and over 150,000 visitors. The true legacy of the Celtic bards, however, may well lie elsewhere.

Norman Davies, in his study *The Isles*, has detailed the way in which, during the eighteenth and nineteenth centuries, the revival of interest in Celtic culture led to Celtic mysticism breaking its traditional bounds and becoming an influence and a force in English culture.[8] Thomas Gray's 'The Bard', the whole Ossian saga, and Blake's 'The Voice of the Ancient Bard' all showed that, however romanticised, the idea of the bard with its overtones of poetry, music and mysticism was not dead. W. B. Yeats was no musician, but many of his poems are cast as songs and there is in his work a mysticism which, in his own mind as well as the minds of many critics, connects him with the bardic tradition. It surfaces also in the work of Rutland Boughton and Joseph Holbrooke at the beginning of the twentieth century. And the idea of the bard as someone who has an ability to see and communicate beyond the ability of ordinary mortals is one that remains powerful to this day. It is not too much to suggest that the prevalence in the English-speaking world of an attitude which regards certain singer-songwriters as sages or prophets, which seeks to extract from their work some message or philosophy, and which regards them as being gifted with a different or higher level of perception, stems ultimately from the concept of the Celtic bard. Bob Dylan is the most obvious example. Others might include Nick Cave, David Bowie, or even Tom Waits.

3 Anglo-Saxons, Celts, and Harps

Meanwhile, in the south and east of what had been Roman Britain, three Germanic tribes – Angles, Saxons and Jutes – which had begun to arrive in waves at the beginning of the fifth century, were now sweeping inland. By 600 AD, they controlled all of what is now England with the exception of Cumbria, Lancashire and Cornwall. These Anglo-Saxons, to use the most convenient term, naturally brought with them their own musical traditions, although precisely what these were is difficult to establish. The storybook image is of a poet-musician, known as a *scop,* standing before his lord in the mead hall and plucking a harp while declaiming *Beowulf* or the story of some glorious victory achieved against all the odds – and it may not be too inaccurate. Percy Young, in his *History of British Music,* suggests that 'the Bardic tradition as established and maintained by the Celts and Britons was readily taken over by the Saxons and the Angles, and scops and gleemen (the former ranking first in seniority) were in consistent employment as long as they obliged their masters.'[1] It is certainly true, as Norman Davies has argued, that while the Anglo-Saxons ruled the land and wielded military and political power, they did not exterminate the Celtic peoples of Roman Britain, nor were they numerous enough to repopulate the country and replace them. The Celts, conquered, and perhaps periodically oppressed, continued to live their lives, speak their own language and follow their own cultural traditions.[2] There must have been plenty of opportunities for crossover between the two ethnic and linguistic groups.

Our understanding of the scop and his role comes principally from Anglo-Saxon poetry. *Widsith* is the oldest Anglo-Saxon poem. It is found in a tenth-century manuscript, the Exeter Book, but probably dates from seventh-century Mercia and may make use of material that is considerably older. The narrator is an itinerant scop whose family are far away and who has no lasting bond to any king or leader.

I followed many
So I may sing — and stories tell
I can in hall rehearse — before the gathering
How men of kingly birth — were kinglike towards me …

When we struck up the lay before our lord in war
Scilling and I with sheer-rising voices
Many men there of unmelting hearts
Who well knew wording their thought
Said this was the best song sung in their hearing.[3]

Deor, which probably dates from the eighth century, is another lament, this time on the part of a scop who has lost his place in his master's hall and consequently feels himself an outcast among men. In *Beowulf*, which was probably written down in the early eighth century but composed earlier, Grendel prowls in the darkness outside Hrothgar's great feasting hall, Heorot, hating what he hears.

The harp was struck
and the clear song of a skilful scop
told bravely of the beginnings of man
how the Almighty had made the earth
a shining plain set about with waters.

After Beowulf has slain Grendel, scops perform 'words and music for their warrior prince / tunes on the harp and tales of adventure'; and later, at the end of the poem, after Beowulf has been killed by the dragon, a Geat woman with braided hair sings a dirge, lamenting his death.

It is worth emphasising that these poems were not composed until two or even three hundred years after the first Anglo-Saxons arrived in Britain, and not written down until many years after their composition, so they may well reflect Anglo-Saxon practice as influenced by Celtic models. It is also worth remarking that both *Deor* and *Beowulf* show signs of later Christian interpolations – tales of the Creation are not really appropriate for Heorot – which may also distort the picture. What is clear, however, is that Anglo-Saxon scops were not bards. They served a king or lord; they were poet-musicians composing and performing battle narratives, laments and elegies, but the scop's focus was the heroic, or the loss of heroic possibility, rather than the mystic. He may have been the keeper of tribal genealogies, but the attempted connection was with a historical rather than a mythical past. He may have offered a moral vision, based on loyalty and heroism, but it was not a prophetic one.

If Celtic traditions influenced the practice of the Anglo-Saxon scops, the Anglo-Saxons influenced Celtic music in a much more fundamental way. Harps have a historical pedigree as long as that of the lyre: they are known to have existed in ancient Sumeria and Persia, and they seem to have been popular in northern Europe by the fifth century. Logic suggests that the Anglo-Saxons brought the harp with them – the name itself has a Germanic origin, meaning 'to pluck' – although, given the lack of records, the evidence can only be circumstantial. The harp, however, was not their main or dominant instrument at the time. At the beginning of the seventh century, the Bishop of Poitiers noted that the preferred instrument among the Saxons was the unbowed crwth (effectively a kind of lyre).[4] And, of course, it was a lyre that was found at the late sixth- or early seventh-century ship burial at Sutton Hoo in Suffolk.

Whatever the precise sequence of events, the harp grew in popularity and rapidly spread right across the British Isles, so that carvings of harpers appear on an eighth-century Pictish stone found at Monifieth in Angus in Scotland, on the ninth-century Dupplin Cross in Strathearn, Perthshire, and on a tenth-century cross at Durrow Abbey in County Offaly in Ireland.[5] The harp may have been an Anglo-Saxon import and it may feature in our traditional image of an Anglo-Saxon scop, but over the years it has become almost completely identified with Celtic culture. Thomas Moore's lines, 'The harp that once through Tara's halls / The soul of music shed', are for many people a definition of Irish musical culture; and the harp is the accepted heraldic symbol for Ireland, as well as providing the logos for Ireland's national drink and national airline. The Welsh musical tradition is almost wholly defined, at least for outsiders, by the harp and the eisteddfod. In Scotland, however, while the Celtic harp, or clarsach, remains popular from the Borders to the Western Isles, and features in national graded music exams, it is less iconic as a representation of the nation's musical culture.

Somewhere around 600 AD, a small army of warriors from the lands of the Gododdin, which comprised Northumberland and parts of south-east Scotland, crossed Hadrian's Wall and marched south to confront the growing power of the Anglo-Saxons. Their overwhelming defeat at the Battle of Catraeth[6] occasioned one of the great bardic poems, *Y Gododdin* – a series of elegies for the dead heroes composed by the Aneirin, who, along with Taliesin, is one of the few names to have come down to us from the period. Yet if the old order was still fighting for survival in the north – though defeated on this occasion – a wholly new order, that was to alter the direction of religion, politics and music in Britain, had arrived in the south, in the Kingdom of Kent, just three years earlier.

A Child's History of Great Britain, published around 1910, has an illustration of St Augustine arriving on the beach of the Isle of Thanet in 597 and being welcomed by King Æthelbert.[1] The saint, recognisable by his halo, and holding a Bible in one hand and a cross in the other, appears to lurch forward uncertainly towards the waiting King, while his entourage, in traditional monkish robes with ropes round their waists and each holding some kind of vocal score, praise the Lord in song. As a representation of what actually happened, one can find fault with such a picture, but it does contain certain essential truths. Christianity was in the air among the fragmented, pagan kingdoms of Anglo-Saxon Britain – for political and dynastic reasons as much as for reasons of faith – but with the arrival of Augustine, armed with full authority from Pope Gregory the Great, the process of conversion began to acquire momentum. Augustine's version of Christianity came from Rome, and so did the music that accompanied it. Tradition has it that he and his companions entered Canterbury, King Æthelbert's capital, singing the processional antiphon, *Deprecamur te, Domine.* Whether literally true or not, the arrival of Augustine marks the point from which we can chart some level of continuity in the development of music in the British Isles.[2]

Augustine brought with him plainsong and the eight modal scales that were to remain the basis of European music for the next nine hundred years. As Augustine's influence grew, through the conversion of Æthelbert and the Kingdom of Kent and then through the conversion of the East Saxons, so the approved, Roman version of church music took root. Instruments had long been forbidden in church music because they were associated with pagan rituals, but a number of very different vocal traditions had grown up, influenced by Greek, Jewish, Armenian, even Egyptian models. The second half of the sixth century saw an effort by the Church authorities in Rome to simplify and bring order into the situation, and it was this Roman initiative that led to the beginning of plainsong. Plainsong probably has its origins in the recitation of prayers or biblical texts. It can be seen as a form of heightened or stylised speech where patterns of phrasing are more rhythmic, and the words themselves more clearly enunciated, than in normal speech. Musically, it is based upon a simple, unaccompanied, melodic line – the *cantus firmus* – moving around a central reciting-note to which it returns. No form of musical notation was yet available, but some attempt seems to have been made, within the oral tradition that passed music and musical practice from one place to another and from one generation to the next, to establish basic rhythms and note durations. And the establishment of eight approved modal scales provided a clear framework within which music might continue to develop.[3]

At the time, the importance of these developments was as much political as musical. Neither Augustine nor Pope Gregory would have seen church music as an end in itself: it was intended to serve religion, to heighten the receptivity of its hearers to the message of God contained within the Mass. But the Church was fragmented: the Pope was only one of five Christian patriarchs and any assertion of Roman authority – whether in doctrine or in music – had political implications. One motive for sending Augustine to convert the Anglo-Saxons was to ensure that they were not converted by the Celtic Church first. Over the centuries, music has, in general, proved resistant to attempts by the authorities – secular or religious – to impose rules or discipline. If the musical forms and disciplines favoured by Rome in the sixth century took root across Western Europe and enjoyed an unusually long period of dominance, it was largely because political developments conspired to strengthen the authority of Rome. In Britain, Augustine's mission effectively allied Rome with the Anglo-Saxons, who continued to be the most dynamic political force in Britain until the ninth century; and in the wider world, Rome and its sphere of influence in Western Europe was less threatened than the rest of the Christian world by the sudden explosion of Islam.

Plainsong – which has become known, it would seem inaccurately, as Gregorian chant[4] – remained the basis of church music for the next four hundred years; and in the British Isles knowledge and practice of plainsong spread, for the most part, with the authority of the Roman Church. Our main source of information about this process is Bede's *History of the English Church and People.* Bede tells us, for example, how when Paulinus, the first Bishop of York, moved south to Rochester in 633, he passed the care of his church to one James the Deacon who 'had a wide knowledge of church music, and … began to teach many people to sing the music of the Church after the Uses of Rome and Canterbury.'[5] He also notes that Putta, who became Bishop of Rochester in 669, was 'a most skilled exponent of the Roman chant, which he had studied under the disciples of the blessed Pope Gregory.'[6] One key event of the period was the Synod of Whitby, called by King Oswiu of Northumbria in 664, which decided that Northumbria would follow the practice of the Roman Church rather than that of the monks of Iona and their Celtic followers when it came to matters such as the monkish tonsure, the calculation of the date of Easter and certain ascetic monastic traditions. And where Roman authority in such matters was established, Roman musical practice followed – although Percy Young draws attention to a claim by Welsh historians that knowledge of the 'Keys of Music' (presumably modal scales) had reached Wales, which was within the zone of the Celtic Church, before the death of King Cadwaladr in *c.*634,[7] suggesting that in some areas the 'new' music may have spread faster than the 'new' religion.

Plainsong is popular with modern audiences for its simplicity and for its capacity to evoke a distant age. At its best, it has a remote, otherworldly, even magical quality. Whether this is what an Anglo-Saxon congregation would have heard must be a matter for speculation. Bede notes one or two exceptional teachers, and St Aldhelm, who was Bishop of Sherborne in Wessex from 675 to 709 and a well-known poet and musician, comments positively on the quality and quantity of music to be heard in Princess Eadburga's new church on the Isle of Thanet. However, we can only guess what the general level of performance was like. One thing we do know is that the monks who participated in services sang from memory – and they were required to memorise a huge amount of material. The *Regularis Concordia,* a manual compiled during the reign of King Edgar (which lasted from 959 to 975), sets out what was expected from Benedictine monks in England at that time. Among many other things, all the monks were expected to commit to memory the entire psalter – effectively *The Book of Psalms,* perhaps with some additional related material – plus hymns, introits, antiphons, and other music. The musical parts of the Mass would be either responsorial, where a priest or a cantor was answered by the assembled monks and the laity, or antiphonal, where two groups or choirs of monks answered each other. In theory, plainsong allowed for greater participation in the sung parts of the Mass by the laity, but, as everything was sung in Latin, it must be unlikely that many of the congregation would have been able to join in.

In 686, King Arwald of the Isle of Wight was killed in battle against King Caedwalla of Wessex. Arwald was the last pagan Anglo-Saxon King, and with his passing only parts of northern Scotland and its Scandinavian-ruled islands remained unconverted. Converted or not, the British Isles remained politically divided. The Church, by contrast, rapidly achieved a coherent administrative structure which both established Roman practice as standard – always allowing for a few exceptions along the Celtic fringe – and drew the Church in Britain into a Continental system that shared and regulated that practice. Rules were rules, yet the regulations surrounding plainsong and the role of music in church services still allowed some latitude for the development of regional styles. A recognisable English style of singing must have evolved, for towards the end of the eighth century we find Alcuin of York sanctioning its export to the singing schools of major abbeys on the Continent. This was a vote of confidence in its quality and authenticity, for Alcuin, although born in York, was also both teacher and adviser on cultural matters to the Emperor Charlemagne at his court in Aachen. Charlemagne wanted his new Carolingian Empire to benefit from uniformity of practice based on high standards, not only in religious matters, but also in the arts that served religion. Alcuin, who was something of a polymath, writing poetry as well as treatises on mathematics and developing a new, more readable script for use by Charlemagne's scribes, was the man charged to deliver it. During his years at Charlemagne's court, he wrote a justification of church music based on the eight Gregorian modal scales, and sought to ensure that contemporary plainsong was sung in accordance with the official guidelines. Britain was not part of Charlemagne's empire, of course, but it certainly felt the influence of the new European power – not least because Alcuin, as a churchman and a native of the Kingdom of Northumbria, looked beyond political boundaries and regularly communicated his ideas to clerical colleagues in York and elsewhere.

That the Anglo-Saxon lands continued to view themselves as part of a European cultural unity even in the ninth century, when the political landscape had been thrown into turmoil by Viking raids and Danish invasions, is shown by the figure of Alfred the Great (849–901). Traditionally seen as a great Anglo-Saxon patriot and a champion of the Anglo-Saxon tongue, he is more likely to have seen himself in a European context. He was educated in Rome from the age of four, receiving an education in music as well as all the other subjects appropriate for a member of the royal house of Wessex. He also spent time in Paris at the court of Charles the Bald, King of the Franks and later Holy Roman Emperor. During Alfred's reign, the Carolingian Empire, faced with Viking attacks and riven with internal power struggles, began to fall apart. Many Frankish scholars, artists and musicians seem to have migrated to Wessex and to his court. He installed at least one of them at Oxford.

Through Alfred the Great, we can also catch a glimpse of the secular music of the time. There is, of course, the famous legend that he disguised himself as a minstrel – the implication being that he was a competent performer – in order to penetrate the camp of his Danish enemies. Alfred also recorded the story, later repeated by William of Malmesbury, of St Aldhelm. Distressed that the people of Sherbourne either did not come to church or, if they did, gossiped throughout the service, Aldhelm disguised himself as a gleeman and stood on the bridge in the centre of the town. There, he attracted attention by singing popular ballads and then gradually introduced hymns and a more serious Christian message into his performance. Some years later, in 747, we find the Council of Cloveshoe – one of a series of Anglo-Saxon synods – not only insisting that chanting should be in accordance with Roman practice, but also forbidding priests to perform secular music, which perhaps indicates that the Church authorities feared a blurring of the boundaries between the sacred and the secular. Such glimpses are tantalising rather than instructive, but they demonstrate that secular music was alive and well.

In January 793, 'heathen men made lamentable havoc in the church of Holy Island by rapine and slaughter.'[8] It was the first Viking raid on the British Isles. Others followed, targeting monasteries because of their wealth – Jarrow, Monkwearmouth, Iona, and Rechru off the coast of what is now County Dublin. The raids became more frequent and longer-lasting until 865, when invading Danish forces began to overwinter in England and then took control of large swathes of territory on a permanent basis. For the next two hundred years, all parts of the British Isles suffered raids, invasion and settlement by pagan tribes from various areas of Scandinavia. The Viking raids were violent. The subsequent waves of invasion and settlement brought death, destruction and a complete disruption of the existing social order. Political and social upheaval naturally implies cultural upheaval and there is no doubt that the Scandinavian invasions had a significant cultural impact. Yet, as far as music is concerned, while development might have slowed, few new forces seem to have been brought to bear.

The Scandinavian invaders destroyed monasteries and disrupted Church organisation to the point where vacant sees in the Danish-occupied areas of England were left unfilled, but, pagan though they were, the Danes do not seem to have subjected Christians to any form of systematic persecution. The Church continued to function, and clerics soon began the work of Christianising the invaders. One of the most important Danish leaders, Guthrum, accepted Christian baptism as one of the terms he was forced to accept when he surrendered to Alfred the Great in 878. Others succumbed over time, quite probably for reasons which were as much to do with prestige and power as with faith and Christian teaching. By the standards of the time, the Church was impressively well organised and had an international reach beyond that of any local ruler. To be associated with the imposing theatricality of Christian services, their liturgy and music, was also a useful addition to the trappings of power.[9] By the turn of the millennium, the Church had re-established a unity of structure and organisation that overrode political divisions and continued to control the performance and development of all formal music. In Scotland, still divided and unstable, and in Ireland, where Brian Boru was in the process of uniting the lands of some one hundred and fifty kings and tribal chiefs, it was the abbots of the major monasteries who held ecclesiastical power. In England, it was bishops or archbishops, such as St Dunstan, who was Archbishop of Canterbury between 960 and 988. Dunstan, another polymath cleric and also a recognised musician, worked hard to ensure that, whatever the changes in the secular world, the Church in Britain would remain in conformity with the rest of Europe.

5 Organum, Notation, and Organs

Conformity with long-established guidelines did not preclude change. We know, for example, that by the year 1000 church music included not only responses and antiphons, but also a range of hymns, tropes, sequences, alleluias, amens and other kinds of specialised musical genres. These reflected not only the growing sophistication of worship, but the growing importance of the Church in a society where prayer, blessing, or other forms of religious endorsement short of a full Mass were required to mark essentially secular occasions. We know also that within the agreed bounds of plainsong, there had been developments, such as the introduction of more adventurous melodic lines – probably stemming from Byzantine and Irish influences – and greater use of melisma (where one syllable is stretched out over a series of notes) to extend vocal lines and increase the possibility of emphasising particular words in the text.

Such developments could still – just – be explained as ways of reinforcing the meaning of the words that conveyed the all-important message of God. What followed could not. With the introduction of *organum*, the world changed. *Organum* was a simple harmonisation of the melodic line, the *cantus firmus*, with parallel parts following the melody a fourth above and a fifth below. And if boy sopranos sang the *cantus* an octave above the main body of the choir, this resulted in a four-part harmony. *Organum* may originally have arisen out of the vocal limitations of certain singers but it soon became an accepted musical technique, giving more weight to the role of the music and the musicians. Precise dating is impossible, but *organum* is discussed in a late ninth-century French manuscript, *Musica enchiriadis*; and no less than one hundred and sixty examples, attributed to a monk of Winchester known as Wulfstan the Cantor, appear in the second of two manuscripts known as the *Winchester Troper*, dating from *c.*1000. So an educated guess is that the technique arrived in Britain during the tenth century.

Organum was the beginning of harmony and a watershed in the development of modern musical forms and structures. The introduction of fourths and fifths meant that it was only a matter of time before someone introduced thirds and sixths. And once we had music in which the different vocal parts followed the *cantus firmus* at a fixed interval – whether a third, fourth, fifth or sixth – it was only a matter of time before someone started asking questions. Why could those intervals not be varied, allowing for the harmonic reinforcement of the main melody to vary at different stages of the piece? And if intervals between parts could vary, why not the rhythm? Ultimately, it would be possible for the parts to become independent – to become separate melodic lines, interweaving with each other, provided only that they fitted together rhythmically and harmonically. The way was open for polyphony and counterpoint, the building blocks of the western classical tradition. Of course, it would take centuries for these developments to take place and to reach their full potential – indeed, that potential would change as musical styles changed across the years – but once plainsong gave way to *organum*, the dam was breached and the rest was only a matter of time.

The long dominance of plainsong may go some way to explaining why musical notation was so slow to develop in Europe. Simple plainsong could be memorised and transmitted orally between monasteries and between generations of singers. With the development of *organum* and multi-part music, a reliable method of notation became necessary. The system of neumes (from the Greek for *breath*) was probably derived from Byzantine models which first appeared *c.*680. In its earliest form, it consisted of a series of wavy or curling lines placed above the text, which could perhaps have been based on the hand gestures made by the conductor or leader of the choir. The problem with these gestural (or cheironomic) neumes was while they might indicate the direction of the melodic line, they could not indicate precise pitch or rhythm. They were thus an aid to memory rather than a way of ensuring accurate reconstruction and reproduction of the music. Moreover, there was no agreed set of markings, so that neumes written in one monastery and read in another would not necessarily be understood or interpreted in the same way.

Once again, we can identify the trend and certain moments within it rather than precise dates. The best available evidence suggests that neumes were first used in Western Europe *c.*800, stimulated by Charlemagne's passion for uniformity and authenticity in Church matters.[1] However, it seems to have been Irish monks who introduced neumatic notation to the Abbey of St Gall in Switzerland at the end of the ninth century; and the first appearance of neumes in Britain, in the *Pontifical of Sherborne* dating from the second quarter of the tenth century, apparently followed the arrival of Breton monks displaced from their homeland by the Norman invasion of 919. By the time the *Winchester Troper* was written, *c.*1000, the use of neumes was well understood.

Gradually, the system developed so that it became possible to indicate the relative pitches between one neume and the next, but the next real breakthrough, which spread across Europe during the middle decades of the eleventh century, was the invention of the stave or staff. This is usually credited to an Italian Benedictine called Guido d'Arezzo, whose *Micrologus*, dating from *c.*1025, was the most widely read treatise on music of its age. Beginning as a single line with neumes scattered above and below, the stave was originally regarded as a teaching aid. However, it soon became standardised at four lines – only achieving its current five-line form in the sixteenth century – and an essential part of musical notation. Melody could be written down, but there was still a long way to go. It was the thirteenth century before individual notes were written as square blocks on the stave, and music began to look like something that we might recognise today. It was the fourteenth century before there was a reliable and generally accepted indication of relative note length and thus of rhythm; the fifteenth century before time signatures began to be widely used; and the sixteenth before the bar line was invented.

The period that saw the development of *organum* and neumes also saw the appearance of new and different kinds of musical instruments. Most of the evidence comes from representations on crosses and other religious sculptures, or from illustrations in a few surviving manuscripts, but a combination of erosion and uncertain draughtsmanship mean these images are not always easy to interpret accurately. Nor is the situation helped by a lack of agreement on what these new instruments – often very similar in shape and often still evolving – should be called. All we can do is recognise that instruments gradually became more diverse and more sophisticated, but any more precise historical narrative is largely speculation. The remarkable Vespasian Psalter, which came from St Augustine's Abbey in Canterbury in the eighth century, portrays King David surrounded by musicians and dancers. The King plays a plucked psaltery; four of the musicians play what could be shawms or possibly medieval cornets (or cornetts);[2] another plays what appears to be a bagpipe. The first bowed instruments also appeared around this time. One, possibly tenth-century, Anglo-Saxon psalter shows St Asaph (a somewhat elusive Welsh bishop who was recognised as a saint because of his ability to carry burning coals in his apron) playing a bowed crwth. Another eleventh-century manuscript shows that the three-stringed bowed instrument commonly called a rebec, but at the time, confusingly, also called a *lyra,* had migrated across Europe as far as Britain. Gradually, one form of bowed instrument emerged and became dominant as the *fithele* or fiddle (a precursor of, but not the same as, the violin), which, we can safely say, was a well-known and popular instrument by the time of Chaucer, in whose works it appears without comment or explanation.

The use of instruments in church services continued to be looked on with suspicion and disfavour by the Church authorities, mainly because they were played by and associated with itinerant minstrels. Later, in the thirteenth and fourteenth centuries, minstrels gained a recognised role at court and in society. During the Anglo-Saxon and early Norman period, however – while they and their music might be appreciated by the populace and, no doubt, privately by some priests – they were subject to repeated condemnation by the Church authorities. They were seen, correctly, as having their origins in the pagan world of bards and scops, and were thus held to represent all that was worldly and ungodly. The harp, in particular, was held by the Church to be a symbol of pagan culture. It has been suggested that when King Alfred disguised himself as a minstrel in order to penetrate the Danish camp, he chose to carry a harp because its pagan associations were enough to prevent him from being identified as a Christian. The Church regarded instrumental music and instrumental accompaniment as potentially sinful. This attitude was reinforced by linguistic changes which meant that, from the early Middle Ages onwards, instruments were described in less technical language than formerly. Rather than being 'blown', 'strummed', 'plucked', 'struck,' or 'sounded', in English as in the other principal European languages, they were generally described as being 'played', associating them with pleasure and time-wasting. One instrument, however, did find favour with the Church authorities and that was the organ.

The earliest reference we have to the use of organs in the British Isles is when St Aldhelm, who died in 709, says that the Anglo-Saxons gilded the front pipes of their instruments. In 814, an organ burned in a church fire at Cloncraff, not far from Athlone in central Ireland. In the tenth century, St Dunstan erected an organ with brass pipes at Malmesbury Abbey, and is said to have encouraged the use of organs in other churches and monasteries. Around the same time, Count Elwin spent the sum of £30 on copper pipes for an organ at a convent in Romsey Abbey. An illustration of a tenth-century organ in the *Eadwine Psalter* shows a strange contraption where four blowers use long sticks to work the bellows, while two musicians stand above them operating a series of pipes which sit within a decorated frame. The greatest organ of this period, however, was to be found at Winchester. Begun by Bishop Æthelwold, who died in 984, and completed by his successor, Bishop Alfege, it was described in excited detail in a Latin poem by Wulstan or Wulfstan, who was Precentor of the Cathedral. According to him, the Winchester organ had twenty-six bellows worked by seventy perspiring men, while its four hundred pipes were managed by two organists 'of concordant spirit.' There were forty 'tongues' or sliders which controlled the flow of air to the pipes. The whole thing made an incredible noise – 'Like thunder the iron tones batter the ear.... The music is heard throughout the town, and the flying tone thereof is gone out over the whole country.'[3] A century or so later, the technology appears to have advanced. An eleventh-century manuscript shows a '*Bumbulum cum fistulâ aereâ*', where a single hand-bellows is sufficient to meet the needs of a single organist who appears to be controlling matters by means of levers.[4] Sliders and levers soon gave way to keys – although the first keys were twenty centimetres wide and needed to be struck with the fist – and by the thirteenth century an organ could be played on a recognisable, if somewhat clumsy, keyboard or manual. Pedals were probably first used in the late fourteenth century and pedalboards developed from there. There must have been an element of novelty and spectacle about these early organs. Certainly, the one in Winchester must have been thunderously loud and the use of sliders would have made any fast or complex passage (had such a thing been composed) almost impossible to play. Yet the musical value of organs cannot be doubted. By the tenth century, they would have been present in many of the larger churches and would have been used in church services – although how much, at this early stage, they were used to accompany singing and how much they were used to provide a musical background to and continuity between the different parts of the Mass remains an open question. One thing, however, is certain: organs were a force for change. They could play more than one note at once. Perhaps, at first, organists followed the controlled principles of *organum*, but it must very soon have become apparent that the instrument offered greater possibilities; that more complex harmonies and more complex musical structures were now a reality and were, quite literally, in the hands of a single musician.

6 Normans, Cathedrals, and Giraldus Cambrensis

In terms of music, the two most important aspects of the Norman Conquest were that it was a conquest, not a migration, and that, unlike their Anglo-Saxon and Scandinavian predecessors, the new arrivals were Christian. Estimates vary, but the number of Normans who followed Duke William across the Channel to become feudal overlords in the newly conquered kingdom was comparatively small: his army at Hastings was probably no more than 7,000 strong. England and most of Wales soon fell under Norman control – attempts to conquer or at least cow the Scots continued for hundreds of years, and Ireland had to wait its turn. It was a violent and bloody process. Again, estimates vary widely, but even by 1100 it seems unlikely that there were more than 15,000 Norman knights to rule over and control a population of one-and-a-half million.

William understood the weakness of his position; and he understood that the best way to strengthen it was to obtain the support of the Church, which was by far the most powerful organisation in Europe. He arranged for the Pope to endorse his invasion; he appointed his long-term ally, Lanfranc, Archbishop of Canterbury; and he made sure that all new ecclesiastical appointments were filled by those who would be loyal to him. One of these loyalists, named Osmund and later beatified as St Osmund, became Bishop of Salisbury in 1078. He was responsible for introducing the Sarum Rite or Use of Salisbury, which standardised the order and form of Christian worship throughout the kingdom and which remained current until the Reformation. According to the *Anglo-Saxon Chronicle*, William and his followers also 'filled the land with castles ... and when the castles were made, they filled them full of devils and evil men.'[1] They built cathedrals, too, and both were expressions of Norman control.

Canterbury, Chichester, Durham, Ely, Gloucester, Hereford, Lincoln, Norwich, Rochester, St David's, Winchester, York – the Norman cathedrals of England and Wales were statements of political and cultural superiority. They were also great, visionary architectural achievements and, as settings for worship and for hearing the music associated with it, they were beyond anything previously known in Britain. They had a full, resonating acoustic which allowed the voice to carry through the long volume of the nave. They were perfectly suited to the slow, extended melodies of unaccompanied plainsong or *organum*. At the same time, the scale of the enclosed space meant that the louder and grander tones of the organ could be heard to their best advantage. For the clergy and laity of the early medieval period, hearing music in the vastness of these surroundings must have been a moving and awe-inspiring experience.

During the two hundred and fifty years that followed the Norman Conquest, religious music flourished, not only in the great cathedrals, but also in the many new monasteries that were founded, and in the new stone churches that sprang up across the country. There were no dramatic developments, rather a slow working through of the possibilities opened up by *organum* and simple polyphony. Plainsong and the *cantus firmus* remained the foundation, but vocal lines became more complex and more ornamented. One particular feature was the hocket – a technique equivalent to a vocal hiccup. Imported from the singing school at Notre Dame, it involves breaking up a vocal line with short rests, or rapidly transferring the melody between voices without reference to the verbal sense. Vocal *tremolando* was introduced, again probably from Notre Dame. Instrumental music began to be heard in and around the church, or even during services. One manuscript, copied in England about 1200 and now held by Cambridge University, contains a number of early liturgical pieces. At this distance we cannot tell how representative they are, but they range from uncomplicated monophony to more complex polyphonic pieces (*Cantu miro*) and Christmas songs with elaborate descant parts (*Divino maduit*). Some of these pieces have been recorded under the title *The Earliest Songbook in England*, although there is nothing definably English about the music.[2]

These developments in church music were probably popular with the laity and those clergy who sang and played, but there was a significant and highly assertive faction among the Church authorities that voiced disapproval, even anger. In the middle of the twelfth century, Aelred of Rievaulx fulminated against 'that terrible blowing of belloes, expressing rather the crashes of thunder than the sweetnesse of a voice,' against singing which sounds like 'a horse's neighing'; and against 'masculine vigour being laid aside … sharpened with the shrillnesse of a woman's voice … [and] writhed and retorted into a certain artificial circumvolution.' John of Salisbury, who died in 1180, took a similar view, blaming the state of church music on secular music which had become dangerously decadent. He deplored vocal ornamentation practised for its own sake, believing that such music 'is more likely to stir lascivious sensations in the loins than devotion in the heart.' Gilbert of Sempringham agreed. Nuns at his convent in Lincolnshire were forbidden to sing for fear that it might 'pervert the minds of the weak with lascivious strains.'[3] From the same period, there survive a number of strange carvings of animals playing instruments. In the crypt of Canterbury Cathedral, for example, we find a bird-donkey hybrid playing some sort of pipe, while a standing goat plays a rebec. Not far away at Barfreston in Kent, we find a carving of a man with a fiddle flanked by a bear playing a pipe and another strange hybrid creature playing the panpipes. There may well be more here than moral disapproval reinforced by ridicule. There may also be fear. The English cleric, Alanus Anglicus, writing in Bologna at the end of the twelfth century, stressed the magical powers of music. Throughout the medieval period and beyond, certain kinds of music and dancing were associated with witchcraft and attempts to summon the Devil. Whether stated or not, the Church's hostility to new developments in music was rooted in the fact that music, with all its emotional power, had the potential to become an independent art form, practised without reference to religion or the Church. Outbursts of hostility to 'modern music' and to the secular values the phrase implies were to continue for several centuries. Yet music continued to develop, suggesting that a significant part of the Church hierarchy must have accepted change – or were at least resigned to their inability to resist it.

That there is comparatively little relevant information about music during these years, and that most of what there is concerns the court and the upper echelons of the Church, can easily give the impression that development was homogenous throughout the British Isles, but that was not the case. Giraldus Cambrensis, Archdeacon of Brecon and chronicler of life in the British Isles in the late-twelfth and early-thirteenth century, gives several glimpses of musical practice away from the ecclesiastical mainstream. As a provincial cleric, he is not particularly critical of new musical styles, although he does object strongly to the practice of singing and dancing in churches. As a Welshman, however, he is clearly proud of the music of his native land.

> In their musical concerts [the Welsh] do not sing in unison like the inhabitants of other countries, but in many different parts; so that in a company of singers, which one very frequently meets with in Wales, you will hear as many different parts and voices as there are performers, who all at length unite, with organic melody, in one consonance.... [They have not] acquired this peculiarity by art, but by long habit, which has rendered it natural and familiar; and the practice is now so firmly rooted in them, that it is unusual to hear a simple and single melody well sung; and, what is still more wonderful, the children, even from their infancy, sing in the same manner.

The English, he notes, 'in general do not adopt this mode of singing', except in the north, 'beyond the Humber', but the singing there has less variety, being limited to two parts, and it was 'from the Danes and Norwegians, by whom these parts of the island were more frequently invaded, and held longer under their dominion, that the natives contracted their mode of singing as well as speaking.'[4]

Giraldus also travelled widely in Ireland and found that in

> playing upon musical instruments ... [the Irish] are incomparably more skilful than any other nation I have ever seen. For their modulation on these instruments, unlike the Britons to which I am accustomed, is not slow and harsh, but lively and rapid. It is astonishing that in so complex and rapid a movement of the fingers, the musical proportions can be observed.... They enter into a movement and conclude it in so delicate a manner, and play the little notes so sportively under the blunter sounds of the base strings.[5]

He also notes that the Irish, like the Spanish, 'mix plaintive music with their funereal wailings, giving poignancy to their present grief.'[6] But perhaps his most interesting observation is a comparison of popular music in the three Celtic nations.

> Both Scotland and Wales strive to rival Ireland in the art of music; the former from its community of race, the latter from its contiguity and facility of communication. Ireland only uses and delights in two instruments, the harp and tabor. Scotland has three, the harp, the tabor, and the crowth or crowd; and Wales, the harp, the pipes and the crowd.... Scotland at the present day, in the opinion of many persons, is not only equal to Ireland, her teacher, in musical skill, but excels her.[7]

Scotland's difference from the rest of the British Isles is further evidenced by the *Hymn to St Magnus*, which exists in a thirteenth-century manuscript, but may well have been written a hundred years earlier to coincide with the building of St Magnus' Cathedral in Kirkwall. The hymn consists of seven stanzas sung to a repeating melody and employing a particular two-part harmony (or heterophony), in which the parts follow each other closely a third apart. The technique is recognisably Scandinavian in origin and a reminder that Orkney was still under Scandinavian rule at the time. The Normans landed in the south and moved north, rapidly becoming the dominant political and cultural force in the British Isles; but it was not until the fifteenth century that Scandinavian rule was finally dislodged from the northern islands of Scotland – and Scandinavian influence remains a core element in the cultural identity of the region. It is evident in the differing folk-music traditions of the Western Isles, Orkney and Shetland; and its enduring strength is shown by the way in which Scandinavian-influenced stories, folk traditions and folk music feature strongly in the work of Salford-born Peter Maxwell Davies, who lived in Orkney from the 1970s until his death in 2016.

7 The Chapel Royal, Medieval Lyrics, and the Waits

The Normans had been Scandinavians themselves in the none too distant past, but the influences they brought were those of Continental Europe. This was true politically: William the Conqueror (r. 1066–87) built a lean and efficient administration, modelled broadly on Carolingian lines, staffed by his Norman henchmen and centred on himself; culturally, because the Normans naturally brought their own language with them, so Norman French became the language of the court and the spoken language of the administration (Latin being its written counterpart); and in the Church, where only one native English bishop was appointed between 1070 and 1140.

As time went on, however, things changed. In 1172, Henry II added Ireland to his possessions. In 1204, King John lost Normandy, Maine, Touraine and his family's ancestral homeland of Anjou. The Plantagenet kings continued to speak French, to see themselves in a European context and (until the fifteenth century) to rule Aquitaine; but for the nobility, on whose support they depended, Continental ties were loosening. Gradually, too, the Anglo-Saxon language began to re-emerge, transformed by time and its contact with Norman French into what we now call Middle English, which was to become the basis of a major literary and cultural revival in the fourteenth century. The Church, however, continued to see itself as part of a pan-European body, taking its orders from the Pope in Rome and resisting attempts by several Plantagenet kings to curb its powers and tax its wealth. Music, too, linked as it was to the Church, continued to develop broadly in line with European models. Only slowly did signs appear that music with an English character was beginning to emerge. It would be the fifteenth century before a recognisably different English musical style burst, quite suddenly, onto the European stage.

The English Chapel Royal began as an imitation of Continental models, but would later become one of the foundations of Englishness in music. As soon as William had established himself upon the throne, he required a group of priests to follow him on his travels in order to sing Mass (and also, of course, to demonstrate the close relationship between Church and State).

As William's successors realised the role that ceremonial, particularly musical ceremonial, could play in projecting an image of power and dignity, so the priests' presence gradually became formalised and their musical role gained in importance. During a royal visit to Salisbury in the reign of King John (r. 1199–1216), we find 'clerks of our chapel' paid for singing *Christus vincit* – one of the three liturgical acclamations, known as *Laudes Regiae*, which had been sung at the Coronation of Charlemagne in 800 and adopted by the Normans long before the Conquest. In the long reign of Henry III (r. 1207–72), the Chapel Royal acquired a clearer identity. The clerks were organised into a fellowship and subject to the command of a principal – one Robert of Canterbury from 1231, followed by William de Larches. We know the names of several of the clerks whose singing was commended, and at least one of them was sent to study at Oxford as recompense for his services. By the beginning of the fourteenth century, the primacy of the musical function of the Chapel Royal was acknowledged when choirboys were employed to supplement the clerks, and in 1312 it acquired its first Dean.

Having originated as part of the Church, the Chapel Royal became an institution more closely allied to the monarchy. In 1521, when Henry VIII visited France for his Field of the Cloth of Gold summit with King Francis I, its members were an essential part of his entourage. Their purpose on such occasions was more about exhibition than devotion. The French Chapel Royal had the highest possible musical reputation. Its English opposite number was there to compete, to uphold the honour of England and the standing of the English king. And the Chapel Royal would go on to achieve its greatest glories under Elizabeth I (r. 1558–1603), producing music of unrivalled quality which would play a part in establishing England's national and political identity.

As early as 1159, there was music that was recognised as sufficiently English enough to be used in a quasi-diplomatic manner. When Thomas Becket travelled to France to negotiate a marriage between King Henry II's eldest son, Prince Henry, and King Louis VII's eldest daughter, Margaret, he took with him a retinue of choir boys, who 'sang English songs after the custom of their country.'[1] However, it is only at the end of the thirteenth and the beginning of the fourteenth century that we have concrete musical examples that allow us to begin to guess what Englishness in song might consist of. *Stond wel moder under rode* is a simple but affecting dialogue between Christ and his mother in which he explains why it is necessary for him to die upon the cross. The use of a dramatic form to express a complex doctrinal truth in human terms suggests that it might owe something to the medieval mystery plays, in which music featured prominently. *Foweles in the frith* is a short, reflective, polyphonic song in which the poet/singer looks at the natural world and compares the carefree life of birds in the wood and fish in the water with his own lovesick state. *Sumer is icumen in* is certainly the best-known English song from the medieval period,[2] a joyous celebration of the coming of spring, and also the earliest surviving six-part polyphonic piece.

All three represent the emergence of a new literary and musical form – the lyric – in which words and music combine to express individual feelings of sorrow, love or happiness. Because it was personal (or appeared to be), the lyric could include subject matter beyond religion, beyond what was traditionally sanctioned by the Church. It thus broadened the basis of the art and increased the possibilities for secular music and poetry. *Stond wel moder under rode* remains firmly within a religious context, but by turning Christ and Mary into characters and allowing the singers to 'act' them, it has moved a long way from traditional Church practice. A similar movement is reflected in the treatment of nature in the other pieces. Traditionally praised as a reflection of the glory of God and of His creation, nature has now become something that can mirror, express or stimulate human emotions independently of the religious impulse. We are still a vast distance from the great, nature-inspired tone poems of the nineteenth and twentieth centuries, but breaking the automatic link between religion and the appreciation of nature was a first step along the way. At the same time, the music of all three lyrics remains recognisably close to church models. *Sumer is icumen in* shows a melodic similarity to a slightly earlier French canon, yet it remains a wonderful example of English synthesis and development – of the way in which classic church-music forms, such as the canon or round and the rondellus (where voices will swap or interchange parts), could now be combined and adapted for use outside an immediately religious context.

Church music continued to evolve. England produced its most prolific composer to date in William de Wycombe, from the Hereford-Worcester area, who produced a significant amount of polyphonic music, particularly four-part alleluias, and who has been tentatively proposed as the composer of *Sumer is icumen in*. Everything naturally continued to revolve around the Mass and the music to accompany it. The invariable order of service –

Kyrie, Gloria, Credo, Sanctus (sometimes Sanctus and Benedictus), and Agnus Dei – became known as the Ordinary of the Mass and has formed the basis of more musical compositions than any other structure of ideas. At the same time, new musical forms were appearing. There was the *conductus,* designed to be sung while the sacred books processed into or out of the church; but more important was the motet, an independent, multi-part piece, which is not an antiphon (or an anthem) or a lyric, but otherwise defies precise definition. These and other developments, such as changes in notation, were recorded by a series of thirteenth- or early fourteenth-century musical theorists, three of whom – John Garland, Walter de Odington, and an anonymous monk from Bury St Edmunds – were English; and all of whom give the impression of reacting after the event, seeking to define or systematise things that were already well established.

Across Western Europe, music outside the Church was developing both rapidly and in a manner that was beyond the capacity of the Church to control. This revived the usual fears that secular music would encourage depravity, and accounts for recurring bouts of clerical hostility and musical conservatism, especially when secular influences were played back into the Church. In 1325, Pope John XXII inveighed against 'certain disciples of the new school … [who] hinder the melody with hockets, they deprave [the melodies] with descants, and sometimes they pad them out with upper parts made out of secular songs.' He was adamant: 'We hasten to forbid these methods … we strictly command that no one shall henceforth consider himself at liberty to use these methods.'[3] But it had no effect.

The Church had long been not only the most powerful organisation in Europe, but also the controlling cultural influence. Now, however, it was faced with an upwelling of secular culture of a kind never seen before. This was not an organised movement, nor was it in any sense opposed to the Church. The vast majority of the population were and remained actively God-fearing, yet as European society developed – as its rulers grew more powerful and its ruling classes grew richer – it felt and responded to the need to develop a secular culture, guided ultimately by Christian principles and parallel, even complementary, to that of the Church, but not subject to clerical discipline. In musical terms, this manifested itself in different ways at different levels of society.

At the pinnacle of society, as royal households grew larger and more splendid in order to bolster the image of the monarch, music became more important and musicians more numerous. Under Edward III (r. 1327–77), the Chapel Royal, maintained and paid for by the King, not the Church, reached an establishment of thirty-seven.[4] The King also kept a group of instrumental players – 'five trumpeters, one cyteler, five pipers, one tabret, one mabrer, two clarions, one fiddler, three wayghts, or haut-bois.'[5] Music was naturally important in court ceremonial. In May 1306, Edward I held the Feast of the Swan, a mass knighting and a call to take up arms against the Scots. It was intended to be a spectacular occasion and the King paid £130, a staggering sum at the time, to eighty-four musicians, who between them played fourteen instruments. As the first person to be knighted was Edward's son, becoming Prince of Wales, he made sure that the band featured a number of Welsh players – a crwth player, a harper and two trumpeters. Music was also used to accompany processions as a means of enlivening and impressing the population. The entry of the monarch into a city or town he was visiting would be accompanied by fanfares and music. Richard II seems to have been particularly fond of musical processions. Just before his accession in 1377, he was welcomed to London with a torch-light procession featuring 'one hundred and thirty citizens, disguised and well horsed, in a mummery, with sound of Trumpets, Sackbuts, Cornets, Shalmes and other minstrels,'[6] and there was another musical procession of a similar size in 1393 to celebrate his reconciliation with the city authorities.

The Scottish king, too, had court musicians who were used in the same manner, to enhance court ceremonial and dramatise the monarch's public appearances, although such evidence as we have suggests that music in the Scottish court remained closer to traditional models, relying more on harps and less on the range of new instruments that were appearing. Where royalty led, the nobility followed; and a number of great nobles of the fourteenth century – John of Gaunt; Lionel, Duke of Clarence; the Earls of Pembroke and of Ulster, whose households were little less than regional courts – also kept bands of musicians to fulfil the same public and social functions.

> Then come forward into the lord's presence the trumpeters and horn-blowers with their frestles (pipes) and clarions, and begin to play and blow very loud, and then the lord with his squires begin to move, to sway, to dance, to utter and sing fine carols till midnight, without ceasing.[7]

At the same time, in England at least, the larger towns and boroughs were growing in importance and status.[8] The emergence of a wealthy, mercantile middle class meant that these towns saw themselves and their representatives in a more dignified light than previously. So it is no surprise that we find boroughs, corporations and ruling bodies following the example set by the king and the nobility and employing musicians to add a degree of pomp to civic occasions. These bands of musicians became known as Waits (sometimes Waites or City Waites). They date back to the thirteenth century – the earliest references being to Waits in York in 1272 and Norwich in 1288 – and in many places they continued to exist into the nineteenth century. Originally, a wait was a shawm- or oboe-like instrument, but the name somehow attached itself to the players. At first, these bands would have consisted mainly of wind instruments and percussion – lutes and viols seem to have been a later addition. The Waits were originally and essentially musicians, but as time went on they were sometimes seen as representatives of the civic authorities and their role expanded to include other civic duties, acting as watchmen or town criers. In the 1970s, 'The City Waites' was adopted as the name of a group of young and subsequently successful musicians seeking to reconstruct and popularise the street music, songs and ballads of the sixteenth, seventeenth and eighteenth centuries.

There was, then, a growth in demand for instrumental music and the people to play it; and it was accompanied by the first appearance of a class of professional or semi-professional musicians, separate from the traditional model of the bard, scop, or minstrel. The same period also saw a rapid and confusing expansion of the number of instruments available. It would probably be true to say that during the thirteenth and fourteenth centuries, instruments developed more rapidly than the music they played. The changing social role of music clearly played a part. So, too, did improvements in the tools and technologies available for instrument-making, and increased foreign influence, particularly from Islamic countries in the wake of the crusades. Ernst Meyer's description of the situation is as concise as any:

> We find almost all the names that are familiar to us now, together with names of instruments like 'nabulum,' 'tintinnabulum' (presumably a small set of bells), 'penniola,' 'bombylium,' the exact nature of which is difficult to define. There are the predecessors of the violin and viol, such as the gigue, rebec, rubebe, rota … vielle or fiddle. The metamorphosis of the crwth can be followed up in a long series of lyra, clarsachs or telyns

> and other harp instruments, while there are innumerable forms of lutes and cithers like the cytele or cythol, with a variety of hurdy-gurdy instruments. The forerunners of the pianoforte as well as of the harpsichord, such as dulcimer, dulsate, psalterie or tympan, are found to have been played in England just as much as on the Continent; and there are many wind instruments: bagpipes such as the cornamuse (also called tympanum, symphony, or sambuca), reed instruments such as the shepherd's pipe, oboe, wait, shalm, pommer and others, instruments of the flute and recorder family, such as pipes or fyfes (tibiae), sardines, rackets; furthermore horns, cornets, trumpets, trombones, and percussion instruments like bells, drums, tabors, nakers, and triangles.[9]

In summary, it was a period of evolution – accompanied by numerous extinctions – when all the main families of musical instruments took significant steps along the way towards their modern shapes and forms.

8 Minstrels, Troubadours, and Courtly Love

Away from a political context, this was the age of the minstrel, although the term *minstrel* covers a range of different roles and functions at different levels of society and so needs to be used with care. The court minstrel, whether at the king's court or in the service of one of the great feudal lords, drew on the tradition of the bard and the scop, but a newer influence was that of the troubadours and trouvères, who were active principally in France between *c.*1100 and 1350. Minstrels at this level were not men who wandered from town to town with lutes on their backs: they were educated, sometimes aristocratic men whose abilities were respected and whose role was to entertain and, through their songs and tales, to add to the regard in which the king or the employing lord was held. In the course of their career, they might move between courts, but they were not travelling entertainers.

The relationship between music and literature was much closer during the late medieval period than at any previous time. The troubadours and trouvères were poets, composers and performers. They left several thousand songs in a range of different genres, and some 1,700 musical settings. Troubadour songs could be bawdy; they could be humorous; some might derive from the older tradition of heroic *chansons de geste,* but the vast majority centred on the concept of courtly love. Whether it arose as a reaction to the prevalence of arranged marriages among the upper levels of European society, or whether it was a form of rebellion against the intense male chauvinism of the Church and of political life, courtly love became the dominant theme in European literature for over two hundred years, from the end of the twelfth century until its substance became diluted in the fifteenth.

Courtly love marks both a stage in the rise of secular culture, and the emergence of romantic love as a major concept in European literature and music. It had nothing to do with marriage, nor was sexual fulfilment, initially at least, an essential part of the scheme. The lady was an idealised figure of beauty, charity and honour. In order to gain her love and her favour, her lover – a knight or a nobleman – would alternately pine, write love lyrics, and seek to perform noble or heroic deeds in her name. His reward was a spiritual and perhaps sexual union: spiritual fulfilment often being presented as more important than sexual conquest. The idealised lady was often represented as having all the perfections that had previously been attributed to the Virgin Mary. This, plus the potential for immorality in the fact that the lady herself might well be married – and not to her lover – meant that the attitude of the Church authorities was at best ambivalent and more often hostile. It is ironic, therefore, that the man responsible for some of the greatest literary and musical expressions of the theme of courtly love should have been a cleric.

Guillaume de Machaut was born in or near Reims *c.*1300 and spent over twenty years in the service first of John I, Count of Luxembourg and King of Bohemia, and then of his daughter, Bonne. At some stage, he took holy orders and although he never rose higher than Canon of Reims, his reputation as a poet and musician spread throughout Europe. He is best known for his sequences of courtly love poems, such as *Le Remède de Fortune, Le Jugement du Roy de Navarre* and *Le Voir Dit,* all of which contain musical settings. *Le Remède de Fortune,* for example, contains a *lai,* a *complainte,* a *chant roial,* a *balladelle,* a *ballade* and a *rondelet,* giving the impression that Machaut is taking all the different popular forms derived from the troubadour tradition and giving a master class in how they should be written. He left settings, both monophonic and polyphonic, for over a hundred poems, most of them belonging to the three so-called *formes fixes* – the *virelai, ballade* and *rondeau* – as well as the simpler, if sometimes longer, *lai* and the motet.

Machaut also wrote church music: his masterly, polyphonic *Messe de*

Notre Dame (*c.*1364) is the earliest complete setting of the Mass that can be ascribed to a single individual, and he was the most impressive composer of the so-called *ars nova* style, which flourished in France and Flanders during the mid-fourteenth century. *Ars nova* featured greater rhythmical freedom and polyphonic complexity than the so-called *ars antiqua* which preceded it,[1] and caused division and controversy within the Church hierarchy. Pope John XXII (r. 1316–34), whose concession to modernity was to allow simple *organum* on feast days, was predictably opposed to it; whereas Clement VI (r. 1342–52) actually recruited *ars nova* musicians from Liège and the composer Philippe de Vitry to serve his papal court in Avignon. But the Church was no longer able to impose discipline on musical developments and, as Machaut's *oeuvre* demonstrates, *ars nova* flourished in both ecclesiastical and secular contexts.

Ars nova made little impact in the British Isles, probably because relations and communications between England and France were badly disturbed for long periods. The century began with famine and political instability. It continued with four or five outbreaks of the Black Death between 1348 and the 1390s, killing up to half the population and causing political and economic turmoil. Then there was the Hundred Years War, which began in 1337 and disrupted many traditional lines of communication. The music of the troubadours and trouvères, however, did become known – at least in court circles – as did the work of Machaut. Both were heard and both sparked imitations in the courts and castles of the British Isles, but the extent of their longer-term influence on literary and musical culture is debatable. The best that one can say is that they contributed to the cultural mix that was to give the secular poetry and music of the late-fifteenth and sixteenth centuries its distinctive flavour.

Fourteenth-century Scotland was subject to repeated English invasions and violent dissent among rival Scottish leaders. Court life was at best fragmentary and its musical life is poorly documented. What subsequently became known as 'The Auld Alliance' with France first came into being in 1295, so we may suspect that French cultural influence would have brought trouvère music and tales of courtly love to Scotland in the years that followed, but there is no solid proof of it. In Ireland, we know that trouvère songs were sung at the Lord Lieutenant's court in Dublin, and that for a period there seems to have been a local school of writing in the genre, although nothing has survived. Although it might seem unlikely that such music would ever spread beyond 'The Pale' – that area, centred on Dublin, which was actually controlled by the representatives of the English kings – later Irish songs, particularly love songs, show a clear awareness of medieval French forms, such as the *carole* and the *pastourelle*. What is not clear is whether this influence originated with the Norman and Plantagenet rulers of the medieval period, or whether it was introduced later by poets familiar with French literature and song as a result of the strong links, based on a shared Catholicism, between France and Ireland which developed during the sixteenth and seventeenth centuries.[2]

It is possible, even probable, that the songs of the troubadours and the ideas and images of courtly love were first introduced to the English court at the time of Eleanor of Aquitaine's marriage to Henry II in 1154, but not until much later do we get any sense of their impact; even then, because so little of the music has survived, we have to look to the poets and the poetry of the period. John Gower (*c.*1330–1408) is normally associated with large-scale moral works such as *Vox Clamantis,* written in Latin, and *Confessio Amantis,* written in English. He was not a nobleman: he was a well-born merchant with a legal training, but he existed on the edge of court circles. Early versions of *Confessio Amantis* tell how the work came about as a result of a meeting with Richard II, although he later seems to have switched allegiance to Henry IV, the man who deposed Richard. And it was to Henry that he dedicated his *Cinkante Balades,* receiving an annual pension of two pipes of Gascon wine in return.

Cinkante Balades is a series of fifty-four poems, written in French – the language of the court and of courtly love. The lover addresses the lady and explores his feelings for her; she responds but ultimately rejects him in favour of another. These are elegant and well-constructed poems, usually consisting of three stanzas of either seven or eight lines, plus a four-line envoi. It is not clear whether Gower intended them to be set to music, but they clearly could have been. They display the influence of troubadour poetry, of Machaut, and perhaps of other French poets, such as Eustache Deschamps (1346–1406). But Gower's approach to the ethos of courtly love (which he calls *fin amour* – a Provençal term) is not the traditional one. The formulae of courtly love are borrowed but transformed, even subverted, to promote a moral purpose, to become an argument for love being effectively legitimised by marriage. This may be characteristic of Gower's approach to literature, but he could not have done it had the ballade form, its origins and its conventional content, not been fully understood by his audience.

William Langland (*c.*1332–*c.*1386) was roughly contemporary with Gower. Although we do not know much about his life, we do know that he was not connected with the court. *Piers Plowman* is both an allegory and a satire on contemporary fourteenth-century society, for Langland's sympathies, unlike Gower's, were with the poor and the oppressed. The minstrels that appear in his work are rough-edged individuals, wandering musicians and story-tellers, living by their wits, getting money for their jokes and their singing. One of them, whose name is Hawkin, calls himself *Activa Vita*. At one level, this is to contrast Hawkin's life on the road with the contemplative life of the true Christian, but it may also be intended as a dig at the scholastic musical tradition or at cosseted court musicians or, indeed, both. Hawkin has none of the skills required of a minstrel – he cannot play the tabor or the trumpet; he cannot fart or fiddle at feasts; he cannot play the harp or the pipe; he cannot joke or juggle; he cannot pluck the psaltery, or sing to the guitar. He makes his living by clever talk, deception, and seduction. Langland's is a deliberately extreme example, chosen to represent the kind of minstrel held responsible for various social disorders, inveighed against by the Church and targeted by Edward II. In 1315, Edward's Order of Restraint identified abuses such as 'feigned business' and demands for excessive payment, and laid down conditions for the reception and employment of minstrels in 'the houses of prelates, earls and barons.'[3] Nearly a hundred years later, in 1402, similar edicts were still being issued in Ireland and Wales, linking minstrels and rhymers with vagabonds and accusing them of fomenting insurrection and rebellion.

Gower gives us some understanding of the musical and literary forms as they were practised in court circles. Langland gives us a pointedly exaggerated picture of musical life at the opposite end of the social scale. Geoffrey Chaucer (*c.*1343–1400) was closely connected with the court from an early age. His sympathies are broader than Gower's, while his outlook is less angry and more ironic than Langland's. As a result, the frequent references and allusions to music and musicians in his work give us a clearer picture of fourteenth-century society and music's place within it. Unsurprisingly for an educated man at court who travelled widely, Chaucer's work shows the influence of French and Italian poetry – Machaut, Deschamps, Petrarch, Boccaccio. He wrote a number of ballades – although, unlike Gower's, Chaucer's are in English – which make full, if sometimes idiosyncratic, use of the conventions of courtly love. We do not know how much, if any, of Chaucer's poetry was or was intended to be set to music, although the ballades certainly offer the possibility of musical accompaniment.[4] That he was fully aware of the forms and techniques of Continental song is evident from repeated references to ballades, virelays, complaints, rondeaux and roundelays – and the fact that these terms are used without explanation or definition suggests that he expected his audience to understand them, too. Chaucer's *Romaunt de la Rose* – a partial translation of the *Roman de la Rose*, one of the central texts of courtly love – is littered with references to various forms of music, in particular the carol, which was then a popular form of circle dance in France, but probably relatively new in England.[5] Again, he feels no need to explain what a carol is. In a curious passage in the dream sequence from Book III of *The House of Fame*, the narrator enters a castle which is full 'Of alle manner of mynstralles, / And gestiours, that tellen tales / Both of wepinge and of game, / Of all that longeth unto fame.'[6] He goes on to list the many kinds of instruments that are being played, and describes the dancing, singing and dream-like activities that are taking place. Although clearly exaggerated to meet the requirements of the dream format, the description has prompted at least one critic to suggest that Chaucer may have visited one of the occasional gatherings of minstrels, or 'schools,' that were known to exist at the time, where minstrels exchanged songs, tunes and news in much the same way that wool merchants would have met up and done business at a wool fair.[7]

Music is also important in *The Canterbury Tales*. In 'The Miller's Tale,' Nicholas the student sings both religious and secular songs and plays the 'sautrye' or psaltery; Alison has a voice like a swallow; Absalom plays the two-stringed fiddle and the giterne and sings in a falsetto voice. In 'The Cook's Tale,' the Apprentice, like many students since, likes dancing more than working and is lost without his fiddle or his giterne. The Prioress sings divine service in the old-fashioned nasal manner. The Pardoner is corrupt, but rants hysterically against the sin and lechery bred by dancing and by secular music, while singing descant in what is apparently the old-fashioned, officially approved manner. The jolly Friar has a good voice and plays the rote or harp. The young, romantically inclined Squire writes and sings apparently in the manner of the troubadours. So, too, does Aurelius, the Squire in 'The Franklin's Tale.' The Clerk of Oxenford, however, thinks more of books than of music. These are vivid, persuasive images, yet it is worth remembering that Chaucer is using his characters' musical attitudes and abilities as an aid to characterisation rather than as literal description.

What we chiefly learn from *The Canterbury Tales* and Chaucer's other works is just how pervasive music was at all levels of fourteenth-century society.

Chaucer was not a poet-musician like Machaut – although there is a suggestion that he may have played the harp and the dulcimer – but he clearly understood and appreciated music. Percy Young suggests that he 'esteemed music, but less for its official than its private virtues ... [which] is symptomatic of the way music was generally cultivated.'[8] This points to a significant change. The Church might intermittently pronounce against secular and instrumental music, but, particularly at the higher levels of society, music was now recognised as an art form, and the ability to perform recognised as a personal accomplishment. The time would come when all educated gentlemen would be expected to appreciate music and to attain some degree of proficiency in singing or playing an instrument. The more ambitious might even try composition. This was a new attitude, encompassing aspiration as well as education: it grew out of troubadour composition and the ethos of courtly love, and it came to be associated with the secular end of the classical music tradition. It also marked the beginning of a divergence between music as practised by the educated classes and the popular dances, tunes and the songs of love and work which developed into what we would now call the folk tradition.

These changing attitudes were particularly relevant to women. The ability to dance had long been seen as a desirable female accomplishment, but from the end of the thirteenth century onwards the number of references to women singers and instrumentalists increases significantly. Francesco da Barberino's treatise on the education of women, *Reggimento e costume di donna,* which was probably written during the first twenty years of the fourteenth century, suggests that

> the lower a woman's status the more freedom she has to sing; girls and women of the lower classes have the greatest liberty to dance and sing. The daughter of an emperor or a king may perform for guests only at the request of a parent; she can sing songs when in her room or with her teacher or with other women, and to pass the time she may also be permitted to study an instrument.[9]

Yet society was changing and, even for their time, these were conservative views. The troubadour tradition was one agent for change – and it was promoted by two very powerful women, Eleanor of Aquitaine and her daughter, Marie de Champagne, both of whom spent much time in England. (There was even a specific term – *trobairitz* – for a female troubadour, although there is no record of any of them reaching the British Isles.) Another was the whole ethos of courtly love in which the idealised figure of the lady possessed all virtues and all possible accomplishments, of which music was one. The early fourteenth-century French work, *La Clef d'Amours,* declares that 'singing is a beautiful and noble thing for a young woman and that playing the psaltery, the *timbre,* the *guiterne,* and the *citole* are highly desirable skills.' The heroine of Chrétien de Troyes' *Philomena,* one of the early works of courtly love, writes poetry and plays at least five instruments. Frêne, the heroine of the thirteenth-century *Galeran de Bretagne,* is not only an excellent harpist, she knows songs from France, Gascony, Lorraine and Brittany. She even knows 'Saracen tunes.'[10] And there are many similar examples throughout the period. Aristocratic ladies would have been aware of these role models and sought to emulate them. An anonymous fourteenth-century English poet writes:

> I teche hem daunce,
> And also, ffor ther lady sake,
> Endyte lettyrs, and songys make …
> Balladys, Roundelays, vyrelayes.
> I teche them ek, (lyk ther ententys)
> To pleye on sondry Instrumentys.[11]

Certainly, by the end of the fourteenth century, and within the bounds of etiquette and decorum, women in the upper levels of society would have had more freedom to play and perform than Barberino recommended.

9 The Morris, and the Ballad

The emergence of music as an art and its acceptance as an accomplishment in aristocratic circles were developments which would, with certain regional variations, have been felt throughout Europe. However, there were other developments in the fourteenth century that were peculiar to British music. One of them came about through John of Gaunt, Duke of Lancaster, who was Chaucer's brother-in-law (although not necessarily, as is often suggested, his patron). As an aristocrat, public figure and feudal overlord of large tracts of central England, Gaunt was much concerned at the amount of public disorder, apparently associated with the presence of a large number of minstrels, in the vicinity of his castle at Tutbury in Staffordshire. In August 1381, he issued a charter creating a King of the Minstrels, who was given authority to appoint officers and keep discipline among all minstrels 'within the honour of Tutbury, viz. Stafford, Derby, Nottingham, Leicester, Warwick.'[1] At the same time, in private life, Gaunt took an active interest in both music and literature. In 1389, returning to England after several years fighting in Portugal and Castile, he brought a troupe of Moorish dancers to Tutbury to entertain his household. The presence and subsequent influence of these Moorish dancers offer perhaps the most likely genesis of the English Morris dance tradition: it is possible that 'Moorish' music and dances were spread by the King of the Minstrels and his officers, combining with existing customs such as the Fool's Dance and May Day celebrations to create the Morris tradition as it subsequently evolved.

This, it must be admitted, is educated speculation. The history of the Morris tradition is almost impossible to pin down – largely because, for over four hundred years, no one saw it as worthy of study, either in musical or in social terms.[2] The first unambiguous record dates from the middle of the fifteenth century – a payment of seven shillings to the Morris men of London's Goldsmith's Company – by which time the Morris had apparently spread as far as Cornwall and, particularly in the Midlands, had taken under its wing many songs and stories surrounding the folk hero Robin Hood. By the sixteenth century, the Morris was firmly established throughout England, and even recognised by the Church as an appropriate manner of celebrating Easter, Whitsun and certain other feast days. It suffered under the Commonwealth in the seventeenth century, when all public dancing and all such folk celebrations were outlawed and suppressed, but revived rapidly with the Restoration. There were clear and well-established regional variations: along the Welsh border, Morris men blackened their faces, perhaps remembering the original dancers; in Oxford and Gloucestershire, they danced with sticks and handkerchiefs; in Yorkshire and the north-east, the Morris had combined with local traditions to produce long-sword and rapper-sword dancing. The Morris remained a central strand of popular musical culture in England until the explosion of industrial and urban culture in the nineteenth century. Tunes, dances and doggerel lyrics were passed between regions and down the generations, so that, with very few and much later exceptions, it is impossible to tell when a given Morris tune was written or who wrote it. The tunes themselves are usually simple melodies (though sometimes with unusual or variable time signatures), based around repeated A and B lines, which allow the musicians – originally pipe and drum or just a fiddle – wide scope for variation and improvisation. But that very simplicity, coupled with their strongly rhythmic character, gives them an appeal that – despite a downturn in popularity that brought the Morris to the verge of extinction in the nineteenth century – ensured that they not only survived but, in the latter part of the twentieth century, actually enjoyed a widespread revival.

Of more significance than Morris dance or Morris music is the folk ballad, although its origins are equally hard to establish and its development equally difficult to trace. Any attempt at a meaningful chronology of the ballad tradition inevitably comes up against the fact that ballads – and, indeed, folk songs – were oral compositions; and that there was a gap, of a length which we cannot really determine, between their composition and circulation and their first appearance in manuscript or print. Nonetheless, the attempt must be made, not least because the ballad tradition was a central strand of popular song throughout the British Isles for several hundred years.

The tradition was strongest in England and Scotland; and the most productive regions seem to have been North-East Scotland, the Scottish Borders, the English Midlands and the West of England. We know little about traditional Irish songs and ballads before the seventeenth century, although what we do know suggests that it was primarily a lyric tradition, which, as mentioned above, had absorbed elements of medieval French song. In Wales, where folk music was closely associated with cultural identity and the eisteddfod tradition, it was natural that many ballads and ballad-like songs should have been written in Welsh, although this tended to diminish their influence on the wider ballad tradition. The folk singer and writer A. L. Lloyd has suggested that between 1250 and 1550 the nature and form of the English ballads were gradually evolving (his use of the word 'English' in this context should be understood as 'English-language'); and that between 1550 and 1800, new ballads were written and performed along what were by then broadly accepted lines – except that, as Lloyd sees it, they became shorter in length and more matter-of-fact in tone.[3] For reasons we shall examine in due course, the ballad tradition in England and Scotland declined during the nineteenth century, often merging with other forms of popular song, while in Ireland ballads and ballad-like songs maintained their popularity into the twentieth century, partly because the tradition had become linked to Irish nationalism. Despite the decline of ballad-writing, many hundreds of ballads survived in the oral tradition right up until the beginning of the twentieth century.

Writing in the 1570s, Sir Philip Sidney recognised that some ballads were already old: 'I never heard the old song of Percy and Douglas that I found not my heart moved more than with a trumpet: and yet it is sung by some blind crowder, with no rougher voice than rude style.'[4] The 'old song' in question was evidently one of those telling the story of the Battle of Otterburn, which took place in 1388. The ballad tradition certainly became increasingly visible from the mid-sixteenth century with the advent of cheap printing technology, and it gradually began to attract scholarly interest. The Oxford-based antiquarian and diarist Anthony Wood (sometimes Anthony à Wood; 1632–95) collected some two hundred ballads in a volume that was presented to the Ashmolean Library in Oxford in 1676. Samuel Pepys amassed over 1,800 ballads. Three anonymously edited volumes entitled *A Collection of Old Ballads* were published in London between 1723 and 1765. Then in 1765 came Bishop Percy's justly famous *Reliques of Ancient English Poetry*, which drew on the so-called Percy Folio[5] as well as on existing collections. This was the work that inspired Sir Walter Scott's three-volume *Minstrelsy of the Scottish Border*s (1802–03) and served as a major source for the first 'modern' collection of ballads by Francis James Child that was published between 1882 and 1898.

The interests of the early ballad collectors were essentially literary and historical. They certainly prevented many ballads being lost altogether, but they collected words, not tunes. This made for a distortion of the tradition because the lyrics were never meant to stand alone, and because we cannot now know with any certainty what tune was associated with any given ballad in the early days of its circulation. Child's collection at the end of the nineteenth century – the contents of which have become known as the Child Ballads – was the first attempt at a systematic presentation of words and music together; but the vast majority of tunes now associated with the old ballads were only collected from the oral tradition in the late-nineteenth or early twentieth centuries. Some of them may be the original tunes, but we cannot tell.

The ballad as we know it now – and which must always be distinguished from the ballade – usually consists of a sequential narrative, told in a series of regular four-line verses which repeat the same metrical pattern and rhyme scheme (A-B-C-B is by far the most common), without – as a general rule – choruses or extended refrains. Occasionally, two-line verses can be found, and sometimes a four-line verse may consist of two lines of narrative interspersed with two lines of refrain which repeat in each verse. Each verse repeats the same song-like tune: there is little variation in melody or rhythm, although there is plenty of room for variations in tempo and dynamic emphasis, as there is for variations of stress and emphasis in the singing. What little evidence we have suggests that Celtic bards and Anglo-Saxon scops performed their narratives to a kind of recitative. It is possible that the first ballads were sung in this way, with the use of strophic tunes a later practice, adopted at some point during the medieval period, possibly reflecting the influence of troubadours and minstrels. Alternatively, and perhaps more likely, the ballad and the medieval lyric may have developed strophic form in parallel. The earliest ballad-like composition is a piece called 'Judas', found in a thirteenth-century manuscript but quite possibly composed earlier, which gives a strange and unusually passionate account of Judas' betrayal of Christ. The 'Lyke-Wake Dirge' is also very old, possibly dating back to the twelfth century. The use of the 'lyke' for a dead body strongly suggests the remains of Scandinavian influence. The narrative describes the journey of a soul departing this life on its way to Purgatory, but – although clearly Christian in intent – the imagery is shot through with pagan references.

Another apparently early ballad is 'Thomas the Rhymer', which tells the story of Thomas's meeting with 'the queen of fair Elfland' who takes him to her domain where he must serve her for seven years. Thomas the Rhymer appears to have been a real person: Thomas Learmonth or Learmont was a landowner and supposed prophet who lived in Erceldoune, now Earlston, in Berwickshire, in the middle years of the thirteenth century. The ballad has been localised to the Scottish Borders, but there are a number of features in the story of how Thomas obtained his prophetic powers – the kiss from the lady, the alternative roads leading to Heaven or Hell or Elfland, the apple received from the lady, the period of seven years' servitude – which find clear parallels in ritual songs collected in parts of Central Europe, possibly suggesting a link to some common pre-Christian source. Similarly, the story told in the Halloween ballad, 'Lady Isabel and the Elf Knight,' has been found in various guises right across the Continent, again indicating a common root and early composition.

Although evidence is scanty, we can at least suggest that the earliest ballads took as their subject matter the mystical or magical edge of religion. Whether the music which originally accompanied the words reflected this we can never know. As time went on, a more heroic tone is evident. The magic is still there, but myth begins to creep in. This shift may have begun in the fourteenth century. Certainly, there are several ballads of apparently early date which combine a royal protagonist with magical elements and find echoes elsewhere in European folklore and mythology. The Shetland ballad, 'King Orfeo', connects to Greek mythology through the late thirteenth- or early fourteenth-century Middle English poem, *Sir Orfeo*. The story of the 'griesly ghost' who appears in the ballad 'King Henry' is a recognisable medieval motif – the 'loathly lady' who is transformed into a beautiful woman – which links the ballad to both Chaucer's 'Wife of Bath's Tale' and the roughly contemporaneous Icelandic *Saga of King Hrolf Kraki*.

Another aspect of this transitional period concerns the Robin Hood ballads, of which forty or more have survived. Whether or not he was a real person, the first ballads featuring the character of Robin Hood were in circulation by the latter half of the fourteenth century. Sloth, the incompetent priest in *Piers Plowman*, confesses that while he is not word perfect on his Pater Noster, he does know the 'rymes of Robyn Hood.'[6] Folklorists have at times sought to identify Robin Hood with Wotan or Mithras or even Jesus Christ, but his real significance is that he is a folk hero, the first to appear in British song. The ballads introduce a new tone which may well stem from the social and economic upheavals that followed in the wake of the Black Death. They are not political or revolutionary, nor even actively subversive, but they do contain a spirit of cheekiness, insubordination and defiance of authority, a championing of the underdog, which is new and which, ultimately, opened the way for the political and protest songs of later centuries.

The great age of the big historical ballads was still to come, but the foundations were being laid. Who then produced these early ballads? The anti-authoritarian spirit of the Robin Hood ballads might suggest that their inspiration came from lower down the social scale, from the kind of minstrels that we have seen associated, at least in the minds of kings and dukes, with social disorder and insurrection. Occasional literary and formal flourishes found in some of the texts may well be later interpolations. What of ballads like 'Thomas the Rhymer,' 'King Orfeo' and King Henry? Could they have been composed by minstrels serving at a nobleman's court? Or by itinerant musicians? Or by a student like Nicholas in

'The Miller's Tale'? There is no reason why not, but we can never be certain. Even with the big ballads of the fifteenth and sixteenth centuries which deal with battles and great events, there is dispute as to whether they originated among educated, professional musicians in castles and great houses, or among the artisan musician class of the markets and taverns. We do know, however, that the ballads were sung in both milieux, among the aristocrats and gentry as well as among the townsfolk and the peasantry. They were the popular music of their day and show just how far the flourishing secular music scene of the age had moved from the dominance of the Church and the forms of church music.

10 Music, Science, and Politics

In secular society, music was becoming an art; in the Church, it remained essentially a science. Troubadours and minstrels sought to engage their audiences by telling stories and expressing emotions; church musicians sought to express mastery of form and technique. Music was taught as a science in the universities of the age. There were three in the British Isles at the turn of the fifteenth century – at Oxford, Cambridge and Dublin. Like other universities across Europe, they had evolved from monastic and cathedral schools and remained firmly ecclesiastical in orientation. Their function was to educate the clergy and certain selected members of the ruling elite; and music occupied a prominent position in the curriculum. It was one of four subjects which made up the *quadrivium*, the second level of university study – the others were arithmetic, geometry and astronomy – and the *quadrivium* was an essential preparation for those who wished to study philosophy and theology.

The fifteenth century was a turbulent period in all parts of the British Isles. In Scotland, it was characterised by prolonged power struggles between the Crown and the Scottish Barons. In England, Henry IV's seizure of the throne in 1399 paved the way for brief glory under Henry V, prolonged instability under Henry VI and during the Wars of the Roses, and then the establishment of an absolute monarchy under Henry VII. And in Ireland, English power, as represented by the Dublin-based Lord Deputy or Lord Lieutenant, was in retreat, faced with the resurgent influence of the Irish lords. Nonetheless, the century also saw a steady increase in the value attributed to education and, at least in Scotland and England, an increase in the number of educational establishments.

In Scotland, three new universities were founded: St Andrews (1412), Glasgow (1451) and Aberdeen (1495). In England, Winchester College was established in 1394 under the patronage of Henry VI. It admitted sixteen choristers and seventy scholars and was intended to begin the education of young clerics who would then move on to New College, Oxford, which also had places for sixteen choristers and boasted an important choir. Eton College, founded in 1440, again by Henry VI, had a similar provision for sixteen choristers and a similar relationship with King's College, Cambridge. Magdalen College, Oxford, founded in 1458, made provision for a choral foundation of men and boys; and several other Oxford and Cambridge colleges already possessed recognised choirs. In 1464, on the orders of Edward IV, Cambridge University began to grant degrees in music. Rotherham Grammar School, founded in 1483 by the Archbishop of York, Thomas Rotherham, made specific provision for musical education. But the trend did not extend to Ireland or Wales – both, in their different ways, English colonies – where there were few comparable developments.

With education still very much in the hands of the clergy, it was natural that main aim of musical education should be to improve the quality of music in the monasteries and religious foundations which dotted the land: there were well over six hundred in England and Wales, roughly the same number in Ireland, and more than two hundred and fifty in Scotland. At the same time, as we have seen, music had an important role to play in boosting the image of the monarchy. It was a role recognised by kings and princes across Europe, and one which grew in importance during the fifteenth century. In England, where the crown was seized by violence on no less than four occasions, the rival families of Lancaster and York both saw music as an important means of projecting an image of power and legitimacy. Royal patronage of music became a significant part of royal support for education, which, it was hoped, would in turn play a part in ensuring the support of the Church for the monarch and his regime.

The Chapel Royal, another aspect of royal patronage of music, now had an overtly political role. During the reign of Henry V, the Chapel increased in size, and under the leadership of John Pyamour followed the King to Normandy whenever he led his army against the French. Nicholas Sturgeon and Thomas Dammet, both members of the Chapel Royal, wrote a *Benedictus* apparently for the occasion of the King's campaign in France in 1416. It may well have been Pyamour who composed the anthem *Quis est magnus,* which was sung before the King in Rouen Cathedral after the city had fallen to the English in 1419. Both Dammet and another Chapel Royal composer, John Cook, wrote pieces praising Henry V and beseeching divine protection for him when he went to war. Compositions in praise of the Royal Family were not, however, limited to Chapel Royal composers. Both Leonel Power (sometimes Lionel or Lyonel; d.1445), one of the leading composers of the age, and the shadowy Walter Frye, who may have been cantor of Ely Cathedral and who may have died at Canterbury in 1474, left ceremonial motets in praise of the House of Lancaster. Enough examples of this kind of musical flattery survive – and it is as certain as such things can be that many more were destroyed during the dissolution of the monasteries – to suggest that it was an accepted (and no doubt prudent) activity among composers of the time.

Henry V's successors continued to recognise the importance of the Chapel Royal. Indeed, it became an integral part of the ritual surrounding the King and his court. Under Henry VI in 1449, William Say, Dean of the Chapel Royal, wrote a book called *Liber regie capelle* for a visiting Portuguese nobleman, Count Alvaro Vaz d'Almada. It instructed him in the precise details of the Chapel's daily, twice-weekly and weekly ceremonies, all of which were designed to ask God to protect the King and his realm. Edward IV formally reorganised the administration of the Chapel in 1483, the last year of his reign. Henry VII, having seized the crown at the Battle of Bosworth in 1485, undoubtedly used it as a tool to boost his legitimacy. And under Henry VIII it gained greater importance in the aftermath of the Reformation. Membership of the Chapel Royal was a path that was to lead many English composers to musical success, but it also offered the possibility of other rewards. From the early years of the fifteenth century, it became common for members of the Chapel to be given jobs, land, or pensions in recognition of their services to the monarchy. Henry V left them £200 in gold. And more senior positions could offer real power and influence: 'By the fifteenth century the dean of the Chapel had assumed extensive powers over the whole [royal] household, estimated to number some twelve hundred. In some matters, he exercised the authority of a bishop, taking full cognisance of criminal cases and proving wills, and he recognised no superior in spiritual matters except the archbishop of Canterbury.'[1]

In England, music and its formal structures thus became something of a political tool, a reflection of growing interdependence between the Church and the State – as represented by the monarch and the barons who backed him – and this situation, which continued until the Reformation, only served to widen the already broad gulf between religious and secular music. In Scotland, however, while music was undoubtedly important in Church and court circles, it did not assume the same political role. James I (r. 1396–1437) was a hostage at the English court for the first eighteen years of his reign. During his captivity, he is reported to have become a skilled musician and composer – though none of his works have survived – and when he returned to Scotland he took with him a number of English and Flemish musicians. In 1460, Mary of Gueldres, widow of James II, founded the collegiate church of Trinity College, Edinburgh, which made special provision for musical education. James III (r. 1460–88) continued to establish collegiate churches throughout his reign, and also reorganised the Scottish Chapel Royal, importing the English musician William Rogers to give direction. If these events did not take on the political colouring they would have done in England, it is largely because – despite wars, rebellions and a succession of violent deaths – the Scottish crown passed directly from one James Stewart to the next over the course of the century. The Church and its music was consequently less important as a legitimising tool.

11 Dunstable, and *la Contenance Angloise*

During the fourteenth century, the Western Church all but tore itself apart. At one stage, the Western or Papal Schism meant that there were rival popes: one in Avignon, one in Rome, and even, for a short while, a third in Pisa. By contrast, the forms of Christian worship and the music that accompanied them suffered no such upheavals. There was evolution: composers continued to develop the possibilities of polyphony; they developed the isorhythmic forms pioneered by Machaut, making use of complex patterns of rhythmic repetition; they developed ever more complicated vocal techniques. But at the heart of everything were settings of the Mass and its component parts, and pieces produced for the other central acts of church ritual, all ultimately anchored in plainsong and the *cantus firmus*. France and Burgundy were the recognised centres of musical development. Then, suddenly, at the beginning of the fifteenth century, we find English music and English composers – of which, with equal suddenness, a significant number appear – receiving recognition and praise in the courts of Europe. English involvement in Continental wars and increasing contact between the English and Burgundian courts certainly meant that English music could now be heard more widely than before. We know, for example, that English music was played and admired during the Council of Constance (1414–18) – in what is now Switzerland and was then part of the Duchy of Burgundy – which elected Pope Martin V and brought the Western Schism to an end. However it came about, English music was now regarded as leading the way, and English composers were in demand in courts, music schools and religious foundations on the Continent. There has even been talk of a 'significant brain drain' of composers during the reigns of Henry IV (r. 1399–1413) and Henry V (r. 1413–22).[1]

This sudden coming of age of English music remains something of a mystery. It came out of nowhere. The Plantagenet kings of the fourteenth century undoubtedly recognised the importance of music and encouraged its development, but there is nothing to suggest that they or the Church authorities did anything to stimulate the change. Improvements in musical education sponsored by the later Plantagenet kings came after the event. Yet both English and Continental sources make it clear that not only were these new composers thought of as leaders in their field, but their output was prodigious. Unfortunately, much of it was lost during the dissolution of the monasteries when the libraries that held their many manuscripts were broken up, sold off, or simply burned.

Much of the best of what has survived is contained in three English manuscripts. The Old Hall MS[2] was originally put together for the Chapel Royal, but then passed to St Edmund's College, one of the oldest Roman Catholic schools in England and since 1793 located at Old Hall Green, near Puckeridge in Hertfordshire. The Lambeth Choirbook[3] appears to have originated at Arundel College (and is sometimes referred to as the Arundel Choirbook) before finding its way to Lambeth Palace, the official London residence of the Archbishop of Canterbury. The Eton Choirbook[4] was compiled in the very early years of the sixteenth century for use at Eton College, where it has remained. To these three may be added the Scottish Carver MS,[5] probably compiled between 1513 and 1520, with one or two later additions, by the Scottish monk and composer, Robert Carver, at Scone Abbey in Perthshire.

In these manuscripts, it suddenly becomes much more common for works to be attributed to named individuals, although there are still numerous anonymous pieces. The traditional medieval view that a piece of music should be an anonymous offering to the glory of God had long been breaking down – though more rapidly in France and Italy than in England and Scotland – and the occasional name slipped through. Now, at the turn of the fifteenth century, individual composers begin to emerge from the shadows: their works are identifiable and biographical details, however limited, can be unearthed. Several factors are at work here: an increased sense of individuality transferring across from secular culture and secular creativity; the increasing institutionalisation of the musical world, leading to named individuals taking named positions; and, of course, the simple survival of documents from the Royal Household and elsewhere which makes research possible. Nonetheless, the emergence of composers as individuals marks a key step in the evolution of music and its place in society. English composers of church music at the beginning of the fifteenth century would undoubtedly have agreed that their talent was God-given, but they no longer saw in that admission any requirement to remain anonymous – and the name that stands out is that of John Dunstable.

We do not know when Dunstable was born and there is even uncertainty about his name – which is variously spelt Dunstaple, Dunstapell, or even Dumstable – but we do know that he died on 24 December 1453 and that, after his death, his reputation 'stood so high that his claim to be regarded as the first great English composer has never been contested.'[6] One epitaph, composed by John Whethampstede, Abbot of St Albans, referred to him as 'an astrologian, a mathematician, a musician, and what not.'[7] A second (in a memorial that was in St Stephen's, Wallbrook, until the church was destroyed in the Great Fire of London) described him as one who knew the secrets of the stars, and a prince of music.[8] The reference to astronomy, mathematics and music suggests the *quadrivium* and a university education, although we cannot be sure. There is, however, a treatise on astronomy in the library of St John's College, Cambridge, which appears to have belonged to Dunstable and describes him as a musician to the Duke of Bedford. This is suggestive because not only is Dunstable in Bedfordshire – and it was common during medieval times for men to be identified by their town of origin – but also because the Duke, who was the third son of Henry IV and thus the younger brother of Henry V, acted as Regent of France during the minority of Henry VI from 1422 until 1429, and as Governor of Normandy from 1422 until 1432. Extended service with the

Duke in France in what was, for much of the time, a diplomatic milieu would explain why Dunstable appears to have made his reputation on the Continent rather than in England. For some ten years between 1427 and 1437, Dunstable was a well-paid retainer in the service of the Queen Joan, widow of Henry IV; and we know that he was subsequently employed by the Duke of Bedford's younger brother, Humphrey, Duke of Gloucester. Other biographical details are largely conjecture.

The only reference to Dunstable during his lifetime comes in a poem called *Le Champion des Dames* (*c.*1442) written by Martin Le Franc. In the course of this 24,000-line attempt to detach the Duke of Burgundy from his alliance with the English, Le Franc coined the phrase '*la contenance angloise*' to describe the new style of the day which characterised Dunstable's music and which he saw as a powerful influence on the leading Burgundian composers, Guillaume Dufay and Gilles Binchois. Twenty years after Dunstable's death, the Flemish composer and scholar, Johannes Tinctoris, was more effusive. In his *Proportionale musices,* he states that the English were the 'fount and origin' of changes that had increased the possibilities of music to the point where it was almost a new art, and that the chief among them was Dunstable.[9] Other references followed, including that by the French composer Eloy d'Amerval, whose poem *Le livre de la deablerie* (1508) contains a description of paradise and the great musicians who are resident there. 'Dompstaple' heads the list.[10] Yet there were no corresponding references from English writers until 1597, when Thomas Morley questioned Dunstable's manner of setting text to music.

Why then was Dunstable considered such a seminal figure? And what was *la contenance angloise* of which he was the leading exponent and which changed the face of music? Approximately sixty works by Dunstable survive, although problems of attribution make it impossible to be precise. The majority are from Italian sources – thirty-one in a single manuscript from Modena, again strongly suggesting that a significant part of his career was spent on the Continent – while only twenty appear in English manuscripts. These surviving pieces include at least two complete settings of the Mass, plus a number of incomplete settings or settings of individual parts of the Mass, as well as motets, hymns, and numerous settings of liturgical texts. He is also reputed to have written secular pieces, although only one of these – *Puisque m'amour,* a rondeau – has been identified with any certainty. In terms of quantity, his output appears to have been similar to other composers of his time: the differences are stylistic and technical.

The most obvious feature of *la contenance angloise* is the use of intervals of a third to build triadic chords and to enable the use of triadic harmonies in creating a new and fuller sound. Whether or not Dunstable was personally responsible for this innovation – other English composers certainly made use of it – it certainly opened up new harmonic and melodic possibilities, and marked a huge step forward in the direction of what we now understand as modern western music. Dunstable combined the use of triadic harmonies with a strong melodic sense. His melodies build smoothly, for the most part avoiding sudden leaps and large intervals, and he limits melodic repetition to concise two- or three-bar phrases, suggesting – despite his academic background – a composer who is thinking about what can be sung rather than working out a mathematical theory. Yet he can be structurally as well as harmonically innovative.

Eric Routley has drawn attention to Dunstable's setting of *Veni Sancte Spiritus,* a four-part motet setting a text for Pentecost that was probably written by the thirteenth-century Archbishop of Canterbury, Stephen Langton. Dunstable's starting point was not a tune usually associated with this text; instead, he turned to the melody – and words – of an older Pentecostal text, *Veni Creator Spiritus,* developing the mixture into a highly complex and forward-looking structure. The result was not only innovative and ingenious, it also openly defied the Church, which was stringently opposed to the idea of setting more than one text at the same time, probably because they feared that musical and textual complexity would distract attention from the meaning of the words.[11] Despite this, *Veni Sancte Spiritus* was performed in Canterbury Cathedral in 1416 in the presence of both Henry V and the Holy Roman Emperor Sigismund at a service of thanksgiving to mark the signing of the Treaty of Canterbury. This was the avant-garde music of the age and Dunstable's technique is impressive. The work is not so much an outburst of passion as a deeply felt but controlled expression of faith. He manipulates the four voices, the different rhythms and the lines of text with great skill, but never to the detriment of the emotion and the deep religious feeling which comes through in the music. Dunstable never shows off, but gives the impression of knowing exactly what he can do and what he can achieve with the new musical possibilities at his disposal. It is a remarkable fact that the use of two texts in this way is something we do not find again in British music until Benjamin Britten's *Hymn to St Peter* in 1955.

Veni Sancte Spiritus is the only composition of Dunstable's to appear in the Old Hall MS, which is the best indication we have of the music that was current in England up to 1421. One can speculate that extended residence on the continent had cut him off from musical life in England and that, as a consequence, his reputation had yet to be established in his own country. By contrast, Leonel Power is represented by no less than twenty-two pieces, and even lesser-known composers such as John Forest, Thomas Byttering, Thomas Dammet and (?Richard) Queldryk are better represented than Dunstable. Little is known about Power's life: he was in the service of the Duke of Clarence; he may possibly have been employed by the same Duke of Bedford who employed Dunstable; and he became Master of the Lady Chapel Choir in Canterbury Cathedral, where he died in 1445. After Dunstable, he was certainly the most influential and progressive English composer of the time, to the point where it is sometimes difficult to tell their works apart. Both made consistent use of triadic harmonies, and they were the first to compose cyclic Masses – settings of the Mass in which the different sections are united by the use of the same or variants of the same *cantus firmus*, making them, in effect, the first multi-movement structures in western music. Power seems to have been somewhat older than Dunstable and this has led to suggestions – not without logic – that Power may have done some of the groundwork from which Dunstable later benefitted.[12]

In the end, it barely matters. Dunstable is the accepted star of the age and Power is a close second. Typp, Tyes, Pycard and Chirbury and the other composers who feature in the Old Hall MS will never be household names, but their music is still worth listening to. The fact that they share certain characteristics – a tendency to treat melodic lines freely, a preference for complex musical forms, notably canons, and, above all, a sense of self-confidence – makes it clear that, from the end of the fourteenth century into the early decades of the fifteenth, there was a group of English composers producing music that had a distinct and recognisable English style.

12 The Eton Choirbook, and the Early Tudors

Johannes Tinctoris acknowledged the primacy of English music in Dunstable's day but claimed that, in the years that followed, the English had shown a miserable lack of invention by continuing to compose in precisely the same manner.[1] Tinctoris's perspective was a Flemish one. In the second half of the fifteenth century, the so-called Franco-Flemish School, led by Johannes Ockeghem and Josquin des Prez but including many other composers of note, such as Orto, Prioris, Obrecht, de la Rue, Isaac, and Tinctoris himself, developed the earlier English style in their own particular way. They showed a fondness for complex forms (Orto wrote a wholly canonic setting of the Mass); a logical, even theory-based approach to their exploration of the possibilities of polyphony; and a move towards imitative polyphony, where all the vocal parts have an equal function and an equal musical value in the piece as a whole. The English, uninterested rather than unaware of what was happening on the Continent, took a step in the opposite direction, towards simplicity. This was not a question of competence; rather because they ranked 'the claims of euphony' above 'intellectual canonic devices.'[2] And in the contrasting approaches of this period, we get the first clear indication of a central, underlying characteristic of much of the music of the British Isles: an inclination to trust melodic invention and musical instinct rather than following a theoretical path.

The Eton Choirbook was compiled at the very beginning of the sixteenth century and contains sixty-four works by twenty-one composers.[3] Although these works differ from those of contemporary Continental composers, they too are descended from Dunstable, Power, and the Old Hall composers. The link is as much one of attitude as of technique, and manifests itself in the freedom and imagination with which they treat their material. Much of the music remains based on a *cantus firmus* in the accepted manner, but there is a new freedom in the way the *cantus firmus* is modified, varied and migrated between parts. At times, it disappears altogether, allowing for the inclusion of new or free material – an indication of the way in which vocal music would develop in the future. Other pieces in the Eton Choirbook appear to be based entirely on new material – such as John Browne's immensely tuneful *Salve regina.* Browne (1453–*c.*1500), yet another composer about whom very little is known, also comes up with new vocal combinations – his *Stabat iuxta Christi crucem* is scored for four tenors and two basses. Yet the most important new element in the Eton Choirbook is a sense of scale and drama. Browne's *Stabat Mater dolorosa* is a remarkable, intensely dramatic piece. The *Stabat Mater* of John Wilkinson (or Wylkynson) is written in nine parts, each representing one of the nine choirs or orders of angels. And Richard Davy's *O Domine caeli* *terraeque creator* is conceived on an impressive scale. A work of some two hundred and sixty bars, it is divided into musically differentiated sections in a manner which perhaps derives from the cyclic Masses of Dunstable and Power, but which can be seen as looking towards a future, albeit a distant one, where the division of works into movements became the norm. These same broad characteristics carry over into the nineteen pieces contained in the Lambeth Choirbook, which was probably put together a few years later than the Eton Choirbook, but which is notable for containing seven settings of the Mass, whereas the Eton Choirbook does not contain any.

In considering the English composers of the late fifteenth century, it is not too far-fetched to see a parallel between their music and their surroundings. This was the age when the last phase of English Gothic, the Perpendicular, reached its architectural apogee. The Perpendicular, with its emphasis on soaring vertical lines, fine tracery, delicate fan vaulting, and huge windows with narrow mullions, can suggest aspiration and a longing for simplicity – at least when compared with the Decorated Gothic of an earlier age. And like the music of the time, it finds no exact echo on the Continent. Eton College Chapel, for which the choirbook was compiled, is a classic example of the style; as are King's College, Cambridge; Magdalen College, Oxford; and St George's Chapel, Windsor. It is surely no accident that many of the composers of the period were connected with these institutions.

The leading establishment composer to emerge from this background was Robert Fayrfax. He was born in Lincolnshire in 1464, became a Gentleman of the Chapel Royal in 1497 and remained one until his death in 1521. His career seems to have been given over wholly to music. His surviving compositions – there are two in the Eton Choirbook and five in the Lambeth – do not generate great enthusiasm among critics today, being seen as less adventurous and versatile than those of his contemporaries, although he was undoubtedly highly regarded in his own time. He obtained doctorates in music from both Oxford and Cambridge and received a series of annuities, positions and generous payments from Henry VIII, who seems to have been a genuine admirer.

William Cornysh (sometimes Cornish; *c.*1468–1523), the other leading musical figure of the period, was a much more colourful character. There is scope for confusion in the fact that his father was also called William Cornysh, and was also a musician. It was the father who was Master of Choristers at Westminster Abbey until his death *c.*1502, and who composed five surviving polyphonic pieces, including an impressive five-part *Salve Regina* and a rich, sonorous *Magnificat*, which appear in the Eton Choirbook. It was Cornysh the Younger who entered the service of Henry VII in 1492, and followed his father in becoming a Gentlemen and, later, Master of the Chapel Royal. In this capacity, he was responsible for the performance of music as well as for the education and welfare of the choirboys at the Chapel, but he does not seem to have composed religious music.

In his youth, the younger Cornysh seems to have been friendly with the poet John Skelton, tutor to the Prince Henry (later Henry VIII), and this may have provided him with an introduction to court circles. However it happened, he rapidly rose to prominence. He was entrusted with producing the musical and dramatic entertainment for the celebrations surrounding the marriage of Prince Arthur to Catherine of Aragon in 1501; and he was also responsible for producing court pageants. His standing does not appear to have been harmed by a short spell in the Fleet Prison for writing a satirical attack on Henry VII's most unpopular tax collector; and with the accession of Henry VIII in 1509, his influence increased. He accompanied the King to France at least twice. During the campaign of 1513, he appears to have been in charge of the musical celebrations to mark the capture of the towns of Thérouanne and Tournai. Then, in 1520, he was probably responsible for the English side of the music at the Field of the Cloth of Gold; his French opposite number was probably Jean de Mouton. A great deal of music – some of which has survived and been recorded[4] – was required for this spectacular diplomatic encounter. Henry travelled with a full complement of choristers (of whom Robert Fayrfax was the senior); with trumpeters, wind players and percussionists to produce appropriately martial music; with a band of musicians to allow for dancing and singing in the evening; and even with a special organ, made of silver with gold ornamentation, for his chapel-tent.

Life at court in the early years of the Tudor dynasty should not, of course, be taken as representative of the British Isles or even of England as whole, but it does display characteristics that point towards later musical forms and practices – and there was interplay between the court and the wider world. Until that time, simple, procession-like pageants and primitive masques based on simple disguises had been a recognised feature of the court. Henry VII, or those around him, drew on a variety of traditions to breathe new life into these existing entertainments and create the distinctive Tudor court pageant. Drama, as such, was in its infancy, but there was a long-established tradition of mystery plays in a number of towns and cities. They were usually cycles of short plays retelling key episodes of the Bible story. They had begun life as liturgical pageants accompanied by hymns and antiphons, but had been liberated from the Church and were now annual civic festivals with each play the responsibility of a particular craft guild. There were also morality plays – independent, allegorical pieces, such as *Everyman*, which grew out of the mystery cycles – as well as the secular and more comic tradition of mummers' (or guisers') plays. Music evidently played an important role in all these productions, whether as preludes or interludes, as songs within the plays, or as accompaniment to the action. Civil pageants on local or historical themes, again accompanied by music, were also staged in some of the major regional centres. In addition to these domestic traditions, Henry VII, who had spent his formative years at the court of the Duke of Brittany, was able to draw on French styles of dancing and his experience of the more sophisticated pageants – masque-like entertainments and mummeries – that were a feature of life at the Burgundian court, which he frequently visited.[5]

Henry VII is traditionally presented as a somewhat dour figure, but he was clearly fond of music. The account books of the Royal Household show frequent payments being made to organists, pipers, bagpipers, instrumentalists and minstrels of all kinds. He also invited companies of actors to perform before the court. More elaborate entertainments marked the major festivals of the Christian year, St George's Day, and important royal events such as the King's birthday. Henry's purpose was clear. Displays of wealth, of artistic appreciation and patronage were all ways of building up his public image, of impressing the country, the court, ambassadors and other representatives of foreign rulers with his status. The responsibility for these entertainments and pageants, or 'revels' as they were known, seems to have fallen to the Master of the Chapel Royal. In 1490, the then Master, Laurence Squire, was required to dress his choristers as mermaids. His successor, William Newark (1450–1509), was specifically tasked with devising and superintending Christmas festivities at court. But it was William Cornysh, with his strong literary and dramatic sense, as well as his musical skill, who became the central figure in the creation of the early Tudor revels.

When Henry VIII came to the throne in 1509, the importance of such entertainments increased. The first pageant of the new reign was at

Christmas when the King, dressed as Robin Hood and accompanied by twelve Merry Men, entered Queen Catherine's apartments and danced with the Queen and her attendant ladies to the accompaniment of a consort of minstrels. In 1511, when a son was born to the royal couple, Cornysh was responsible for the celebratory entertainment. *The Golden Arbour* featured an artificial mountain upon which grew a golden tree, elaborately decorated with Tudor roses and real, and therefore rare, pomegranates.[6] Another, in 1514, was called *The Triumph of Love and Beauty*. These pageants were little more than expensive tableaux with only limited dramatic content. Dancing was important, but so too were the musical interludes between scenes which gave the production a sense of continuity. Court entertainments quickly grew more sophisticated, providing a greater and more assertive role for music. The first actual masque to be produced at court was part of the Twelfth Night festivities in 1512: the players, apparently including the King, wearing golden masks and caps, told a story after the Italian manner through singing and dancing. By 1517, a more ambitious masque, *Troilus and Cryseide*, based on the story as told by Chaucer, marked the beginning of a new fashion and a new musical form, that would lead first to the elaborate and highly produced masques of the Stuart kings and then to the earliest English forays into opera.

It was during the early Tudor period that the first ripples of the Renaissance began to reach English shores. At this stage, the impact was limited, but it did strengthen the foundations of secular music in a way that was to become extremely important in the latter part of Henry VIII's reign when the Reformation and the dissolution of the monasteries overturned structures that had produced and sustained religious music for centuries. As we shall see, this did not necessarily damage the quality of the religious music that was produced, but it marked a major shift towards the secular in national consciousness and culture. That shift built on the changes that occurred early in the Tudor period.

As the fifteenth century drew to a close, minstrels continued to sing songs that reflected the now much-watered-down tradition of the troubadours; merchants and peasants might sing songs about love or work, or ballads about honour and battle. At court and among the aristocracy, however, the approach to secular song was changing. Part-songs were becoming increasingly common, and, while love predominated, it was no longer the only subject. Composers were showing both greater breadth and more discrimination in the texts they set. William Newark, despite being a long-serving Gentleman and, subsequently, Master of the Chapel Royal, is survived by only seven compositions – all of them secular songs in two or three parts. One of them is a wonderfully simple, two-part setting of a moving, philosophical lyric, attributed to the early fifteenth-century poet, John Halsham.

> The farther I go, the more behind;
> The more behind, the nere my wayes end;
> The more I seek, the worse can I find;
> The lighter leefe, the lother for to wend.
> The truer I serve, the farther out of mind;
> Though I go loose, yet am I tied with a line;
> Is it Fortune or Infortune this I find?[7]

The same manuscript, known as the Fayrfax Manuscript and dating from *c.*1500, also contains William Cornysh the Younger's busy, almost raunchy, three-part setting of a colloquial and energetic poem by his friend, John Skelton.

> Ay, besherewe yow, be my fay,
> This wanton clarkes be nyse all way;
> Avent, avent, my popagay!
> What, will ye do no thyng but play?[8]

Formal musical settings across such a range of mood and subject matter would have been inconceivable at any earlier time.

Instrumental music, too, was changing. Around the turn of the century, keyboard instruments began to appear at court and in the richer, aristocratic households, although it took some time for the design and the very names of these instruments to settle. Keyboard playing began to be recognised as an accomplishment. Records show that Elizabeth of York, Henry VII's queen, was given a pair of clavichords in 1502. An inscription on the walls of Leckington Hall in Yorkshire, one of the seats of Henry Percy, 5th Earl of Northumberland, who was brought up at Henry VII's court, suggests the presence of clavichords and virginals at about the same time. William Cornysh mentions the importance of correctly tuning a 'clarrychord' in *A Treatise bitwene Trouth and Enformacion* (written in 1504 while he was in prison).[9] The poet, Stephen Hawes, in *The Passetyme of Pleasure* (1517), talks of 'claricymbals' and 'claricordes'.[10] In 1530, Henry VIII apparently bought five virginals.

The first surviving music composed specifically for these new keyboard instruments – a series of pieces attributed to one Hugh Aston (or Ashton,

Ayston, Asshetone and other variants) – is interesting because it is so clearly written without reference to church music or formal vocal parts, both of which had previously been crucial to the development of music.[11] Instead, it drew on popular speech and popular dance forms. *Aston's Hornpipe* is based on a dance form that may have originated in Lancashire (and in this manifestation is very different from the later sailor's hornpipe), and *My Lady Carey's Dompe* is an arrangement of a hypnotic, rhythmic dance, popular at the time, but usually associated with working people and usually accompanied by a lute. Moreover, musicians were now arranging this material in a way that added a level of sophistication and thus made it acceptable to people of educated taste. Yet this was not a democratisation of music. It was a process driven from the top and intended for the benefit and enjoyment of those in the upper levels of society.

By this stage the English had enjoyed a sequence of actively musical monarchs. The best indication of this is the fact that the 'Roy Henry' who appears in the Old Hall MS as the composer of a *Gloria* and a *Sanctus* – both in three parts and both worthy of inclusion on their own merits – has at various times been identified as Henry IV, Henry V and Henry VI.[12] Henry VII was neither a performer nor a composer, but, as we have seen, he appreciated music and did much to encourage it, spending a great deal of money in both the religious and the secular spheres. However, it was Henry VIII who took the prominence of music at court and the prominence of the monarch's role in music at court to a new level. He himself had great gifts: he was a horseman, an athlete, a sportsman; he spoke Latin and French well, as well as some Italian and Spanish. He had a knowledge of mathematics, theology and astronomy, but

> above all, he was a gifted and enthusiastic musician. He had music wherever he went, on progress, on campaign. He scoured England for singing boys and men for the chapels royal.... Sacred music in the Renaissance style – the work of Benedict de Opitiis and Richard Sampson, later bishop of Chichester – was introduced.... The king acquired a collection of French and Netherlandish music. Henry had many foreign musicians at court, like the violist Ambrose Lupo, the lutenist Philip van Wilder from the Netherlands, as well as trumpeters, flautists and two Italian organists.... The king himself played the lute well; he could manage the organ and was skilled on the virginals.... He had a strong, sure voice, could sight-read easily.... His court was a generous patron to composers

> ... the king wrote at least two five-part masses, a motet, a large number of instrumental pieces, part-songs and rounds.[13]

Opinion remains divided about the merits of Henry VIII as a composer, but there is no doubt that he was technically competent. Pieces such as *Pastyme with Good Companye*, *Grene Growth the Holy*, *Un Vray Amour*, and *Helas Madam* are still sung and recorded.[14]

Henry's range of interests and abilities has frequently led him to be labelled a Renaissance Prince, but J. J. Scarisbrick in his classic biography has argued that 'if anything, Henry was the last of the troubadours ... a youth wholly absorbed in dance and song, courtly love and knight-errantry.'[15] For the first twenty years of his reign, it was this image that dominated and was projected to the nation; but as time went by he became increasingly obsessed with more conventional dynastic concerns, and his determination to provide himself with a male heir would have a huge impact not only on the future of English music but on the country as a whole.

13 Pre-Reformation Ireland, Wales, and Scotland

It is difficult to construct a coherent picture of musical life in Ireland in the period leading up to the Reformation. Some historians suggest the Irish Church was in disarray due to the war-torn state of the country; others see it as holding its own despite the circumstances. Music in many monasteries and at least some churches seems to have been neglected; elsewhere it apparently flourished. The archbishopric of Dublin was held by a series of powerful figures, several of whom went on to combine the office of Lord Chancellor of Ireland with that of Archbishop, so it is no surprise that their attention was largely focussed on political and judicial rather than musical matters.

One of them, however, Michael Tregury (Archbishop from 1449 to 1471), left a will donating two organs for use in St Mary's Chapel in Dublin's St Patrick's Cathedral; and there are sufficient records of the Anglo-Irish gentry giving money to build new organs or repair old ones to suggest that the provision of organs for Irish churches was a feature of the period. Kilkenny seems to have been a centre for organ-building, at least in the second half of the fifteenth century. A Dominican friar called John Rouse who was building organs in England in the 1460s claimed to have learned his craft there in 1455. And another organ-builder, John Lawless, was so highly regarded by both the Earl of Ormond and the burghers of Kilkenny that in 1476 they agreed to pay his rent as long as he lived in the town. Lawless was responsible for organs in some twenty churches and monasteries, including one in Christ Church, Dublin, in 1470. Organ-building aside, however, there is no suggestion of any great dynamism in the field of church music. Discounting suggestions that Leonel Power and John d'Excetre, another Old Hall MS composer, were of Irish origin[1] – for which there is no evidence – no religious music of any consequence seems to have been written. We can only assume that most Irish religious institutions followed the general musical trends that came to them from England or from Scotland.

In the secular sphere, music became an aspect of the political and cultural struggle which continued to tear the island apart. Although no actual music has survived, we know that the majority of the Irish population were sustained by dance tunes and by the bardic tradition. Manuscripts such as The Book of Hy-Mane (or Hy-Many), The Yellow Book of Lecan, and The Book of Fermoy contain bardic poems from the fourteenth and early-fifteenth centuries which would have been sung or declaimed to music; and chronicles such as the Annals of Ulster record the deaths of the men who wrote them: their obituaries emphasise how, within the bardic tradition, history, poetry, genealogy and music were all closely interwoven disciplines. For the English authorities and many of the Anglo-Irish landowning class, the existence of an Irish culture, in which music was a significant component, was an obstacle to the political control they were trying to exert. As far back as 1367, the Statutes of Kilkenny had ordained that 'it is agreed and forbidden, that any Irish agents, that is to say, pipers, storytellers, bablers, rimers, mowers, nor any other Irish agent shall come amongst the English, and that no English shall receive or make gift to such.'[2] Even in the English-dominated Pale, this cultural apartheid could not be sustained. In 1435, Henry VI was outraged to find that the Anglo-Irish gentry, and even some of the aristocracy, were in the habit of paying Irish minstrels and musicians to perform in their houses; so he reinforced the penalties for doing so. There were more attempts to prevent musical fraternisation between the two communities, with Poyning's Law in 1495, and further legislation in 1520 and 1533. However, music, as so often in its history, proved resistant to political control and Irish music continued to cross the borders between the two communities. The regulations only succeeded in undermining the authorities and reinforcing the resentment and sense of oppression felt by the Irish.

A poignant illustration of this situation is the tale of Thomas Fitzgerald, 5th Earl of Desmond, who became lost while out hunting and fell in love with Catherine MacCarthy, the daughter of one of his tenants. A charming Gaelic song, *Deirdre deag-gnuireac* (*The Blooming Deirdre*), which still survives, was composed for their wedding in 1409. A union between a member of the Anglo-Irish aristocracy and an ordinary Irishwoman was actually contrary to the Statutes of Kilkenny. That obstacle might have been overcome, but such was the extent of family and caste disapproval that the Earl was forced to abandon his title and his lands and live out his days in exile in France.

The situation in Wales was very different, principally because there was less opposition to English rule. As a consequence, the revival of Welsh culture and music that took place in the fourteenth and fifteenth centuries was not seen by the English as a threat. It began with Dafydd ap Gwilym, who was reputedly born at Penrhyns near Aberystwyth and buried, according to competing traditions, either a few miles farther inland at the great Cistercian Abbey of Strata Florida or farther south at Talley Abbey in Carmarthenshire. There is no consensus as to when he lived: the date of his birth has been given as between 1315 and 1320, and his death has been put anywhere between 1350 and 1380. What we do know is that he is credited with radical changes in Welsh musical and literary forms. He developed a new metre for Welsh poetry, based on rhyming couplets. He revived a flagging bardic tradition by incorporating elements from the troubadour tradition, not the least of which was to place himself and his feelings at the centre of his work. And he not only sang to the harp, but took harp music in a new direction, making use of pentatonic chords and new harmonies drawn from Ireland and perhaps from the Celtic parts of France. We also know that he wrote a number of poems which, if not actually obscene, contain a strong sexual element: they include an ode to his penis.[3]

Both possible burial places for ap Gwilym are closely connected with the revival of Welsh culture. Strata Florida was undoubtedly a focal point for poetic and musical traditions, both religious and secular, over an extended period. (The fact that poems of love and sexual comedy such as those of ap Gwilym were apparently accepted by those who also practised traditional Cistercian observance argues a remarkable degree of tolerance.) This aspect of the abbey's life contributed to the revival and rejuvenation of the eisteddfod as a Welsh national institution. But it was in Carmarthen in 1451 that the first modern Eisteddfod took place – modern in the sense that it was a large-scale gathering, which set rules for poetic and musical entries and offered separate prizes for poetry, singing, and harp playing, establishing a framework that has continued to the present day. The eisteddfod tradition has remained an expression of a distinctly Welsh cultural identity, but, unlike Ireland (or, much later, Scotland), that identity did not become associated with an assertion of political identity. Consequently, Welsh music was never the subject of suspicion, prejudice and political interference in the way that Irish music was – which may also go some way towards explaining why Welsh music has never seemed to assert itself, even in the context of the British Isles, in the way that Irish and Scottish music have.

The lack of a political context also affected Welsh church music. Monasteries in Wales had never been as rich or as numerous as in other parts of the British Isles and, as a consequence, church music remained comparatively undeveloped. Bishop Adam Houghton founded and endowed the cathedral school at St David's, Pembroke, in the 1360s, and then – together with his patron, John of Gaunt – sought to expand the musical life of the foundation by building a special college or Chantry dedicated to St Mary. But St David's was the only such foundation in Wales, and Welsh church music never developed any independent or distinctive flavour. Wales became politically integrated with England – a process symbolised, if not actually completed, by the 1536 Statute of Union – and the Church in Wales eventually became integrated with Henry VIII's Church of England, suffering badly during the dissolution of the monasteries. During Henry VIII's reign, there were a number of reasonably prominent Welsh musicians: John Lloyd (*c.*1480–1523), composer and member of the Chapel Royal; William Pasche (*fl. c.*1513–37), organist and composer of an interesting *Christus resurgens* Mass; Philip ap Rhys (*fl. c.*1545–1560), organist at St Paul's Cathedral and a composer noted for his contrasting use of rhythms, as well as for writing the only surviving British organ Mass; Richard William (*fl. c.*1525–40), choirmaster at St Mary-at-Hill, one of the London churches where the Chapel Royal sang. All of these might, under other circumstances, have contributed to the development of Welsh music, but they migrated to London and contributed to what was rapidly becoming an English-dominated and London-centric musical world.[4]

Scottish music during the first part of the sixteenth century enjoyed a brief blaze of glory before it, too, died away in the heat of the Reformation. James IV (r. 1488–1513) was probably the most successful of the Stuart kings of Scotland and, like Henry VIII, has often been described as a model Renaissance prince. He took a great interest in the arts and sciences, particularly music. In 1501, he once more reorganised the Scottish Chapel Royal at Stirling Castle, establishing it as a collegiate church with sixteen canons and six choirboys, as well as (apparently) three pairs of organs. Another ten canons were added shortly afterwards. Scotland's traditional enmity towards England meant that the country leaned culturally towards the Continent, and a number of prominent Scottish musicians, such as Thomas Inglis and John Fethy, went to the Netherlands to study – although because so little of their music survives, it is difficult to assess how deeply they were influenced by contemporary masters such as Ockeghem, Obrecht or Josquin des Prez. In 1503, however, with James's marriage to Henry VII's daughter, Margaret Tudor, there was a change of emphasis. He imported clavichords such as those found at the English court for his new bride to play, and may also have arranged for English or English-style music to be performed in the Chapel Royal in order to make her feel at home.[5] The Carver MS, sometimes referred to as the Carver Choir Book, which is the largest collection of music we have from Scotland during the period, certainly shows English influence. It contains works by Cornysh, Fayrfax, John Nesbet and John Brown. It also includes other works, including those of Robert Carver (after whom it is named), that show English characteristics, notably one anonymous *Magnificat*, but whether this was 'written by a Scottish composer in the English style, or by an English composer writing specifically for a Scottish occasion', it is impossible to tell.[6]

14 Robert Carver, and the Scottish Reformation

Carver himself is undoubtedly the outstanding figure of Scottish music in the sixteenth century. We know that he spent thirty-six years at the Augustinian monastery at Scone Abbey in Perthshire and it is reasonable to assume that he is the same Robert Carver who was associated with the Scottish Chapel Royal during that period. The fact that some documents name him as 'Carver alias Arnot' may identify him with a Robert Arnot who held the civil offices of burgess and bailie in the borough of Stirling, or it may suggest that he was the protégé of Archdeacon Arnot of Lothian, who later became Bishop of Whithorn and also had a Chapel Royal connection. He may also have been educated at the University of Louvain, but there are few certainties. His birth is usually given as between 1484 and 1487. And of his death, we know only that it occurred after 1566.

Carver's surviving output – five masses and two motets – is all found in the manuscript that bears his name. His masterpiece is undoubtedly the nineteen-part, votive antiphon, *O bone Jesu,* 'a vast ornamentation of the private prayers of James IV … part of a Devotion of the Name of Jesus that he would have heard in the evening after Compline.'[1] This is the work that defines Carver's style. Rich in harmonic and structural invention, with plenty of decorative, melismatic passages, it develops slowly, building to a brilliant formal resolution in the final bars. He clearly enjoyed composing on a large scale: the ten-part Mass, *Dum sacrum mysterium,* is another big and complex work, and may well have been heard at the Coronation of James V in September 1513. His style may show a degree of English influence, but it is clear that Carver was also fully aware of what was happening on the Continent. From the mid-fifteenth century onwards, the secular tune *L'Homme Armé* was used as a *cantus firmus* for almost fifty Masses in France and the Netherlands. One of the earliest, by Dufay, composed *c.*1460, appears in the Carver MS; and Carver himself followed the trend by composing a four-part Mass based on the tune, the only known example by a British composer.

All but one of Carver's surviving compositions come from the early part of the sixteenth century, the period which marked the brief flowering of Scottish music – although the widespread destruction of musical manuscripts during the Scottish Reformation makes it likely that he composed significantly more than has survived. The exception is the four-part Mass, *Pater creator omnium,* dating from 1546, which sees him trying to adapt to a later, more concentrated musical style with syllabic setting of the text, but still lapsing occasionally into his original more decorative manner. This change in style, which he did not quite achieve, reflects the changes in the political and religious climate that characterised the reign of James V (r. 1513–42), an uncertain and unstable period during which Scotland, and Scottish music, was subject to conflicting pressures.

James V was less than eighteen months old when his father was killed at the Battle of Flodden in 1513. By the time he emerged from the regency, aged sixteen, he was musically educated and able to sight-read and sing well, despite a harsh, even raucous voice. He was passionate, outgoing and licentious, and life at court was enlivened by mimes and masquerades featuring secular music and songs: some, such as *Pansing in hairt* by John Fethy, the Netherlands-trained composer, organist and cleric, were reflective, literate pieces; others, such as the anonymous medley, *Trip and go, hey*, were frankly erotic. Yet James V was also strongly and conventionally religious. Faced with the English Reformation and the growing influence of Protestant thought, he set up an Ecclesiastical Commission for the Extirpation of Heresy – which led at least one composer, Robert Johnson, to flee to England. He also became increasingly dependent on France, relying on his godfather, the French King Francis I, for political support against pressure from Henry VIII, and marrying first Princess Madeleine de Valois, and then, after her early death, Marie de Guise. Meanwhile, the Scottish court aped French manners, and sang and danced to music composed in a recognisably Franco-Scottish manner. In the main, these were short, rhythmical, predominantly chordal part-songs using Scottish texts (or just occasionally a translation of a French poem), with titles such as *Richt soir opprest*, *The time of youth*, or *How suld my febill body fure?* They remain attractive pieces, but at the time their secular nature and their concentration on love and melancholy only served to demonstrate how life at court failed to reflect the temper of the rest of the country.

From the 1520s onwards, there was a growing tide of opinion in favour of ecclesiastical reform. James V resisted and persecuted the reformers. After his death, in 1542, those who held power during the minority of his successor, Mary Stuart or Mary Queen of Scots, tried first conciliation and then incremental change as a means of suppressing the growing discontent. Neither was successful. When the so-called Reformation Parliament convened in Edinburgh in 1560, it was determined to effect change and its impact was both rapid and radical. The Mass was outlawed; choirs were forbidden; the organ, 'a Popish instrument', was banned; the role of music both in worship and in society was drastically curtailed. Two manuscripts give an indication of the changes in Scottish music over the period. The Dunkeld Music Book, or Dunkeld Antiphon, probably dates from the late 1540s, before the Reformation. It is a loose collection of Masses and other pieces, some of them fragments, by Scottish, English and Continental composers, leaving the impression of continuity in the development of Scottish music. Perhaps the most interesting works are two fine, polyphonic Masses, *Cantate Domino* and *Felix namque*, probably by David Peebles or Pables (fl.1530–76), which differ from comparable pieces in the earlier Carver MS in that they are tighter and more succinct in both structure and expression.

The Wode Part-Books are entirely different. They were begun in 1562 when the Regent of Scotland, James Stewart, Earl of Moray, instructed Thomas Wode to provide suitable music for the new Protestant Scottish Psalm Book. Metrical psalmody – the practice of setting the psalms to regular, repeated melodies for singing by the congregation – had been introduced in the 1540s when two brothers from Dundee by the name of Wedderburn published *Gude and Godlie Ballates*. Now, with John Knox's Calvinism triumphant, metrical psalms were almost the only religious music acceptable in Scotland. Wode collected over one hundred metrical settings of the psalms, the majority by Peebles, for use with the new Psalm Book. But he went well beyond his original brief. He had begun life as a Catholic monk and, following the Reformation, he feared that 'musike sall pereische in this land alutterlye.'[2] So he continued collecting music right up until his death in 1592, without obvious religious partiality. Thus the Wode Part-Books also contain works by the Scottish composers John Angus, Andrew Blackhall, John Buchan, John Fethy, Andrew Kemp and, again, David Peebles (whose four-part motet, *Si quis diligit me*, written about 1530 for presentation to James V, is probably the most interesting of the Scottish works). And Wode's attention ranged farther afield as well, to include English and Continental writers from the second half of the sixteenth century, such as Campion, Dowland, Morley, Tallis, Lassus, and van Wilder.[3]

With the Reformation, the traditional forms of liturgical music were effectively discontinued in Scotland. Apart from the Chapel Royal, religious and polyphonic singing had centred on the cathedral schools, the collegiate churches, and what were known as song schools in the main towns. Most of these institutions were swiftly broken up, their choirs expelled and their libraries destroyed. The few survivors were subject to financial pressures which led them to do away with or drastically reduce their musical specialisation. Mary Stuart became Queen of Scotland in 1542 before she was a week old and spent her formative years at the French court where music was part of daily life. Returning to Scotland in 1561, aged nineteen, her attempt to hear a sung Mass in the Chapel Royal in Holyrood Palace caused public outrage and violent protests. The following year, no musicians could be found to sing or play at her Christmas Mass. She was Queen, but she was isolated. She fought back and, by 1565, had gathered a band of musicians to play for her at Easter. By now, however, religious music and Catholicism were firmly associated in the Scottish public mind. Her commitment to religious music thus fed into those factors which fatally weakened her public and political position; and this in turn certainly played a part in the effective disappearance of the Scottish Chapel Royal as a musical entity for almost thirty years. James VI (r. 1566–1625) made an attempt to revive it, building a new Chapel Royal at Stirling Castle and arranging for a programme of traditional, polyphonic music to be performed to celebrate the baptism of his son, Prince Henry, in 1594. But when he became James I of England (r. 1603–25) and moved south, the power of musical patronage moved with him. The Scottish Chapel Royal continued to exist, at least notionally – and formed the basis of a long-running dispute between the King and the Scottish Parliament – but as a musical force it faded away.

Faced with a changed world, composers, almost all of whom had begun life as clerics, had to adapt. Peebles gave up orders, married and raised two children, while still living in the grounds of the Priory of St Andrews. Andrew Blackhall, originally a canon at the Abbey of Holyrood House, became a minister within the new Scottish Church and, together with Peebles and Andrew Kemp, continued to compose, but accepted the confines of psalmody. William Kinloch, principally a composer for keyboards, was heavily influenced by Byrd and wrote some well-regarded dances for virginals. He seems to have been dependent on private patronage, but he was later locked up for helping pass messages to and from the imprisoned Queen Mary. Again, James VI tried to revive things. Blackhall was given a pension and, under James's patronage, was able to compose polyphonic anthems in the English style and a number of secular part-songs, notably *Adieu, O desie of delyt*, a setting of a lyric by the poet Alexander Montgomerie, who was a particular favourite of the King. John Black, one of the musical and religious old guard, had once been master of the Aberdeen Song School, but following the Reformation he renounced holy orders and married. He was given a musical role at James's court. So, too, was James Lauder, who wrote melodic pavans and galliards for consort of viols to be performed at court and in aristocratic households. Musical life in Scotland was certainly not dead, but – except where folk music was concerned – it had lost the capacity for home-grown development and become heavily, if not wholly, dependent on outside influences. Even before James VI became James I and moved south to London, Scottish music had assumed, and for a long while would be resigned to, a parochial status.

15 The English Reformation, Merbecke, and Tye

The English Reformation, unlike that in Scotland, did not begin with doctrine and as a consequence did less damage to musical life than one might have expected. It began with dynastic politics. It was painful and disruptive and it shifted the foundations of English musical life, which had endured since St Augustine arrived on the Isle of Thanet nearly a thousand years earlier. But there was no loss of continuity or inspiration. Choral and educational traditions were maintained and, somehow, despite the inevitable insecurity and uncertainty which pervaded England's religious institutions in the middle years of the sixteenth century, there emerged some of the finest religious music ever written.

Henry VIII wanted a male heir. His wife, Catherine of Aragon, failed to give him one. Neither scripture-based wrangling nor diplomatic manoeuvring would persuade Pope Clement VII to give Henry the divorce or annulment that he sought, and the King was forced to find an English solution. Archbishop Cranmer declared the marriage to Catherine of Aragon null and void and Henry married Anne Boleyn. The Pope, angry at being defied and not uninfluenced by the fact that Catherine's nephew was Charles V, Holy Roman Emperor, King of Spain and ruler of much of Italy, excommunicated both Henry and his archbishop. Henry, equally angry, decided to break with Rome completely; and the 1534 Act of Supremacy declared that 'the King, our sovereign lord, his heirs and successors, kings of this realm, shall be taken, accepted, and reputed the only supreme head in earth of the Church of England, called Anglicans Ecclesia.'[1]

That this led to the dissolution of the monasteries is not, in itself, surprising. English monasticism was in decline and there were many instances of abuse and corruption. Henry and his Chancellor, Thomas Cromwell, who masterminded the dissolution, no doubt exaggerated the extent of the abuse to justify their case, but, equally, there is no doubt that the system urgently needed reform. More importantly, the monasteries were both a huge potential source of wealth for the Crown and a potential source of a religious backlash against Henry's Act of Supremacy. Six small monasteries were suppressed in 1534, but the real business began in 1536 and continued until 1540 by which time over one thousand institutions had been closed.

The architectural and artistic damage was immense, but probably worse was the loss of hundreds of ancient libraries. Many early printed books and hundreds of thousands of manuscripts – including innumerable manuscripts of church music dating back hundreds of years – were lost or destroyed. John Bale (1495–1563), a notably quarrelsome cleric and writer, and certainly no defender of monks, had a rant on the subject of libraries:

> If there had been in every shire of England, but one solemn library, to the preservation of those noble works and preferment of good learnings in our posterity, it had been yet somewhat. But to destroy all without consideration is and will be unto England forever a most horrible infamy.... A great number of them which purchased those superstitious mansions reserved of those library books, some to serve their jakes, some to scour their candlesticks, and some to rub their boots. Some they sold to the grocers and soap sellers, and some they sent over sea to the bookbinders, not in small number, but at times whole ships full, to the wondering of the foreign nations. Yea, the universities of this realm are not all clear in this detestable fact.... I know a merchant man, which shall at this time be nameless, that bought the contents of two noble libraries for 40 shillings price – a shame it is to be spoken.[2]

In human terms, things could have been worse. Of the thousands of monks expelled from their monasteries, the vast majority were given pensions and found vicarages and benefices, or allowed to leave the religious life altogether. In this way, although libraries and manuscripts were destroyed, the accumulated musical knowledge of the monasteries was diffused and may well have strengthened the music of both England's wider religious community and the secular tradition.

Parish churches, cathedrals, cathedral schools and, of course, the Chapel Royal continued to function as normal and the role and nature of music within worship remained largely unchanged. In 1542, Henry VIII reorganised the cathedrals. The reform was structural as much as doctrinal, and resulted in increased importance being given to the position of organist, but it nonetheless reflected the Protestant pressures that were building within the new English Church. In 1536, the lower house of clergy of the Canterbury diocese presented the King with *The Seventy-Eight Faults and Abuses of Religion* which stated that 'Synging and saying of mass, matins, or even song, is but roaring, howling, whistling, conjuring and jogeling; and the playing upon organs a foolish vanitie.'[3] A riposte of a kind was contained in a 1539 book of ceremonies, which had the King's approval and stated that 'the sober, discreet and devout singing, music and playing with organs used in the Church in the service of God are used to move and stir the people to the sweetness of God's word, the which is there sung.' The debate escalated. In 1544, Archbishop Cranmer, having translated some parts of the Prayer Book, wrote to the King that he wanted a musical setting that was not

> full of notes but, as near as may be, for every syllable a note so that it may be sung distinctly and devoutly as be in the matins and evensong Venite, the hymns, Te Deum, Benedictus, Magnificat, Nunc dimittis, and all the psalms and versicles; and in the mass Gloria in excelsis, Gloria Patri, the Creed, the Preface, the Pater Noster, and some of the Sanctus and Agnus.[4]

Cranmer's suggestion had little impact, but the fact that he could press for the full range of liturgical functions to be set to simple, homophonic music again illustrates the direction in which the Church of England was moving.

The political changes that enabled the King to become Supreme Head of his own Church inevitably led to doctrinal reform. Until his fall from grace and execution in 1540, these reforms were implemented by Thomas Cromwell, but Henry, having achieved his political objectives, was reluctant to move too fast on doctrinal issues and did not wish to associate his new Church with the Protestant Reformation on the Continent. His death in 1547 changed the situation. The accession of his nine-year-old son, Edward VI, opened the way for Cranmer and those who thought like him to push through rapid and radical change. In April 1548, a Royal Commission visited Lincoln Cathedral and ordered that

> they shall from hensforthe synge or say no Anthemes of our lady or other saynts but onely of our lorde. And them not in laten but choseyng owte the best and moste soundyng to cristen religion they shall turne the

> same into Englishe settying thereunto a playn and distincte note, for euery sillable one, they shall singe them and none other.[5]

Then, in 1549, the Act of Uniformity affirmed that England was now a Protestant nation; that English was the language of its religion; and that Archbishop Cranmer's new *Book of Common Prayer* was the basis for Anglican worship.

The 1549 *Book of Common Prayer*, and its subsequent revisions in 1552 and 1559, had a long-term influence on English church music that it is almost impossible to overestimate. It established Matins, Holy Communion, and Evensong as the basis of the liturgy; it included 'anthems' as an integral part of the structure of worship; and it thus gave birth to the Anglican Service, as distinct from the Mass, as the basis of worship in the new Anglican Church. Two new forms of musical composition resulted: the 'anthem' – the name derives from the votive antiphon, but musically it evolved from the motet, although it took a very different direction; and the 'Service', a choral setting of all or part of the Anglican liturgy. These are English concepts – they have no counterparts in the Catholic Church or among the Protestant Churches of northern Europe. It was the great names of the Tudor period who established and defined these new forms, and passed them down to later generations of composers.

Such a process, however, took time. The immediate musical response to the 1549 Prayer Book was an extremist one. In 1550, John Merbecke (sometimes Marbeck; *c.*1510–85) produced the *Booke of Common Praier Noted*, which set the new liturgy to a series of simple, rhythmical chants, some based on traditional plainsong, some written by Merbecke himself. Merbecke's work has the beauty of utter simplicity and also of complete conviction. It was intended to be music of a kind which any parishioner could sing without difficulty whether they had a musical education or not. As a clerk and, later, organist at St George's Chapel in Windsor, Merbecke had composed at least one five-part Latin Mass, *Per arma justitiae,* and several motets, but he then became a fervent Calvinist convert. In 1542, he and several others were arrested for compiling an English concordance to the Bible and for being in possession of an epistle by Calvin attacking the Mass. His friends were executed, but Merbecke was pardoned, apparently because he was a musician and known to the Bishop of Winchester, Stephen Gardiner. Once Henry VIII was dead and the country began to move towards Calvinism under Edward VI, Merbecke saw his opportunity.

The Booke of Common Praier Noted, with its unison chanting and strict homophony, emerged from his conviction that music in Christian observance should not only be pared to the minimum, but should also be unified across the country. Cranmer agreed and issued a series of new instructions and injunctions concerning church music. These, however, did not go unchallenged. Conservative pressures, particularly from the cathedrals and colleges who were unwilling to reduce their choirs and their musical establishments, forced him to compromise. Merbecke was popular in some quarters, but England as a whole was not ready for such musical austerity and usage was not enforced. Strangely enough, the mid-Victorian period saw a rediscovery and revival of the *Booke of Common Praier Noted* as a response to debates and pressures within the Anglican community. It may well be that Merbecke's chants were sung more widely during the late-nineteenth and early-twentieth centuries than in his own time.

Metrical psalms arrived in England about the same time as they did in Scotland, but in England the central collection was Miles Coverdale's *Goostly Psalmes and Spirituall Songes* (1543), which included many German translations and German tunes. A series of other psalters followed. In 1549, Robert Crowley published his somewhat long-winded *The Psalter of Dauid newely translated into Englysh metre in such sort that it maye the more decently, and wyth more delyte of the mynde, be reade and songe of al men*, which was the first such publication to include full musical notation. Then in 1553 came Francis Seager's more succinct *Psalter* which, perhaps oddly, arranged the tunes in four parts, like a simple motet. The direction of change was clear. Congregational singing was to be preferred to the kind of choral polyphony that had sustained church music over the centuries. This cannot have made life easy for musicians; yet, in the end, these metrical psalms, altered and developed over time, provided the basis for the great English tradition of hymn-singing.

An interesting perspective on the complexities of the period is provided by Christopher Tye (*c.*1505–72), one of the most highly regarded composers of the age. Beginning life as a choirboy (possibly) and then a lay clerk (certainly) at King's College, Cambridge, Tye gained a bachelor's degree in music in 1536 and a doctorate in 1545. Until 1561, nearly twenty years, he was Organist and Master of Choristers at Ely Cathedral; he had personal connections with the Chapel Royal, although he was probably not a member; and he may well have been Edward VI's music tutor (though there is no evidence to support suggestions that he was also tutor to the

Princesses Mary and Elizabeth). Tye's early work, setting Latin texts, was written during the reign of Henry VIII. Much has been lost or destroyed, but the pieces that have survived, which include a four-part Mass based on the secular tune *Western Wynde*, suggest both a recognisable personal style and a degree of continuity with the imaginative approach of the Eton Choirbook composers. A Latin text, *Domine Deus coelestis,* which survives as a fragment, was probably set at the beginning of Edward VI's reign, for it contains lots of fine, moral advice suitable for a young monarch. Tye appears to have been a convinced Protestant. Among his close connections was Richard Cox, an aggressive Protestant reformer who was, at various times, Dean of Westminster, Chancellor of Oxford University and Bishop of Ely. As the new reign and the tide of reform advanced, Tye began setting English texts and writing in a significantly more restrained style. His *Actes of the Apostles, translated into Englyshe Metre, and dedicated to the Kynges most excellent Maiestye* was sung at the Chapel Royal in 1553. It consists of a series of motet-like pieces, polyphonic yet simple, and clearly reflecting the changed musical circumstances of Edward VI's short reign. Yet the whole concept of setting the Acts of the Apostles to music, with its implication of storytelling and characterisation, seems to point in the opposite direction, drawing on the kind of secular part-songs that were popular at the court of Henry VIII. The work contains some attractive music – including the tune which, much adapted by later generations, became the hymn tune *Winchester New* ('While shepherds watched their flocks by night') – but has never become popular as a whole, probably because Tye's attempt to turn the biblical text into English verse is almost comically inept.

That same year, 1553, saw the death of Edward VI, the accession of Queen Mary, and a sudden reversal of religious and musical direction. Tye, a known Protestant and prominent musical figure who had dedicated works to Edward VI, could well have found himself in an exposed and dangerous position. He appears to have retreated to Ely and given the new regime what it wanted. His masterpiece, the six-part Latin Mass, *Euge bone,* was probably composed during the reign of Queen Mary, and possibly to celebrate the arrival of Cardinal Pole and the formal return of England to the Roman Catholic fold in 1554.[6] It is an exceptional piece, scored for two basses, two tenors, alto and soprano, so that a rich depth of sound is balanced against a soaring, mobile treble part. Although there are four settings of the *Agnus Dei,* the whole work feels remarkably compact and its tight structure is reinforced by confident, assertive rhythms. Another piece from the same period is the seven-part antiphon, *Peccavimus cum patribus nostris*. During the reign of Queen Mary, a number of English composers – William Mundy, Thomas Tallis, John Sheppard – composed large-scale votive antiphons, as if to demonstrate publicly that the old musical forms had returned. Tye's excursion into the genre is an extended and intensely emotional one, which builds deliberately through its different sections to a climactic point of such cathartic power that its overall effect has been compared to a romantic symphony.[7] One can still detect the residual influence of the enforced simplicities of Edward VI's reign, but there is no doubt that Tye had demonstrated his willingness to adapt, reverting happily to Latin texts and more complex musical structures.

Then, in 1558, Mary died; Queen Elizabeth came to the throne; and everything changed again. Protestantism returned, and the Church of England was once again independent of Rome, with the Queen as its Supreme Governor. But Elizabeth's was a qualified Protestantism, a middle way between Mary's Catholicism and the Calvinist extremes which had threatened under Edward VI. It was not uncontested – there were challenges from both Puritans and Catholics during the course of the reign – but it survived. Doctrinally, the Elizabethan Settlement clearly suited Tye: he took holy orders in 1560, resigned from his post at Ely Cathedral, and received the living of Doddington-cum-Marche in the Isle of Ely. This may have been a kind of retirement: he certainly gave up composing church music, although he maintained contact with the court – there is a much-repeated story that when Queen Elizabeth complained about his organ-playing, he replied that her ears were out of tune. Or it may be that, having been buffeted by the demands which conflicting doctrines had placed on his music, he simply wanted to follow a more personal musical direction, for Tye is in a very real sense the father of English chamber music. During the sixteenth century, the name *In Nomine* was given to instrumental pieces for groups of four or five instruments, often consorts of viols. One instrument plays the main theme – as if it were the *cantus firmus* of a choral work, though *In Nomines* could be, and very often were, original compositions. The other instruments then join in, elaborating the theme, usually in imitative counterpoint. Tye left no less than twenty-four of these pieces, many with titles such as *Reporte* or *Trust* or *Crye*. Some echo his vocal compositions, but the majority are freer and more imaginative in feel, with ranges and melodic lines beyond the capability of a soloist or a choir. These pieces are not as well known as his choral works, but the fact that a composer of the stature of Tye should place such an emphasis on instrumental music as a separate genre indicates that change was coming: composers were starting to look at musical self-expression in a new and different way.

Tye died in 1572. By all accounts a peppery individual, he nonetheless managed to survive the religious upheavals of four reigns. He did so by adapting, by keeping his personal views to himself and composing the kind of music the authorities of the day required of a professional musician in a public position. By contrast, Richard Sampson (*c.*1495–1554), a minor composer noted principally for a long motet in praise of Henry VIII,[8] was accused of treason and locked up in the Tower of London; but he was Bishop of Chichester at the time and it was the influence he could exert as a religious figure rather than his status as a composer that led to his incarceration. He was later released. The other composer to get into trouble with the religious authorities was John Taverner.

16 John Taverner

Taverner was the first in a succession of great composers who illuminated English music throughout the sixteenth century and on into the seventeenth. Very little is known about his life, something which has given rise to much, often ill-judged, speculation. Neither his birthplace nor his date of birth is certain, although somewhere in the region of Tattershall in Lincolnshire about 1490 seems a reasonable supposition. A certain John Tavernar, recorded as a new member of the Fraternity of St Nicholas, the London Guild of Parish Clerks, in 1514, has in the past been identified with the composer, but there is no evidence to support this. In an age when a man's surname was often taken from his family's profession, 'John Taverner' was not an uncommon combination. Nor is there any mention of him in court records – although some of his works appear in manuscripts which were copied in or around the Chapel Royal between 1515 and 1525. Our first confirmed sighting comes in 1525 when he was in residence at Tattershall College, a prestigious school for choristers, founded in the previous century by Lord Cromwell.[1] That same year, Cardinal Wolsey, then at the height of his power, began the construction of Cardinal College, Oxford, the institution which he hoped would perpetuate his reputation as a patron of learning and the arts. The following year, Taverner was asked to be

Master of Choristers at the new college. It was an important and well-paid post – £10 a year, plus £5 expenses – but he was reluctant to accept, explaining in a letter to Wolsey in October 1526 that he had a profitable living at Tattershall and was about to marry. Wolsey, however, was not a man to be resisted and a month later Taverner took up his new appointment.

He was in sole charge of establishing and building up a musical establishment to match Wolsey's ambitions for the new college, and there is nothing to suggest that his efforts were anything but successful. In 1528, however, he and a clerk of the chapel called Radley were found to be hiding forbidden Protestant literature belonging to one John Clark in their rooms. Clark was arrested and interrogated. Taverner and Radley were brought before the Dean of the College for questioning, but, contrary to what has often been suggested, they were neither accused of heresy, nor imprisoned, nor punished. The Dean's view was that they were 'unlearned, and not to be regarded.' Wolsey agreed: Taverner was 'but a musician.'[2] And that was that. Some members of the college were actually excommunicated, but Taverner simply carried on with his work. He was praised by the up-and-coming Thomas Cromwell. He accompanied Wolsey to Hampton Court to audition choristers. There is not the slightest indication that he was tainted by the incident or that it contributed to his resignation two years later in April 1530. By that time, Wolsey had fallen from power; his other, smaller collegiate foundation at Ipswich had been seized and suppressed by Henry VIII; and a similar fate must have seemed likely for Cardinal College. In the event, Henry chose to re-establish the college, which we know today as Christ Church, but that did not happen until 1532. As far as we can judge, therefore, Taverner's decision to resign seems to have been a pragmatic one, unconnected with matters of religious conviction.

Taverner then disappears for nearly seven years, until 1537, when he is listed as a new member of the Guild of Corpus Christi in the town of Boston, in Lincolnshire, some fifteen miles from Tattershall. From 1538 to 1540, he acted as an agent of the crown, a civil servant, answering directly to Thomas Cromwell and involved in the dissolution of some of the smaller monastic foundations in Lincolnshire. Other official duties, some less congenial than others, were connected with enforcing the changes which Cromwell and Henry VIII were bringing to religious practice in England. Yet, as Colin Hand has demonstrated, Taverner's attitude to the dispossessed friars with whom he was required to deal was one of compassion.[3] He was not the fanatical convert portrayed in Peter Maxwell Davies' 1972 opera, *Taverner*, which has had an unfortunate effect on our understanding of the real man – though, to be fair, Maxwell Davies said clearly that his portrayal was not a realistic one.

Taverner died in Boston in 1545. Some years later, in 1563, when John Foxe published his history of the Protestant movement, *Actes and Monuments* – better known as *Foxe's Book of Martyrs* – he added a marginal note stating that 'Taverner repented him very much that he had made songs to popish ditties in his time of blindness.' If, in later life, Taverner did say such a thing, he was probably doing no more than expressing a view appropriate to the time. Whether as Wolsey's appointee at Oxford or Cromwell's civil servant, Taverner was essentially an establishment figure; and, like Tye, he gave the establishment what it wanted.

We do not know when Taverner began composing music or when he finished. It is generally assumed that he was no longer writing during the final period of his life in Boston, but even that is supposition. Some forty works – including eight settings of the Mass; four major votive antiphons; and twenty-two motets – survive in a range of manuscript sources. All were written for the pre-Reformation church. Stylistic differences suggest they were written over an extended period of time, although it is difficult to establish with any certainty when any given work was written. Like his life, Taverner's work reflects a period of transition, when the certainties which had underpinned church music for centuries began slowly to unravel.

Taverner's work has been described as representing 'the high point of Henrician music, and the effective terminal point of the English later medieval tradition'[4] and it is true that Taverner is grounded in the medieval tradition. The connection with the Eton Choirbook generation of composers is evident in the florid style of the antiphons *Ave Dei patris filia* and *Gaude plurimum*, and the festal Mass, *Missa Corona spinea*: all of which display a fondness for complex polyphonic structures, independent voice parts and heavily melismatic word settings. At times, in what are probably earlier works, his use of melisma is such that one can almost understand the views of the reformers who wanted simpler musical expression: in the *Sanctus* of the Mass *O Michael*, the third syllable of 'Benedictus' lasts for seventeen bars. His settings of the Mass also derive from traditional models in that they retain both a *cantus firmus* and use a head-motif to link the different movements.

It would be wrong, however, to see Taverner's music as backward-looking. It is imaginative, innovative and open to Continental influences, while remaining resolutely English. If the connection with the fifteenth century is clear, so, too, is the movement towards the simpler imitative style of choral polyphony which characterised mid- and later-sixteenth century composers – such as Sheppard and Byrd. And Taverner's influence extends way beyond the next generation of composers. He is a powerful figure on the musical landscape, all the way down to his descendant John Tavener (despite the changed spelling) and other twentieth and twenty-first century composers, such as Peter Maxwell Davies, James Macmillan, and Gabriel Jackson. One reason for this is that his work contains certain elements that were to become familiar as part of the mainstream language of English music. His great, sweeping, lyrical melodies contribute to his essential Englishness, but there is more to it than that. In the *Gloria* of *O Michael*, for example, a soaring treble part, carefully balanced against the lower voices, combined with a succession of checks and flows in the contrapuntal movement, create a strong sense of lyrical and mystical yearning. As we have noted previously, while not unique to English or British composers, this hard-to-define sense of yearning, of transcendental longing – frequently, although not always, derived from or associated with the natural world – is the emotional heartland of much British music.

Of Taverner's eight settings of the Mass, three – *O Michael, Corona spinea* and *Gloria tibi Trinitas* – are festal settings. These are big works, all probably written while he was at Cardinal College, with *O Michael* probably the earliest. Colin Hand has noted the influence of Dutch techniques from the fifteenth century and suggested that some of the part-writing displays an uncharacteristic immaturity.[5] Admittedly, *O Michael* is a less polished work than the *Gloria tibi Trinitas* Mass, but it is nonetheless both innovative and inspirational. *Gloria tibi Trinitas* shows more fluency of melodic movement, a greater sense of balance between movements, and displays a greater use of changing time signatures within the overall structure. It also demonstrates the way in which Taverner takes the imitative techniques commonly employed on the Continent – where a phrase or melody begins in one part and is then echoed or imitated by the others – and varies them: in this case using imitation within as well as between parts. Another example occurs in the antiphon *Fac nobis* where imitation features at the very beginning of the piece, a practice previously very rare in England; Taverner employs it again in his *Meane Mass,* and Tye and Byrd both adopted it. *Gloria tibi Trinitas* was clearly highly influential in its time. The central section of the *Benedictus* appears in various transcriptions – for keyboard, viols, solo voice and lute, and four-part unaccompanied with English words. What is more, the *cantus firmus* of this Mass was adopted as the basis for arrangements and for *In Nomine* compositions by almost every composer up to the time of Purcell, who wrote both a six- and a seven-part setting based on the theme.

Of the non-festal Mass settings, the best known is the *Western* (originally *Westron,* but henceforth *Western*) *Wynde* Mass. It is a wonderfully melodic work, shorter than the big, festal Masses and scored for four rather than six voices, but also very carefully structured. It takes its title from a folk song with elegant, but distinctly secular lyrics.

Westron wynde, when wilt thou blow,
The small rain down can rain.
Christ, that my love were in my arms
And I in my bed again.

On the Continent it was more or less common practice to use a secular tune as the basis for a Mass. In England, the *Western Wynde* folk tune was the only one so used. In Taverner's Mass, it is repeated no less than thirty-six times, giving shape to the four main movements so that the *Gloria* and *Credo* mirror each other in structure, as do the *Sanctus* and the *Agnus Dei.* Apparently influenced by Taverner's choice of tune, both Christopher Tye and John Sheppard also wrote Masses based on *Western Wynde.* Indeed, Tye's Mass appears to be a direct response to Taverner's in that, while Taverner concentrates the melody in the trebles, passing it at times to the counter tenors and basses but never to the altos, Tye keeps the tune with the altos throughout.

Although the chronology is uncertain, it would seem that Taverner's *Meane Mass* was written in the latter part of his career. Scored for five voices, without a treble part and with the melody concentrated in the alto or meane – hence the name – it marks a distinct stylistic change. Again, Taverner appears as something of a trend-setter. Having followed his example by writing a *Western Wynde* Mass, Tye wrote his own *Mean Mass*; while both Sheppard and Tallis may well have been following Taverner when they wrote Masses without treble parts. Taverner's *Meane Mass* is based on original material rather than a pre-existing *cantus firmus* (which explains its alternative title of *Sine Nomine Mass*) and appears to show him responding to the changed musical expectations of the religious establishment in the later years of Henry VIII's reign. The *Meane Mass* could not be called austere, but it is certainly simpler in concept and approach than its predecessors: the long, vaulting melodic lines have given way to shorter, rhythmical phrases, while imitative techniques rather than counterpoint become the dominant structural drivers. The long, melismatic phrases which were characteristic of *O Michael, Corona spinea* and *Gloria tibi Trinitas* have been replaced by an almost syllabic approach with melisma largely restricted to emphasising certain key words or phrases. Taverner died in 1545, four years before Henry VIII, but both the *Meane Mass* and another technically advanced and imitative five-part setting – *Small Devotion* or the *Sancti Wilhelmi* Mass – were later set to English words and sung during the reign of Edward VI, again indicating that, although Taverner may have begun as the last of the medieval composers, his later, less ornate style was sufficiently forward-looking to be accepted by the new Protestant Church of England.

17 John Sheppard

John Sheppard is the least known of the major Tudor church composers. Matthew O'Donovan of the group Stile Antico has suggested a number of reasons for this neglect:

> First, Sheppard's music survives almost exclusively in manuscript form; much of Tallis's music was published. Secondly, many of his Latin works are preserved in an incomplete source, requiring time-consuming editorial reconstruction in order to produce performing editions.... Thirdly, the successful resurgence of many Tudor composers partly rested on their English anthems which, until recent decades, were far more welcome in the Anglican liturgy than Latin motets. Although some enduring anthems have lasted from Edward VI's time (1547–53), it was really under Elizabeth that the Tudor anthem reached its zenith; Sheppard died barely a month after Elizabeth's accession. Fourthly, Sheppard's music is frequently simply more difficult to sing than that of his contemporaries, often spanning a vast vocal range, with disjunct vocal lines and unexpected harmonic progressions common features; furthermore, he had a penchant for writing music in many voice parts: six is common in the Latin motets, and he further subdivides the parts on a regular basis.[1]

To this cogent summary may be added the fact that we know almost nothing about Sheppard's character and career – even less than we know about Taverner. We have no idea of his origins; of when or where he was born. He may possibly have studied at St Paul's School, but our first confirmed sighting is as Master of Choristers (*Informator Choristarum*) at Magdalen College, Oxford – a position to which he was probably appointed in 1542, although even this date is uncertain.[2] He seems to have been a Fellow of Magdalen College between 1549 and 1551. He was certainly one of the Gentlemen of the Chapel Royal by 1552, though he may have been appointed a year or two earlier. On 21 April 1554, he made a formal application – or 'supplication' – to Oxford University for a doctorate in music, stating that he had studied and composed music for twenty years, which suggests a date of birth somewhere between 1515 and 1520. It is not clear whether or not he actually received the degree – no subsequent record refers to him as 'Dr Sheppard' – but he does seem to have enjoyed a certain prominence at court: Chapel Royal records show him presenting 'three rolls of songs' to Queen Mary on New Year's Day 1557. For a long time, even determining the date of his death was difficult. Court records suggest that he was present at Queen Elizabeth's Coronation in January 1559, but it now seems as certain as these things can be that he made a will on 1 December 1558, died on or shortly before 20 December, possibly of the influenza that was sweeping through London at the time, and was buried in St Margaret's Westminster the following day.

Despite his short life, Sheppard was a prolific composer, more so, for example, than Tallis, who lived to the age of eighty and is far better known. The contemporary partbooks and manuscripts in which Sheppard's works survive suggest that his compositions were popular and performed both at Oxford and in the Chapel Royal; and the fact that in his will he felt able to request burial in Westminster Abbey clearly indicates that he knew himself to be highly esteemed. His reputation survived his early death. Forty years later, Thomas Morley – who was born about the time Sheppard died – described him as one of the leading composers of his time, and his work was being copied into new partbooks as late as the 1640s. By the later years of the seventeenth century, most Tudor church music had fallen into neglect. Interest began to revive at the end of the nineteenth century, but Sheppard, probably because of the editorial difficulties of piecing together his works, somehow missed out on what became known as the Tudor Revival. Only more recently, with the advent of groups such as The Tallis Scholars, The Sixteen, and Stile Antico has his reputation begun to revive.

Recent scholarship has identified Sheppard's Second Service, which may have been written between 1549 and 1552, as one of the precursors of William Byrd's *Great Service*.[3]

As with Taverner, dating individual works is difficult, if not impossible, but one can still get a sense of how Sheppard's music developed over time, and of its relation to external events. As with Tye and Taverner, Sheppard's main creative years were those during which the religious landscape of England was in turmoil, although there is nothing in any surviving records to suggest that he became personally caught up in the religious upheavals of the time or that his career was adversely affected in any way. If a birth date of between 1515 and 1520 is correct, then he would have come to maturity in the years of Henry VIII's Reformation – and his appointment at Magdalen College certainly dates from that period. He was appointed to the Chapel Royal – a mark of favour – in the Protestant years under Edward VI; but he remained at the Chapel Royal and apparently still in favour during the reversion to Roman Catholicism under Queen Mary.

The *Western Wynde Mass* seems to be an early work, although there is no evidence to suggest – as some critics have maintained – that it was a student composition. It was almost certainly written after Taverner's and Tye's settings, but it is musically less interesting with the tune mainly in the treble and the harmonies below. There are melismatic passages with an early sixteenth-century feel to them, but the setting is, for the most part, syllabic. It is also short – only half the length of Taverner's setting – with nearly half of the restatements of the main tune abbreviated and significant cuts made to the text of the Mass. All this suggests composition at some time during 1540s while Sheppard was at Magdalen College, when Protestant ideas about musical simplicity and textual clarity were becoming more influential, but before the insistence on English texts, which came during the reign of Edward VI. The *Plainsong Mass for a Mene* (or *Mean*), which is again comparatively simple in style and construction and has similarities with Taverner's *Meane Mass*, seems likely to belong to the same period.

To judge from his music, Sheppard seems to have been unworried by the introduction of the 1549 *Book of Common Prayer*, the vernacular liturgy and other radical Protestant measures which followed the accession of Edward VI. Subsequent reversals of religious and musical policy mean that much music from this period is missing or incomplete, but we know that he wrote at least fifteen English anthems, most of them in four parts and following the new requirements for syllabic setting and simplicity of form. He also wrote four services – settings of texts for use at Matins, Holy Communion and Evensong, the central pillars of worship in the new Church of England. While none of them has survived complete, the *Magnificat* and the *Nunc Dimittis* from the Second Service are pieces of considerable interest, their strictly syllabic settings and compressed power showing just how far Sheppard had moved from the *Western Wynde Mass*, for example, in a comparatively short time. His beautiful, five-part setting of the *Lord's Prayer* presumably also dates from this period, although in style it is more elaborate, with occasional melismatic phrases, and despite its brevity allows more room for the individual parts to develop.

This level of adaptability enabled Sheppard to revert, with no apparent problem, to setting Latin texts and writing for the Sarum Rite, the traditional Catholic form of worship, which had lasted from the eleventh century until 1549 and was revived by Queen Mary. In fact, he seems to have been one of the musical mainstays of the new Queen's Roman Catholic revival. His output during Mary's five years on the throne – which were also the last five years of his life – was prodigious. There are numerous responsories and hymns, many of them in *alternatim* form, where sections of five- or six-part polyphony alternate with sections of chanted plainsong. Like his English anthems and services, these were compositions intended for daily use in the Chapel Royal and elsewhere, but at least two larger works demand particular notice. It is (again) not clear when the *Missa Cantate* was written. It is a big, rich, six-part, festal Mass, recalling Taverner's *Missa Corona spinea* and *Gloria tibi Trinita*, which might argue for early composition, but its maturity and complex polyphony (it is probably Sheppard's most complex score) make it more likely to have been written during Queen Mary's reign for some important event or occasion – in which case, those aspects of the Mass that recall Taverner may be interpreted as conscious references to a time before the intervention of Protestantism.

Richard Turbet, one of the leading contemporary experts on Tudor church music, has speculated that Sheppard's huge antiphon *Media vita* might possibly have been written in memory of the composer Nicholas Ludford, who died in the summer of 1557. Ludford was not only a fellow composer, but also a fellow parishioner at St Margaret's Westminster, and it must be probable that Sheppard would have known him well.[4] Today, Ludford's name is even less likely to be recognised than Sheppard's, but he was another of those composers who made the Tudor period so rich in religious music. Born *c.*1485, he seems to have spent his whole working life in London. He joined the Fraternity of St Nicholas, effectively the guild of musicians, in 1521 and, as far as we know, worked mainly at St Margaret's Church and then St Stephen's Chapel, both in Westminster. He was a prolific composer, writing no less than seventeen settings of the Mass, including a unique cycle of seven three-part Masses in praise of various aspects of the Virgin Mary. His music is often heavily textured and sometimes he adopts a grand, almost florid style, but it is also powerfully melodic and can at times show a strong sense of structural cohesion. The fact that Ludford was known as a highly religious man and that he seems to have ceased composing around 1535 suggests an inability or an unwillingness to adapt to the musical changes which accompanied Henry VIII's Reformation.

Whether or not Ludford's death was the occasion for its composition, Sheppard's *Media vita* is a major achievement, an antiphon on a scale unmatched in Tudor church music. There is no thought of simplicity of form, syllabic setting, or textual clarity. It is a complex and extended musical meditation on the idea that 'In the midst of life we are in death'. Lasting some twenty-five minutes, it builds slowly, with full note lengths and a slow tempo, section by section, to a massive and moving climax. It makes a fitting conclusion to his work. Sheppard was perhaps unlucky to live at the same time as Taverner and Tallis. His music is less consistent than theirs, both in terms of melodic invention and in imaginative force, and also in its ability to reach those great, inspired climactic moments which convey such a sense of exultation. His technical skills are not in doubt. He knew what he could do and he did it extremely well, although there is a sense that he was almost too much in control and, as a result, rarely took risks. Nonetheless, he left a body of intricate, beautiful and often neglected polyphony. His contribution to sixteenth-century English music should not be overlooked.

18 Thomas Tallis

Thomas Tallis was probably ten years older than Sheppard, but outlived him by nearly thirty. Tallis's date of birth is usually given as *c.*1505,[1] and by the time of his death in 1585 he would have been one of the last links with the musical world as it existed before Henry VIII's Reformation. He was a professional and a survivor. He sang, played the organ and composed under four different monarchs, all of whom had very different (and often changing) views on both the nature of religion as it should be practised in England and on the music that should accompany it. Like others in his profession, Tallis bent with the wind, writing the music that the church authorities asked and expected of him. In all probability, he remained a Roman Catholic – an adherent of what became known as the 'Old Faith' – although this is an inference based on the company he kept and the kind of music he wrote in his later years, rather than on documentary evidence or any direct statement from Tallis himself. He had known people who were burned at the stake for their beliefs, and, unlike his much younger pupil, friend and business partner, William Byrd, he avoided parading his personal views. Seen in this context, it is perhaps not surprising that his undeniable status as one of the greatest of English church musicians should rest on his abilities as an adapter and developer of musical forms, rather than as a radical innovator.

It seems likely that Tallis was born in Kent, somewhere not too far from Dover. In 1532, he is recorded as earning £2 a year as the organist at Dover Priory, a small Benedictine community, which is only remembered these days because the railway station built on top of it bears its name. In theory, these were the untroubled days before Henry VIII's Reformation, but Tallis may well not have seen them in such terms. Dover Priory had an annual income of just £170. The brothers were sufficiently interested in music to employ an organist, but there were only twelve of them, and even if Tallis was allowed to step out from behind the organ and work with the choir his resources would have been very limited. The fact that the Priory was one of the very first to be dissolved by Henry VIII's commissioners – in 1535, before the main programme of such closures began – suggests that there was something seriously amiss either with its governance or with its morals, or possibly both.

Whether Tallis left Dover before or after the Priory's dissolution, we do not know. He next appears in London in 1537 at the church of St Mary-at-Hill (close to London Bridge and the Tower of London) where he was probably employed as organist, although he may also have sung in the choir. It was clearly a step up. The church had had a new organ installed twenty years earlier, and the choir would have been more sophisticated than anything he had had in Dover, capable of singing Masses in five parts and fulfilling all the other musical functions required by a church in the heart of the capital. Records show that from 1510 into the 1520s, members of the choir of the Chapel Royal occasionally sang there. The fact that it was a well-connected church raises the possibility that Tallis may have met people who were able to help him later in his career – though only Robert Okeland, organist at St Mary-at-Hill in Billingsgate between from 1534 to 1535, as well as a composer and later a Gentleman of the Chapel Royal, can be positively identified.

Tallis did not stay in London long. In 1538, he moved to the Abbey of the Holy Cross at Waltham in Essex. Was he seeking promotion or security, or both? The abbey was the most important Augustinian foundation in England. It had an annual income in excess of £900. It had three organs and maintained its own Lady Chapel choir of boys and men, among whom Tallis was one of the most senior. It was also a favourite retreat of Henry VIII: a place where he went to discuss the problems surrounding his marriage with Archbishop Cranmer and with other influential advisers, among them its Abbot, Robert Fuller. But the world was changing and Tallis's arrival at Waltham coincided with beginning of the final phase of the dissolution of the monasteries. Abbot Fuller's influence with the King – not to mention a £50 bribe to Thomas Cromwell – might delay but could not prevent the inevitable. In January 1540, Waltham Abbey became the last English abbey to surrender itself to the Crown. The Abbot received an annual pension of £200. Tallis received 20 shillings arrears of salary and a further twenty shillings redundancy pay.

And yet, as Nicholas Sandon has pointed out, 'The dissolution of the monasteries itself created some attractive opportunities. About half of the cathedrals of medieval England – Bath, Canterbury, Coventry, Durham, Ely, Norwich, Rochester, Winchester and Worcester – had been Benedictine priories. When these were dissolved, most of them were promptly refounded … and in their new guise they were equipped with larger professional choirs than they had ever been able to maintain during their monastic existence.'[2] Whether through luck, talent or influence, Tallis managed to turn the situation to his advantage and take another step up the professional ladder. By the summer of 1540, he had become a senior member of the choir of Canterbury Cathedral, a position which must surely have been much sought after. Yet he stayed only three years – perhaps even less – and by 1543 he appears as a Gentleman of the Chapel Royal, a position he was to retain for over forty years until his death.

However scanty our knowledge of Tallis's early life, we are at least able to trace his ascent to the top of his profession. It was progress born of the fact that he was undoubtedly a highly talented organist and singer. It was also shaped by the politically-induced changes affecting religious foundations at the time and, from what one can deduce, by a strong sense of personal ambition on Tallis's part. In ten years, he went from being the organist at an undistinguished provincial priory to being a member of the Sovereign's hand-picked musical elite. What we do not know is at what stage in this process Tallis started composing. There has been speculation and debate – balancing internal musical evidence against the date of the sources in which the works are preserved – as to whether such apparently early works such as the antiphons *Ave dei patris filia* and *Ave rosa sine spinis* were composed in the 1520s or in the 1530s. The texts are characteristic of limp, early Tudor antiphons to the Virgin; the music lacks direction and distinction and there is a natural inclination to assign them to his apprentice years in Dover. Yet another apparently early work, the five-part antiphon *Salve intemerata virgo,* while clearly written after the other two, shows an entirely different Tallis. The text is a long, prose prayer to the Virgin with no verse structure, rhythm or rhyme to support a musical setting. Using imitative and motif-based techniques, Tallis argues his way musically through the wordy text, and creates a coherence and transparency which the words themselves do not possess. It is a work that is both careful and ambitious; and it comes off – giving an early glimpse of the mind that created *Spem in alium.* Tallis went on to rework the same material into his earliest surviving setting of the Mass, which also bears the name *Salve intemerata virgo.*

Whenever these works were actually written, it seems that Tallis's career as a composer developed slowly. It was only at Canterbury and on his arrival at the Chapel Royal that his music began to appear and gain prominence. By that time, Henry VIII's Reformation was well under way and the pressures for church music to adopt simpler forms were growing. Tallis's *Mass for Four Voices*, set to a Latin text, would seem to come from this period. With the accession of Edward VI, those pressures became demands – for syllabic setting and English texts. Tallis responded with works such as *Hear the voice and prayer; If ye love me;* and *A new commandment* – antiphons, which were now, with the triumph of English, called anthems; and, above all, with his five-part *Te Deum for Meanes.* The English text of the *Te Deum* consists of thirty lines of unequal length and uneven rhythm, with no natural dynamic structure. As with the antiphon *Salve intemerata virgo,* Tallis triumphs over his text. Indeed, given the restrictions imposed upon him by the ruling ideals of clarity and plainness one can argue that his achievement is that much greater. The work is big in conception and in emotional impact, yet at the same time it is deeply understated. The balance and the exchanges between the parts are carefully managed to create an almost surprising momentum. Tallis separates key lines from the body of the text ('Thou art the king of glory, O Christ') and uses repetitions of key lines ('Day by day, we magnify thee') to give both the text and the work as a whole a definite, but again understated, dynamic structure.

The 1549 *Book of Common Prayer* was followed in 1552 by an even more strongly Protestant version. Cranmer, with Thomas Cromwell as his Vicar General, was establishing a Protestant Church of England as swiftly as he could, creating a new style of observance and a new, English-language liturgy. New music was necessary; and because doctrinal change was being imposed from the top, musical change also had to come from the top (despite the fact that there were some at the extreme end of the reforming spectrum who regarded any music in church as an unnecessary distraction from the word of God). Much of the new music was thus composed by the Gentlemen of the Chapel Royal and their associates. Tye and Sheppard contributed, as did lesser-known figures such as Robert White (*c.*1538–74) and Robert Parsons (*c.*1530–72), but it was Tallis who led the way and appears to have done most of the groundwork. It is difficult, if not impossible, to establish which of his English language compositions were written during Edward VI's reign and which were written when the Anglican Church was re-established under Elizabeth I – and some, of course, may have been written under Edward VI and revised or cannibalised later.

What we do know, however, is that Tallis was the main contributor to the musical framework of the new Anglican Church. He wrote choral settings of the Preces, the exchanges between the priest and the congregation, such as 'O Lord, open thou our lips / And our mouth shall shew forth thy praise.' He wrote Responses and Collects, the exchanges between a cantor and a choir or congregation, for daily use and for particular festivals, such as Easter and Christmas. He wrote settings for Morning and Evening Service and for Holy Communion, some of them heavily pared down (one setting of the *Sanctus* lasts barely thirty seconds). He wrote anthems, hymns and settings of the psalms. For Tallis – as for his colleagues and, indeed, anyone whose life was bound up with the Church – it was a strange and unsettling time. The music which had formed the basis of his education and of his whole professional life was suddenly proscribed, and he was being asked to create a substitute. All he could do was keep his head down and carry on, which is what he seems to have done – even getting married in 1552 or thereabouts to a lady called Joan and going to live in Greenwich.

Having invested so much in the Edwardian Reformation – indeed, having risen to pre-eminence among English musicians during Edward's reign – how would Tallis react in 1553 when Edward expired of tuberculosis and Mary Tudor turned the whole situation on its head once again? The answer seems to have been a burst of creative relief. Latin was back. Traditional Catholic observance, the Mass and the Sarum Rite were back. Full scale choral polyphony and votive antiphons were back, too, and although, as ever, precise dating is a problem, everything points to Tallis's massive votive antiphon *Gaude gloriosa Dei mater* having been written for the accession of Queen Mary. It is a big, exuberant, celebratory work – 'the greatest unbroken span of florid polyphony created by any Tudor composer, literally breathtaking in performance'[3] – with a text carefully chosen so as to seem to rejoice in both the role of the Virgin Mary and the accession of Mary Tudor at the same time.

This technique of celebrating a sacred and a profane subject simultaneously occurs again in the seven-part Mass, *Puer natus est nobis,* which was probably composed for Christmas 1554. When Mary became Queen, overcoming Protestant attempts to install Lady Jane Grey in her place, she not only returned the country to Catholicism, but sought to ensure a Catholic succession. The best way to do this was to find a Catholic husband and have Catholic children. In July 1554, she married Philip, Prince of Asturias, King of Naples, Duke of Milan and future Philip II of Spain. The wedding took place in Winchester Cathedral with three choirs participating in the special Mass – the Chapel Royal; the Capilla Flamenca, its Spanish equivalent; and the choir of Winchester Cathedral. As Christmas approached, it was widely believed that Mary was pregnant. Tallis's new Mass could thus celebrate the Nativity of Jesus Christ and the prospective birth of a male heir, and the work does seem to make some kind of statement about continuity and traditional values. It takes the form of a traditional English Festal Mass, the kind Taverner was writing some thirty years previously. The choice of a plainchant *cantus firmus* is equally backward-looking, and Tallis's slow, sustained writing for the tenor line, which carries the theme throughout, seems positively medieval. Yet the text chosen – 'For unto us a child is born, unto us a son is given: and the government shall be upon his shoulder'[4] – gives it clear contemporary relevance. Nicholas Sandon has speculated that 'the unusual scoring for two altos, two tenors, baritone and two basses could suggest that Philip's chapel choir, which evidently lacked trebles, took part in the performance.'[5] All in all, we see again just how closely music and politics were bound together at the time. And in the end, of course, there was no pregnancy. The cynical Venetian Ambassador, Giovanni Michieli, appears to have been correct when he quipped that it would end in 'wind rather than anything else'.[6]

Under Edward VI and Cranmer, Tallis had led the way in composing for the new Protestant Church. Now, under Mary, it was Sheppard who took the lead in writing for the re-established Catholic Church. Not that Tallis suffered any retribution as a result of his participation in the Edwardian Reformation. His reputation remained unequalled and he continued to enjoy royal favour: Queen Mary granted him a half-share in the lease of the manor of Minster in Thanet. On a personal level, he was probably glad at the return of Catholicism – although, as we have seen, he was not given to public expression of his religious views – and we probably owe the exuberance of the music that he composed following Mary's accession to the fact that he could now compose without nitpicking restrictions, a relief almost certainly shared by his colleagues in the Chapel Royal. And, in terms of music, there were other reasons for welcoming Mary's accession. The hostility to religious music of many of the Protestant reformers had left choirs weakened and depleted. Musical manuscripts had been destroyed, thrown away or, at best, left to gather dust in a corner; organs were allowed to rot or were actually broken up; and there were plans to revoke the charters of collegiate churches and choral foundations. The situation was not uniform across the country, but in some ways that only made things worse because neither clergy, nor congregations, nor the musicians themselves knew where they stood. The Marian Counter-Reformation, if it could not repair the damage, at least stopped the rot and allowed the old musical traditions to re-establish themselves – though any such positives have to be balanced against the three hundred or so lives lost as Mary rooted out, and frequently burned, her political and religious opponents.

Mary died in November 1558 and Elizabeth, her half-sister, Henry VIII's daughter by Anne Boleyn, came to the throne. She was known to be a Protestant, but how she would respond to the challenges facing the English Church and the English body politic was anybody's guess. She moved quickly, and within months of her accession had created the basis of the so-called Elizabethan religious settlement. In reality, it was less a settlement than a way of balancing opposing forces, but it endured throughout her reign and laid the groundwork for the broad church Anglicanism of later centuries. The Act of Supremacy gave her the title of Supreme Governor of the Church of England; while the Act of Uniformity required everyone to attend a Church of England service on Sunday and ensured that the service would be based on the new 1559 *Book of Common Prayer*. It was a settlement that was Protestant in doctrine – the 1559 book differed little in essentials from Cranmer's 1552 book – but Catholic in appearance, retaining traditional vestments and ceremonial procedures, such as making the sign of the cross and kneeling to accept Communion. These were important points. No less than her medieval ancestors, or, indeed, her father at the Field of the Cloth of Gold, Elizabeth understood the importance of ceremony and ritual. In a religious context, it set Christian worship apart from daily life, and set the clergy who practised its mysteries (and who, of course, owed their allegiance to the Supreme Governor) apart from the congregation. In a royal context, it created awe and emphasised the difference between the monarch and her subjects. Again like so many of her predecessors, Elizabeth understood that in both contexts music was essential.

Issued in the Queen's name in June 1559, Injunction 49 stated that there would be no interference with collegiate churches or choir schools; that 'a modest and distinct song' might accompany 'all parts of the common prayers in the church' as long as it did not impair understanding of the words; and that 'for the comforting of such that delight in music … in the beginning, or in the end of common prayers, either at morning or evening, there may be sung an hymn, or suchlike song to the praise of Almighty God, in the best sort of melody and music that may be conveniently devised, having respect that the sentence of the hymn may be understanded and perceived.'[7] This was the great Elizabethan compromise. In practice, and within reason, the clergy could do what they liked – as could Tallis and his fellow composers.

Tallis lived another twenty-five years after Elizabeth's accession. It was a period when he enjoyed unprecedented creative freedom, royal favour, and the respect and admiration of his colleagues; and he produced a string of remarkable compositions. He wrote for the Elizabethan church, for the Chapel Royal and for private patrons. He wrote anthems and motets to English texts, and to Latin texts, and he wrote pieces which were originally for Latin texts but then rearranged for an English translation (known as contrafacta). He wrote psalm tunes, nine of which were collected for *The*

Whole Psalter, compiled by the Archbishop of Canterbury, Matthew Parker, in 1567. One of these – *Why fum'th in fight*, a setting of Psalm 2 – was famously used by Vaughan Williams as the basis for his 1910 homage, *Fantasia on a Theme by Thomas Tallis*. It was probably in the 1560s that Tallis wrote his two settings of texts from *The Lamentations of Jeremiah*, which are usually associated with Holy Week. This was not an unusual choice at the time and Tallis follows established practice by setting the introductory words, the Hebrew letters which preface each section and the concluding refrain, and the text itself. It seems likely that these works were written for private use by Catholic supporters, but they are among Tallis's most impressive compositions. Each Hebrew letter is given a melismatic setting, which is followed by an austere, syllabic setting of the text. The effect is one of emotionally charged but also deceptive simplicity, the work of a composer who is absolutely in control of his material.

Royal favour was evident in 1575, when the Queen granted Tallis and his young business partner, William Byrd, a twenty-one-year monopoly on the printing of music in England. As a business venture this proved a failure, as we shall see shortly, but it did result in one remarkable volume. *Cantiones Sacrae*, published in 1575, immediately after the granting of the monopoly, was a collection of thirty-four motets (seventeen by each composer) dedicated to the Queen. It did not sell, but it remains – and was intended to be – an unambiguous statement of the power and quality of English music at the time.

Although Tallis was a Gentleman of the Chapel Royal for over forty years, his precise role there is not always clear. Given his early background, one assumes that he was employed as the Chapel Royal's organist, although there is no formal record of him having that title until the 1570s; and shortly afterwards – by which time he would have been in his late sixties – he seems to have shared the position with Byrd. As well as his many choral works, he composed a significant amount of organ music for use in the Chapel Royal; and he also composed secular music for keyboards, viols or for larger consorts of instruments (the manuscripts in which these pieces survive rarely indicate the intended instrument or instruments). These secular works are an odd mixture, including keyboard pieces such as *The Lesson of Mr Tallis: two partes in one*; a number of *In Nomines* of the kind written by Tye; and secular part-songs with titles which anticipate Dowland, such as *When shall my sorrowful singing slack* or *Like as the doleful dove*. These works – some of which are secular adaptations of tunes that appear in his religious works – may have been written for the choirboys of the Chapel Royal, for private patrons, or, as has been suggested, even for performance by the Queen herself. Times were changing and a composer such as Tallis, whose career had focussed on sacred choral music, could now allow himself – with the apparent approval of the Chapel Royal and court – a certain latitude where secular music was concerned. This was a situation which, as we shall see, Byrd in particular would turn to his advantage.

The one work not considered so far is, of course, is Tallis's ultimate masterpiece, the forty-part motet *Spem in alium* – surely one of the greatest musical works ever composed. And yet it has a different starting point from most of Tallis's mature work. His compositional signature, particularly in his later work, was economy of means, quite possibly reflecting the way in which it was sensible to approach composition when extreme Protestant attitudes were in the ascendant. The music might be sad or penitential; it might be exultant; but whatever the mood, he created clarity, a sense of space between the parts, a sense that limited forces were being deployed to convey a clear message and create a defined emotional effect. *Spem in alium* is quite different: it is a massive piece, employing eight choirs of five voices (soprano, alto, tenor, baritone, bass). The text is a somewhat uninspiring adaptation from the Book of Judith – 'I have never put my hope in any other but in You, O God of Israel' – but the text does not matter: the aim is to overwhelm the listener with pure musical sound. When, about two-thirds of the way through the piece, all forty voices enter simultaneously, the impact is astonishing. Working in Los Angeles in the 1960s, record producer Phil Spector used multi-track techniques to create his 'Wall of Sound'; it is no exaggeration to say that Tallis got there first.

The usual account of the work's origins is that it came about as a result of a commission, possibly even a bet. The story goes that the Italian composer Alessandro Striggio (1536–92) came to London on a diplomatic mission in 1567, bringing with him the score of his massive motet for forty independent voices, called *Ecce beatam lucem*. The Duke of Arundel challenged Tallis to match Striggio's work and the result was *Spem in alium*, first performed at Arundel House in the Strand in 1570. An alternative version maintains that the work was first performed on Queen Elizabeth's fortieth birthday in 1573. But this is untenable if the Duke of Arundel were really involved, as the Queen had had him executed in 1572. A second alternative is that *Spem in alium* was commissioned by the Duke of Arundel, but in honour of Queen Mary, who had restored the dukedom to his family. This places its composition around 1556, which is plausible not only because its scale and magnificence fits the Catholic triumphalism of Mary's reign, but also because Mary's courtiers had deliberately chosen to identify her with the biblical heroine, Judith.[8] The truth will probably never be known.

Spem in alium is very much alive today, perhaps more so than any other work of its time. It continues to inspire contemporary composers. In 2005, Gabriel Jackson wrote his *Sanctum est verum lumen* as a companion piece to Tallis's work. In 2010, David Lang premiered *I never*, his own forty-part homage to Tallis, at the Sage, Gateshead. Three years later, and just next door in Gateshead's Baltic Centre, Janet Cardiff's art installation recreated *Spem in alium* with the aid of forty separately recorded voices played back through forty individual speakers. Then in 2015, *Spem in alium* reached the top of the British classical music charts after it was featured in the soundtrack of the erotic film *Fifty Shades of Grey*. This sense of relevance and accessibility can tempt a twenty-first-century audience to see the work as in some sense 'modern'. Perhaps in some ways it is; yet familiarity and accessibility should not obscure the fact that *Spem in alium* is also firmly linked to the medieval tradition which regarded music as more science than art. There is, for example, a cryptogram embedded in the structure of the work, based on the entries and movements of the vocal parts. These are plotted with mathematical precision in order to create a pattern which, interpreted using the correct numerical formula, spells out Tallis's name – and allows him to identify himself with his great work.[9]

19 Early Byrd

And then there was Byrd, the last in the great sequence of Tudor composers. Byrd is an intriguing and enigmatic figure. Undoubtedly something of a maverick, he manages to wear several different hats. He appears at once a figure of musical continuity in age of change; an exemplar of the social changes of the Elizabethan age – and the consequent changes in what it meant to be a musician; and a dissident, allying himself to the forces of Catholic reaction. A great deal of research has been done in recent years into his origins and early life, but, as ever with Tudor composers, certainties remain elusive. The Byrd family had connections with Essex and Kent, but by the time William was born (somewhere between 1539 and

1543), they were probably tradesmen living in London. Byrd was probably the third son, after Symond and John, and he had four sisters – Alice, Barbara, Mary and Martha. His brothers were choristers at St Paul's Cathedral and he may have joined them there, though his name does not appear in the surviving lists. Byrd's early keyboard works have been thought to show the influence of the composer John Redford, who was choirmaster at St Paul's from 1532 until his death in 1547 (although that influence could equally have derived from a manuscript owned by Byrd's brother, Symond).[1] Sebastian Westcott (or Westcote; *c.*1524–83), who became organist in 1550, and later Master of the Choristers at St Paul's, may have been his first teacher and may have sent his especially promising young pupil to be trained at the Chapel Royal by Tallis, whom he probably knew. Alternatively, Byrd may have shown such promise as a chorister that the Chapel Royal recruited him directly. It is often stated that Tallis was Byrd's teacher – and it would be a convenient way of explaining the later closeness between them – but in fact there is no proof that he was.[2] Unless the dates for his birth are wildly wrong, our Byrd was not the Wyllyam Byrd who was a chorister at Westminster Abbey in 1542 – although even this theory has its adherents. The truth may yet be discovered, but at present we simply do not know.

Whoever supplied it, Byrd's musical education was excellent. By 1563, when he was probably no more than twenty-seven or twenty-eight, he took up the prestigious post of organist and choirmaster at Lincoln Cathedral. Before that, however, at some point and for some reason, he made an important, even momentous, decision. He became a Catholic. He was not born into a Catholic family, but once converted he maintained his new convictions for the rest of his life in the face of great personal difficulty and even danger. Perhaps he was convinced by the Marian Counter-Reformation of his teenage years. We know he composed music for the restored Catholic Church. Somewhere towards the end of Mary's reign, he collaborated with John Sheppard and another composer, William Mundy (sometimes Munday; *c.*1529–91), who would later be a colleague at the Chapel Royal, on a setting of Psalm 113, *In exitu Israel.* Perhaps there was a particular teacher or mentor who influenced him. Sebastian Westcott is one possible candidate. A stubborn Catholic, who was responsible for arranging the music for the ceremony which formally marked the restoration of Catholicism under Queen Mary in 1553, Westcott never disguised his adherence to the Old Faith. This caused trouble with the church authorities on various occasions during Elizabeth's reign and he was stripped of some of his appointments, but he remained Master of the Choristers at St Paul's until his death in 1582, probably because he retained the favour of the Queen herself: she particularly enjoyed the dramatic performances featuring young choristers he organised at court.

It seems likely that the Dean of Lincoln, Francis Mallett, played a significant part in Byrd's appointment at the Cathedral there. He was a known lover of music and may well have had Catholic sympathies: he had been imprisoned under Edward VI for celebrating Mass and then appointed to Lincoln by Queen Mary. Byrd received a generous salary, approaching £13 a year, which by some accounts was double that of his predecessor, though he may have taken on extra duties. He was also given, or managed to negotiate, a rent-free house, 6 Minster Yard, in the shadow of the Cathedral. Byrd seems always to have had a frank and assertive attitude in financial matters. During his time in Lincoln, he appears to have been personally happy and professionally successful. In 1562, he married a lady called Juliana Birley and the first two of their seven children – Christopher and Elizabeth – were born while he was still working at the Cathedral. Professionally, he appears to have worked hard as choirmaster and organist, while consolidating his reputation as an up-and-coming composer and branching out into new areas. There are, of course, the usual difficulties in dating individual compositions, but it is clear that, by the time he left Lincoln in 1572, he already had an impressive body of work.

The young Byrd was obviously prodigiously talented, but it was an open talent, ready to absorb the full range of influences available to him. He would have begun his training by learning to compose, develop and manage lengthy passages of music based on pre-existing chants. This was the traditional starting point for a composer of church music – though it was a tradition that would not long survive his generation. The doyen of English composers at the time, and thus the effective guardian of this traditional approach to composition, was Tallis, whose influence is evident in a number of works from Byrd's early years, notably his keyboard settings, such as the short instrumental piece based on the chant *Gloria tibi trinitas*, and his writing for consort of viols. However, Byrd's simple but attractive settings of *Christi qui lux es* in four and five parts appear to show a debt to Robert White; while some early keyboard works may have been influenced by John Blitheman (*c.*1525–91), who became Master of Choristers at the Chapel Royal in 1564 and organist there after Tallis's death. Two of Byrd's five-part *In Nomines* written about this time are said to show the influence of the young Italian composer Alfonso Ferrabosco (1543–88), who visited England several times in the 1560s and again in the 1570s. Ferrabosco was something of a favourite with the Queen and introduced the first madrigals to the court, although the great English madrigal craze did not begin until the late 1580s. Then there is Robert Parsons, a minor composer, who was appointed as a Gentleman of the Chapel Royal in 1563. Parsons certainly knew Byrd – he may even have been his teacher – and Byrd used one of his pieces as the basis for another five-part *In Nomine*. It was Parsons who, inadvertently, opened the way for Byrd's appointment to the Chapel Royal. On his way north from London in January 1572, apparently to visit Byrd in Lincoln, he fell into the flooded River Trent at Newark and drowned. Byrd was appointed in his place. Yet if Byrd in his early years was something of a magpie, collecting different influences, he soon synthesised what he found and developed his own individual voice. At least one major work – the stately, eight-part *Ad Dominum cum tribularer*, a setting of Psalm 120 ('When I was in trouble I called upon the Lord') – can be securely dated from this period.

Byrd stayed nearly ten years at Lincoln. It was a successful period, but the contentious religious issue still hovered in the background. The Archdeacon, appointed just a few months before Byrd, was John Aylmer, a zealous anti-Catholic. According to his biographer (who may have been fond of a pun), he 'first purged the Cathedral church of Lincoln, being at that time a nest of unclean birds; and next in the county he so prevailed … that not one recusant was left.'[3] Byrd seems to have been less open about his Catholicism at this stage than he became later, but as time went on (and, quite possibly, as the influence of Dean Mallet declined – he died in 1570), he found himself in trouble with the Cathedral authorities on musical grounds. To zealous Protestants such as Aylmer, decorative and elaborate organ arrangements would have signposted the road to Rome, and in November 1569, Byrd was summoned to appear before the Cathedral Chapter. His playing during services and in accompanying the choir had gone beyond what was considered seemly. He was reprimanded and his salary suspended for a short period. Perhaps paternal pride played a part, for the incident happened just the day after his son Christopher was christened. In the end, however, Byrd managed to leave Lincoln without any major rift with the authorities and – characteristically – in a manner which was financially to his advantage: he agreed to continue to compose for the

Cathedral, while the Cathedral agreed that his replacement should be appointed only as his deputy. This meant he could continue to receive a proportion of his salary. It was an arrangement that lasted for ten years.

Tye, Sheppard and Tallis began and ended their lives as church musicians; Byrd began in that role, but even within his own lifetime he became almost as well known for his secular as for his religious works. He was the first cross-over composer of any stature. While at Lincoln, he devoted a significant amount of time to secular music, particularly for keyboards: *Parson's In Nomine*, *A Horne Pipe*, the *Galliard Gygge* and *The Hunt's Up* are among works that have been dated to this time.[4] Byrd also seems to have written music for Twelfth Night celebrations in Lincoln. (One wonders what the hard-line Protestants made of that.) Yet it was his return to London and his appointment as a Gentleman of the Chapel Royal that allowed him not only to fulfil his promise as a composer of both sacred and secular music, but also to develop and extend the role that a musician could expect to play in society.

In 1575, as mentioned earlier, Tallis and Byrd were granted a twenty-one-year monopoly on the printing of music in England, whether in 'English, Latin, French, Italian, or other languages that may serve for music either in church or chamber'. Their licence also extended to the use of what was termed 'ruled paper' for printing music.[5] The first instance of moveable type being used to print music was the *Constance Gradual*, probably dating from 1473, and produced either in Konstanz or in Augsburg. The first example in England was in 1495, when the remarkably named Wynkyn de Worde, who had taken over Caxton's workshop that same year, printed eight notes in an edition of Ranulf Higden's *Polychronicon*. Progress was painfully slow. In the late 1520s, one William Rastell printed a handful of liturgical pieces and a ballad, *Time to pas with goodly sport*, of his own composition. Not until the 1550s, when William Seres and John Day received licences to print music, did music publishing take a step forward. Working as partners, they printed a number of volumes which provided music for the Elizabethan Church – including a collection of services and anthems, Day's *Certaine Notes* in 1560, and Sternhold and Hopkins' *Whole Book of Psalms* in 1562. They were responsible for publishing Archbishop Parker's *Whole Psalter* (to which Tallis contributed) and also for *Songs in three, fower and five voices* (1571) by Thomas Whythorne. Whythorne's work was the only secular musical work published in England between 1530 and 1588, and that is probably its main claim to fame. Perched somewhere between part-songs and madrigals, Whythorne's small output and his name disappeared from view until resurrected by Peter Warlock in the 1920s.[6] A few years later, in 1932, E. J. Moeran used his song *As Thy Shadow Itself Apply'th* as the basis for his wonderfully melodic orchestral piece, *Whythorne's Shadow*.[7]

Music publishing should have been a growth industry. Byrd, with his keen interest in business and in money matters, probably saw that. Tallis's status and influence no doubt smoothed the path at court, but as a business venture the whole enterprise reflects Byrd's character rather than Tallis's. In fact, it was not a success and, after two years, Byrd and Tallis – though one imagines Byrd leading – petitioned the Queen that the 'lycense for the printinge of musicke … hath fallen oute to oure greate losse and hinderaunce to the value of two hundred markes at the least.'[8] The Queen was sympathetic and granted them compensation in the form of income from certain manors in East Anglia and the West Country.

As we have seen, the one publication to emerge from the monopoly was *Cantiones Sacrae* (1575). It was a rather grandiose project, quite explicitly designed to present Tallis and Byrd as the leaders of English music and capable of holding their own against foreign competition. There were seventeen motets by each composer – the number apparently chosen to reflect the number of years that Elizabeth had been on the throne. Tallis's contributions are the stately pieces that one would expect from the greatest composer of the age towards the end of his career. Byrd's are more mixed. Some are impressive pieces that look forward to the 1580s and beyond (*Domine, secundum actum meum; Siderum rector; Emmendemus in melius*); some we know to have been keyboard pieces before words were added (*Laudate pueri*); while others seem to look back to pre-reformation models and patterns (*Tribue dominum; Libera me dominum*), suggesting that he may perhaps have struggled to make up his seventeen pieces. That is not to deny the quality of Byrd's writing or the popularity which some of these pieces have achieved, rather to point out that he had not reached the level of consistency that was to be the hallmark of his later work.

One wonders whether at one level *Cantiones Sacrae* represents another attempt by Byrd – who had been in London only some three years – to use his association with Tallis to forward his career. If so, it does not seem to have created any tension between them. They shared the role of organist at the Chapel Royal without any apparent friction; Tallis stood godfather to Byrd's second son in 1576; and when Tallis died in 1585, Byrd wrote *Ye*

Sacred Muses, a simple, but heartfelt and moving tribute to his mentor, ending with the words 'Tallis is dead and music dies.' And with the death of Tallis, Byrd succeeded to the role of England's leading composer. In a dedicatory epigraph in the second volume of *Gradualia* (1607), Byrd was described as 'cultivated by many and admired by all … Father of British Music', a phrase which recurred on his death in 1623 when he was lamented by a Chapel Royal colleague as 'a Father of Musick.'[9]

As a Gentleman of the Chapel Royal, Byrd carried out his duties, playing the organ, teaching the next generation of composers, and composing. He seems to have worked happily within the disciplines of the Anglican Church, producing various psalms and anthems as well as two settings of the *Magnificat* and *Nunc dimittis* for Evensong (known as his Second and Third Services). He wrote two complete settings of music for Matins and Evensong – a *Short Service* ('short' meaning 'simple' and thus leaning towards Cranmer-style demands for simplicity) and the famous *Great Service.*[10] These are works of the highest standard. The *Short Service* is concise and controlled, even understated, but it makes a powerful emotional impact, building to a climax with the *Magnificat*, before moving to a still firmly controlled conclusion with the *Nunc dimittis.* However, it is the *Great Service* that has attracted most attention. Probably written around 1590, it was not rediscovered until 1922. Julian Fellowes, the historian of English cathedral music, has judged it 'the finest unaccompanied setting of the Service in the entire repertory of English Church music.'[11] It would have been too long for daily use, and few choirs, apart from the Chapel Royal, would have had the ability to take on such a work – although it does appear to have been sung in York around 1618, and the fact that the manuscript was rediscovered in Durham Cathedral suggests that it may have been performed there. Scored for ten parts, it is a work that develops through contrast and opposition: soloists against full choir; sopranos and altos against tenors and basses; the two sides of the choir against each other. There is drama in its scale and in the complex movement of the vocal lines, but it maintains throughout a great clarity of purpose – and Byrd never loses sight of his text. He never allows drama or volume to obscure or drown the words.

One major difference between Byrd and previous composers was the amount of his work that was published in his lifetime. Of course, he had a vested interest in publication, but it was also an indication of changing times. The Chapel Royal, the cathedral schools, and aristocratic patrons remained the main sources of income for Elizabethan composers, but the increasing wealth of the mercantile middle classes was slowly becoming a factor. They bought themselves spinets, virginals and clavichords to play at home; they learned the lute and the *viola da gamba*; and, of course, they sang. Music was becoming a leisure activity – and the fact that Elizabeth I, an early exponent of the cult of personality, was an enthusiastic performer did nothing to diminish this new enthusiasm. Performance at home led to a demand for published music, and composers began to see publication as a source of income.

20 Catholic Byrd

It took thirteen years, following the commercial failure of *Cantiones Sacrae,* for Byrd to return to music publishing, but he did so in style. Between 1588 and 1591, he published four major collections: *Psalms, Sonnets and Songs of Sadness and Pietie* (1588), and *Songs of Sundrie Natures* (1589), followed by two further volumes of *Cantiones Sacrae* (1589 and 1591). The publication of so much music by a single composer was unprecedented. The first two volumes were Byrd's response to a sudden change in the market for music that could be sung at home. At the beginning of 1588, Nicholas Yonge published his collection of Italian madrigals, *Musica Transalpina.* It was an immediate popular success. Byrd was not the man to pass up a business opportunity. *Psalms, Sonnets and Songs of Sadness* was a retrospective collection, consisting, in his own words, of 'divers songs being originally made for instruments to express the harmony, and one voice … now framed in all parts for voices.' These were not madrigals, but they were clearly designed to appeal to the market Yonge had opened up. As the title suggests, the mood is wide-ranging, from a lullaby and settings of sonnets by Sir Philip Sidney to settings of metrical psalms taken from Sternhold and Hopkins. *Songs of Sundrie Natures*, which followed, is equally diverse in its musical style and its mood. There are settings of seven penitential psalms, but also carols, an anthem, and some lighter five-part songs. This was Byrd the voice of the Elizabethan era, the man who understood and could cater for the tastes of his time.

The two volumes of *Cantiones Sacrae* show a somewhat different face. They contain motets, Latin settings of religious texts, demonstrating that Byrd was a master of the form. The 1589 collection moves effortlessly from

Aspice Domine, a *cantus firmus*-based piece, which is clearly intended to sound like Tallis – and thus to suggest that Byrd is continuing alone the work that they began jointly in 1575 – to *Vigilate*, which uses all the techniques of the newly popular madrigal form to call on people to be ready for the coming of Christ. This was the new sound of the 1580s and 1590s, but its quicker tempo and brighter musical texture can deceive: the mood of Byrd's texts is resolutely sombre – 'My life has wasted away in grief, and my years in sighing'; 'O Lord, we look for your coming: come quickly and dissolve the bonds of our captivity.' The 1591 volume continues in similar vein, though here perhaps there is just a glimmer of hope in the idea that Christ will come and free people from their suffering and slavery – 'Remember, Lord, your intention, and say to the murderous Angel / Stop now your work, so that the earth is not left desolate'; 'Tribulation is near and there is no help at hand / But thou, O Lord, defender of my life, do thou avenge me.' Why should Byrd, at the top of his profession, a success with the public and a favourite of the Queen, be obsessed with misery and suffering? The answer lies in his Catholicism.

Elizabeth I's main priority was stability. She fully understood that a significant minority of both the nobility and the gentry were either actively Catholic or had Catholic sympathies, and her instinct was to tolerate private Catholicism in exchange for public loyalty. In 1569, however, the Earls of Northumberland and Westmoreland rose in rebellion with the aim of installing the Catholic Mary Queen of Scots on the throne. And the rising was supported by the Pope, Pius V, who issued *Regnans in Excelsis* (1570), which not only excommunicated Elizabeth I but absolved 'all and singular the nobles, subjects, peoples' from any requirement to obey her. Elizabeth could no longer afford to be tolerant and it became increasingly difficult to be a Catholic in England. Byrd was not shy about his Catholicism, nor was his wife Juliana; and in 1577 when John Aylmer, last seen as a zealously anti-Catholic Archdeacon of Lincoln, reappeared in their lives as Bishop of London, they became the subject of official scrutiny: this may explain their move to the village of Harlington, Middlesex, a few miles outside London. By 1580, recusancy fines – imposed on those who refused to attend Church of England services as required by the Act of Uniformity – had risen from their original level of one shilling to an astonishing £20. In 1581, the Catholic priest Edmund Campion was arrested while conducting a secret ministry in England, tried for treason, and hanged, drawn and quartered at Tyburn. In 1584, Byrd was formally cited as a recusant. (Juliana had appeared on the list as early as 1577.) He was known to mix with other Catholics whose agenda was far more political than his own – men like Lord Thomas Paget, who was implicated in a number of plots against the Queen and eventually fled to Spain. By 1585, the evidence against him had accumulated to the point where he was temporarily suspended from his Chapel Royal duties and his house was searched. His wife and three of their children were actually declared outlaws for their persistent recusancy.

The contents of *Cantiones Sacrae* 1589 and 1591 have to be seen against this background. On a superficial level, they are simply motets based on rather gloomy texts, focussing on suffering, slavery and imprisonment, but, for the initiated, Byrd is speaking on behalf of a Catholic community who feel themselves a persecuted, isolated group surrounded by a hostile culture and longing for some form of release. This was potentially very dangerous ground. There is no evidence to suggest that Byrd was ever anything but loyal to the Queen, but it would have been perfectly possible to interpret some of his texts as bearing a political message.

Byrd was, to some extent, protected by his fame: he was England's greatest composer and recognised as such. He was also protected by a network of powerful Catholic friends and patrons, chief among whom was Sir John Petre of Thorndon Hall in Essex, a known Catholic, but also recognised as a loyal servant of the Queen. Byrd dedicated *Cantiones Sacrae* 1589 to the Earl of Worcester and the 1591 volume to Lord Lumley. Both were powerful Catholic loyalists – Lumley was also Elizabethan England's greatest art collector and bibliophile – and both were known to be in favour with the Queen. The Attorney General, Sir John Popham, intervened with the authorities twice, in 1589 and 1591, on Byrd's behalf; and then, decisively, in 1592, the Queen herself told them to leave Byrd alone. It did not end his acts of religious defiance, but it did put an end to significant trouble with the authorities.

Byrd completed one other volume in 1591. Or rather, a lay clerk named James Baldwin at St George's Chapel, Windsor, finished copying it for him. It was called *My Lady Nevell's Book*. The Lady Neville in question was another of Byrd's well-connected friends, as well as being the sister of Sir Francis Bacon, and the manuscript Byrd dedicated to her was an anthology of forty-two of his finest keyboard pieces. Had the technology been available, Byrd would surely have published *My Lady Nevell's Book* along with his other four volumes, but at the time printing keyboard music was a much more complex task than printing vocal music. The technique of copper plate engraving did not arrive in England for another twenty years.

Byrd's surviving keyboard works – over one hundred and forty of them – represent a significant part of his output. Davitt Moroney, who recorded a complete edition of the keyboard works, has drawn attention to the role that these compositions, and particularly Byrd's fifty-six surviving pavans and galliards, played in his inner musical life: 'They may be seen as a sort of laboratory in which he wrestled with new concepts of melodic structure supported by innovative harmonic schemes, and gave renewed life to older English ideas of rhythmic development … he demonstrably put the experience thus acquired to good use in non-keyboard music.'[1]

Byrd was obviously a complex character. He was a businessman with an eye for profit; a studious man with a library of notably heavyweight intellectual tomes; a courtier, even a flatterer, with a natural ability to exploit his connections in case of need. He could write the most beautiful words and music in praise of the Queen – 'O Lord, make thy servant Elizabeth our Queen to rejoice in thy strength / Give her her heart's desire, and deny not the request of her lips' – while remaining a lifelong recusant, stubborn in his defiance of the Queen's laws. He was also an almost obsessive litigant: legal proceedings surrounding the manor of Langney in Gloucestershire (granted to him by the Queen in 1577 following the commercial failure of the first *Cantiones Sacrae*) lasted nearly thirty years, and those relating to his estate at Stondon Massey in Essex something like fifteen. None of this, however, prevented him from pursuing his musical ends, which were more far-reaching than just composing appropriate music for a particular audience. Much more than with earlier composers – quite probably because more documentation is available – we can sense Byrd moving stage by stage through his musical life, always seeking to develop the possibilities of his art. Certainly, his actions in pulling together a wide spectrum of past compositions and assembling them into five volumes of music in the space of three years gives the impression of stocktaking or clearing the decks, a deliberate preparation for the next phase.

In 1595, Byrd sold his house in Harlington and bought Stondon Place at Stondon Massey, where he was to live for the rest of his life.[2] Despite the move, which put him some thirty miles from London and sixty from Windsor, he seems to have remained a member of the Chapel Royal. Given his status, one imagines he was allowed to take leave from the court, a kind of semi-retirement, as long as he continued to produce appropriate music and be present on important occasions. We know he spent a considerable amount of time at court during 1601 and we must assume, again given his status, that he sang at the funeral of Queen Elizabeth and the Coronation of James I in 1603. We know that his music continued to be performed by the Chapel. His anthem *Sing joyfully* was sung at the baptism of James's daughter, Princess Mary, in May 1605; and his song for solo voice and viols, 'Fair Britain Isle', was written to mourn the death of the King's son and heir, Prince Henry, in 1612. Approaching seventy by this stage – and semi-retired or not – the public Byrd kept producing music. In 1611, he published what turned out to be his last solo collection, *Psalms, Songs and Sonnets*. It showed no falling off in quality – *This day Christ was born* and *Praise our Lord, all ye Gentiles* are among a number of remarkable pieces that retain their popularity to this day. Two years later, he contributed to *Parthenia*, an influential collection of music for the virginals dedicated 'To the high and mighty Frederick, Elector Palatine of the Reine and his betrothed Lady, Elizabeth the only daughter of my Lord the King.' Alongside Byrd, *Parthenia* contained works by John Bull, whom Byrd had taught, and Orlando Gibbons, the up-and-coming star of English music. And in 1614, four of Byrd's songs appeared in *The Teares or Lamentations of a Sorrowfull Soule*, an anthology of contemporary composers compiled by Sir William Leighton. These were the last pieces published in his lifetime.

But Byrd was also a private composer – not private in the sense that his work was not published, but private in that he was pursuing a personal ambition and a personal conviction. From about 1590 until 1607, he was engaged on a massive project, which was at once ambitious and extremely dangerous. There is no doubt that he chose his new home at Stondon Massey because it lay within three or four miles of Ingatestone Hall, the seat of his Catholic patron and protector, Sir John Petre. And it was almost certainly at the instigation of Petre and other members of the English Catholic community that Byrd embarked on the composition of a full cycle of music for the Latin Catholic rite. This consisted of settings of the Mass, and settings of texts suitable for each of the main feast days of the Catholic year.

These were the first settings of the Mass to be composed in England for something like thirty years – and they make a clear statement about the history, continuity and legitimacy of the Catholic tradition in which he is writing. The use of motifs to link movements and the pattern of frequent interplay between full choir and semi-choir sections refer back to the early

Tudor period. The *Mass for Four Voices* actually takes its structure and at least one tune from Taverner's *Meane Mass*. There are Continental influences, notably the inclusion of a *Kyrie* in each Mass, a rarity in Masses composed for the traditional English Sarum rite, but these are very much Masses for the beleaguered Catholic community of the 1590s. The sense of anguish and longing Byrd imparts to the *Agnus Dei* from the *Mass for Four Voices* echoes the sense of isolation and desperation that characterised the two later volumes of *Cantiones Sacrae*. Between 1593 and 1595, Byrd published a new setting of the Mass every year. On the face of it, he was taking a very great risk. It was done discreetly: the printer was not named and no publication date was given, but Byrd did nothing to disguise his authorship – and he got away with it.

It was ten years before the next part of Byrd's great project saw the light of day. He had already taken huge risks in publishing his three Masses, but in the uncertain atmosphere of Elizabeth's last years, when Catholics were again cast as bogeymen who threatened the succession, to go further would have been to court disaster. Moreover, there was a distinct hope among the Catholic community that James VI of Scotland, when he succeeded to the English throne, might be more sympathetic to their cause. And then, of course, there was the sheer scale of the undertaking. When the two volumes of Byrd's *Gradualia* did eventually appear – in 1605 and 1607 and dedicated to the (Catholic) Earl of Northampton and to Byrd's patron, the recently ennobled Lord Petre – they contained no fewer than one hundred and nine motets. Seen from today's perspective, these are obviously Catholic pieces. Byrd 'provides settings of the Propers at Mass, that is, those texts (Introit, Gradual, Tract or Alleluia, Offertory and Communion) which change from day to day according to the Feast being celebrated. He also provides some Antiphons … and Hymns for Divine Office.' They are concise pieces, suited to performance by small groups of singers, such as would gather for the secret – and highly illegal – celebration of Mass in a recusant household. And Byrd's own introduction, with its references to the Blessed Virgin Mary, seems determined to emphasise their essential Catholicism. Yet perhaps we are too aware of Byrd's Catholicism and his recusant lifestyle. As with two later volumes of *Cantiones Sacrae,* so the two volumes of *Gradualia* were apparently capable of a less controversial interpretation. Richard Carwood suggests that 'for the purposes of publication these relatively short, Latin-texted pieces could easily be presented as spiritual entertainment for the home, innocent pieces, to be sung after supper perhaps, allowing one to exercise vocal, instrumental and linguistic skills. This is certainly how a Protestant household would have perceived them.'[3] And the fact that Byrd actually asked and received permission to publish these two volumes from Richard Bancroft, the Archbishop of Canterbury, suggests that this position was at least defensible. It is worth noting that Byrd never sought to publish any of the music he wrote for the Anglican Church.

The *Gradualia* motets are shorter and less elaborate than those of the *Cantiones Sacrae* volumes. As one might expect from such a large collection, there is a huge stylistic range – from those that look back to the pre-Reformation period to those that adopt contemporary madrigalian techniques – but the common characteristic is restraint. Byrd's artistry is implied rather than stated: there is more tune and less decoration and thus greater attention placed upon the words. Byrd's great project – his three Masses and the *Gradualia* motets – is a statement of passionate religious belief expressed in words and music and extended over some one hundred and twenty pieces of music. It is a remarkable achievement, not least because of the importance Byrd gives to his texts. He was one of those composers – one thinks of Warlock and Finzi despite the huge gulf in time and style between them – who recognised the interdependence of words and music: a master of word-setting, and not just in a technical sense. He claimed that he liked to meditate on the texts until a theme suggested itself almost spontaneously; and he would surely have accepted that the coherence of his musical vision owed much to his understanding of the texts he was setting. Byrd was seeking the perfect marriage of words and music, something he believed was only possible when vocal music was, as he put it in his introduction to *Psalms, Songs and Sonnets*, 'framed to the life of the words.' It is, arguably, in the *Gradualia* motets that he came closest to achieving that aim.

21 Madrigals

The great Tudor composers of church music – Tye, Taverner, Sheppard, Tallis, Byrd – stand like monuments on the landscape of English musical history. Ever since the rediscovery of Tudor music in the late-nineteenth and early-twentieth centuries, they have been seen as the accepted masters, and today their works are regularly performed by groups such as the Tallis

Scholars, the Cardinall's Musick, the Hilliard Ensemble, Stile Antico, and the Sixteen.[1] But in reality, of course, the landscape was much more crowded. A number of names from the early Tudor period – Cornysh, Fayrfax, Ludford, Aston, Redford, Newark – have already been mentioned. Richard Bampston (*c.*1485–1554) also deserves to be remembered for his impressive motet, *Recordare, Domine;* as does Richard Pygott (*c.*1485–*c.*1549), who wrote the elegant carol, *Quid petis, o fili?,* and who in 1517 was pardoned for breaking a law regulating the use of handguns and crossbows.

The Elizabethan period saw an explosion of musical talent and activity. Tallis and Byrd may have dominated, but there were numerous other composers, many of them gifted and not all of them attached to the Chapel Royal, who wrote for the Elizabethan Church. There was the unfortunate Robert Parsons, whose drowning in the River Trent opened the way for Byrd to become a Gentleman of the Chapel Royal. He wrote for both Queen Mary's Catholic Church and its Protestant successor, leaving a collection of Latin works, two impressive Anglican services, and a number of English anthems. There was William Mundy (*c.*1529–91), a member of the Chapel Royal for some thirty years, who wrote some fine psalm settings – notably *Adolescentulus sum ego* (Psalm 118) and *Adhaesit pavimento* (Psalm 119) – and some striking English anthems – *O Lord the maker of all things* and *O Lord, I bow the knees*. Then there was Robert White (whom we've already met); born in Holborn in London, the son of an organ builder, White spent most of his career in Cambridge, Ely, and Chester before returning to the capital as Master of Choristers at Westminster Abbey in 1570 and dying of the plague just four years later. He, too, began his writing under Queen Mary (he must have been still in his teens at the time) and appears to have made the transition to the Elizabethan Church without undue difficulty – though, privately, like Tallis, he seems to have remained a Catholic. Only in his mid-thirties when he died, he still left a considerable body of work, including seventeen Latin motets, a large scale *Magnificat*, two sets of *Lamentations*, and no less than four settings of the hymn *Christe qui lux es et dies*. He was highly regarded both by his peers during his lifetime and in the period after his death.

In the last decades of the century, a new generation of composers came to maturity. These included Thomas Morley (*c.*1557–1602), John Bull (*c.*1563–1628), Thomas Tomkins (1572–1656) and Thomas Weelkes (1576–1623) – all of them probably taught by Byrd – and, of course, Orlando

Gibbons (1583–1625). The list could be extended to twenty or even thirty names, and together they constituted a large and loose-knit fellowship of composers, many of them knowing each other, listening to and feeding off each other's music, all contributing to the corpus of music available to the Elizabethan and the Jacobean Church. Members of this post-Byrd generation followed his example by composing at least as much secular as religious music, and the principal focus of their secular music was the newly-fashionable madrigal.

Around 1540, one Jeronimo Bassano from the village of Bassano del Grappa, some fifty kilometres north-west of Venice, moved to England with five of his six sons and formed a wind consort that played at the court of Henry VIII. In 1561, Nicholas Lanier the Elder, a flute and cornett player at the court of Henry II of France, came to England to escape persecution as a Protestant and found employment at court, eventually being given the title Master of Flutes by James I. Joseph Lupo, a Venetian viol player and composer, arrived around 1563 and served the court for forty years; and the presence of Alfonso Ferrabosco, originally from Bologna, at Elizabeth's court has already been mentioned. These families intermarried, giving rise to several generations of court musicians (and, a long way further down the line, to Tennessee Williams). Their presence in England at that time is proof that, despite religious and political differences with much of the rest of Europe, the cultural and musical outlook of Elizabeth's court was anything but insular.

The first published collection of madrigals appeared in Venice in 1539, credited to Jacques Arcadelt, a Dutch composer working as a singer and composer at the Sistine Chapel in Rome, and it proved so successful that it was still being used as a textbook a hundred years later. The madrigal itself was Italian in origin, having evolved from a number of existing types of Italian popular song. It was a highly polyphonic, unaccompanied vocal composition, usually written for three to six voices. It differed from folk songs and from the lute song or ayre, which would become the next popular musical form, in that it was usually through-composed. That is to say, the music for each verse was different, so that the piece developed as it progressed with the aim of creating a musical whole. Despite its popularity in Italy and the English court's openness to Continental music, the madrigal was slow to reach England and then slow to catch on. Bassano, whose sixth son was a musician in Venice, must surely have kept abreast of the latest musical developments in Italy; as would Lanier and Lupo with their extensive Continental connections. But it was Ferrabosco who is credited with bringing the madrigal to Elizabeth's court, probably in the 1560s. He was certainly popular with Queen Elizabeth, who granted him a pension of £100 a year (perhaps because she liked his music or perhaps, as was rumoured on the Continent, because he had acted as a spy for her), but this was not enough for his madrigals to achieve popularity outside court circles.

It needed Nicholas Yonge's *Musica Transalpina* in 1588 to launch the new genre successfully. Among the fifty-seven pieces by eighteen composers, Yonge granted pride of place to Ferrabosco, who died that same year, having long since returned to Italy where his music was almost unknown. Today, we are more convinced by the contributions of the Italian masters Marenzio, Palestrina, Donato and de Lassus (di Lasso), but when the collection was published, it was Ferrabosco's skilful if somewhat conservative offerings which seem to have been responsible for the volume's commercial success. Two years later, Thomas Watson, the poet and friend of Christopher Marlowe, brought out a similar volume, *The First Sett of Italian Madrigalls Englished.* Watson restricted himself to four Italian composers, giving Marenzio the greatest prominence, and noted that his was a free translation, 'more after the affection of the note than the dittie,'[2] a particularly important statement given the interaction between words and music that was to be so characteristic of the English madrigal school. He did, however, include one English composer. As a scholar and Dean of St John's College, Cambridge, Watson presumably had more influence than Yonge, a mere lay clerk at St Paul's, and, in order to ensure the success of his volume, felt able to ask Byrd for a contribution. Byrd obliged with two settings of 'The Sweet and Merry Month of May', but these were his only excursions into the form. He never referred to any of his other secular songs as madrigals and, although he was quite clearly a master of the necessary techniques, he preferred to employ them in his sacred writing.

The tradition of trained composers setting English texts was still relatively new. It only really began with Henry VIII and the focus had been on church music. Of course, as we have seen, composers had set secular English texts as part-songs for the aristocracy to sing, but they were mainly incidental pieces to accompany court celebrations, regarded as of secondary importance. During Elizabeth's reign, however, the changed status of the Church, the emergence of music as a leisure activity among the newly wealthy middle classes, and the emergence of a new generation of composers who had *not* grown up with the Church as the dominant presence in their musical world, made for rapid change. These new composers no longer saw secular music as lightweight or second best. The arrival of the madrigal at just this moment was providential. Here was a new genre, secular in origin, which offered them the chance to pursue their art and achieve recognition for their talents in the secular sphere.

The reign of Elizabeth I marked the high point of the Renaissance in England. Italian influence was visible everywhere – in the comedies and tragedies which played to packed houses in theatres and inn yards up and down the country; in the sonnets of Sir Philip Sidney, Edmund Spenser, Shakespeare and many others; and, in the musical sphere, in the sudden emergence and dominance of the madrigal. Foreign models were accepted, absorbed and adapted in a very English way. The madrigal was an opportunity that English composers seized. It appealed not just to one or two of them, but to a whole school (if a group of composers united by practice rather than theory can be called a school). And the boom, which was to last some thirty years, demonstrated two important characteristics of the English musical imagination: a gift and preference for melody; and a particular interest in and genius for vernacular word setting.

It was Thomas Morley who took the madrigal beyond translation and imitation and laid the foundations for a genuine English madrigal school – just as he was also one of the first to publish lute ayres and music for instrumental groups. Born and brought up in Norwich, where he was Master of Choristers at the Cathedral from 1583, Morley moved to London in 1591 to take up the position of organist at St Paul's. That same year he not only visited Spanish-held Flanders, apparently acting as a spy among English recusants who had fled there,[3] but was also noticed by Queen Elizabeth when one of his pavans was played during a royal visit to Hampshire. Whatever the connection between these events, in 1592 Morley found himself appointed a Gentleman of the Chapel Royal, a role he filled for the next ten years, but which does not represent the main thrust of his musical activity. Membership of the Chapel Royal enabled him to start publishing music; like Byrd, Morley was a businessman as well as a composer. Between 1593 and 1601, he published eight volumes of madrigals.[4] Three were collections of his own original work;[5] two were transcriptions and reworkings of Italian originals;[6] two were anthologies of previously published Italian work;[7] and one, *The Triumphes of Oriana* (1601), was an anthology of specially-commissioned English pieces. This represented a huge contribution to the development and the popularisation of the form both in England and in the rest of the British Isles.

Morley's own work is immensely tuneful. There is a liveliness and a freshness which sets him apart from many of the Italian madrigal writers who were his models. This is most clearly seen in his fondness for dance rhythms and in the bright, polyphonic constructions which accompany his famous (and much caricatured) 'Fa la la la la' refrains. Morley's subject matter tends, like his tunes, to be bright and cheerful, although the pains of love also feature frequently. He concentrates on love, May mornings, praise of his mistress, and rustic scenes with shepherds and milkmaids. 'See, see, myne own sweet jewell', 'O Flye not, O take some pittie', 'Good morrow, fayre ladies of May', 'Blow, shepherds, blow', are all representative titles from his first collection, *Canzonets to Three Voyces* (1593). Madrigals and madrigal singers have been much satirised over the years – not least by Kingsley Amis in *Lucky Jim* – and to twenty-first-century ears Morley's titles and lyrics can conjure up chocolate-box images of Merrie England, but a 1590s audience would have found these songs new, exciting, romantic, even faintly exotic by reason of their Italian connection. We know this because Morley and many other madrigalists enjoyed a degree of commercial success. Their published work continued to sell in significant quantities for the next thirty years.

By the time Morley died, in 1602, in his mid-forties, the madrigal craze was at its height. Less than ten years before, his *Canzonets to Three Voyces* had been the first collection of English madrigals to be published. The year before his death, he edited *The Triumphes of Oriana*, a collection of twenty-five madrigals by twenty-three composers, all but one of them English (Thomas Tomkins was proud of his Welsh birth), in honour of Queen Elizabeth. Once again, modern taste may struggle with the artificiality of the subject matter – 'The nymphs and shepherds danced', 'Sing shepherds all', 'All creatures now are merry-minded', 'Come, gentle swains' – but the lyrics, based on elaborate metaphors or conceits, are no more or less artificial than those of Victorian parlour ballads or 1950s rock'n'roll. They were simply the discipline of the age; and composers were judged by their ability to work within the prescribed framework to musical and emotional effect. Within that framework, *The Triumphes of Oriana* contains a range of differing styles and responses, including works by Ellis Gibbons (elder brother of Orlando), and John Milton (the father of the poet), as well as Thomas Weelkes and John Wilbye.

Thomas Weelkes (1576–1623) came from the village of Elsted, near Chichester, and may well have been the son of the vicar there. Apart from a period studying at New College, Oxford, where he was awarded a degree in music in 1602, his working life was spent within the orbit of Winchester and Chichester Cathedrals, though he was clearly no stranger to London. Although he was a church musician and wrote a considerable amount of very fine church music, which we will look at in Chapter 28, he is best known for his madrigals. Weelkes' behaviour does not fit with the general conception of a church musician. He was constantly in trouble with the authorities for drinking and behaving badly when drunk. On one occasion, he is supposed to have urinated on the Dean from the organ loft during Evensong and, on another, he was so drunk that he shouted obscenities during a service. This led to his dismissal, though he was later reinstated.

Weelkes published four volumes of madrigals in his lifetime, all between 1597 and 1600, but the two volumes entitled *Madrigals for 5 and 6 parts, apt for viols and voices*, both of which appeared in 1600, contain his most important work. He was inventive in a restless, sometimes erratic manner. He recognised that madrigals need not be restricted to voices alone and wrote with the idea that they could be accompanied by viols or other instruments; and that parts could be changed round or substituted as required. He was certainly capable of enjoying himself in his madrigals, some of which may indicate why he was constantly in trouble with the church: 'Come, sirrah Jack ho / Fill some tobacco / Bring a wire and some fire … I swear that this tobacco / Is perfect Trinidad-o / By the very very Mass / Never never was / Better gear / Than is here.' But, as so often, an exuberant exterior seems to have masked a more complex and uncertain personality. 'O Care, thou wilt despatch me' and the three-part 'Cease sorrows now' are expressions of intense emotional pain. 'Death hath deprived me of my dearest friend', written following the death of Morley, whom Weelkes knew well, is an outpouring of desolation and sadness. If Morley saw the madrigal as a light, entertaining form, Weelkes developed its emotional and descriptive range. His word-painting – the ability to make his music match the meaning of the words – goes beyond Morley's in both the enormous range of his subject matter and his imaginative approach to it. He can even make the traditional 'Fa la la la la' refrain carry a tragic meaning. One senses a man pushing the boundaries of what he and the madrigal could achieve. No other English madrigalist would have attempted the text of 'Thule, the period of cosmography' and its second part, 'The Andalusian merchant', let alone turned them into a masterpiece of descriptive music.

> Thule, the period of cosmography,
> Doth vaunt of Hecla, whose sulphurous fire
> Doth melt the frozen clime and thaw the sky;
> Trinacrian Etna's flames ascend not higher:
> These things seem wondrous, yet more wondrous I,
> Whose heart with fear doth freeze, with love doth fry.
>
> The Andalusian merchant, that returns
> Laden with cochineal and china dishes,
> Reports in Spain how strangely Fogo burns
> Amidst an ocean full of flying fishes:
> These things seem wondrous, yet more wondrous I,
> Whose heart with fear doth freeze, with love doth fry.

Nonetheless, it is John Wilbye, not Weelkes, whose work is regarded as the highest achievement of the English madrigal school. Wilbye (1574–1638) is the odd man out. He was neither a church musician, nor a businessman. Nor did he occupy any public position. The son of a tanner from Diss in Suffolk, he spent his entire adult life in the service of a number of well-to-do Suffolk families – the Cornwallises, the Kitsons, and the Rivers. He never married and ended his days a well-off and well-respected family retainer within the household of the Countess Rivers. His circle of friends included George Kirbye and Michael Cavendish, both madrigalists and both contributors to *The Triumphes of Oriana*. He may also have known the madrigalist and composer of lute sings, Thomas Greave. Wilbye published only two works, a *First Set of Madrigals* in 1598 and a *Second Set of Madrigals* in 1609 – a total of sixty-four pieces – but they assured him an enduring place in the history of English music.

Wilbye was a perfectionist. If he lacks the bouncy vitality of Morley and the edgy creativity of Weelkes, he makes up for it with a combination of superb technique and complete poetic understanding. Tunes, harmonies, rhythm, the interplay of parts, the mood of the text, and the setting of individual words and phrases are all held in careful balance. Take two examples: 'Lady your words do spite me' and 'Cruel behold my heavy ending', both from the 1598 volume. In the first, the opening note and first syllable of 'Lady' leads one to expect a calm and polite address, but the second leaps up and begins a tune which itself rises and falls on each syllable to suggest the disconcerting impact of her spite. In the second, the word 'Cruel' is sung slowly, its two notes drawn out to emphasise its meaning and its emotional impact. The tune which emerges initially stays close to those first two notes, again pressing home the idea of cruelty and the inability of the writer to escape its consequences. Then it builds into something more rhythmic and expressive of resentment or anger. Both songs are excellent examples of Wilbye's approach to through composition. Although only two or three minutes long, their development is organic – there is an inevitability in the way each new section emerges from its predecessor – and, at the end, both tune and text return to their beginning in a modified and resolved manner that almost suggests symphonic movement. There is something about his controlled execution that recalls Jane Austen's little bit of ivory, a sense that great art does not have to be on a grand scale. Certainly songs such as 'Flora gave me fairest flowers', 'All pleasure is of this condition', 'Weep, weep, mine eyes' and, perhaps above all, 'Draw on, sweet night' are miniatures in which technique and understanding combine to form a unity unequalled by many larger works of this or any other period.

Wilbye represents the high point of the development of the English madrigal, but the vogue for madrigals continued into the 1620s and many other composers contributed to the genre. John Ward (1571–1638) was another whose musical career depended on patronage. After being a chorister at Canterbury Cathedral, he entered the household of Sir Henry Fanshawe, whom he served as both a musician and a legal functionary at the Exchequer. Ward published a single collection of madrigals in 1613, borrowing Weelkes description that they were 'apt both for Viols and Voices'. Unlike Weelkes, who seems to have written most of his lyrics himself, and Wilbye, who wrote all his, Ward sets lyrics by a number of well-known poets – Sir Philip Sidney, Michael Drayton and Francis Davison – in a bold, descriptive style which is effective, but less subtle than his predecessors'. Orlando Gibbons also published a single collection of madrigals, *A First Set of Madrigals and Motets of 5 parts* (1612). 'The Silver Swan' is justly famous, but while they display great technical mastery, particularly of counterpoint, Gibbons's madrigals are serious, even moralistic in tone – and by drawing a lesson from the text rather than describing or illustrating an emotion, they move away from what the madrigal does best.

Thomas Tomkins' 'Fauns and Satyrs Tripping' was included in *The Triumphes of Oriana* in 1601, but he did not publish a collection of secular work until 1622. When he did, he avoided the word madrigal and called it simply *Songs of 3, 4, 5 and 6 parts*, including a number of anthems as well as madrigals. One cannot deny the quality of Tomkins' work. The anthem 'When David heard that Absalom was slain', dedicated to his teacher, Byrd, is a remarkable outpouring of grief, and quite possibly the finest thing he ever wrote. He is equally at home with a light four-part ballett, a kind of madrigal meant for dancing, such as 'O let me live for true love', and can put convincing emotion into a love song such as 'Cloris, as when I woo', which – with what must surely have been ironic intent – he dedicated to the serious Orlando Gibbons.[8] Tomkins could be appealing and entertaining, but there was little new in his collection: the Italianate texture of the writing looked backwards to Morley and the earlier madrigalists. Indeed, none of the composers who followed Wilbye found a way of taking the madrigal form further. The achievements of the English madrigalists were considerable, but by 1622 enthusiasm for the genre was waning rapidly. Tomkins' volume was the last collection of any consequence to be published.

The madrigal boom originated at the English court and depended for its continuation on the interest and income of the English middle classes. Elsewhere, its impact was limited. It does seem to have spread to Anglo-Irish society in and around Dublin, and at least two madrigal composers were active in the city at the time. James Farmer (*c.*1560–*c.*1601) was organist at Christ Church Cathedral from 1595 to 1599, and composed a number of fine madrigals, including 'Fair Phyllis I saw sitting all alone' and 'Fair Nymphs' which appeared in *The Triumphes of Oriana*. Like Weelkes, Farmer seems to have had a knack of getting into trouble with the Church authorities. At one stage he simply abandoned his post, leaving his deputy in charge, to go to London and negotiate the publication of his madrigal collection, *The first set of English Madrigals to Foure Voyces* (1599). Thomas Bateson (*c.*1570–1630) began his working life as organist at Chester Cathedral, but moved to Christ Church Cathedral, Dublin, in 1609, first as a singer and organist and later as Master of Choristers. Although he did compose some church music, he is best known for his *First* and *Second Book of English Madrigals* (1604 and 1608), both of which were popular at the time.

In Scotland, madrigals were certainly sung, but they were confined mainly to the court and to one or two cultivated and aristocratic families. In the late 1580s, James VI conceived the idea of promoting a revival of

Scottish cultural life and gathered around him a group of poets and poet-musicians which became known as the Castalian Band, taking its name from the Castalian Spring at Delphi, which was seen as a symbol of inspiration. Music was very much secondary to poetry in the concerns of this group and little of it survives, but we do have a handful of madrigal lyrics from the 1590s, perhaps written by James Lauder, or by James VI's favourite, Alexander Montgomerie (later exiled for his Catholicism), or even by the imprisoned William Kinloch.

22 The Waits, and the Theatre

The expansion of music affected all areas and levels of Elizabethan society. In the public sphere, and particularly outside London, the Town or City Waits took on a new level of importance, reflecting the increasing prosperity and self-confidence of provincial centres throughout the country. We know, for example, that as early as 1524 the Leicester Waits were granted a livery of scarlet gowns trimmed with silver and lace; and that they were expected to play in the gallery of Leicester's fourteenth-century Guildhall at Easter, May Day, Michaelmas, Christmas, or indeed whenever the Mayor asked them to. By 1582, they were expected to play every night and every morning winter or summer; their salaries had been raised to reflect their new duties; and they were now paid from local taxes authorised by the Mayor and Corporation of Leicester. They played at weddings and other private functions, but only with the permission of the Mayor. Most Waits consisted principally of wind instruments. The Norwich Waits were one of the larger bands; in 1572 they numbered fourteen – five recorders, three hautboys (early oboes), four sackbuts and two trumpets – and were considered one of the finest groups in the land. By 1600, strings had been added. When Will Kemp, the actor and dancer famed for his roles in Shakespeare's plays and for his signature jigs, Morris-danced all the way from London to Norwich in nine days, the Waits were there to greet him on his arrival. 'Few cities in our Realme have the like,' he wrote, 'none better … besides their excellency in wind instruments, their rare cunning on the Vyoll and Violin: theyr voices be admirable.'[1]

The Waits were professional musicians, but civic music was not considered equal to church music and there was little formal training available. The majority were probably self-taught, or came from musical families, and honed their skills on the job – though in some towns, such as Leicester and York, there were arrangements for an apprentice to be attached to the band and learn what was, in effect, a trade like any other. Nonetheless, their talent and their skills were clearly impressive. Some of Morley's instrumental works may have been intended for the London Waits. Certainly, he dedicated his *First Booke of Consort Lessons* (1599) to them, praising the quality of their playing and declaring his 'love towards them.' Awareness of the Waits, their function and their music, has all but disappeared today, yet they were an integral part of musical life in Elizabethan England, even of daily life: the citizens of the bigger towns and cities probably heard the Waits at least as often as they heard their church choir. The Bristol Waits, for example, are credited with having a virtual monopoly on musical performances within the city.[2] That was probably exceptional, but there is no doubt that in the larger towns and cities of the day the Waits played a bigger and more influential role than is often acknowledged. Sir Francis Drake even took Waits musicians with him on his round-the-world voyage (1577–80); and, again, when he set off on his ill-fated expedition to Spain and Portugal in 1589. On that occasion only two of the five musicians returned.

An additional and occasional role for the Waits was to provide incidental music for dramatic performances. In the first half of the sixteenth century, these would have been the cycles of mystery plays or the morality plays. We know that the Coventry Waits accompanied the city's annual cycle of mystery plays, and, although direct evidence for the involvement of the Waits elsewhere is scanty, given that the mystery plays were put on by working men in provincial towns and cities, it is difficult to see who else could have provided the provided the necessary musical support. Certainly, many of the cities that had well-established mystery cycles – Newcastle, York, Wakefield, Chester, Coventry, Lincoln, Norwich, Exeter – were also those that had well-established Waits. In 1552, Trinity College, Cambridge, made an official payment 'unto ye Wayttes upon our feast day when ye show was played called *Anglia deformata*,'[3] which seems to have been an allegorical play of broadly moral and political intent. In 1562, the Bristol Waits – who seem to have made a habit of travelling widely – journeyed all the way to Chelmsford to play at a summer festival when four biblical plays were performed. But the era of the mystery and morality plays was drawing to a close, and the Elizabethan theatre, with its more strongly secular orientation, was taking shape. In 1576, the Norwich Waits actually received a licence from the Corporation allowing them to perform 'comedies, and upon interludes, and such other playes and tragedies which shall seem to them mete,'[4] as long as the performances did not clash with church services. And in London, as one might expect, the growing popularity of the new theatres had a direct impact on the Waits, who became so involved with this new and comparatively well-paid work that they sometimes did not turn up for their official duties.

Elizabethan and Jacobean theatre was an unusual cultural phenomenon. It was accessible to and appealed to almost all levels of society. It was enjoyed equally by the court, where leading companies of actors were regularly invited to perform before the Queen and, later, King James, and by the groundlings who would pay a penny to crowd into an inn yard or into the pit of a theatre. It was also a national phenomenon. The leading companies were London-based and the most famous theatres – the Globe, the Rose, the Swan – were on the south bank of the Thames, just outside the jurisdiction of the City of London. But there were numerous companies outside the capital that spent their time touring the provinces. Indeed, two of the better-known companies, Lord Strange's Men and the Earl of Worcester's men, made their name in the provinces before settling in London. And the London-based companies also went on tour, particularly during outbreaks of the plague when their home theatres were forced to close. These performances took place in inn yards, town squares, sometimes in the houses of wealthy patrons; and they would have occurred in towns right across England and Wales, although naturally with less frequency in more remote areas. In Ireland, too, though records are scarce, a theatrical tradition based on religious plays seems to have given way to occasional productions of secular plays in the houses of the nobility and in the larger towns. Only in Scotland, where the puritan tradition ran strong, was drama confined almost completely to the court.

Between the early 1550s, when the headmaster of Eton, Nicholas Udall, wrote *Ralph Roister Doister*, generally regarded as the first English comedy, and 1642, when public theatres were closed by order of Parliament, over six hundred plays were published; and we can name some eighty playwrights active in the period. An educated guess suggests that the total number of plays actually written and performed could exceed three thousand. How many people saw them is even more difficult to assess. The total capacity of London theatres in the early 1580s has been estimated at around 5,000. As new theatres were built – the Rose (1587), the Swan (1595), the Globe (1599), the Fortune (1600) – each with a capacity of between 2,000 and 3,000, it must have approached 15,000. The first performances of *Henry VI Part I* at the Rose in March 1592 attracted audiences of 10,000 a week. In a city with a population of 200,000, these are impressive figures. In addition, the later years of Elizabeth's reign saw seven or eight performances a year at court; a figure which shot up to twenty under James I. Outside London, audiences probably did not exceed a few hundred, but populations were correspondingly smaller: Norwich, for example, probably had a population of 16,000 in the 1580s, while York's population rose from 8,000 in the mid-sixteenth century to 12,000 by the early seventeenth. However one interprets the figures, Elizabethan and Jacobean drama was the first cultural movement to reach a mass audience – and, although practice naturally developed over the years, music was and remained an essential component of it.

Plays would typically begin in mid-afternoon and were heralded by a fanfare, usually played three times with intervals in between, presumably to encourage latecomers to hurry. Descriptions, often by foreign visitors to London, suggest that music would often precede and end a performance. According to Frederic Gershow, Secretary to the Duke of Stettin-Pomerania, who went to the Blackfriars Theatre in September 1602 to see a play performed by a company of boy players, 'for a whole hour before, a delightful performance of *musicam instrumentalem* is given on organs, lutes, pandores, mandolines, violins and flutes.'[5] Visiting London in 1598, the German lawyer, Paul Hentzner, wrote in his diary that 'English actors represent almost every day tragedies and comedies to very numerous audiences; these are concluded with Music, variety of Dances and the excessive applause of those that are present.'[6] And it was common practice, however serious the play, for the proceedings to close with the players performing or improvising a jig – a practice adopted by London's reconstructed Globe Theatre today – or indulging in some more rowdy, even bawdy, form of dancing. There would have been music, too, between the acts, even sometimes a song or a dance. There is no way of knowing at this distance whether this music was composed especially for particular plays, or how dramatically relevant it would have been. One suspects, particularly if the Waits were involved, that the music was improvised, or at least based on certain stock tunes. As with the Waits, one imagines that in the earlier years of the period the music would have been based around wind instruments. As theatre and musical life became more sophisticated, viols and even organs – as in Gershow's description – would have appeared, but for most performances it is likely that wind instruments would have provided the main accompaniment.

The plays of the period thus began and ended with music, but they were also – and this is often overlooked – absolutely full of incidental music, songs and musical references. Shakespeare includes or quotes from well over a hundred different songs in his plays. Comedy, naturally enough, offered more scope for music than tragedy, and it is remarkable how quickly the writers of comedy realised its potential. *Ralph Roister Doister*, which dates from the very beginning of the period, includes a dozen or more opportunities for songs and dances and this set the tone for the next ninety years. David Whitwell identifies the opening of Thomas Heywood's *English Traveller* which points to the rarity of a play without music:

> A Strange Play you are like to have, for know,
> We use no Drum, nor Trumpet, nor Dumbe show;
> No Combat, Marriage, not so much today,
> As song, Dance, Masque to bumbaste out a Play.[7]

Whitwell also suggests that 'since one of the goals of Elizabethan theater was to imitate real life on the stage, these stage directions offer not only information on how music functioned in the theater but to some degree reflects musical practice in real life.'[8] Certain musical interventions may, indeed, be associated with particular characters and events, and that may perhaps be seen as an indicator of social attitudes, but the idea should be treated with caution. Rather than imitate reality, playwrights were often seeking to create an impression of reality, and music was one of the tools used in this deception. Musical indications come from stage directions or from the text itself. Trumpets, most obviously, sound fanfares or flourishes to announce the entry of kings and rulers. Trumpets, cornets, shawms, sackbuts and other wind instruments in various combinations play processional music, which can also mark the arrival of kings, nobles or civic dignitaries. Trumpets and drums, flutes and drums, or fifes and drums are used to suggest armies on the march, military preparations, battles or other dramatic happenings offstage. Horns are associated, naturally enough, with hunting but also with characters journeying by horse or arriving from far off. Flutes are often called for in funeral scenes or when characters are mourning.

Such associations are broadly naturalistic, but the playwrights of the period also began to use music in other ways: to support, comment on, and develop the action on stage; and also – in a manner which may seem perfectly normal to generations of film-watchers, but which was new at the time – to create atmosphere and support the mood of the action. Music thus served the full range of dramatic and emotional purposes: from innumerable love scenes where music 'gives a very echo to the seat / Where Love is throned'[9] to the many battle scenes where the stage directions call for 'A charge sounded',[10] and 'Alarums and Excursions'; from the riotous, boozy fun of Marston's *What You Will* where 'Music, tobacco, sack, and sleep / The tide of sorrow backward keep'[11] to the formal song to Cupid in Lyly's *Mother Bombie*;[12] from angelic voices to dancing devils in Marlowe's *Dr Faustus*; from the pastoral evocations of *As You Like It* or Peele's *Old Wives' Tale* to the dead march at the end of *Hamlet* or the music Zenocrate calls for to ease her passing in Part Two of Marlowe's *Tamburlaine*; from the ironic commentaries of Feste in *Twelfth Night* to the music of marriage and resolution at the end of *Much Ado About Nothing* or *As You Like It*; from the solid reality of a peal of bells in Udall's *Ralph Roister Doister* or Morris dancers on stage in Dekker's *Witch of Edmonton* to the evocations of magic and supernatural surrounding Ariel and Prospero in *The Tempest*.

Some of this music would have been played on wind instruments of the kind used by the Waits; some would have required a consort of viols. Tavern songs might have been accompanied by a fiddle or a violin, both usually associated, at this stage of their development, with the rougher end of society. Love songs and songs sung by clowns or other solo figures might well have been accompanied by a lute. Stage directions occasionally give an indication of what instruments are preferred, and sometimes indicate the kind of music required – 'A sad song,'[13] 'Flutes sound a mournful senet,'[14] 'Still music,'[15] 'Caliban sings drunkenly.'[16] More often, directors have to interpret from the text, and there is little to guide them. Beyond a few songs, most notably those by Robert Johnson, almost no theatre music from the period has survived.

Born *c.*1583, Johnson came from a musical family – his father, John, was a lutenist at the court of Queen Elizabeth – and by the age of twenty or twenty-one he was lutenist in James I's personal chamber ensemble, the Private Musick. He was heavily involved in the world of the theatre, working with the King's Men between 1610 and 1617 when they were based at the Blackfriars Theatre, which, being an indoor theatre, offered more opportunity for solo voice and accompaniment than a big outdoor auditorium such as The Globe. Johnson is known to have worked with Shakespeare on several plays and to have made the original settings of songs from *The*

Tempest ('Full Fathom Five', 'Where the Bee Sucks') and from *Cymbeline* ('Hark! Hark! The Lark!'). And it is possible that his role might have been even more significant. Jonathan Holmes, Artistic Director of the innovative Jericho House theatre company, has seen the structure of *The Tempest* as resembling 'a musical court masque' and suggested that Shakespeare and Johnson should share the credit for the play. This idea has received support from the Shakespeare scholar, Stanley Wells, who has said that he could 'quite believe *The Tempest* might have been conceived as a musical entertainment.'[17] Robert Johnson also collaborated with other leading playwrights of the time: Ben Jonson ('Have you seen but the bright lily grow' from *The Devil is an Ass*), John Fletcher ('Care-Charming Sleep' from *The Tragedy of Valentinian*), and Thomas Middleton ('Come Away, Hecate' from *The Witch*). Thomas Morley is the only other composer who left contemporary settings of Shakespeare's songs – notably 'It was a lover and his lass' from *As You Like It* and 'O Mistress Mine' from *Twelfth Night*. Morley and Shakespeare lived in the same London parish at one time and may have known each other, but Morley's settings, unlike Johnson's, cannot be linked to actual productions of the plays from which they come.

23 Folk Music, Ravenscroft, and Ballads

The Elizabethan and Jacobean theatre offered the possibility for a tune or a song to become known right across those parts of the country where the companies of players toured their productions. The only other musical channel which could spread a tune so widely was the folk tradition, though in practice that often operated on a regional basis. The history of folk music is often undocumented and obscure. There are numerous references to individual songs and dances during the medieval period, but it is difficult to build them into a coherent narrative, especially as we cannot be sure when the music that has come down to us was composed. All we can really say is that in all parts of the British Isles, the different strands of folk music – ballads, love songs, ritual songs, laments, dances – continued to evolve throughout the medieval period and on into the fifteenth and sixteenth centuries. And it is clear also that, while there undoubtedly was a degree of cross-fertilisation, the four nations – England, Ireland, Scotland, and Wales – maintained recognisably different musical styles.

Nor did folk music exist without any reference to other kinds of music.

We have seen that the folk song 'Western Wynde' was adopted by Taverner, Sheppard and Tye as the basis for settings of the Mass. And as the Tudor century progressed, certain characteristics of popular folk music crossed over into more formal musical traditions. Traditional English dances, such as jigs, dompes and hornpipes were practised at Henry VIII's court, and even when these were supplemented or replaced by Continental imports, such as the courantes, bransles and pivas, the new arrivals were frequently danced to popular English tunes. The Waits, of course, would have adapted popular songs and dances for their own use. Carols, too, show a tendency to blend traditional tunes with more formal arrangements. The *Fitzwilliam Virginal Book*, one of the principal sources for keyboard music between roughly 1562 and 1612, contains nearly three hundred pieces by a range of composers. A number of the tunes are adapted from or influenced by folk music, including an 'Irish Ho-hoane' or lament. Even Byrd was happy to adapt an Irish tune, turning it into the song 'Casturame'.[1] But the name that stands out in this respect is Thomas Ravenscroft (*c.*1582–1635).

Ravenscroft began life as a chorister, first at Chichester Cathedral and then from 1594 to 1600 at St Paul's. He took a degree in music at Cambridge, probably in 1605, before returning to London to teach music at Christ's Hospital School in Newgate between 1618 and 1622. This outwardly conventional strand of his career led to the production of a number of more or less conventional anthems and motets, and of a metrical psalter, *The Whole Book of Psalmes* (1621), which achieved a degree of popularity in its day. He was also active in London's theatrical world: he knew many of the leading actors and playwrights of the time and wrote music to accompany some of the plays that were produced at the Globe Theatre, though not, it seems, any of Shakespeare's. Yet it is not for his compositions that Ravenscroft is remembered, but for three collections of popular vocal music. *Pammelia* (1609) contains a hundred rounds or catches, canons and songs. Some are in English; some are in Latin – often bad or dog Latin. There are sacred songs, thoroughly profane songs about lost maidenheads, drinking songs, songs about oysters, songs about walking out of a May morning. It is a complete mixture, even a muddle. *Deuteromelia* (1609) is shorter, sticks to English-language songs and catches, and contains a number of songs that have remained in the folk-song canon down to the present day – 'We be soldiers three'; the drinking songs 'Of all the birds' and 'Martin said to his man'; and one of the best known of what we would consider nursery rhymes, 'Three Blind Mice'. *Melismata* (1611) is shorter still and contains songs from the court, the city and the country. These include street cries from Cheapside; a warning to 'He that will an alehouse keepe'; the well-known song 'Three Ravens', and the beautiful carol, 'Remember, O Thou Man.' All three volumes were hugely successful, appealing to the same middle-class audience that had responded to Yonge's *Musica Transalpina* and fuelled the English craze for madrigals.

In the history of English music, Ravenscroft is important because he was the first collector of folk songs and folk melodies. Not all the pieces in these three volumes can be classed as folk music, and Ravenscroft altered and embellished tunes and rewrote lyrics in the manner of many other early collectors. Nonetheless, he was undoubtedly offering something new. He soon had his imitators, such as John Hilton, whose volumes, *Ayres or Fa La's for Three Voyces* (1627) and *Catch that Catch Can* (1652), are clearly modelled on Ravenscroft's work; and even Orlando Gibbons was soon setting London's street cries. John Playford's seminal *The English Dancing Master* (1651), to which we shall return, surely owes something to Ravenscroft's example, too. Ravenscroft's catches were immediately popular in taverns, contributing to the music-and-drinking culture, particularly prevalent in England, which eventually gave rise to both the eighteenth-century music club and the male voice choir.[2] He demonstrated that folk music in its various forms was worthy of collection, publication and serious consideration by educated people. In doing so, he opened up new ideas and new musical possibilities that would lead, ultimately, to the folk tunes woven into the fabric of *The Beggar's Opera*, Vaughan Williams touring Norfolk on a bicycle, and folk rock groups like Fairport Convention and Steeleye Span in the 1970s.

The area of the folk tradition about which we have most evidence from the Elizabethan period – and which appears to have followed the rest of the musical world in expanding rapidly – is the ballad. Ballads were both entertainment and a recognised way of commenting on public events. In Beaumont and Fletcher's *Humourous Lieutenant* [*sic*], the eponymous lieutenant's reaction to losing a battle is to fear that

> Now shall we have damnable Ballads out against us,
> Most wicked madrigals: and ten to one, Colonel,
> Sung to such lowsie, lamentable tunes.[3]

Of the three hundred and five ballads in Francis Child's 1882 and 1898 collections, sixty-nine refer to identifiable historical events or individuals. Thirteen of these refer to the period before 1500, six to 1500–1550, forty-eight to 1550–1700, and only two to the years after 1700, suggesting that the ballad came into its own in the middle of the Tudor century. Printing was a key factor. The first printed ballad, 'The Geste of Robyn Hood', appeared about 1475, and, somewhere around 1500, Wynkyn de Worde printed a series of Robin Hood ballads. Once printing technology spread, and became more accessible, broadside ballads rapidly became part of popular culture.

They were called broadside (or broadsheet) because they were printed on one side of a single sheet of paper. They contained the text of the ballad and often a woodcut illustration. There was no music, but there might sometimes be a note suggesting that the words could be sung to an already well-known tune. In 1556, the Stationer's Company of London started its Register, allowing booksellers and others to pay a fee (usually fourpence) to register their right to publish a given work, thus leading eventually to the idea of copyright. In theory, the publishers of broadsides were meant to pay their fee and register their ballads. In practice, many or even most of them ignored the regulation; but even so, over two thousand ballads were registered between 1556 and 1600, and another thousand in the period up to 1709. Estimates vary widely but, by the 1650s, anything between 300,000 and 400,000 broadsides were being sold annually in England and Wales; and, unlike the madrigal, this was a craze that spread north to Scotland and over the sea to Ireland.

Broadside ballads were sold at stalls in the streets or in the town square; they were sold by itinerant merchants of cheap goods (hence 'chapmen'), who travelled the towns and villages; they were sold by itinerant musicians who toured the fairs and the markets. They were popular entertainment for ordinary people, whether in the town or the countryside. And there was a communal element: broadsides would be stuck to walls for people to learn, or displayed in the inns and ale-houses for people to read and sing. The appeal of the ballad crossed social boundaries: they came from the streets, but they were heard in the houses of the aristocracy, and even at court.

Despite their popularity, we have no clearer idea who wrote the ballads that have come down from the sixteenth and seventeenth centuries than those from the time of Chaucer. Nor can we tell with any greater certainty whether the tunes accompanying these ballads that were collected in the nineteenth and early-twentieth centuries bear any relation to the original tunes. What we can say is that the explosion in the popularity of ballads is related to the rapid expansion and sudden popularity of theatre in that both reflect a popular demand for narrative. Shakespeare names or makes reference to more than twenty different ballads in the plays. And although the ballads of the period, unlike the plays, are almost all located in Britain, there are major thematic similarities. Both explore the nature of heroism; the nature of kingship and leadership; issues of rebellion and outlawry; betrayal in love; betrayal in war; issues of family honour; revenge; the consequences of fate and malice. Even allowing for variations in quality and for the conventions of ballad narrative – the repeated lines, the progressive variations, the standard adjectives and descriptions – the ballads depict these concerns and the characters who bring them to life with a realism which stands in stark contrast to the madrigal lyrics of the same period.

It was Scotland that produced, or at least provided the setting for, a significant number of great ballads. One example will have to stand for many. 'Sir Patrick Spens' is one of the most popular of the great historical ballads and survives in a number of different variants. Sir Patrick himself is probably a fictional character and the story in which he features may or may not be based on the expedition to bring Margaret, the Maid of Norway, back to Scotland in 1281, but we are moved by the reality of his predicament. He laughs at the idea that he should captain a ship; then weeps as he realises he has been set up by an enemy and has no choice but to obey the King's command. The detail carries a powerful sense of reality: the arguments between the Scots and the Norwegians about money; the bolt of silk used to try and block the leak in the ship's side; the reluctance of the Scots lords to get their expensive shoes wet. And the storytelling would have been strengthened (as it is in modern recordings by Nic Jones, Fairport Convention, or June Tabor) by a tune which had the capacity to carry the narrative forward; that is to say, a tune which was melodic and memorable enough to help a singer who did not have (or could not read) the music, but was at the same time simple enough not to overwhelm the words. Ballads were stories set to music. They could, and can, be sung and arranged in different ways, but, unlike madrigals once again, the core of the ballad is the story, not the arrangement.

The most powerful group of ballads comes from the Anglo-Scottish borderlands. Many of them first appeared in printed form during the Elizabethan and Jacobean period, but some may have been in oral circulation as early as the fifteenth century. Until 1603, when the Union of the Crowns made it possible for a single monarch to exercise his or her authority on both sides of an often disputed boundary, the Borders were home to a clan-based society that lived by violence and theft. For the families who lived on either side of the border, the raid was a central fact of their lives: the English raided the Scots and the Scots raided the English. Douglas, Montgomery, Percy, Graeme, Murray, Armstrong, Johnstone, Maxwell – the family names are scattered throughout the border ballads. They are upright heroes and faithless villains, cruel murderers and noble avengers; like many violent and lawless societies, the Borders not only built up their own elaborate code of honour, but somehow contrived to have it recognised and romanticised by those who stood outside their world.

Some of the border ballads are based on identifiable, historical events. 'Lord Maxwell's Last Goodnight' depicts the 9th Lord Maxwell departing into exile in 1608, having killed Sir James Johnstone in a family feud. 'The Douglas Tragedy' can be located to Blackhouse in Selkirk and tells of the elopement of Margaret Douglas with a local nobleman; they are then intercepted by Lord Douglas and his seven sons and cut down, thus saving Douglas family honour. 'Johnnie O'Breadislee'[4] is supposed to have originated with the owner of Morton Castle above Nithsdale, and demonstrates again the anti-authoritarian attitude which characterises so many ballads. Johnny O'Breadislee is both poacher and hero. He is asleep after poaching deer when he is attacked and mortally wounded by seven cowardly foresters. He wakes and kills six of them, while the seventh, though wounded, escapes to tell of his heroism. Other ballads have a greater ring of truth about them. 'Hughie Graeme' is full of anger. Hughie Graeme steals the bishop's horse but is caught, taken to Carlisle and killed, claiming as he dies that his wife was seduced by the bishop and exhorting his family to take revenge. Still others have a sense that they represent the reality of Border society. In 'The Border Widow's Lament', the widow laments the death of her husband who has been killed by the King. 'The Fair Flower of Northumberland' tells of a Scottish knight, a prisoner of the Earl of Northumberland, who promises to marry the Earl's daughter if she will release him and come with him to Scotland. Once across the border, he tells her he is already married and sends her home. For once, the ending is not tragic and the returning daughter is told by her mother that 'you're not the first that yon Scots have beguiled.' Some of the border ballads were probably written shortly after the events they describe. Others will have been written later, after King James's men managed to impose some kind of order in the Borders – from about 1610 onwards – when the events and names were still in living memory but distant enough to be looked back on from a position of safety. Taken together, and despite uncertainties about the nature of the original tunes, the Border Ballads, with their stories of love and hate and grief, create an emotional world which, in its own way, is as complete and as powerful as any Schubertian song cycle.

24 The English Ayre, and Thomas Campion

Ballads may at times have been accompanied by a fiddle or violin as a form of simple continuo, or perhaps by a lute or a cittern, using simple chords to emphasise the rhythm and structure of the vocal line, but they were essentially unaccompanied songs, narratives sung to simple tunes. Madrigals, as we have seen, were originally unaccompanied, but as time went on – and in Britain rather more than on the Continent – it was accepted that they would often be accompanied by whatever instrument or instruments were available to the family or group who were performing. The English ayre – 'the chief glory of the Jacobean era'[1] – was different: it was an equal partnership between vocal melody and instrumental accompaniment.

The English ayre was a synthesis. Its origins, and in particular the choice of the lute as accompanying instrument, lay in the French *chanson*, but there is no doubt that the English composers and practitioners were strongly influenced by Italian singing styles. Where the madrigalists concentrated on word painting, the composers of ayres adopted and adapted the Italian declamatory style, choosing words as much because their sound and rhythm fitted the music as for their meaning. The English ayre also drew on the folk-song tradition for its strophic form (where all verses are sung to the same music) and for the simplicity of its lyrics, in particular the absence of the elaborate classical and pastoral imagery characteristic of so many madrigals. This synthesis resulted in a uniquely English musical form which flourished for some twenty years – less than the madrigal, although its long-term influence on British music was much greater.

The term *ayre* had been around since the 1560s, but the English ayre as a recognisable genre evolved only during the last years of Elizabeth I's reign. Thomas Morley's 1597 volume was called *Canzonets or Little Short Aers to Five and Sixe Voices*, although these ayres were really part-songs for which Morley provided lute transcriptions for some of the lower parts. That same year, John Dowland published his *First Booke of Songes or Ayres of foure partes*. Some of the twenty-one pieces Dowland included had begun life as part-songs; others seem to have been dances to which words were added; and some were composed as solo lute songs. Common to all of them, however, was the fact that – as published – the highest part (the *cantus*) always carried the tune and had to be sung. This was emphasised by the highly original manner in which Dowland caused the music to appear on the printed page. In a large format volume, the *cantus* and the tablature for lute accompaniment appeared on the left-hand page, while the alto, tenor and bass parts appeared on the right-hand page, facing, as it were, north, east and south. The music could thus be read and the song performed by four performers gathered round a single copy of the book placed on a small table or stand.

Two important points emerge from this. The first concerns modern perceptions of the ayre, which is often thought of as essentially a combination of solo voice and lute. That is the most common format for performance today and may well have been the preferred format at the time, but it was far from the only one. Dowland was not unique in offering one or more different formats for performance. Indeed, it was the norm among English composers of ayres to do so – a practice which, as we will see, links them to the wider world of consort music. The second point concerns the whole nature of music-making in late Elizabethan and Jacobean society.

On the face of it, the idea of four people facing inwards round a table would seem to exclude the possibility of an audience – and appears a little odd from the perspective of an age in which the concert or the gig is the accepted context for live musical performance. In fact, such private music-making for private pleasure was absolutely normal among the prosperous middle classes of England and Wales (and, to a lesser extent, in Ireland and Scotland where the middle class had not grown so large or so prosperous). The same process of social change which stimulated the popularity of the madrigal and the ayre meant that religious music was increasingly confined to its own sphere. Byrd was aging, and despite the achievements of Orlando Gibbons, the great age of English church music was drawing to a close. In Italy, under the direction of Monteverdi, the idea of an orchestra and orchestral music was taking shape, but it would not reach the British Isles for some years. True, public music in the form of the Waits and music for the theatre was flourishing, but during the early decades of the seventeenth century, most of the music being published, whether vocal or instrumental, was for individuals or small groups – fitting the original definition of chamber music: that it should be suited for playing in a room. The family or the extended family group was thus the centre of musical practice – whether they sang madrigals or ayres, played the virginals or together constituted a consort of viols. Morley's *Consort Lessons* (1599) is dedicated to 'a Gentleman for his private pleasure, and for divers others his frendes which delight in Musicke.' In 1620, Martin Peerson (or Pierson; *c.*1571–1651), perhaps best known today as a composer of Latin motets, published a collection of secular works – madrigals, songs for one or two voices with virginals or viol accompaniment – under the title *Private Musicke*.

All this naturally affected the way musicians were seen and how they saw themselves. By the time James I came to the throne of England in 1603, secular musicians were no longer regarded as inferior to church musicians. They were artists in their own right, who could follow a successful career outside the church, allying themselves and their art to other secular art forms, particularly poetry and drama. They were no longer expected to give expression to conventional religious sentiments; they had the same freedom as poets to express their feelings and perceptions. This was a situation that would have been unthinkable when Mary Tudor came to the throne fifty years previously. The madrigal, with its ability to combine music and poetry and convey a strong emotional burden, was ideally suited to this new situation, but the ayre took the relationship between words and music a stage further. It gave equal weight to the vocal line and the accompaniment; it did away with contrapuntal fireworks and complex imagery; it increased the audibility of the lyric and put greater emphasis on its meaning.

The interplay between poetry and music is clearly seen in the work of Thomas Campion (sometimes Campian; 1567–1620).[2] Campion was neither a professional musician nor a professional poet: he was – or, more accurately, eventually became – a doctor. Born in London where his father was a clerk in the Court of Chancery, he seems originally to have been intended for the law. In 1581, at the age of fourteen (by which time his parents were dead and he was in the charge of his stepfather) he was sent to Peterhouse College, Cambridge, but left three years later without taking a degree. In 1586, aged nineteen, he entered Gray's Inn in London to study law. There is a possibility that he interrupted his studies to serve in the army that the Earl of Essex led to support the French Protestants in 1591, and saw action at the siege of Rouen. Whether or not this is true, Campion does not seem to have applied himself to his studies. He left Gray's Inn after eight years without any legal qualification and for the next few years seems to have remained in London, living in the area of Fleet Street, in the parish of St. Dunstan-in-the-West. This was an area frequented by the poets, playwrights and musicians of the period, as well as one of the most influential families of the time, the Sackvilles, who were well known for their patronage of the arts. We know that he became friendly with John Dowland during this period because he contributed a dedicatory poem to Dowland's 1597 *First Booke of Songes.*

By this time, Campion was earning a literary reputation. *Poemata, a collection of Latin panegyrics, elegies and epigrams* appeared in 1595 and seems to have made his name known in London circles. Then in 1601 came *A Book of Ayres.* This was a collaboration with Philip Rosseter (1568–1623), a talented musician from the provinces (origins as far apart as Somerset and Lincoln have been suggested) who had come to London a few years previously and who went on to become lutenist at the court of King James I and manager of a company of boy actors. Rosseter wrote the music and Campion wrote the words. Campion also wrote the preface which makes his views on the English ayre quite explicit.

> What epigrams are in poetry, the same are airs in music: then in their chief perfection when they are short and well seasoned. But to clog a light song with a long *præludium* is to corrupt the nature of it.... There are some who, to appear more deep and singular in their judgement, will admit no music but that which is long, intricate, baited with fugue, chained with syncopation;... as in Poesy we give pre-eminence to the Heroical Poem; so in music we yield the chief place to the grave and well-invented Motet; but not to every harsh and dull confused Fantasy, where, in multitude of points, the harmony is quite drowned.[3]

In contrast to the madrigal, then, ayres should be short, light, and accessible, and in large measure Campion and Rosseter followed this advice. Rosseter's tunes to songs such as 'My sweetest Lesbia, let us live and love', 'I care not for these ladies', 'My love hath vowed' and 'Turn back, you wanton flyer' are elegant and expressive. Campion's lyrics are effective portrayals of various aspects of love, well rhymed and well written, though without any sense of deep emotional involvement and not, perhaps, as closely matched to musical rhythms as they became later. It is all the more surprising, then, that in the following year, 1602, Campion published *Observations in the Art of English Poesie*, a theoretical work which attacks rhyming in poetry as 'tedious affectation' and 'childish titillation.' Rhyme, he suggests, is responsible for poets extending their metaphors 'beyond all bounds of art'.[4] He also embarks on a complicated argument that seeks to demonstrate the superiority of Latin quantitative metrical forms over the qualitative forms characteristic of English verse. These are very odd arguments to come from an English poet – especially one such as Campion, whose most successful work depends on the flexibility of English rhythms and rhymes – although it is worth noting that, of Campion's strictly literary output, something like one third consists of Latin poetry. These ideas were attacked by the then influential but now largely forgotten poet, Samuel Daniel, but even more effectively demolished by Campion himself who, in all his later work, completely ignored his own theories.

Having begun to establish a reputation, Campion suddenly took himself off to France to study medicine. He chose the University of Caen, which may, perhaps, add weight to the idea that he had served in Normandy with Essex's army. Caen was a respectable university, founded in the fifteenth century by John of Lancaster, with a respected medical school, as well as a famous annual poetry competition. Campion studied there for three years and, this time, actually qualified. He returned to London in 1605 aged thirty-eight and began to practice as a doctor. How much time he actually gave to his practice is unclear. He seems to have been rapidly absorbed into the artistic elite which enjoyed aristocratic and court patronage. His introduction into this world was probably mediated by his long-term friend and patron (also the dedicatee of the 1601 *Book of Ayres*), Sir Thomas Monson, who enjoyed a degree of political influence under James I. It was certainly successful. Between 1607 and 1614, Campion provided the librettos for three court masques – a form of entertainment which enjoyed a brief and expensive period of popularity under James I and Charles I, and to which we will return. He also wrote a short series of songs lamenting the death from typhoid fever in November 1612 of James I's eldest son, Prince Henry, the same event that led to the composition of Byrd's *Fair Britain Isle*.

Campion's songs were published in 1613 as *Songs of Mourning: Bewailing the Untimely Death of Prince Henry*. Like *A Book of Ayres*, this was a collaboration, but the composer this time was John Cooper (1575–1626), a Londoner who had studied in Italy and changed his name to John (even occasionally Giovanni) Coprario (or Coperario), apparently in the belief that a fashionable Italian name would help his career. It certainly did no harm. He became Private Secretary to the Earl of Salisbury; he was heavily involved in the musical life of James I's court; he may have tutored Prince Henry for a short period; and he certainly taught the future Charles I. He also enjoyed the patronage of the Earl of Hertford who brought him the young William Lawes as a student – and it was through Cooper/Coprario that Lawes met Charles I, at whose court he was to be a favoured musician until his death in the Civil Wars. Like Campion, Coprario was involved in court masques; he also wrote madrigals and over ninety fantasias – another musical speciality of the early-seventeenth-century period to which we shall return. His collaborations with Campion, however, were 'set forth to bee sung with one voice to the lute, or viol'.[5] Coprario's tunes, while not particularly memorable, are perfectly professional offerings, but it is clear that the formality of the situation, in which each song is addressed to a different member of the Royal Family, did not suit Campion. Some of the lyrics have a complexity of form that suggests madrigals rather than lute songs, while others can only be described as grim: 'Heaven's hostage which you bred / And nursed with such great care / Is ravish'd now, great King, and from us led / When we were least aware.'

And yet, in that same year of 1613, Campion also published *Two Books of Ayres*, which shows him in an entirely different light. The collection is retrospective – Campion maintains that he is merely publishing a few songs at the request of friends – and divided into the 'grave and pious' and the 'amorous and light', but the big difference is that he has no collaborator: both words and music are his own, although where and when he obtained his musical education is a mystery. In this volume and in *The Third and Fourth Book of Ayres*, which followed in 1617, Campion's art reaches its maturity. 'I have chiefly aimed,' he says in the 1613 preface, 'to couple my words and notes lovingly together' and that is the heart of his achievement. 'Never Weather-Beaten Sail' is a popular piece for individual singers and for groups. The lyric consists of only eight lines and the melody has the deceptive simplicity of a hymn tune, but the balance between words and music, the way in which the vowel sounds are carefully linked to the musical accents, and the way the careful crescendo is joined to the repetition of 'O come quickly' to create an urgency almost more appropriate to a love song than a religious lyric, all make it a small masterpiece. 'Jack and Joan' is another example of deceptive simplicity. Ostensibly a celebration of country and peasant life, it has a sting in the tail wholly appropriate for those in court circles – 'Though your tongues dissemble deep / And can your heads from danger keep / Yet for all your pomp and train / Securer lives the silly Swain' – yet the sting hides itself in what appears to be, but is not quite, a round-the-maypole folk dance tune. 'Fire, Fire' develops the classic comparison between fire and desire by calling on all the main rivers of England and the ocean to drown him if they cannot quench his desire. It is a light, witty, faux-dramatic song which is made effective by a setting that matches the mood of the words and adds to the sense of absurdity of the whole. 'Oft have I sighed' sets a lyric of utter simplicity to a tune which at once supports and develops its meaning. And at least two songs in the 1617 collection – 'Think'st thou to seduce me then' and 'Fain would I wed' – deserve mention too because they make a leap of imagination unusual at the time and present the lyric from a female point of view.

Campion published nothing after 1617 and died in 1620, probably of the plague. In addition to over a hundred ayres, he left behind his librettos for court masques, poetry in both Latin and English, his *Observations in the Art of English Poesie* and a parallel volume on music *A New Way of Making Four Parts in Counterpoint* (1610). There was little else. Philip Rosseter, the beneficiary of his will, received just £23.

Campion's is a civilised art. His work, at its best, shows great technical mastery: small stories and recognisable human situations are set to music in a way that entertains and satisfies. But it does not take risks; it does not challenge and it rarely seems to engage emotionally. Although we lack detailed information about much of Campion's life, one still arrives at the sense of a man adopting a particular pose or outlook on life: that of the gifted non-professional, the gentleman amateur. It is a type that could not have existed before the beginning of the seventeenth century – socio-economic conditions would not have allowed it – and Campion may well have been one of the first, but it crops up regularly in the history of both arts and sciences throughout the British Isles from this time onwards. John Bartlet (dates unknown), another composer of ayres who enjoyed the patronage of Edward Seymour, Earl of Hertford, seems to display a similar attitude. We know very little of Bartlet and his life, but the title page of his one published work, *A Booke of Ayres with a Triplicitie of Musicke* (1606), describes him as 'Gentleman and practitioner in this arte'. The *triplicitie* indicates that his ayres were published in three separate arrangements: for the lute, the *viol da gamba*, and the orpharion (a rather odd metal-stringed relative of the cittern). Michael Cavendish, who published *Ayres in Tabletorie* as early as 1598, was another amateur, but, coming as he did from an aristocratic family (which gave rise to the ducal families of Newcastle and Devonshire) and spending much of his life in royal service, his status was more that of a courtier-amateur, harking back to the idea that noblemen at court were expected to have artistic accomplishments.

Despite its popularity at court and its connection with larger genres such as the masque, the ayre was essentially a domestic art form. It is not surprising, therefore, that it was favoured by gentlemen who found themselves with the liberty and the education to pursue music outside a professional context – although that, of course, did not prevent professional musicians from composing ayres. Between 1600 and 1611, Robert Jones (*c.*1577–*c.*1617), a Gentleman of the Chapel Royal and theatrical collaborator with Philip Rosseter, published no less than five collections of attractively simple ayres, as well as a collection of madrigals. Francis Pilkington (*c.*1565–1638), who spent his life in and around Chester, first as a chorister, then as canon and rector, was another notable composer of ayres, some of which, such as 'Rest, sweet nymphs', 'Music, dear solace to my thoughts', and 'Underneath a cypress shade', are still sung and recorded. William Corkine (dates unknown) published two books of ayres in 1610 and 1612 before disappearing to Poland, after which nothing is known of him. Thomas Ford (*c.*1580–1648), was another court-based composer who composed ayres, as well as anthems, part-songs, fantasias and instrumental works for viols. As with composers of madrigals, the list could be extended to thirty names or more.

25 John Dowland

The greatest composer of English ayres was John Dowland (1563–1626). Like Taverner, Tallis and Byrd, Dowland towers over his contemporaries and is one of the great figures of English music. With the possible exception of Dunstable, he was also the first English musician to have a truly European reputation. Dowland's music is renowned for its pervasive melancholy. This was something he recognised himself and was prepared to joke about – 'Semper Dowland, semper dolens' is the title of one pavan for lute – and there is no doubt that he was a melancholic, moody character, apt to see himself as a victim of prejudice and conspiracy. Melancholy also reflected the spirit of the age. The last years of Elizabeth's reign were characterised by uncertainty over the succession and the future of the Church of England. The accession of James I marked the end of the old order and the slow birth of a new one. This was the age of *The Tempest*, the King James Bible, Donne's 'Anatomy of the World', and Burton's *Anatomy of Melancholy*. New ideas were certainly in the air, but confidence was lacking. Doubt, uncertainty and melancholy can be found in the work of a number of writers and composers, but in Dowland they reach an intensity of expression which is at once personal and cosmic.

Dowland's name and music are well known, but his life and career throw up a series of mysteries. Nobody knows where he was born, although we can be sure that he was English, not Irish as was once suggested,[1] and that he was brought up in the Church of England. We know nothing of his origins or his early life. Diana Poulton, the lute player and Dowland scholar, has investigated Dowland families from Devon to Sussex and found them to be masons, printers, tailors or fisherman, but there is nothing to link him to any of them. She suggests that his silence about his origins might stem from an unwillingness to admit to humble antecedents.[2] His first confirmed appearance is in 1580 when, at the age of seventeen, he went to France as part of the entourage – he described himself as a 'servant' – of the new English Ambassador to Paris, Sir Henry Cobham. The one certain result of his sojourn in France – he seems to have returned in 1584 – was his conversion to Catholicism, which would have an influence on his future career.

The nature and circumstances of his musical education are equally obscure. We have to assume that it was well under way by the time of his return from France, for in 1588 he received a degree in music from Christ Church, Oxford. Moreover, that same year he was also cited by John Case, the commentator on Aristotle and writer on music, in his *Apologia Musices*, as one of the contemporary musicians most deserving of praise, alongside Byrd, Mundy, Bull, Morley and Johnson. Clearly, he had already established a considerable reputation as a composer, but what he had written and how he had established himself we have no idea. There are no extant compositions from this early period. Somewhere around this time, Dowland also married, but the circumstances of his marriage and the identity of his wife are no clearer than his birthplace or his education. We know that he had a son, Robert, born in 1591 or thereabouts, but his wife is no more than a hazy presence, mentioned, without any detail, in three or four documents until 1601, after which she disappears.

In 1590, it seems that Dowland's song 'His golden locks time hath to silver turned' was played before the Queen at the annual celebration of her accession – though he may not have been the singer. In 1592, he almost certainly played and took part in an entertainment put on for the Queen at Sudeley Castle in Gloucestershire. Then, in 1594, on the death of John Johnson, one of the court lutenists, Dowland applied for the newly vacant post, but did not get it. Why he was unsuccessful has been the subject of speculation. Dowland himself claimed it was because he was a Catholic, but, as we have seen, the Queen was not inclined to discriminate against Catholics as long as they were loyal to the throne. Only a couple of years previously she had intervened personally on behalf of Byrd. Diana Poulton suggests that Dowland's personality may have played a part: he was known to be self-centred, emotional and highly sensitive to criticism. Or, more prosaically, he may have been the victim of cost-cutting: the post for which he applied was apparently not filled for four years.[3] Whatever lay behind it, the rejection was important because it led directly to Dowland's decision to leave England and travel on the Continent.

He went first to Wolfenbüttel in Lower Saxony, the seat of the Duke of Brunswick. The Duke seems to have offered him employment, but Dowland declined and travelled on to the court of the Landgrave of Hesse-Kassel, accompanied, at the Duke's suggestion, by the Duke's own lutenist, Gregorio Howet. These were intellectual German princes, patrons of the arts, who were actively interested in literature and music. They gave Dowland both a warm welcome and generous payments – although he was not always an easy guest, apparently upsetting the court at Wolfenbüttel by his open criticism of the standard of musicianship there. From Kassel, he travelled south, crossing the Alps and visiting Venice, Padua, Genova and Ferrara before arriving at the Medici court in Florence, where he played for Grand Duke Ferdinando and met the composer Giulio Caccini. At Florence, he received letters from Luca Marenzio, one of the leading composers of the day, credited with some five hundred madrigals and an influence on some of the later English madrigalists. Marenzio was based in Rome and Dowland had planned to go and meet him, but while in Florence something happened to change his plans.

By his own account, he was approached by an English Catholic priest, John Skidmore (actually Scudamore, son of one of Queen Elizabeth's courtiers, Sir James Scudamore), who attempted to draw him into an English Catholic network based in Italy, dedicated to enlisting Spanish help to overthrow Elizabeth. Unwilling to become involved and fearful that he might be suspected of treason by association, Dowland fled to Nuremberg where he wrote a long letter to Sir Henry Cecil, the Queen's Secretary of State. Dowland presents himself as a convinced Catholic, but nonetheless a loyal subject of the Queen, who feels it his duty to inform Cecil of the conspiracy he had encountered in Italy, but the whole story is full of inconsistencies and contradictions. If he was a high profile 'papist' capable of being used by those opposed to Elizabeth, why was he allowed to travel abroad in the first place? And why did he receive such a warm welcome in the strongly Protestant courts of Germany? Why (unlike Byrd) was he never accused of recusancy in England? And why had he been awarded a degree at a time when this was not permitted to professing Catholics? All of which has led to the suggestion that he might have been engaged in some kind of espionage work. And certainly Cecil, his chosen correspondent, was responsible for intelligence gathering under both Elizabeth and James I. We do not know what response – if any – Dowland's letter received. He seems to have made his way back to the Landgrave's court in Kassel and remained there until late 1596 when he received word from Henry Noel, a friend at court in London, that he might expect a post as a court musician if he returned. Dowland obeyed the summons, but Noel died suddenly. He was much lamented by the musical fraternity – Dowland wrote the music for his funeral service in Westminster Abbey; Morley wrote one memorial piece and Weelkes wrote another – but Dowland was left friendless at court and the post he so much desired failed to materialise.

It was at this point, in 1597, that Dowland published his *First Booke of Songes or Ayres of Foure Partes with Tableture for the Lute.* He had contributed six pieces to Thomas Est's *Whole Booke of Psalmes* in 1592 (a compilation of markedly Protestant character), and a number of lute solos had appeared (probably without Dowland's permission) in William Barley's *New Booke of Tabliture*, but this was his first solo publication and the first real collection of English lute songs. The elaborate dedication, usual for the time, is addressed to Sir George Carey, 2nd Baron Hunsdon, who may have been Dowland's employer or patron at the time. Carey was certainly a notable patron of the arts – the first performance of *The Merry Wives of Windsor*, also in 1597, is supposed to have been staged to mark his elevation to the Order of the Garter – but he was also a prominent anti-Catholic, which raises more questions about Dowland's religious position.

If he was the notorious Catholic he claimed to be, why would an anti-Catholic like Carey employ him or even accept a dedication from him? The volume's introduction ('To the courteous Reader') seems to express Dowland's feelings about his career, for it is at pains to emphasise the high regard in which he is held by both his Continental patrons and by his German and Italian contemporaries. It also adds one more mystery with regard to his education, since it suggests that he has a degree in music from both Oxford and Cambridge – something he would be unlikely to claim were it not true. Whatever its precise context, the *First Booke of Songes* was a runaway success, being reprinted four times by 1613.

At the beginning of 1598, Dowland received a fulsome letter from the Landgrave asking him to return to Kassel, but he chose instead to accept an offer to become court lutenist to King Christian IV of Denmark. Christian, who had come to the throne aged only eleven, was now twenty-one and would reign for another fifty years. He was an odd mixture: astute and energetic, reforming, obsessive (particularly about witchcraft), passionate (twenty-four children by five different women), cultured and boozy. He was hugely fond of music and Dowland became one of the best-paid servants at the Danish court with a salary of 500 *dalers* a year. Nor was he the only English musician employed by Christian. Among those who overlapped with him were the composer and viol player, William Brade (1560–1630); the lutenist and composer, Daniel Norcombe (1576–1626); and the singer and lutenist John Myners (d.1615). Also present was an Irish harper, Charles O'Reilly, who we know was paid only 200 *dalers* a year. O'Reilly was one of a series of Irish harpers at the Danish court. He was followed by Donald Dubh O'Cahal, who was later sent on to London and the court of James I, whose consort, Queen Anne, was Christian's sister. A third harper, Darby Scott, is also known to have worked at the Danish court from 1621 to 1634.

Initially at least, Dowland seems to have to have felt at home in this environment. It was certainly his most productive period. In 1600, he sent the manuscript of his *Second Booke of Songes* home to his wife ('From Helsingoure in Denmarke the first of June 1600') to arrange for publication. He returned to England in 1601 to buy instruments for the Danish court musicians. He travelled with King Christian and may have visited Norway. The *Third and Last Booke of Songes* was published in 1603. Dowland returned to England that same year and met Queen Anne at Winchester, probably in the context of a court masque that was being staged to mark the new reign; and we can assume that he sought to persuade the Queen to seek an appointment for him at the English court – something which had by this stage become almost an obsession with him. While in England, he completed work on another collection, this time of instrumental music: the remarkable *Lachrimae, or Seaven Teares,* which was published the following year. He also seems to have bought a house in Fetter Lane in the City of London. Back in Denmark in the early months of 1604 – he claims to have set out twice but been forced back by bad weather on both occasions – everything seemed normal, but it soon became apparent that he had money problems. Given his salary, it is hard to work out quite how he could have got into debt, but, despite the King's attempts to help him, he was effectively sacked at the beginning of 1606 – though quite possibly by court officials rather than the King himself. Dowland probably returned to Fetter Lane to live with his son. During his father's absence abroad, Robert Dowland (1591–1641) had been living and receiving his early musical education in the household of Sir Thomas Monson, a leading courtier whose positions included Master of the Armoury at the Tower of London and Master Falconer to the King. In 1609, Dowland published a translation of Andreas Ornithoparus' *Micrologus,* which he called *The Art of Singing.* The following year, two more publications emerged from the Dowland household – a *Variete of Lute Lessons,* and *A Musical Banquet,* an anthology of lute songs by several composers. Both were credited to Robert Dowland, but it is more than probable that Dowland had a hand in both, not least because Robert was only nineteen at the time. Then, in 1612, came Dowland's last published work, *A Pilgrim's Solace.*

Dowland used the preface to *A Pilgrim's Solace* to give full vent to his persecution complex. He was a man of sorrows: forced to work abroad, where he was appreciated, because he could not get even the meanest job at home, he has returned home but is still neglected, sniped at by younger musicians who do not, he implies, show him sufficient respect. None of this is entirely accurate. By 1612, Dowland had become lutenist to Lord Howard de Walden, who was rich, cultured, heir to the Earldom of Suffolk, and very much in royal favour. It was a far from contemptible appointment. And Dowland's music remained popular: his collections were reprinted; his songs were heard at court, arranged by other composers, and quoted by playwrights. The most likely explanation is that he was still embittered by his failure to obtain a court appointment. True, there was undoubtedly backbiting within the musical profession – when was there not? – but all the evidence suggests that Dowland was still considered in the very front rank as both composer and performer.

One section of the preface suggests a concern that musical fashion may be turning against the lute. Dowland attacks (although not by name) the Scottish composer, Tobias Hume (*c.*1579–1645), who, in the preface to a 1605 collection of ayres entitled *Musicall Humors* had written that 'the stateful instrument Gambo Violl shall with ease yeelde full various and as devicefull Musicke as the Lute.' Hume was a remarkable man, another amateur composer, but this time a soldier-amateur, apparently a mercenary who had fought at various times for the King of Sweden and the Czar of Russia. He sometimes claimed the rank of colonel although there is no evidence that he ever rose above captain. He was a fine musician; his ayres, such as 'Fain would I change that note' and 'Cease leaden slumber', are well written and distinctive; and he was renowned as a first class performer on the *viol da gamba*, for which he composed a large number of pieces. He was clearly also a loud and extrovert character, writing a song in praise of tobacco – 'Tobacco is like love' – and 'an Invention for two to play upon one Viole' which demanded that one musician should sit on the other's lap. Dowland's hostility to any claim that the viol could equal the lute was only going to be deepened by the expression of an outgoing personality so completely opposed to his own introverted self.

Shortly after the publication of *A Pilgrim's Solace*, in October 1612, Dowland was at last appointed as a lutenist at the court of King James. His salary was twenty pence per day. At the age of fifty, he had achieved his ambition, but it was too late. In one of those mysteries that characterise his life, his court appointment marked the end of his career as a composer. Was this a deliberate choice? Was it simply that his invention had run out? The Inns of Court sponsored two great masques at the beginning of 1613, the music was written by John/Giovanni Cooper/Coprario and by Robert Johnson. Dowland was one of the leading players, but not the composer. He fulfilled his duties at court; he continued to be named as one of the country's leading musicians; his music was widely known (and reproduced) on the Continent; from 1621 onwards, he is referred to as Dr Dowland (although it is not known which university conferred the degree on him); but nothing new flowed from his pen. In May 1625, he was among the musicians who played at the funeral of King James I. Less than a year later, in February 1626, he was buried in the churchyard of St Anne's Blackfriars. Characteristically, the precise date, cause, and circumstances of his death are uncertain: surviving documents suggest that he was buried nearly a month after he died. Robert Dowland immediately succeeded his father as court lutenist.

Dowland's music is characterised by simplicity, or the appearance of simplicity. It is music an amateur can approach and play, but which requires a master to convey its full depth of meaning and subtlety of expression. Yet this simplicity is based on a capacity for synthesis. Many of his dance tunes, from the 'Frog's Galliard' to 'The King of Denmark's Galliard' or 'Mrs Winter's Jumpp', clearly draw on the folk tradition, as do a number of songs in the earlier collections – 'Away with these self-loving lads', 'Fine knacks for ladies', 'What poor astronomers are they'. Yet he also makes use of contrapuntal techniques – creating a tension between the vocal line and the accompaniment to drive the music forward – of Italian declamatory techniques, of dissonance and chromaticism. The end in view is always the song and how it can express the overall meaning that arises out of the combination of words and music. Dowland is unusual in that, while his work does develop stylistically in the fifteen years between the *First Booke of Songes* and *A Pilgrim's Solace,* his characteristic style and mastery of the lute song form was apparent from the beginning. Even in his early works, one could scarcely call Dowland's approach to life light-hearted. Some of the early songs do contain instances of an approach more metaphysical than melancholic, and of a sexuality ('Come away! come, sweet Love!') which can recall John Donne, but the dominant theme is melancholy: failed love and the failure of the world to live up to the singer's hopes. As he grew older, his vision of the world darkened still further. The later songs, in particular those in a *Pilgrim's Solace* dwell increasingly on God and death, sometimes – as in the case of 'In darkness let me dwell', which appeared in 1610 – presenting a picture of utter despair.

> In darkness let me dwell; the ground shall sorrow be,
> The roof despair, to bar all cheerful light from me;
> The walls of marble black, that moist'ned still shall weep;
> My music, hellish jarring sounds, to banish friendly sleep.
> Thus, wedded to my woes, and bedded in my tomb,
> O let me living die, till death doth come, till death doth come.

Like his music, Dowland's lyrics, the vast majority of which he probably wrote himself, have the appearance of simplicity – at least when compared with those of contemporary madrigals and some of his fellow composers of ayres. His tends to avoid convoluted syntax and complex imagery, and, by the standards of the day, classical allusions are notably few. This directness increases accessibility, certainly for the modern listener and no doubt also for Dowland's audience. It intensifies the sense of loss, passion and suffering which suffuses his work; and it also increases the sense that Dowland himself is speaking, that the songs are in some sense confessional, giving vent to his own, real emotions and dilemmas. This may well be the case some of the time, but it is just as unwise to associate the song and singer too closely with Dowland as it would be with modern, melancholic singer-songwriters, such as Dylan, James Taylor, or Morrissey.

Dowland has been called 'a pioneer but without successors,'[4] and it is true that the English ayre did not long survive his death in 1626. John Attey's decidedly mundane collection of ayres, *First Booke of Ayres of Foure Parts, with Tableture for the Lute*, published in 1622, was the last such publication for over thirty years. Dowland had imitators, among them his son Robert, and lute songs continued to be heard in and around the court, but the vogue was over. Dowland's innovations transformed the ayre as a musical form, but by the time of his death no one had emerged to take that new form forward in a manner to suit the changing musical tastes of the time. Unable to adapt, it faded away and Dowland's name slipped into obscurity – only to be rescued at the beginning of the twentieth century by composers such as Frederick Keel, Peter Warlock (who somehow managed to arrange some of Dowland's dances for brass band) and Percy Grainger.

The lute song disappeared, but the broad concept of the song as shaped by Dowland did not. That a song should be a composition capable of performance by a solo performer; that it should be in strophic form, have an accessible lyric and a harmonic accompaniment designed to complement and balance the lyric: these are basic characteristics which fed into English song as it evolved throughout the eighteenth and nineteenth centuries; and they surfaced even more strongly in popular song in the nineteenth and twentieth centuries. Even today, four hundred years on, Dowland's songs remain accessible in a way that the madrigals of Weelkes and Wilbye – wonderful though they are – do not. Songs such as 'Come again, sweet love doth now invite', 'Now, oh, now I needs must part', 'Behold a wonder here,' and his best-known song, 'Flow my tears', are popular today because the form is recognisable and the appeal is universal. And Dowland's appeal reaches well beyond the classical sphere. In 1974, the Dutch rock guitar virtuoso, Jan Akkerman, recorded *Tabernakel*, an album based around Dowland's dance music; in 2006, Sting recorded *Songs from the Labyrinth*, consisting of songs by Dowland and his contemporaries; the jazz saxophonist John Surman has recorded music by Dowland; and singer-songwriter Elvis Costello has recorded at least one Dowland song.

One other aspect of Dowland's work deserves consideration at this point. By the end of the Elizabethan era, vocal music had long been written for a given number of parts with the nature of each part – soprano, alto, tenor, bass – clearly designated. With instrumental music, it was very different. Many distinguished works had been written for solo instruments, particularly for keyboards of various kinds, but where larger bands or groups of musicians were concerned, composers generally did not specify any particular combination of instruments or sounds. The English 'consort', a term which first appeared in the 1550s, was usually made up of whatever instruments and whatever players happened to be on hand. Anthony Holborne (*c.*1545–1602), a composer much respected in his day – Dowland dedicated one of his songs to 'to the most famous Anthony Holborne' – but now largely forgotten, was an influential composer of consort music. His *Pavans, Galliards, Almains, and other short Aeirs both grave, and light, in five parts, for Viols, Violins or other Musicall Winde Instruments,* published in 1599, is a good example of how instrumental music was treated. It contains sixty-five pieces, many of them inventive and melodic, but at no stage does Holborne indicate or even suggest which instruments should play which pieces or which parts. Writing in 1619, Michael Praetorius, the German composer and musicologist, described an English consort as 'several persons with all kinds of instruments.'[5] This free-for-all approach continued well into the seventeenth century. The terms 'whole' or 'closed' consort were used to describe groups consisting solely of stringed instruments, while 'broken music' or 'broken consort' were used to refer to consorts containing instruments from more than one musical family – strings, woodwind, wind, lute, or harp.

Given that the nature and, indeed, the success of the ayre depended on the balance between voice and accompaniment, it was logical that composers of ayres should seek to define the accompaniment more closely by taking a more prescriptive approach towards instrumentation and scoring. The first moves in this direction came around the turn of the seventeenth century. Three names stand out: Thomas Morley, Philip Rosseter, and Dowland. Morley's *Consort Lessons* of 1599 specifies a consort consisting of treble lute, cittern (or gittern; a predecessor of the guitar), a bandora (or pandora; best described as a bass cittern), flute or recorder, treble viol and bass viol – and the music is scored specifically for that combination. Rosseter's 1609 collection of consort music, *Lessons for Consort*, follows Morley's example closely. Dowland's reputation, as we have seen, rests on his lute songs, but he also wrote pavans, galliards and other instrumental pieces for consorts of various shapes and sizes – and these are presented with clear indications of instrumentation and scoring. Although their example was not necessarily followed immediately, these three composers stand out as demonstrating the first approach to proper scoring and orchestration in English music.

In 1596, Dowland wrote an instrumental piece called 'Lachrimae pavan' featuring a four-note, falling-tear motif. This was reworked as the ayre 'Flow My Tears', which appeared in his 1600 collection. Then in 1604, he published *Lachrimae, or Seaven Teares, Figured in Seaven Passionate Pavans*. The pavan, of course, was originally a dance, but these seven pavans are certainly not meant for dancing. They are short pieces, none of them much over four minutes in length, and all of them variations on the original 'Lachrimae pavan' theme with its four falling notes. They are scored for lute and five viols (treble, alto, tenor, bass and 'quintus' or fifth viol) and each has a title based on a different kind of tears – 'Old Tears', 'Old Tears Renewed', 'Sighing Tears', 'Sad Tears', 'Forced Tears', 'Lover's Tears', and 'True Tears'. Whether these titles had some significance for Dowland's life or whether they were intended to represent some sort of metaphysical progression, we cannot know, but the music has a private intensity which goes beyond anything else in Dowland's work and is almost of the order one finds in the late Beethoven quartets. The writing is absolutely precise. Melancholy has become grief and every note of every part contributes to its expression. Desolate though it may be in its emotional landscape, there is a strong case for *Lachrimae* to be considered the first great instrumental masterpiece of English music.

26 King James, King Charles, and the Masque

James Stuart was born in Edinburgh castle in 1566 and succeeded to the Scottish throne as James VI at the age of only thirteen months. When his minority ended, he had to struggle for several years to gain full control of his kingdom, but once he succeeded, he ruled Scotland in his own right for twenty years before he became King of England as well. Scotland thus formed his character and his intellectual and cultural outlook. Of his intellectual abilities, there is no doubt. He wrote a series of books and pamphlets on theological and political issues. He took a great interest in poetry, writing a treatise on the subject when he was only eighteen and encouraging the formation of the so-called Castalian Band as part of his project for a revival of Scottish cultural life. As befitted a prince of the age, he also had a general interest in music, although he did not have the musical education or abilities of England's Tudor monarchs, nor, indeed, their exposure to music.

James's mother, Mary Stuart, had loved singing and dancing – for which she was publicly taken to task by John Knox – and she played both the virginals and the lute. But James was separated from his mother at the age of only ten months. His childhood and early adolescence were spent in the austere atmosphere of Stirling Castle, where his tutor sought to turn him into a God-fearing, Protestant monarch. There would have been metrical psalms; there would have been instrumental music for keyboards and consorts of viols; and there would also have been traditional Scottish songs and traditional Scottish dances – which in Scottish Protestant eyes were less likely to encourage sin than more fashionable French or Italian measures. When James formally entered Edinburgh as King in 1579, there were only four viols and a few singers to welcome him, and one of his first acts on attaining his majority was to send James Lauder to London to buy a pair of virginals. He inherited or re-employed some of the musicians who had been at his mother's court, among them five members of an English family called Hudson – memorably described by Donald Macleod as a kind of Scottish von Trapp family[1] – who sang and played viols and wrote verse. William Hudson became the King's dancing master and taught him the galliards and pavans that had previously been regarded as unacceptable. As we have seen, James offered royal patronage to several composers, such as Black and Blackhall who had their roots in the old world of polyphonic, sacred music, and he encouraged the writing of madrigals and instrumental music. He also did his best to reinvigorate the song schools which had played a major part in Scottish musical life. This was a worthy attempt to revive Scottish music, as well as an effective method of imposing his personality on the court, but it was only when he arrived in London in 1603 that he was able to experience a genuinely rich musical society and exercise musical patronage on a significant scale.

James had thought and written about the nature of monarchy and, like the Tudors, understood the value of music as a means of projecting power and legitimacy. He was a new monarch, imported from a country which many English people regarded as essentially hostile, so legitimacy was of particular importance. His coronation procession in 1604 began with trumpets, was accompanied by at least three separate musical groups, and also featured a performance for wind ensemble and choir in St Paul's Church, and a musical pageant in Fleet Street. He made full use of the musical resources of the Chapel Royal and, one assumes, appreciated Thomas Weelkes' somewhat sycophantic seven-part anthem, 'O Lord, grant the King a long life.' His own musical tastes were not sophisticated, but he was generous with his musical appointments. The court was soon supporting some forty musicians – flautists, recorder players, a consort of oboes and trombones, and, of course, numerous viol players and lutenists – a number that would increase to one hundred and forty by the time of his death in 1625. As it happened, despite his own limited interest in the art, James presided over a particularly rich period of musical history, when the vogues for madrigals and for lute ayres were at their height, but the musical form over which he exerted most direct influence was the court masque.

Masques, as we have seen, were devised and performed at the court of Henry VIII, and musical entertainments of a similar kind were regular features of Elizabeth's court, but it was under James I and Charles I that the form reached its own particular zenith. The masque is often seen as the precursor of English opera. It was – at least in so far that a number of its constituent parts became familiar during the period of its popularity and were then carried over and developed when opera finally appeared in England later in the century – but it would be a mistake to overstate the connection. The masque was anything but a coherent art form: it was a collection of diverse artistic elements – design, costume, verse, dance, song, instrumental music – harnessed together to provide entertainment for the court. The entertainment, however, was not narrative-based. A masque would have a story, usually a well-known, classical tale or some allegorical conceit designed to flatter the king, but the plot was very much a secondary consideration.

Some masques were staged away from London, usually by powerful aristocrats seeking to impress the King during a royal progress. In 1617, the Earl of Cumberland staged an entertainment at Brougham Castle which was devised by Thomas Campion. In 1620, William Cavendish put on a masque written by Ben Jonson at Welbeck Abbey, after which he was created Viscount Mansfield. Thirteen years later, by which time he had already risen to the rank of Earl of Newcastle, he put on another Jonson masque, *Love's Welcome at Welbeck*, for Charles I. And the following year, 1634, the good Earl put on a third masque, *Love's Welcome at Bolsover* at Bolsover Castle. In 1621, one of James's favourite masques, *The Gypsies Metamorphosed*, also by Jonson, was staged at the Duke of Buckingham's country home at Burleigh-on-the-Hill, and then repeated a few days later at Belvoir Castle, seat of the Duke of Rutland. Masques might also be put on by institutions, such as Christ Church, Oxford, or the Inns of Court in London, to express their gratitude for royal support and patronage. However, the vast majority of the masques produced during the reigns of James I and Charles I – and there were well over fifty in all – were staged in the Banqueting Hall in Whitehall. This was originally a temporary structure put up by Queen Elizabeth, but in 1606 James ordered it to be rebuilt in stone, specifically for the staging of masques. It burned down in 1619 and was rebuilt to a design by Inigo Jones as the structure that still stands today.

The masque was an exclusive entertainment, completely different and divorced from the public theatre – although elements of the masque did spill over into the theatrical world. The most obvious example is Shakespeare's *Tempest*; there are also masque sequences in both *Romeo and Juliet* and *Henry VIII*; and it has been suggested that the idea of the witches' ritual in *Macbeth* may have been borrowed from Ben Jonson's masque *Oberon* (1611). Most masques were funded by the King, staged at a venue to which only the court had access, and featured members of the court circle on stage. They were very expensive – *Oberon* cost £2,100, which was costly enough, but *The Triumph of Peace* (1634), the most extravagant of the period, cost ten times that amount. Masques were also Stuart propaganda: their classical or allegorical themes often sought to link the reigning monarch with King Arthur or with Imperial Rome. *The Masque of Flowers* (1613) went even further, identifying James with the sun, having the power to turn young men into flowers and then return them to human form. James knew that the combination of exclusivity and sheer splendour was a way of binding people to him. A new golden age had arrived and they were part of it.

The masque brought together all the arts; and the generous sums made available by both James and, later, Charles I ensured that England's leading designers, writers and musicians were all involved. Inigo Jones (1573–1652), who today is thought of principally as an architect, was at least as well known in his time as a designer of court masques. His first designs, for *The Masque of Blackness* (1605), were already elaborate, showing an awareness of Italian use of perspective in creating scenery and of Italian stage mechanics; and, as time went on, his sets grew even more lavish and the stage machinery more complex, geared to creating ever more spectacular visual effects. For many years, Jones's principal collaborator was Ben Jonson. Jonson, of course, is remembered as a playwright and contemporary of Shakespeare, but he was also the court's preferred writer of masques. Indeed, he wrote nearly twice as many masques as he did plays, and it was his masques that earned him his appointment as Master of the Queen's Revels. An intricate plot was not required for what was essentially a series of musical scenes linked by dialogue and narration, but Jonson's wit, his lyric gift and his classical learning all made him a prolific provider of what were more than scripts but less than librettos. He and Inigo Jones eventually fell out badly, but in their respective disciplines they certainly did more to shape the masque than anyone else. Whereas other writers – Samuel Daniel, Campion, Francis Beaumont, James Shirley – made notable contributions, Jones seems to have had no competition.

Set and costume designs have been preserved and librettos were published, but we have no complete score from any masque of this period. Individual songs survive; so do many dances and some consort pieces; yet among the wealth of instrumental music from the reigns of James and Charles I, it is difficult to say with any certainty what may or may not have been written for, or adapted from, the score of a masque. What is clear, however, is that there was no single composer who could match the dominance of Jones or Jonson. Campion wrote the music for several masques. Other leading masque composers were Robert Johnson, John Coprario, Nicholas Lanier (1588–1666) and Alfonso Ferrabosco the Younger (*c.*1575–1626; son of the Alfonso Ferrabosco who introduced madrigals to Elizabeth's court). It was also common for the music to be shared between two or three composers: *Oberon* (1611) had music by Robert Johnson and Ferrabosco; *The Masque of Augurs* (1622) by Ferrabosco and Nicholas Lanier; *The Triumph of Peace* (1634) by William Lawes, Simon Ives (1600–62) and Bulstrode Whitelocke (1605–75). Such cooperation was possible because masques did not demand a coherent or thematically connected score. They consisted of a range of diverse musical forms – instrumental interludes, songs, choral pieces, dances – which could be contributed individually by different composers.

A masque would commonly begin with an instrumental prelude for a consort of viols or of viols and wind instruments, allowing the audience to settle and the cast to ready themselves; and there would also be instrumental interludes at various points during the performance to cover scene changes. These pieces represented something of a conceptual development. They had a practical function: they had to engage the audience – or at least prevent them from being bored – while they waited for the next spectacle. At the same time, they were not tied to any other musical form: they were not songs, accompaniments, or dances; nor were they tied to the story – we are still a very long way from a score conceived as in any sense unifying the scenes and characters of a drama. So the composer had both the opportunity and the need to innovate, either structurally or aurally, developing new sounds, using instruments in new ways or in new combinations.

These preludes and interludes are linked to the development of the instrumental fantasia, a specialised and more interesting form of composition which also reached the zenith of its popularity in the early decades of the seventeenth century. In fact, the fantasia was an attitude as much as a musical form. In his *Plain and Easy Introduction to Practical Music* (1597), Thomas Morley says that in a fantasia

> the musician taketh a point at his pleasure and wresteth and turneth it as he list, making as much or as little of it according as shall seem best in his own conceit. In this may be more art than shown in any other music because the composer is tied to nothing but that he may add, diminish and alter at his pleasure.

Although the term originated with the lutenists, fantasias were soon being written for keyboards, for lutes, for consorts of viols, and for wind instruments. Orlando Gibbons even wrote one specifically for 'the great dooble bass' or bass violin. A number of the leading writers of fantasias – Byrd, Gibbons, Morley – kept wholly or largely aloof from masques, but most of the leading masque composers – Ferrabosco, Coprario, Lanier, William Lawes, Simon Ives – also wrote fantasias. The common ground appears to have been the need or the wish to express an emotion or an idea instrumentally. The status of instrumental music was rising and the popularity of the fantasia both reflected and fed upon this. Dowland had shown that instrumental music could in all respects equal vocal music – although there is nothing in these early fantasias to compare with a work such as

Lachrimae – but the idea was still comparatively new and would not reach its full musical expression for many generations. Nonetheless, the seed had been planted and it is possible to see the composers of fantasias, and of masque preludes and interludes, as pushing at the boundaries of what instrumental music could achieve. Perhaps, though one should not exaggerate this, they can even be seen as taking the first steps, however small and tentative, towards the great, romantic expressions of the self in the nineteenth century.

After the prelude, the masque proper would commence with a song from one of the leading characters, usually setting out the symbolic or allegorical framework of the piece. And there would be songs of different kinds throughout – from lute songs to catches and rounds, from songs which approached ballad form to part-songs and madrigals. Many settings survive and all the main composers of the period clearly had some competence in this area, but Nicholas Lanier, Robert Johnson and John Wilson stand out in their ability to combine an easy tune – at least some of the singers, it should be remembered, would have been courtiers, not professionals – with an effective and accessible setting of the words. And the words had to be heard if the masque was to make sense. They were displays of wit and, to the extent that the masque had either, they provided narrative logic and character development. Percy Young has actually compared some of the four-part songs in the *Masque of Flowers* to the kind of thing that appeared in Gilbert and Sullivan's Savoy Operas over two hundred years later.[2] At some stage, the declamatory linking passages spoken by the leading characters gave way to early recitative. In the published text of *Lovers Made Men* (1617), Ben Jonson suggests that 'the whole Maske was sung (after the Italian manner) by Master Nicholas Lanier.' Scholars have questioned this statement – which was written twenty years after the event – but we can at least be sure that first examples of English recitative occurred in the masques of the early Stuart kings.

Although the music might have little thematic connection with the action of the masque, it was nonetheless fully integrated into the staging. The movements of singers and musicians were carefully planned and choreographed to achieve maximum dramatic effect or maintain continuity. In Jonson's *Pleasure Reconciled to Virtue* (1618), for example, we are told that at one point in the performance 'the whole grove [of trees] vanished, and the whole music was discovered, sitting at the foot of the mountain, with Pleasure and Virtue seated above them.' And in the *Masque of Queens*

(1609), the connection between the music and the action is quite explicit: 'loud music sounded as before, to give the masquers time of descending'. Such details of production would have been under the control of a professional dancing master. These men – Nicolas Confesse, Jacques Bochan, Thomas Giles and Jerome Herne were among the best known – were in effect directors, and were often the most highly paid professionals involved. When *Love Freed from Ignorance and Folly* was first produced in 1611, Ben Jonson received £40 for the libretto; Inigo Jones £40 for the set and costume designs; Alfonso Ferrabosco £20 for composing the music; Thomas Lupo and Robert Johnson £5 each for musical arrangements; while Confesse and Bochan shared £70 for the choreography and teaching the dances. The pay scale reflects the fact that dancing lay at the heart of the masque, something largely obscured these days by the need to read the text or reconstruct the music rather than actually see a performance. Indeed, the centrality of dance as an illustrative and expressive medium – although its expressive aspects were still very much in their infancy – can support the argument that the masque looks forward to classical ballet as much as to opera. But there is an additional element, because dance in the sense that it appeared in court masques went beyond mere entertainment: dancing before the King in a prescribed manner was an exercise in submission, in fealty.

The term *masque* derives from *masquerade*, and once the masque was under way, groups of masked dancers or masquers would make their entry in a formal procession, often accompanied by torchbearers. To begin with, men and women would often be in separate groups. They would merge and the main dances would follow, interspersed with songs and declamations. These were carefully choreographed dances, based on slow and deliberate movements, the dancers forming patterns on the stage – diamonds, squares, circles, figures-of-eight – the better to display the elegance of their movements and the splendour of their costumes.

The masque had Italian origins and drew on French ideas, notably in design and costume, but under James and Charles I it developed into a particularly English genre that encapsulated the changes which the early Stuart kings brought to the English court. Queen Elizabeth's parsimony evaporated in these extravagant and glittering displays. The decorum of Elizabeth's court also disappeared. Dancing gradually became more vigorous, even suggestive. An extra element was added by Ben Jonson when he wrote the *Masque of Queens*. This was the antimasque, which often featured as an *entr'acte* and was designed to contrast with the formality of the masque itself. Antimasques dwelt on the grotesque or the ridiculous. *Pleasure Reconciled to Virtue*, for example, has two antimasques: the first is 'danced by men in the shape of bottles, tuns, etc.', the second by pygmies who disappear into holes at its conclusion. As time went on, and particularly in those masques staged during royal progresses in the provinces, there were occasions when antimasques not only began to multiply, but became increasingly wild in content and expression, so that they risked overwhelming the masque proper. Such displays would have been seen as vulgar in the previous reign, but they probably reflect James's character: his intellectual abilities were not matched by sophisticated musical or artistic tastes. Displays of wealth and splendour were part of his strategy for kingship, perhaps as a reaction to the constraints of life at the Scottish court, whereas lively performances, robust humour and heavy drinking – he is reported to have been too drunk to make it to the end of the performance on a number of occasions – were probably a reflection of the tastes he formed as a young man in Scotland.

As the masque approached its end, it was customary for the dancers on the stage to select partners from the audience to join in some more high-spirited measures, such as galliards, corantos, even jigs. These were the Revels. They were not choreographed in the same way as the rest of the masque and might last for a considerable time, depending on the interest of the King and the stamina of the dancers. When the Revels ended and the masque was ready to conclude, the masquers would perform a going-off dance, often echoing their entry procession and intended to re-establish an air of stateliness and formality.

One significant development associated with the masque, though not a specifically musical one, was the fact that women, both actresses and the ladies of the court, appeared on stage. Even James's Queen Anne took part. In one of the earliest Jacobean masques, *The Vision of the Twelve Goddesses* (1604), she was Pallas Athene, wearing a costume which was considered by some to be too revealing; and in *The Masque of Blackness* (1605), she was not only six months pregnant but also blacked up for the part. Charles I's queen, Henrietta Maria, also appeared on stage, most notably in *The Shepherd's Masque* (1633), which marked the first occasion when the Queen and her ladies took on speaking roles. Such antics from the Royal Family, combined with the fact that Henrietta Maria was a Catholic, that backstage behaviour among some of the ladies of the court was reported to be significantly less than chaste, and, of course, the sheer scale of expenditure, all led to puritan outrage. The most obvious instance was the publication of William Prynne's *Histriomastix* (1633), a thousand-page tome attacking all forms of dramatic performance as sinful, but held by Charles I to attack the Queen in particular. Prynne was tried for seditious libel, fined and imprisoned, but his was only one voice in a growing wave of opposition to the King, his court, and his politics. By 1640, relations between the King and Parliament had deteriorated and Charles' financial position was growing desperate. The masque was an early casualty. *Salmacida Spolia*, performed that January, was written by Sir William Davenant, with sets and costumes by Inigo Jones, music by Lewis Richard, and featured Queen Henrietta Maria in the role of an Amazon. It was the last of its kind to be produced before the country slid into civil war.

27 Orlando Gibbons

In 1564, a delegation of officials from Oxford University travelled to Cambridge for the visit of Queen Elizabeth, taking with them the Oxford Waits, whose function was probably to assist with the incidental music for the plays that were performed in the Queen's honour. One of the band, William Gibbons (*c.*1540–95), did not go home: he married a Cambridge girl and earned a living playing and teaching music in the city. His career was not without incident – at one point he was fined the substantial sum of forty shillings for running a dancing school within the boundaries of the town – but he was clearly well known and widely respected; and he produced a highly musical family. Of his five sons, the eldest died in infancy. The second, Edward (1568–1658), took a degree in music at Cambridge and went on to become organist and Master of Choristers at King's College. He later fulfilled the same role at Bristol Cathedral, and then served as a priest-vicar and organist at Exeter Cathedral from 1609 to 1644, when the organ was destroyed and the choir disbanded during the Civil Wars. The third, Ellis (1573–1603), we have already met as a promising composer of madrigals whose work appeared in the *Triumphs of Oriana*. The fourth, Ferdinando, was born in 1582 after the family had returned to Oxford and his father had rejoined the Oxford Waits. Ferdinando has been identified with Ferdinando Gybbins, a member of the Lincoln Town Waits in 1611. The fifth was Orlando, born in 1583 and apparently named after the

Dutch composer, Orlando di Lasso. The family moved back to Cambridge in 1590 where William now became leader of the Cambridge Waits, but his health was poor and, following an extended period when one of his sons, presumably Ferdinando, acted as his musical deputy, he died in 1595.

There are few records of Orlando Gibbons's early life. The year after his father's death, he joined the choir of King's College, where he was under the supervision of his brother Edward. Two years later, in 1598, he left the choir and enrolled as a student at the college. On five occasions between 1601 and 1603, he was paid small sums for occasional compositions, apparently intended for performance at Michaelmas and Christmas. He must also have been studying the organ, for in 1605, at the age of only twenty-one, he was appointed Gentleman and Organist at the Chapel Royal. From that point onwards, his career never faltered. In 1606, he received his degree from Cambridge. In 1611, he received grants of money from the King and Queen in addition to his Chapel Royal salary. In 1617, he was commissioned to write the ceremonial music for King James's return to Scotland, and he may well have accompanied the King on this visit. In 1619, he was appointed 'one of his Majesty's Musicians for the virginalls to attend in his highness privie Chamber,'[1] and in 1622 he may also have received a doctorate from Oxford University – although doubt has recently been thrown on whether the degree was actually awarded, and it is true that he was never styled 'Dr Gibbons'. The following year he added organist at Westminster Abbey to his list of positions. He composed some of the music for James I's funeral in 1625 and for Charles I's wedding that same year. He and the rest of the Chapel Royal had actually travelled down to Canterbury and were ready to perform a special programme welcoming King Charles's new bride, Henrietta Maria on her arrival from France, when on Whit Sunday 1625 Gibbons was struck down by an apoplexy and died. He left a wife, Elizabeth, whose father had been a yeoman of the vestry of the Chapel Royal, and seven children, one of whom, Christopher, would go on to become one of the most active musical figures at the court of Charles II. Elizabeth Gibbons died just a year after her husband.

In his lifetime, Gibbons was probably better known as a player of keyboards than as a composer. On his death, he was lamented as 'the organist of the chapel that had the best hand in England'.[2] Many of his keyboard compositions have been lost, but some forty-five pieces survive. They include fantasias, preludes, galliards, pavans, and other dance forms such as the ground and the alman (or allemande). The Canadian pianist,

Glenn Gould, rated Gibbons as his all-time favourite composer, even above Bach. With Gibbons, he said,

> one is never quite able to counter the impression of music of supreme beauty that lacks its ideal means of reproduction. Like Beethoven in his last quartets, or Webern at almost any time, Gibbons is an artist of such intractable commitment that, in the keyboard field, at least, his works work better in one's memory, or on paper, than they ever can through the intercession of a sounding-board.[3]

Gould is right in that, at its best, Gibbons's instrumental music, whether for keyboards or for viols, manages to remain recognisable within the forms and structures of seventeenth-century music, while at the same time offering an edgy, mysterious quality, which seems to suggest some undefined reference point beyond the music. And Gould is adept in bringing out this quality in his performances of works such as the keyboard *Fantasia in C major;* the allemande, *Italian Ground;* and the *Lord of Salisbury's Pavan and Galliard*. Gibbons's eight variations on a popular Tudor tune, *The Woods so Wild*, are unusually expressive for the time, pushing the boundaries of keyboard music to the point where, taken as a single work, they have actually been compared to a tone poem.[4]

Gibbons's achievements in writing for viols centre on the evolving form of the fantasia, of which he proved himself a master. Twenty-seven fantasias survive: four of them are *In nomine* adaptations of earlier tunes, and at least one, as noted above, was for the double bass or bass violin (although no less than eight actually feature a double bass part). The fantasia suited Gibbons. An intensely musical background had given him such versatility and capacity for invention that one of his four-part fantasias can include a morris dance tune, while others incorporate fugato or fugue-like passages. At the same time, he approached music in a very formal manner: his fantasias are anything but loosely structured, having a strong sense of coherence and proportion. In 1613, at the time when six of his pieces for virginals were included in *Parthenia* alongside works by Byrd and John Bull, Gibbons published *Fantasies of III Parts*. These nine fantasies show how his understanding of the potential of the form progressed. He starts with a model based on the kind of early fantasias that had appeared during the reign of Elizabeth. Essentially these pieces consist of several sections linked together by repetition and restatement to create a single work. This was the structure favoured by his contemporaries, John Bull, Thomas Lupo and Alfonso Ferrabosco, and later developed by John Jenkins during the Commonwealth period and the reign of Charles II. However, the later works in *Fantasies of III Parts* show Gibbons moving to what is effectively a multi-movement structure (although the term 'movement' did not become current until 1683, when it was used to describe Purcell's sonatas). The different sections are separate and self-contained, with different time signatures and often contrasting moods, but they are constructed and organised in such a way as to constitute a single work. In *Fantasia no. 7 à III*, for example, Gibbons creates a sense of unity not only by using similar thematic material in all four sections, but also through a basic cyclical structure, returning at the end to a theme and mood which recall the beginning. This concept of a multi-movement structure may perhaps have derived from settings of the Mass in an earlier age, but, applied to instrumental music in the way Gibbons does, it clearly looks forward to sonata form, the symphony, the concerto and other classical genres that were to emerge in the eighteenth century. Yet both approaches to the fantasia were attempts to create unity within a single musical work and, as such, are evidence of an increasing awareness of theoretical issues relating to the development of musical forms.

Gibbons, as we have seen, was often considered a rather serious character, and this side of him comes across strongly in his collection of madrigals, *A First Set of Madrigals and Motets of 5 parts*, published in 1612. He chose, or was complicit in the choice of, some very moral, even severe, texts – much more metaphysical and less concerned with love than those set by his contemporaries[5] – and while Gibbons's music is, as one would expect, of undoubted quality, the resulting madrigals have neither the brightness of Morley nor the eccentricity of Weelkes. Gibbons was not, however, a completely austere and humourless individual. Some of his dance tunes demonstrate that he can write brilliant ornamental passages to match any of his contemporaries'. A set of fourteen variations on the popular tune 'The Hunt's Up', known as 'Peascod Time', and a ground with the title 'Whoop, do me no harm, good man' show that he did have some sense of humour. As does his extraordinary composition, *The Cryes of London*, clearly influenced, if not inspired, by Thomas Ravenscroft. Solo voices singing the everyday cries of street sellers in the capital are set to a viol consort accompaniment which is clearly designed to recall the *In nomine* tradition. No doubt the court would have found the juxtaposition funny, though it may be that by presenting the piece as a pseudo-madrigal, Gibbons was aiming a barb or two at the shallowness of some contemporary vocal compositions.

It is worth emphasising Gibbons's positive and forward-looking contributions to secular music because it is for his church music that he is principally remembered, and in that context he is invariably represented as the last great polyphonic composer, coming at the end of the succession of great church composers which began with Tye and Taverner. This may be true, but it is a judgement made with hindsight. Gibbons was the natural successor to Byrd, and his work marks the extension and the development of the great tradition of Tudor church composers into the Stuart period. He was Byrd's equal in deploying contrapuntal techniques – not only in church music – to maximum effect. And he went further than Byrd in adopting a powerful declamatory style derived from Italian music and the madrigal tradition to add drama to his anthems. *See, see the Word is incarnate* represents the high point of his experiments in this direction: it has even been described as a miniature oratorio on the life of Christ.[6]

But Gibbons's world was not the world of his predecessors. He was the first of the great church composers to have been born into the Church of England and to have had a wholly Protestant upbringing. Unlike Taverner, Tallis and Byrd, he never had to struggle with his religious conscience or with the religious authorities. He never wrote a setting of the Mass and he never set a Latin text: all his texts were English. Living and working in court circles, he would surely have had some knowledge of musical developments elsewhere in Europe – this was the age when Monteverdi's first operas were being performed in Italy; when Heinrich Schütz in Germany and Jan Sweelink in the Netherlands were breaking new ground in keyboard music and establishing a new tradition of organ playing which spread across northern Germany. Yet Gibbons's work does not reflect Continental influences in the same way or to the same extent as that of his predecessors; they were men who had known or lived with the legacy of England as a Catholic country and felt a connection with Europe which made the transmission of musical ideas both easy and natural. Against this background – and also given that, although he was born in the reign of Elizabeth, his entire working life was spent under James I – it is not surprising that Gibbons's sacred music should show a progression from that of previous generations. He did not send Anglican church music off in a new direction, but he did change its emphasis.

He wrote several settings of the Anglican Service – including the *Morning and Evening Service in F*, also known as the *Short Service*, which is still sung today. This is a very individual setting, where the four parts are frequently not in unison, but the words still come through with great clarity. Although uneven at times, it remains inspiring. Gibbons also wrote a number of hymn tunes, which appeared in *Hymns and Songs of the Church*, edited by George Wither in 1623. This compilation was published with the strong support of the King, and it came at a time when James was trying to inject a little more ceremony and beauty into Church of England services. It was intended to supplement the congregation's regular diet of metrical psalms with more melodic hymn tunes. Some of Gibbons's tunes are still in use in the Church of England and one of them, called simply *Number 13*, provided the basis for a piano prelude by Vaughan Williams. His involvement in what was certainly not a career-bettering, high-profile task is evidence not just of his willingness to do the King's musical and religious bidding, but also of a genuine commitment to the Church of England.

Gibbons's most important contributions to church music, however, were his anthems. Church of England anthems evolved out of motets, and the traditional anthem was a piece for full choir. Gibbons wrote several memorable examples. *Great King of Gods* is a piece with a big sound, written for King James's visit to Scotland in 1617. *Hosanna to the Son of David* is equally outgoing, exuberant and celebratory in character. His eight-part anthem, *O clap your hands together,* takes its text from Psalm 47 and generates a complex momentum of sound which, in its overall texture (rather than the details) seems to look back to Tallis's anthems. By contrast, the six-part *O Lord in my wrath rebuke me not* has a particular delicacy and restraint, its unusual harmonies and moments of discord giving it an almost modern sound.

Yet it was with the verse anthem that Gibbons seems to have had a greater natural affinity; and this was where he made his most important contribution to the Anglican musical tradition. The verse anthem alternates sections for full choir with sections for solo voice or a small group of voices. It also includes instrumental passages for consort of viols or for organ. In comparison with the full choir anthem, it feels closer to – though still at some considerable distance from – the modern, verse-plus-chorus idea of a song. Verse anthems emerged at the end of the sixteenth century: Byrd wrote several, including *Christ rising again* and *Teach me, O Lord*, and the form was taken up by Weelkes, by Thomas Tomkins, and also by John

Bull, whose *Almighty God, which by the leading of a star* (the so-called *Star Anthem*) survives in more sources than any other verse anthem of the Jacobean period. Gibbons wrote twenty-four verse anthems – as opposed to fifteen full anthems – and, in doing so, turned what was essentially a variant of the full anthem into a recognised and accepted part of the Anglican musical repertoire. This paved the way for the popularity of the verse anthem during the Restoration period; for Purcell's glorious expansion of the form; for Handel's *Chandos Anthems*; and for works (of admittedly varying quality) by a whole series of composers stretching through the eighteenth and into the nineteenth century – among them John Blow, William Croft, Maurice Greene, William Boyce, and Sebastian Wesley.

The strength of the verse anthem is that it is inherently dramatic. The contrast between the passages for full choir and those for solo voice or for a small group creates a natural momentum. It also offers the composer a dynamic structure that can respond to, support and even illustrate the text which is being set. Gibbons recognised this. He saw the flexibility that the form offered him and he had something of a genius for managing the contrasts. Dense contrapuntal passages and full polyphonic scoring alternate with solo or instrumental passages of great simplicity and clarity. Yet Gibbons's approach is never formulaic. He constantly varies the number and the combination of voices used for the verse passages – indeed, only three of them are scored for a single soloist – and he plays with the structure, altering the verse-chorus pattern and the emphasis between the two.

His best known verse anthem is probably *This is the record of John*, a setting of words from John's Gospel describing the ministry of John the Baptist. Its origins mark Gibbons as the establishment figure he certainly was. It was written in honour of William Laud, royal favourite and later Archbishop of Canterbury, on his return to St John's College, Oxford, but nothing could be further from the triumphalism of Gibbons's royal anthems. A solo verse is followed by a full choir chorus, which picks up the last line of the verse, and the pattern is repeated three times. It is a triumph of restraint and simplicity. By contrast, *O Thou the central orb* (sometimes also known as *O All true faithful hearts*), written in 1619 to celebrate James I's recovery from illness, is more outgoing. The tune is hymn-like and more uplifting; the chorus almost bouncy; and the piece ends with the chorus repeated three times, followed by an elaborately extended amen. From a modern perspective, it is easy to underestimate the importance of the texts of these anthems, to see the anthems themselves as essentially musical exercises, when they were intended and were understood as devotional pieces. Anthems could serve many purposes. *Blessed are all they* was 'A Wedding Anthem first made for My Lord of Somerset'. *Lord grant grace* is a paean of religious praise. *If ye be risen again with Christ* and *The secret sins* dwell on the mysteries of the Christian faith. Yet the tone remains reflective: the music is written to bring out the meaning of the words, to encourage prayer and meditation. One anthem, *Behold, Thou hast made my days,* was written 'at the entreaty of Dr Maxie, Dean of Windsor' as the Dean approached his death.

In any assessment of Gibbons's life and work, there must be an element of 'what might have been'. Tallis lived to the age of eighty, so did Byrd. What might Gibbons have achieved had he not died so suddenly at the age forty-one? In his keyboard music and his fantasias, he was an innovator whose music suggested new possibilities which he did not live long enough to realise. In his church music, he was a developer rather than an innovator; he did what previous generations had done: he drew on the tradition in which he had been educated and modified it in the time-honoured, English, evolutionary manner. And there is no doubt that Gibbons's contribution, particularly his championing of the verse anthem, strengthened the Anglican tradition – which, even by the time of his death, had been in existence for little more than sixty years. He was Byrd's natural successor, but there was no one to succeed him, and with his death the tradition stalled. This may have been because he died relatively young, before he had had time to pass his knowledge on to the next generation. It may simply have been a question of the talent available. But his death came at a time when continuity in any form would have been valuable: at the beginning of a reign that would see Queen Elizabeth's now sixty-year-old religious settlement challenged, relations between the King, the Church, and Parliament thrown into disarray, and, as part of the chaos that ensued, some fundamental questioning of the role of music both in religion and in society.

28 Thomas Tomkins, and Church Music

If longevity were a factor, Thomas Tomkins would have been the man to carry the musical torch forward. Born in 1572, eleven years before Gibbons, he survived him by thirty-one years. He not only bridged the Elizabethan and Jacobean periods, but survived to see the beheading of Charles I and the installation of Oliver Cromwell as Lord Protector, dying in 1656 at the age of eighty-four. Yet he never attained the musical stature of Byrd or Gibbons.

Like Gibbons, Tomkins came from an intensely musical family. His father, also named Thomas, moved from Lostwithiel in Cornwall in 1565 to take up the position of organist and vicar-choral at St David's Cathedral in Pembrokeshire. He married twice, had a significant number of sons – many of whom showed musical talent – and complicated matters by naming two of them Thomas. The elder Thomas was briefly a vicar within the patronage of St David's, but was dismissed for misconduct, ran away to sea, enlisting on the gallant ship *Revenge* under Sir Richard Grenville, and was killed in action. Giles Tomkins (?1588–1668) was organist of King's Chapel, Cambridge, organist of Salisbury Cathedral, Musician in Ordinary for voices and virginals at the court of Charles I, and organist of the Chapel Royal. John Tomkins (1589–1638) was also organist of King's Chapel, Cambridge, before becoming organist at St Paul's Cathedral, and eventually a Gentleman and Organist of the Chapel Royal (a position he appears to have shared with his brother). Robert Tomkins (dates uncertain) also became Musician in Ordinary to Charles I and made a brief reappearance under Charles II following the Restoration. And the family continued to produce musicians throughout the seventeenth century.

The younger of the two sons named Thomas, with whom we are concerned here, was born in Pembroke and was proud of his Welsh birth. Details of his early life are sparse, but at an early stage he seems to have been a pupil of Byrd – perhaps as a chorister at the Chapel Royal – and to have become friendly with Thomas Morley, who would later publish one of his madrigals, 'Fauns and Satyrs Tripping', in *The Triumphs of Oriana*. By 1596, at the age of twenty-four, Tomkins was appointed organist at Worcester Cathedral and he maintained his association with the city and the cathedral for the rest of his life. The next year, following the accepted practice the age, he married the widow of his predecessor. They had a son, Nathaniel, born in 1599, who also became a respected Worcester musician. Somewhere around 1602 or 1603, Tomkins was appointed Gentleman Extraordinary of the Chapel Royal. Although this represented a degree of recognition, it was an honorary post and his centre of gravity remained firmly in Worcester where, in 1612, he supervised the construction and installation of a new organ by Thomas Dallam, the leading organ-builder of the day, whom we shall meet again shortly. It was not until 1620 that Tomkins became a full member of the Chapel Royal. The following year, he was appointed organist, sharing the post with Gibbons. Even then, he did not abandon Worcester for London, but split his time between the two.

The mid–1620s were the high point of Tomkins's career. It is probable that he was among the members of the Chapel Royal who were at Canterbury when Gibbons died. Certainly, Gibbons's death seems to have given his career a significant boost. Charles I's Coronation was delayed for a year because of plague in London, but when it took place, in Westminster Abbey in February 1626, almost all the music was composed by Tomkins, for which he received the sum of twenty-five shillings. Yet in 1628, when the position of Composer of His Majesty's Music fell vacant on the death of Alfonso Ferrabosco the Younger, it went not to Tomkins, but to Ferrabosco's son, Henry, who is not known to have been a composer at all. This was a major disappointment and there is some evidence that Tomkins spent more time in Worcester as a result, although he continued to carry out his duties at the Chapel Royal until 1639. By then in his late sixties, he retired from most of his public duties, but he continued to live in Worcester, close by the cathedral, and he continued to compose.

Tomkins was a prolific composer, leaving a large body of liturgical music, more anthems than any other seventeenth-century composer, a substantial body of work for consort, for organ and for virginals, and the single volume of madrigals, *Songs of 3, 4, 5 and 6 parts*, which was mentioned earlier. The risk in making any overall assessment of his work is to damn with faint praise. If, in terms of church music, Gibbons was a developer rather than an innovator, Tomkins was a disciple. Byrd was his teacher and to Byrd's teaching he remained faithful for the whole of his composing life. This is not to deny him any originality or to devalue his work – Tomkins was a highly talented composer – but rather to explain why his work so often sounds as if it belongs to a somewhat earlier period. It does seem to have been Tomkins's fate to have always been composing at the end of things. His collection of madrigals was the last of any significance to be published; his many compositions for virginals came at the end of the great English virginals tradition, just as the instrument's popularity was giving way to that of the harpsichord. Hence, one supposes, the epithet 'the last Elizabethan' which has often, and not always fairly, been applied to both the man and his work.[1] There is, of course, an element of hindsight and historical accident here. Had the established order of Church and State not broken down, had the Civil Wars not occurred, English music might have taken a different direction and Tomkins might have been seen in a different light. As it is, his huge body of work is poised awkwardly between the emerging and evolving Anglican tradition in which he himself was educated, and its near destruction during the Civil Wars which he witnessed in old age.

Tomkins is known principally for his church music, most of which was collected in a volume called *Musica Deo Sacra* and published by his son, Nathaniel, in 1668, by which time Charles II had restored the Church of England to something approaching its former state. The characteristics that immediately stand out are his fondness for old-fashioned polyphony and an immense skill, almost comparable with that of his teacher, Byrd, in contrapuntal technique. Tomkins wrote five complete settings of the Anglican Service. The Third or *Great Service* is the best known. Like Byrd's *Great Service* – which was clearly its inspiration – it is written in ten parts. There are also certain similarities in the scoring, though most of the time Tomkins uses the voices in a different way. The entry of the full choir in the *Te Deum* and the rich polyphony of the *Magnificat* show Tomkins at his best – throughout his work it does seem that many of his most effective and moving passages are written for full choir – but compared with Byrd's masterpiece, Tomkins's *Great Service* lacks fire. The *Magnificat* from the Fifth Service also deserves a mention for its beautifully structured contrast between solo bass voice and melodic passages of choral polyphony. And, like another of Tomkins's most moving pieces, the setting of the *Funeral Sentences* from the 1606 *Book of Common Prayer*, it provides a lesson in careful and sensitive word-setting.

Tomkins wrote more than a hundred anthems. Given the number, it is hardly surprising that they vary in both style and quality. *Be strong and of a good courage*, written for the Coronation of James I in 1603, is a celebratory piece with a full, uplifting polyphonic sound which looks back towards Tallis rather than Byrd. *When David heard that Absalom was slain* is more dramatic, with dissonance giving way to harmony as a way of paralleling and illustrating David's move to understanding and acceptance of his situation. The eight-part anthem *O God, the proud are risen against me* is one of his finest pieces. It is characteristic in that it takes an earlier age as its starting point and also in the way Tomkins uses the strength of the full choir to create a huge, polyphonic wall of sound. However, there are occasions when his work seems to anticipate the later sound world of Purcell and the Baroque – for example, in the concluding passages of the anthem *Almighty God, the fountain of all wisdom,* or in the remarkable *O Woe is me,* a six-part anthem which mixes contrapuntal treatment of long, sustained lines with brief bursts of repeated motif-like melodies and sharp dissonances.

Tompkins is far from forgotten. He wrote some beautiful music and some of it, quite justly, remains within the Anglican canon, yet he cannot be regarded as a composer of the calibre of Byrd or Gibbons. His work still divides critical opinion, some extolling his achievements, others damning him for being insufficiently progressive. In the end, one is left with the feeling that technical accomplishment triumphs over inspiration; that he is at his best when writing what was expected of him, demonstrating his technical abilities within a familiar framework. This musical conservatism may reflect the fact that most of his career was spent in Worcester rather than London: he was approaching fifty by the time he was appointed a full member of the Chapel Royal. Or it may be that be was simply comfortable with the older aspects of the tradition in which he was writing. It is worth remembering that he was thirteen when Tallis died, and over fifty when Byrd passed away: it would have been natural for him to seek inspiration in the works of those who were the leading composers during his formative years. Perhaps he was simply pleasing himself, writing what he liked rather than what was fashionable.[2]

The trouble with Tomkins is that it is hard to get a sense of the man. His life, like his music, seems to have lacked a sense of adventure, of risk – at least when compared to some of his contemporaries. John Bull, whom we have already met as composer of the popular *Star Anthem*, was undoubtedly a more controversial figure. Some ten years younger than Tomkins, Bull also had a provincial background. He seems to have been born in or near Hereford – perhaps in Radnorshire across the Welsh border. In 1573, he is recorded as being a member of the Hereford Cathedral choir, but was soon whisked off to London as one of the Children of the Chapel Royal, returning to Hereford as organist in 1582. To begin with, his career followed the classic pattern: a degree from Oxford in 1586; appointment as a Gentleman of the Chapel Royal in the same year; appointment as Organist of the Chapel Royal in 1591 (on the death of John Blitheman, who had succeeded Tallis); a doctorate from Oxford in 1592. Then, in 1597, Bull was appointed as the first Professor of Music at the newly opened Gresham College in London's Bishopsgate (on the site now occupied by the immense

National Westminster Tower). Finding the rooms in which he expected to live still occupied and the occupant unwilling to move, rather than break down the door, he employed a stonemason to break a hole in the wall. His excuse was that if he had not formally occupied the room on the day of his appointment, he would have been in breach of the terms of his employment and his job would have been at risk. Naturally enough, this landed him in trouble. In 1601, he departed for the Continent and stayed abroad for eighteen months. Such trips were far from uncommon among musicians of the period and Bull claimed that he was going because of his health, but, apart from Brussels, it is not known where he spent his time and there have been persistent suggestions that he was acting as some kind of intelligence agent for Queen Elizabeth.

Bull returned not long before the old Queen's death, and, with the new reign, rapidly established himself in court circles as a highly regarded composer and performer of keyboard music. But he was in trouble again in 1607, when he got a young woman by the name of Elizabeth Walter pregnant and was dismissed from his post at Gresham College as a consequence. He married the girl and they had a daughter, but the College did not permit its professors to marry, so he had no chance of being reinstated. His Chapel Royal appointments, his popularity as a performer, and the favour of King James seem to have sustained him, and in 1611 he entered the service of Prince Henry at an annual salary of £40. The following year he was appointed music teacher to Princess Elizabeth, for whose marriage in 1613 – the same marriage celebrated by the publication of *Parthenia*, which included a number of Bull's compositions – he composed an anthem, *God the Father, God the Son*. But he was soon in trouble again. This time it was more serious, so he fled to Brussels, where he claimed religious asylum, although there is absolutely no evidence that he was ever a Catholic. The truth, at least according to William Trumbull, the senior British representative at the court of Archduke Albert VII, ruler of the Netherlands, was that Bull 'did in that dishonest manner steal out of England … to escape the punishment, which notoriously he had deserved … for his incontinence, fornication, adultery, and other grievous crimes.'[3] The Archbishop of Canterbury was particularly outraged: it is impossible to resist repeating his much-quoted remark that Bull 'hath more music than honesty and is as famous for marring of virginity as he is for fingering of organs and virginals.'[4] Nevertheless, the Archduke gave Bull work as an organist and he remained in Brussels until 1617, when he moved to Antwerp, working as organist at the cathedral there and living in a state often bordering on poverty until his death in 1628.

Unlike Tomkins, Bull did not have a devoted son to collect and publish his work. The seven pieces which appeared in *Parthenia* were the only works to be published in his lifetime. As one would expect from a musician of his stature and in his position, Bull composed choral music for religious and for state occasions, but much of what he wrote appears to have been lost or destroyed following his flight to Brussels. Today, he is best known for his instrumental compositions, largely because nearly forty such pieces survive in the *Fitzwilliam Virginal Book*. These range in mood from the thirty short variations on the tune *Walsingham*, and arrangements of tunes from his church music, to lighter works, such as *The Kynge's Hunt*, various jigs and dance tunes. Like the man himself, Bull's music has an extrovert quality; it is robust, exuberant and somewhat uneven. It is technically accomplished and often requires a skilled musician to do it justice, but it does not achieve the level of melodic invention and the sense of control that one finds in Byrd or Gibbons. Even in exile, however, Bull continued to be well regarded. He became friendly with Sweelinck, certainly the most influential keyboard composer on the Continent at the time. Sweelinck included one of Bull's many canons in his manuscript setting out his rules for composition. Perhaps in gratitude, after Sweelinck's death in 1621, Bull wrote a fantasia on one of Sweelinck's fugues.

The troubled and troublesome Thomas Weelkes was another composer who was at his most active during the reign of James I. He published his four volumes of madrigals very quickly between 1597 and 1600. A fifth, characteristically boisterous collection, *Ayres or Phantasticke Spirites*, followed in 1608, but, in fact, after 1600, he appears to have concentrated on religious music. He wrote no fewer than ten full settings of the Anglican Service. None has survived wholly intact, but musicologists have been able to reconstruct at least three complete settings and enough of the remaining works to demonstrate that he was a gifted composer of church music. He also wrote some forty anthems. Of the verse anthems, *If King Manasses* is particularly interesting in that it shows Weelkes employing madrigalian techniques in a religious context, and managing to be both reflective and restless at the same time. But it is the full anthems that are more memorable. *Hosanna to the Son of David; When David heard; All people clap your hands,* and *Alleluia, I heard a voice* all contain some wonderfully rich choral writing and were clearly intended for big choirs.

During the early decades of the seventeenth century, England's provincial cathedrals were home to a number of interesting and talented composers who did not become part of the court circle – either out of choice or because they were not invited. Weelkes may have wanted a position in the Chapel Royal – and his verse anthem *O Lord, how joyful is the King*, produced in thanksgiving for King James's deliverance from the Gunpowder Plot in 1605, suggests he was not above flattering his way in – but his reputation was against him and he remained at Chichester. Tompkins, as we have seen, achieved some success as a court musician, but his centre of gravity was always Worcester. And there are many others, most of them cathedral organists, who wrote organ pieces, anthems and settings of the Anglican Service for use in their own cathedrals. John Amner (1579–1641) spent most of his life in Ely, where he was organist at the cathedral for thirty years from 1610 until his death. He composed at least three settings of the Service, settings of the Preces and of the psalms, and a large number of anthems, twenty-six of which were published as *Sacred Hymns of 3, 4, 5, and 6 Parts* in 1615. Conservative in his approach – in much the same way as Tomkins – Amner was undoubtedly talented: *Come, let's rejoice* is a particularly cheerful and melodic piece, and *Hear, O Lord* contains a highly effective duet for treble voices. Elway Bevin (*c.*1554–1639) is traditionally held to have been a pupil of Tallis, though there is no documentary evidence to support the claim. He spent most of his life as organist and Master of Choristers at Bristol Cathedral and is known to have composed at least three services and a number of anthems. His reputation today rests on his output of canons, most of which are preserved in his theoretical work, *A Brief and Short Introduction to the Art of Musicke*, published in 1631. Matthew Jeffreys (dates uncertain) was vicar-choral at Wells Cathedral. Three of his services, seven full anthems and five verse anthems survive – although we have no way of knowing how much more may have been lost – and the full anthems, such as *Rejoice in the Lord*, show him to have been both technically competent and imaginative. Francis Pilkington, Precentor of Chester Cathedral, and Thomas Bateson, organist at Chester then in Dublin, have both been noted as composers of madrigals, but they both also wrote anthems and partial or complete settings of the Service. So, too, did Robert Ramsay at Canterbury and John Heath at Rochester.

John Holmes (?–1629) was organist at Winchester Cathedral and later Master of Choristers at Salisbury. As well as madrigals (one of which was featured in *The Triumphs of Oriana*), he wrote anthems, settings of the psalms, the canticles and other parts of the Service, many of them for the organ. Holmes's main claim to fame, however, is that he was the teacher of Adrian Batten (1591–1637). Batten was the son of a joiner from Salisbury. He probably studied under Holmes at Winchester before moving to London as vicar-choral at Westminster Abbey in 1614. He stayed there until somewhere around 1626 when he became vicar-choral and organist (sharing the position with John Tomkins) at St Paul's Cathedral. Batten was a prolific composer – as many as sixteen services and nearly seventy anthems – but, while anthems such as *O Sing joyfully* and *O Praise the Lord* do have an attractive, buoyant quality, his music is not often sung or recorded these days. His importance today lies in the fact that, at his death, he left a manuscript – four hundred and ninety-eight quarto leaves, which he had copied over the course of some twenty years. He may well have begun it when he arrived in Westminster, for we know that he used to copy music to earn a little extra money. Whatever its origins, 'The Batten Organ Book', as it has become known, is a unique document: the single most extensive source of Anglican anthems and services from the pre-Restoration period.[5] Very little of the church music of this period, especially that written outside London, was ever published; and much of it was either destroyed during the Civil Wars or simply lost over the course of time. Even though, in the manner of the day, Batten's manuscript is a collection of sketches and outlines rather than full scores, it is invaluable as the only known source for many of the services and anthems of the period.[6] Another curiosity of the manuscript is that it shows Batten as one of the first to make consistent use of bar-lines in his scores.

That this was such a rich period for English church music is in large measure due to the fact that Queen Elizabeth's religious settlement had worked and endured. All the composers we have been considering here were born and had their educational and musical roots in her reign. When James came to the throne in 1603, his policy was to support the Church of England as he found it – its bishops, its hierarchy and its institutions – as a way of strengthening his own position in his new kingdom. In musical terms, this meant a magnificent coronation with music by Byrd and Tomkins. It meant not simply the continuation of Elizabeth's Chapel Royal, but money spent to strengthen and expand it, to find and recruit the best new talent in the country. Thus the signal went out to cathedrals and churches up and down the land that the musical life of the Church of

England could and should continue as before – and so it did, or seemed to, for most of James's reign. As time went on, however, cracks began to appear in the political and religious framework that made such continuity possible.

29 King James, King Charles, and Archbishop Laud

By the end of his reign, James I was employing at least one hundred and thirty musicians at court, more than four times the number employed at the end of Elizabeth's reign. If this expansion was driven more by the King's longing for personal and political prestige rather than a deep-seated love of music, it is unlikely that the musicians complained. They were part of something special. Taken together, the members of the Chapel Royal, the musicians of the King's Private Musick, the instrumentalists and composers in the King's pay, the writers of preludes and interludes, songs and dances for the court's masques, represented a formidable and – in the British Isles at least – unprecedented concentration of musical talent.

In the English provinces, while the aristocracy and the gentry may have taken an interest in recreational music, professional musicians were, as we have seen, mainly employed in the cathedrals and major churches. In the other parts of James's newly united kingdom, musical life was developing slowly. Dublin was just beginning to develop a modest reputation as a musical city; Thomas Bateson was active at Christ Church Cathedral. As noted earlier, apart from his madrigals, he is known to have written a number of anthems, although only one survives: *Holy, Lord God Almighty,* which is thought to have been written in 1612 when he received a degree in music from Trinity College. Bateson was followed by Randall (sometimes Randolph) Jewitt (1603–75) and Benjamin Rogers (1614–98), who ensured a high standard of music in the Cathedral until services were suspended under the Commonwealth in 1647. Outside Dublin, what Londoners would have regarded as musical life centred on some of the larger churches and the houses of the Anglo-Irish aristocracy. Elsewhere, the native folk tradition remained dominant. Indeed, it was probably strengthened by continuing hostility on the part of King James and Parliament to the Catholic population in general – this was the period when there were numerous Protestant plantations in Ulster and elsewhere – and to bards in particular, who were regularly proscribed and threatened with execution. One of the most famous Irish musicians of the period, the blind harper, Rory Dall O'Cahan (Ruaidri Dáll Ó Catháin), seems to have spent much of his life in Scotland, perhaps fleeing persecution. O'Cahan is supposed to have visited King James in Scotland before James's accession to the English throne, and may well have died there sometime during the 1640s. He is popularly credited with writing the 'Londonderry Air' (better known today as 'Danny Boy') and another well-known tune, 'Give Me Your Hand.'

In Scotland, James sought to restrict Presbyterian influence and reintroduce bishops, but the kind of church music that he encouraged in England, and which had become an accepted and integral part of the Anglican Church, was rarely heard. When he visited Scotland in 1617, James had to take with him both the music (by Gibbons and others) and the musicians to play it. Otherwise, metrical psalms were the limit of religious music for the majority of the population. The Scottish Chapel Royal lived a shadowy, often notional existence. Song schools continued to exist in the larger cities – notably in Glasgow, Aberdeen and Stirling – but they faced financial difficulties and bouts of hostility from the Presbyterian Church, and their connection with public worship, which had been their original *raison d'être*, was effectively severed. Of course, ayres and madrigals, pavans and galliards from England, France and Italy were performed and enjoyed, particularly among the aristocracy and the middle and merchant classes (a larger and more influential part of the population in Scotland than in Ireland). But with the court of James VI no longer there to act as a focal point, Scottish musicians were left without patronage, without employment, and without any shared sense of direction. As a result, music in Scotland during the seventeenth century became the province of gifted amateurs and enthusiastic collectors.

One positive aspect of this was the emergence of interest in Scotland's own musical tradition. This seems to have come about as part of the slow questioning process that came over Scottish cultural life with the removal of James's court to London. As such, it was a wholly different phenomenon from Thomas Ravenscroft's discovery of the English folk tradition, which was an assertion of identity born of confidence. It was different also from the same process in Ireland, where the impulse was less scholarly and more political. A number of Scottish manuscript anthologies have come down to us, some containing art music, some containing folk music, and some a mixture of both.[1] A key figure was Sir William Mure of Rowallan in Ayrshire (1594–1657). Like his uncle, Alexander Montgomerie (already mentioned on p.74), Mure seems to have been essentially a poet and lyricist, but he also owned and added to two important musical manuscripts. The first, which is dated 1615 but was almost certainly compiled over a number of years prior to that, contains some fifty dance, ayre and song tunes. There are no words and all the tunes are arranged for the lute, which Mure himself played, mixing pieces apparently suitable for polite society (although not, of course, the court which was in distant London) with others which have a more rustic quality. Some of the dance tunes – such as 'Katherine Bairdie' and 'The Battle of Harlaw' – are still current among Scottish folk musicians. Although not all the pieces are of Scottish origin, and although many of them are mere fragments, this was the first collection of its type. Then, about 1620, Sir William Skene of Hallyards in Fife made a collection of over a hundred pieces, including many Scottish airs and dances, all arranged for the mandora (a small, treble lute). Collecting and arranging Scottish tunes in this way did not preclude an interest in the outside world. Mure's second manuscript, perhaps dating from the 1630s, is a single surviving part-book from a set which may have numbered five or six. It contains the *cantus* or upper line from a collection of part-songs. Again there are no words – except in one case – but the tunes are drawn from Scotland, England (including some by Morley, Weelkes and Wilbye), from France and, in one or two cases, perhaps from Italy.

Meanwhile, musical life at James I's court and in London generally was characterised by its confidence. The King was generous – or profligate, depending on your point of view – in his spending on all aspects of court life. In less than ten years on the throne, he came close to doubling Elizabeth I's peacetime expenditure. In terms of music, James's wish to bask in the reflected glory of the musical community he had created was supplemented by genuine musical interest on the part of his sons. Prince Henry, who fancied himself something of a Renaissance prince, encouraged the formation of mixed ensembles. We have seen how a varied or *ad hoc* mix of instruments was recognised as an 'English' or 'broken' consort. Prince Henry's interest, probably sparked by knowledge of what was happening in France and Italy, seems to have been in larger bands. The idea of violins, viols, flutes, flutes, trumpets, horns, early trombones, even organs, all playing together was something novel; and it was, of course, a step along the way towards the modern orchestra. When Prince Henry died of typhoid, an event much lamented by the musical community and the occasion for compositions by Byrd and Tomkins, Prince Charles took over his brother's musical establishment. He was himself a competent performer on the viol, having been taught by the younger Alfonso Ferrabosco. As King, he continued his father's strategy of promoting religious music to support the Church of England and masques to flatter and entertain the court. One of his first acts on becoming King was to recognise the importance of music at court and create the post of Master of the King's Musick (which endures to this day) for Nicholas Lanier. Nonetheless, his personal preference was for music that did not depend on public participation – works which, in David Starkey's words, were 'intimate, private, sober and subtle, much like Charles himself.'[2]

In fact, Charles's belief in the value of music in supporting religious and royal ceremonial was even greater than his father's. His Coronation in 1626 was a huge affair, lasting five hours with an extensive musical accompaniment, most of it – as we have seen – composed by Thomas Tomkins. Many of the texts chosen for the occasion were intended to glorify Charles and the concept of kingship as well as God. These included not only the first appearance of *I was glad* at a coronation (set by different composers over the years, it has maintained its place ever since), but another of Tomkins's anthems which Charles would no doubt have found apposite:

> Behold, O God our defender, and look upon the face of Thine anointed.
> Great prosperity givest Thou unto Thy king
> And will show loving kindness unto Thine anointed for evermore.

King James had had firm beliefs on the issue of the divine right of kings, but his Scottish upbringing, during which his right to rule was challenged by both the Scottish Church and the Scottish aristocracy, and his wish to consolidate his position on the English throne, had led him to temper their expression. Charles had no such inhibitions. He had been brought up in a court which revolved around the figure of his father. He firmly believed that he owed his throne to God and to God alone; and that it was his duty to employ his own aesthetic sense and the artistic resources of his kingdom in celebration of that fact. Under his guidance, the arts were thus to serve both a political and a religious purpose. Charles was a perfectionist: he wanted the best and believed that money, pressure and persistence could obtain it. He was also absolutely convinced of the rightness of his own judgement. These were qualities that made him an ideal patron of music and the arts. Unfortunately, the same qualities made him a disastrous king.

The man who gave expression to Charles's beliefs within the Church of

England was William Laud. In 1626, the year after Charles's accession, Laud became both Bishop of Bath and Wells and Dean of the Chapel Royal. The fabric of the Chapel did not need renovating – it had benefitted from the attention of successive monarchs and was probably the most richly decorated place of worship in the country – so Laud began by smartening up its Gentlemen, forbidding them to wear cloaks, boots or spurs during services. He also instituted a more ritualistic, theatrical form of worship: kneeling, bowing to the altar, turning to the east, kissing the altar cloth. And as Laud rapidly climbed the ecclesiastical ladder – Bishop of London in 1628, Archbishop of Canterbury in 1633 – so he first encouraged and then ordered the adoption of what we would now call High Church practices. Cathedrals and churches across the country replaced their communion tables with richly decorated altars and began to restore or replace stained glass windows which had been damaged or destroyed during the Reformation. Ministers began to call themselves priests and wear beautiful vestments. Services were conducted in a blaze of candlelight and to the rich smell of incense. The key phrase was 'the beauty of holiness,' which both Charles and Laud believed should resonate through all aspects of Christian worship. Neither of them were Catholics – Charles was the first monarch to be born and brought up in the Church of England – but they sought 'to conjure up all the splendour, solemnity and sacred mysteries of the medieval Catholic rite, while still maintaining Protestant doctrine.'[3] And a key component of this conjuring was, of course, music.

Tomkins's rich, nostalgic, polyphonic works were ideal for Laud's purpose and, while the dating is not conclusive, it seems that a number of Tomkins's more elaborate, multi-part works may well have been composed during the period of Laud's ascendancy. Two other composers contributed to the Anglican repertory at this time: the Lawes brothers, Henry (1596–1662) and William (1602–45). The sons of a vicar-choral at Salisbury Cathedral, they studied under John Coprario, and gained places at court once Charles, with whom they seem to have had a close relationship, became King. Both of them are better known these days for their secular works. Henry was a friend of John Milton and composed the music for Milton's masque, *Comus*, which was performed at Ludlow castle in 1634. He was also a prolific composer of songs – well over four hundred survive – the best known of them a setting of Edmund Waller's poem, *Go, lovely rose*. William is recognised as the composer of some quite remarkable suites for consort of viols or for viols and organ. He also wrote a famous setting of Robert Herrick's *Gather ye rosebuds*. In their own time, however, both brothers would also have been recognised as composers of choral music for the Church. Henry wrote some fifty anthems, mainly three-part settings of the psalms, which were popular in their day and sung regularly in the Chapel Royal. William composed forty anthems, many of them in the same format as Henry's, but also including the unusual *Let God arise* which is written for bass solo and organ, with a soprano, alto, tenor and bass chorus. We know that some of William's anthems were used by the King for his own private worship, which suggests that the choral style adopted by the brothers – simple but not sparse, harmonised but without complex counterpoint – was consistent with the conception of music in worship favoured by Charles and Laud.

Laud's need, however, was not so much for new compositions as for a method of disseminating his and the King's preferred form of worship across the kingdom. Music was a part of this, but the process was not easy for several reasons. The Elizabethan religious settlement had allowed for music to accompany Church of England services. It had even encouraged the use of music, but it had not insisted: Elizabeth was too wise to demand uniformity. The result was that there were many places up and down the land – often, but not always, the cathedrals and the collegiate churches – where full choral services were the norm. But there was an equal number of places which had never replaced the organs that had been removed or destroyed during the Reformation, and where anything beyond the chanting of metrical psalms was viewed with suspicion. And there was another issue. The big religious institutions received a substantial part of their income from central government. Elizabeth had been notoriously parsimonious and extremely reluctant to grant any increase in the subsidies. Nor did James I do anything to ease the financial pressure. He spent money freely, but he spent it in London. So the musical world became increasingly centred on the capital. A talented musician might stand a better chance of gaining royal patronage under James than under Elizabeth, but he would have to go to London to get it. As a consequence, musical standards in many provincial cathedrals and churches had slumped. In 1623, John Bridgeman, Bishop of Chester, found attendance at services in his own cathedral so poor that he instituted a fine of tuppence for canons, clerks, organist and choristers who missed a service. The organist was also formally admonished for not carrying out his teaching duties and threatened with dismissal if he did not mend his ways. When Giles Tomkins took up his post as organist at Salisbury Cathedral in 1629, he found that there were no choristers for him to teach. In 1634, Robert Neile, the Archbishop of York – a close ally of Laud – found services in Chester Cathedral still disorganised. The *Te Deum*, *Benedictus*, and *Magnificat* were rarely heard in any of the churches of the diocese, and Manchester Cathedral and All Saints' Church in Wigan appeared to have no choirs at all.

Laud instituted a programme of organ-building across the country, many of them – and certainly the finest of them – being built by the Dallam family. Thomas Dallam, the father of what became an organ-building dynasty that lasted well into the eighteenth century, migrated from his native Lancashire to London as a young man and was almost certainly apprenticed to an organ builder, although the only certain record we have of him is as a liveryman in the Blacksmiths' Company. In 1598, the complexities of European politics led Queen Elizabeth to send a present to the Turkish Sultan, Mehmet III. He was known to be fond of music so she decided upon an organ – a massive, elaborately constructed, ornate affair featuring a chiming clock, bejewelled mechanical figures that moved with the music, and a clockwork mechanism that allowed the organ to play by itself for six hours. Dallam, aged just twenty-four, was selected to lead a small team of craftsmen on the eventful six-month sea voyage to Constantinople where they assembled and demonstrated the Sultan's present. The mission was a huge success, resulting in the Sultan offering Dallam a job and two virgins (all of which he declined) as well as granting England important trading privileges.

Back home from his adventure, Dallam gradually established his reputation, building new organs for King's College, Cambridge, in 1606, for Worcester Cathedral in 1613, and for Wells Cathedral and Wakefield Parish Church in 1620. It became a family concern sometime during the 1620s when Thomas's son Robert began to work alongside his father. Thomas then either retired or died somewhere around 1630, and Robert and his sons continued the business. It was under Charles I and Laud that the family truly made its name and became acknowledged as England's leading organ builders. Dallam organs commissioned during Charles's reign included the Chapel of Whitehall Palace (1628); Bristol Cathedral (1630); Jesus College, Cambridge (1634); York Minster (1634); St John's College, Cambridge (1635); St Asaph Cathedral (1635), Manchester Parish Church (1635); Magdalen College, Oxford (1637); and Gloucester Cathedral (1641). It is an impressive list and no doubt these and other new instruments built during the period earned the gratitude of organists up and down the country – but they provoked a negative reaction, too.

Laud's programme of organ-building was accompanied by a drive to improve the quality of church music, the appearance of the choir, the decor of the church, the conduct of services, which all contributed to 'the beauty of holiness'. He conveyed his concerns and his wishes to the bishops who, in turn, passed them on down the Church of England hierarchy and out into the parishes. The Puritan wing of the church was predictably outraged. They objected to music as part of church services in general and to organs in particular. They saw the return of music and of ritual as the beginning of an attempt to reintroduce Catholicism. Their suspicions can only have been strengthened by the fact that the Dallams were known to be a Catholic family, and that Robert Dallam was known to have played the organ for Charles's Catholic Queen, Henrietta Maria. Nor did it help that full choral Masses were sung in Durham and Exeter cathedrals, and possibly also in Worcester. Yet it was not just the message, it was the messenger. The Puritans not only disliked receiving orders from bishops, whose authority they disputed; many of them also disputed the right of the King to tell them how to worship. Charles, confirmed in the belief that he ruled by divine authority, and considerably less wise than Elizabeth, sought to impose uniformity of worship through his kingdom. And thus the battle lines were drawn.

In 1629, just four years after his accession, Charles dissolved Parliament and embarked on an eleven-year period of personal rule. This concentrated political power ever more firmly on the court and the figure of the monarch, and had a similar effect on cultural and musical life, strengthening the centralising tendency which had been evident under James I. During those eleven years, at a time when he was finding new and unusual ways of financing his government, Charles staged no less than eleven expensive and elaborate masques. Madrigals were still widely sung and enjoyed, although the height of the madrigal boom was long past. Ayres and lute songs were still heard also, but Campion and Dowland were dead and the songs and ayres that featured in court masques were of a different quality. Charles did not economise either on the Chapel Royal or on his court musicians. In the circle around the King, there was a particular emphasis on instrumental music – on fantasias and suites written for consorts of varying kinds. There was even a revival of the *In Nomine* form which had been popular in Elizabethan times. This was not the song and dance music that had appealed to James I. This was art music. It required concentration and an educated ear. As such, it reflected Charles's personal taste. It was also music that heightened the sense that, with its exclusive tastes and privileged insiders, the court was out of touch with the rest of the country.

Many of the musicians around Charles had served his father, but a number of new faces appeared. The Lawes brothers have already been mentioned. William seems to have been particularly close to the King. His suites of instrumental music were undoubtedly popular in their day, but later fell into neglect due to their equally undoubted oddity. Whether Lawes was a fearless experimenter, or simply bored and playing around to achieve new effects, or flouting all the musical rules as part of some kind of in-joke among court musicians, we cannot know; but these eccentric, restless works, full of dissonant effects and odd structural juxtapositions, have been rediscovered and become justly popular in recent years. The lute player and composer, John Wilson (1595–1674) made his entry into court circles at this time. So, too, did John Jenkins (1592–1678), a virtuoso on the lyra or small bass viol and a prolific composer of instrumental suites. Both were among the King's favourite musicians. Davis Mell (1604–62) also deserves a mention as one of the first violinists to achieve recognition as a virtuoso performer in court circles. He was a noted composer of instrumental music – as well as a clockmaker, the trade to which he had been apprenticed as a boy. Following the death of his father Orlando, Christopher Gibbons (1615–76) had gone to live with his uncle Edward, who was Master of Choristers at Exeter Cathedral, but he returned to the Chapel Royal in the 1630s before departing a few years later to become organist at Winchester. These were talented musicians, many of whom would return to fulfil their musical promise and important roles at court in the years after the Restoration, but they were not as gifted as the generation of Orlando Gibbons, Campion, Dowland, Weelkes, and Wilbye which preceded them.

It was not only England that perceived Charles as remote and out of touch. In Scotland, the feeling was stronger. Although born there, he had neither sympathy for nor understanding of the country and its people. In 1633, he travelled north for his Scottish Coronation, but insisted that the ceremony should be conducted according to the Anglican rite with full musical accompaniment – and to ensure that the music would be performed to the appropriate standard, he brought much of the English

Chapel Royal with him. This created offence all round. Four years later, he ordered the Scottish church, the Kirk, to use a new prayer book, closely modelled on the English *Book of Common Prayer*. This would have caused outrage under any circumstances, but the fact that neither the Kirk itself nor the Scottish Parliament had been consulted made things worse. There was rioting in the streets of Edinburgh. Offence became organised opposition and the long, slow slide into civil war began.

30 Civil War, Playford, and the Beginnings of Opera

Between 1640 and 1660 – that is, between Charles I being forced to recall Parliament and the Restoration of King Charles II – the musical life of the British Isles went through several different phases of turmoil. It suffered disruption, loss of life, and physical destruction; it faced prejudice, prohibition, and regulation. The damage was immense, yet during the Civil Wars (1642–49) music and musicians, as always, found ways to survive; and during the Commonwealth period (1649–60) they not only survived, but began to adapt in ways that were to have important implications for the future.

Most professional musicians sided with the King rather than with Parliament. The finest musicians in the country were concentrated in or around the court; others depended on the patronage of aristocratic families or rich, rural landowners; while cathedral organists, choirmasters, vicars-choral and a whole population of choristers and others derived their income from the established Church. For motives of self-interest, if for no other reason, it would have been natural for these groups to support the status quo and fall in behind the Royalist cause. Royalist armies marched to the fife and the drum, and it was normal for companies to have a trumpeter or a small band of three or four men playing hautbois and other wind instruments. Henry Cooke (*c.*1616–72), a Gentleman of the Chapel Royal, was among those who joined up on the Royalist side, reaching the rank of Captain, surviving the wars and becoming an important figure in the musical life of both Chapel Royal and the court under Charles II. Christopher Gibbons, no longer able to act as organist at Winchester Cathedral, was another who joined the Royalist ranks. He also survived and was later rewarded by Charles II for his loyalty. William Lawes was less lucky. He was appointed commissary, effectively an administrative post, in the King's Life Guards, but in 1645 during the Battle of Rowton Heath, as the King's cavalry sought to break the siege of Chester, he was killed by a stray bullet.

The status quo suffered badly from the moment hostilities began in 1642. By October of that year, following the Battle of Edge Hill, Charles was obliged to withdraw to Oxford, leaving London in the control of the Parliament. Oxford became the Royalist capital and the home of the court until Charles's surrender in 1646. In his *General History of Music*, published in four volumes between 1776 and 1789, the great historian of music, Charles Burney, says:

> Oxford, in the time of the Civil War, seems to have been the only place in the kingdom where musical sounds were allowed to be heard; for that city, during a considerable time, being the royal residence, not only the household musicians, but many performers, who had been driven from the cathedrals of the capital, as well as those of other parts of the kingdom, flocked thither as to a place of safety and subsistence.[1]

Burney is overstating the case here, but it is true that the King's need to create the illusion of normality helped Oxford become, for a time, the centre of the kingdom's musical life. Consorts of viols played fantasias. The much-reduced court danced. The university continued to function. John Wilson, one of those who had followed the King from London, was awarded a doctorate in music in March 1644, just a matter of weeks before the city was besieged. There was even a proposal to stage a masque. But it came to nothing.

Attitudes to music on the parliamentary side were more complex. The majority of Puritans were not hostile to all forms of music, but there was a common core of agreement that, apart from the singing of psalms, music in church should be prohibited, and there was a broader dislike of certain forms of public musical entertainment. Parliamentary armies certainly used music in the traditional manner to give heart to their men. Before the Battle of Leeds in January 1643, General Fairfax sent a trumpeter to demand the surrender of the town. At the same time, he ordered a minister to pray for victory and then to lead the troops in singing Psalm 68: 'May God arise, may his enemies be scattered / May his foes flee before him.'[2] In 1642, Parliament ordered the closure of all theatres, many of which, including Shakespeare's Globe, were subsequently demolished. Stage plays and the music that accompanied them were formally suppressed – and were to remain so for eighteen years. The same year also saw Parliament proscribe the celebration of festivals held to have heathen origins (such as May Day) and those held to be papistical in origin (such as Christmas). By 1644, choral services had effectively ceased. Choirs were disbanded and many musicians found themselves without work. There followed attempts to suppress ballad singers and musicians who played in public places, taverns or alehouses; while in many towns the Waits, who had played such a prominent role in municipal life under Elizabeth and James, were either disbanded or reduced to the role of watchmen. It was not a happy time.

The religious focus of the war is evident in the way that parliamentary forces, when they gained control of a city or town, vented their anger on the cathedral or the main church. Organs and even organists suffered badly. The organ in Canterbury Cathedral was played with such violence that it was damaged beyond use. In Worcester, the Dallam organ which Thomas Tomkins had played for thirty years was completely destroyed (and Tomkins himself, now over seventy, was forced to seek shelter when his house was hit by a cannon ball during the siege of the city). Organs were smashed right across the country, in Bristol, Carlisle, Chichester, Exeter, Peterborough, Romsey, Westminster and Wigan, and in hundreds of other cathedrals, abbeys and churches. A few cathedrals escaped: in St Paul's Cathedral, York Minister, Lincoln Cathedral, and some of the Oxford and Cambridge Colleges, the organ was silenced but not actually destroyed. And in Salisbury, it was dismantled and stored away until such time as it could safely be reassembled. Many collections of hymn books, service books, and musical manuscripts were also burned or destroyed. The Dallam family fled to Brittany where their craftsmanship and their Catholicism made them welcome. Arthur Phillips, organist at Bristol Cathedral, was another who fled the country, also to France, where he became organist to Queen Henrietta Maria. Others suffered a harder fate. Edward Gibbons, organist at Exeter, was thrown out of his home at the age of seventy-nine for having lent money to the King. William Child, organist at St George's Chapel in Windsor since 1630, became a farmer.

This was not a time for new music. Only Thomas Tomkins, by this time the grand old man of English music, seems to have used music to speak out against what was happening. He wrote a big, forceful, verse anthem setting the words of Psalm 79 in protest at the damage done to Worcester Cathedral (and to his own house):

O god, the heathen are come into thine inheritance
Thy holy temple have they defiled
And made of Jerusalem an heap of stones.

In 1647, looking back to the beheading of Archbishop Laud two years previously, Tomkins took an old-fashioned dance form and adapted it to become something approaching a lament. It was entitled simply *Pavan: Lord Canterbury*. And when King Charles was beheaded in 1649, he again used his art to make his opinion clear: this time with the slow, reflective *Sad Pavan: For These Distracted Times*. This was potentially dangerous stuff. Perhaps, in his late seventies, he felt he had nothing left to lose, though in fact he lived on for another seven years, dying on his country estate in the village of Martin Hussingtree, north of Worcester, in 1656.

John Jenkins, too, used his art to respond to the war, but in a different way. When the fighting began, he left London and was employed as a musician and music teacher by two Royalist families – the Derehams and the L'Estranges – in the largely Puritan county of Norfolk. With the loss of King's Lynn in 1643, Norfolk was effectively controlled by parliamentary forces, and both families were keenly interested in the fate of the strategically important Nottinghamshire town of Newark. For three weeks in March 1644 it was besieged by parliamentary forces until the King's nephew, Prince Rupert of the Rhine, swept down to relieve it. Jenkins wrote *The Newark Seige*, a suite consisting of a pavan and a galliard, each divided into two parts, which paints a picture of the siege, the bombardment of the town, Prince Rupert's arrival, his battle charge and victory. Programme music – the use of music to describe events or situations rather than emotions – was not an entirely new idea: Byrd had written a nine-part piece called *The Battell* which appears in *My Lady Nevell's Book*, but Jenkins's work is nonetheless an impressive, and highly specific, early example of the genre.

Charles I was beheaded on 30 January 1649. Just over a week later, Parliament formally abolished what he had regarded as a divine appointment but which they referred to as 'the office of king.' Oliver Cromwell became Lord Protector. Burney wrote that 'ten years of gloomy silence seem to have elapsed before a string was suffered to vibrate, or a pipe to breathe aloud.'[3] There certainly were Puritan elements within the parliamentary coalition which took extreme positions – even to the point of suggesting that all music was sinful and should be banned – but Burney was writing less than twenty years after the Restoration and was keen to blacken the reputation of the Commonwealth. The truth is more nuanced.

The structures of traditional musical education were all but obliterated. The members of the Chapel Royal were dispersed. The cathedral choirs were disbanded and the cathedral schools closed. No more young men were taught or trained. A generation of choristers who might have gone on to become organists and composers went missing. At the same time, there were composers and musicians who appear to have supported the Puritan cause – or at least bent sufficiently with the prevailing wind to receive official favour – and a certain amount of musical superstructure was maintained. John Wilson, who had followed the King to Oxford, became Professor of Music in 1656, his appointment formally approved by Cromwell. Benjamin Rogers was awarded a degree in music from Cambridge University on the direct instructions of Cromwell himself, and also granted a state pension. Charles Coleman (1605–64), a known anti-Royalist, was awarded a doctorate in music from Cambridge in 1651. Davis Mell became one of Cromwell's musicians; and John Hingeston (1612–83) was appointed State Organist. All these figures had had some form of official employment under Charles I, and all were received back into the official fold at the Restoration. Nonetheless, the overall situation was sufficiently serious for a group of well-known musicians – mainly from the broadly pro-Puritan ranks, but also including the definitely Royalist John Jenkins – to petition the Lord Protector for the establishment of a national school or college to maintain some level of musical education in England. Cromwell appears to have been sympathetic and the Council of State set up a committee, but nothing happened.

Cromwell's own attitude to music was inconsistent to the point of hypocrisy. Publicly, he supported the parliamentary and Puritan position, but privately his actions were much more liberal. Having taken over Hampton Court, to the west of London, as a weekend and holiday residence, he arranged for the Dallam organ from Magdalen College, Oxford, to be transported and reassembled there – where it was played by Hingeston and also, quite probably, by Cromwell's Secretary for Foreign Tongues, John Milton. Cromwell also employed his own personal musicians – seven instrumentalists and two boy singers, in addition to Hingeston as organist – and liked to listen to the Latin motets of Richard Dering (sometimes Deering; 1580–1630), a known Catholic who had been organist to the Catholic Queen Henrietta Maria. He commissioned Hingeston to write keyboard music, instrumental fantasias, and even dance suites for cornets and sackbuts, some of which were published in part-books bearing the Cromwell coat of arms.[4] That much might just have been acceptable within the Puritan code, but to sanction, as Cromwell did, the publication of John Wilson's *Psalterum Carolinum: The Devotions of His Sacred Majestie in His Solitudes and Sufferings* (1657) would seem to require some special justification.

However, the main musical developments of the Commonwealth period took place well away from political circles. In 1644, Milton (whose father, it should be remembered, was a composer) wrote his pamphlet, *Aeropagitica*, an attack on parliamentary plans to require the formal licensing of all published work, in which he argued against state control of music in the private sphere: 'And who shall silence all the airs and madrigals that whisper softness in chambers?' he asked. It was in private houses that music thrived during the Protectorate. Many of the organists, singers and composers who had worked in court and cathedral circles were now employed in the houses of the aristocracy or the land-owning gentry. Here they taught, performed and composed, again giving the lie to Burney's 'ten years of gloomy silence.'

A change in the social context in which music was heard naturally changed the character of the music that was produced. With no choirs and no large consorts to perform their work, composers had to rely more on the resources of the family group around them, or on their own individual skills, for performance. At a time when writing or performing religious music had become a potentially dangerous business, it was natural for them to concentrate on instrumental music, which for the first time – indeed, for the only time before the twentieth century – became the most popular form of art music. Moreover, dispersed as they were around the country, removed from the competitive context of cathedral or court, the music that they produced lost something of its common or collective purpose. Its prime objective was no longer the glorification of God, or even the glorification of the monarch. John Jenkins, a virtuoso viol-player himself, produced some of the best music of the period – lyrical, descriptive fantasias and suites for consort of viols – while living in comparative isolation in Norfolk. For the composer, this was a professional duty; for his employers – the Derhams and the L'Estranges – it was a form of entertainment. It was not music they could sing or dance to – though, no doubt, there was plenty of that – rather, it was music they could sit and listen to, a pleasant pastime divorced from other considerations, and a welcome, even valuable one at a time when many forms of public entertainment were suppressed or controlled. The Puritan ascendancy did not so much suppress music as limit and alter its role. Severely reducing its public functions meant placing increased emphasis on music as entertainment, as something which – among the aristocracy and gentry at least – could be purchased for private pleasure. One should not exaggerate the impact of this – music had, after all, been detaching itself from the Church, and musicians gradually moving towards independent professional status, ever since the Reformation – but, in terms of attitude, the changes that occurred under the Commonwealth marked a first step along the road towards the commercialisation of music in the eighteenth century.

A different aspect of the process is illustrated by the story of John Playford (1623–87). The son of a Norwich mercer, Playford was probably educated at the choir school attached to Norwich Cathedral. At the age of sixteen, after his father's death, he was apprenticed to John Benson, a London publisher with premises in St Dunstan's Churchyard, just to the north of Fleet Street. After his seven-year apprenticeship, in 1647, Playford was able to register as a publisher in his own right with the Stationer's Company and cross to the south of Fleet Street, trading from a shop in the porch of Temple Church. He was a convinced Royalist and in 1649 was arrested in connection with *A Perfect Narrative of The Whole Proceedings of the High Court of Justice in The Tryal of The King in Westminster Hall* which, while not revealing the name of the author, stated clearly (if ungrammatically) on the cover that it was 'Printed for John Playford, and are to be Sold at His Shop in The Inner Temple. Jan. 23. 1648.' Precisely what happened next, we do not know. He escaped trial and imprisonment, but with his Royalist enthusiasm much dampened and his publishing policy radically altered. His next publication was *The English Dancing Master* (1651).

The first edition contained one hundred and five popular dances, giving what the title page describes as 'Plaine and easie Rules' for their performance and a simple, single-line notation of the tune. It was a huge success. Initially, it was seen as a kind of self-help book: by following Playford's instructions, dances, like instrumental music, could now be performed at home, which was important at a time when people were uncertain about entertainment in a public context. Even after the Commonwealth, when social attitudes to dancing relaxed, the book remained popular. Later editions, of which there were eighteen in all up to 1728 (enlarged to include some non-English tunes), were entitled simply *The Dancing Master.* As the first attempt to assemble and notate English dances, it also represents an extension of Thomas Ravenscroft's work of collecting folk songs forty years previously. Although there may still be some disagreement about how 'traditional' a number of the dances actually were, there is no doubt that *The Dancing Master* proved highly influential. It was a source on which Cecil Sharp relied heavily in the early years of the twentieth century in his labours to revive the English folk-dance tradition; and it inspired many artists during and after the 1970s folk revival, including Ashley Hutchings (one of whose albums is called *The Compleat Dancing Master*), Philip Pickett, the Broadside Band, and The City Waites.

Playford went on to publish a series of other books of or about music, showing a fine sense of awareness of what the public wanted and what the authorities would allow. These included *Catch that Catch Can* (1652), *A Booke of New Lessons for the Cithern & Gittern* (1652), *Select Musical Ayres and Dialogues* (1653), *Musick's Recreation on the Lyra Viol* (1652), *A Breefe Introduction to the Skill of Musick* (1654), *Court Ayres* (1655), and *Choice Musick to the Psalmes of David* (1656). In fact, he was so successful that he virtually monopolised music publishing during the Commonwealth. He continued publishing right up to his death in 1686. The respect in which he was held, and, indeed, the influence he exerted, were such that, on his death, Purcell was moved to write his *Elegy on my friend, Mr John Playford.*

Both the popularity of instrumental music and the success of John Playford came about as a response to changed social conditions under the Commonwealth. The other main development of the period was essentially an attempt to get round the rules. English opera took a long time to develop and had several antecedents. One was the farce jig, which in the late-Elizabethan and Jacobean theatre had become the accepted and expected conclusion of a theatrical performance. It was originally just an afterpiece, a jig danced by a clown with perhaps a few extemporised words. It grew and evolved until it could consist of anything between two and eight characters singing two or three hundred lines of text and lasting up to half-an-hour. The farce jig became, in effect, a kind of primitive, miniature, comic opera. Then, as we have seen, there was the court masque with its loose assemblage of songs, dances and spectacle. There is, however, a general consensus that the first English opera worthy of the name was *The Siege of Rhodes*, performed in September 1656 at Rutland House, on Aldersgate Street in the City of London, the home of Sir William Davenant.

By the 1650s, opera was well established in Italy: Jacopo Peri and Claudio Monteverdi were already dead and Francesco Cavalli was the leading composer in the genre. It had spread to Poland-Lithuania in the 1640s and would arrive in France at the court of Louis XIV in the 1670s where the Italian-born Jean-Baptiste Lully would establish a clearly defined French operatic tradition. Opera's arrival in England was a less ordered and more commercial process. Theatres had been officially closed since 1642, but that had not prevented plays from being performed privately. Play readings became popular and there were various other attempts at evading restrictions. In 1653, James Shirley wrote a masque called *Cupid and Death* with music by Christopher Gibbons and the young Matthew Locke (of whom we shall hear more later), for private and semi-public performance. But it was Davenant who made the breakthrough.

Davenant was born in 1606 in Oxford, where his father was a successful vintner and the proprietor of the Crown Tavern; he later became the city's Mayor. Shakespeare is reputed to have stayed at the Crown en route between London and Stratford and at some stage a rumour grew up that Davenant was Shakespeare's illegitimate son. There is no evidence to support the idea, although Davenant himself never denied it. He seems to have been a thoroughly commercial animal and it may well have been to his advantage to let the rumour circulate. He moved to London and made a name for himself during the 1630s writing poetry, plays and masques. He fought for the King, was knighted during the siege of Gloucester and, when Charles was defeated, fled to France where he converted to Roman Catholicism. In 1650, on his way to Maryland, he was captured at sea, imprisoned in the Tower of London and sentenced to death. Spared execution – possibly on the intervention of Milton – he was released in 1652 and pardoned in 1654. He immediately petitioned John Thurloe, Secretary to Cromwell's Council of State, that he should be allowed to mount public entertainments which would have a moral purpose – such as dwelling on the barbarous behaviour of the Spaniards in the West Indies – as well as benefitting the public purse. The authorities may be forgiven a degree of scepticism.

Davenant's schemes matured rapidly. In May 1656, without official approval, he staged *The First Dayes Entertainment*: a mix of music and declamatory dialogues making the case in favour of both opera and the restoration of stage plays. If this was intended to test the reaction of the authorities, it worked: nothing happened. So he moved ahead with *The Siege of Rhodes*.

What was sufficiently different about *The Siege of Rhodes* to merit the title 'opera'? In the first place, it presents a far more coherent story than any masque. The narrative is based on actual events in 1522, when the armies of Suleiman the Magnificent (Solyman in the opera) expelled the Knights of St John from their Aegean stronghold, but behaved in a chivalrous manner, allowing the defeated knights to depart unmolested. The story is divided into acts (called "entries" in the opera), but the narrative is carried by a mixture of songs and recitative, allowing Davenant to claim that it was a musical performance, not a play. The use of recitative was not wholly new in England – it had featured in Lanier's masques, *Lovers Made Men* and *The Vision of Delight*, both performed in 1617 – but it had never been used to such an extent. Musically, it is difficult to make too many judgements as the score has not survived, but we do know that it was a through-composed work and that the music was shared between five composers: Henry Lawes, Henry Cooke (who liked to keep his military rank of Captain), Matthew Locke, Charles Coleman and George Hudson (*c.*1615–72). It was common enough for the music for a masque to be split between two or three composers, but to involve five was unusual – and potentially troublesome, given that some of them held diametrically opposed political views. The involvement of five composers makes it clear that musical consistency and coherence was not part of the design. At the same time, there was only one librettist – Davenant himself – emphasising the fact that in the early days of English opera, as with the court masque, the writer was the prime mover. The composer (or composers) followed his lead. When it came to the actual production, however, Davenant was sufficiently concerned about the quality of the music to insist that the cast be made up of singers rather than actors. One of them was Henry Persill (Purcell), probably the father of the composer; while another, remarkably, was a woman. As far as we know, this was the first time outside court circles that an English lady had appeared in a dramatic role on stage. The lady in question, Mrs Edward Coleman, played Ianthe, who is married to Alphonso, which part was taken by her husband, thereby, one presumes, reducing the possibility for moral outrage on the part of the authorities.

One other – non-musical – aspect of *The Siege of Rhodes* deserves attention. The proscenium stage that could be fitted into Rutland House was small. Davenant was able to enlist the services of John Webb, nephew and pupil of Inigo Jones, to design and construct special moveable scenery of the kind that was already used in Italy but had never previously been seen in England. Using 'shutters' at the back of the stage, which could open or close, and 'relieves' which slid in and out of the wings, Webb created a full depth of perspective in a very restricted space – the novelty of which must surely have contributed to the opera's success.

Having successfully staged an opera in a private house without arousing the ire of the authorities, Davenant determined to risk opening a public theatre, the Cockpit in Drury Lane, for his next production, *The Cruelty of the Spaniards in Peru*, staged in the summer of 1658. It was a less innovative piece than *The Siege of Rhodes* in that it abandoned recitative and reverted to the declamatory style of *The First Dayes Entertainment* – the format that became known as a semi-opera. The next year saw *The History of Sir Francis Drake*, with six entries and recitative, again at the Cockpit Theatre. Both works enjoyed modest success. The librettos by Davenant have survived, but no music; nor is there any record of who wrote it – although it seems likely that Matthew Locke was involved in both. By this time, the Commonwealth was crumbling and, in the way of failing regimes, sought to reassert its authority. Davenant was arrested and the opera closed, but it was only a temporary setback. He was soon released, and within months Charles II was back in England and on the throne. Rapid, sweeping social changes would open up new possibilities for opera and for all forms of music, but would not be able to undo the major shifts in musical life which had taken place during the Civil Wars and under the Commonwealth.

31 The Return of the King

On the morning of Thursday 22 April 1661, King Charles II set out from the Tower of London at the head of a magnificent procession which took five hours to travel the three miles (five kilometres) to Westminster. It was an extravagant progress, designed to put London in the mood for the Coronation ceremony which would take place the following day – St George's Day – in Westminster Abbey. The planning and production was the work of John Ogilby (1600–76). Like Davenant, Ogilby seems to have crammed a lot of activity into a single life. He was a Scottish-born dancer and dancing master turned theatrical producer; an entrepreneur who had made money opening the first theatre in Ireland and then lost it in the wars; a Royalist and sometime Master of the Revels in Ireland who had survived the Commonwealth by translating classical literature; a man who would go on to become His Majesty's Cosmographer and Geographic

Printer and publish the first road atlas of England and Wales. Along the route of the procession, Ogilby created a series of entertainments, rich in music, elaborate costumes, symbolism and sycophancy, clearly derived from the court masques in which he had danced as a young man. Much of the music was written by Matthew Locke. Unfortunately, apart from an oddly restrained suite 'For His Majesty's Sagbutts and Cornetts', none of it has survived.

On leaving the Tower of London, the King encountered first one and then another band of Waits, whose musical functions had now been restored to them. In Aldgate was the first of four huge and richly decorated ceremonial arches, this one depicting the theme of Rebellion and Monarchy. Rebellion on one side of the arch was surrounded by drummers; Monarchy and Loyalty on the other were supported by trumpeters. The second arch in Cornhill was the Naval Arch, extolling the King's mastery of the seas. Singers and musicians – trumpeters and wind players – were dressed as sailors. On Charles's arrival they sang 'From Neptune's Wat'ry Kingdoms' and, after flattering words from Father Thames himself, 'King Charles, King Charles, Great Neptune of the Main' as he left. Along Cheapside, there was military music, then a wind band, then more Waits. Near Wood Street, the Arch of Concord featured living, allegorical statues representing Prudence, Justice, Temperance, Fortitude and other virtues. As the King passed through the arch, Concord, Love and Truth, accompanied by the monarch's personal band of Twenty-Four Violins, sang 'Comes not here the King of Peace?' and then 'With all our wishes, Sir, go on'. After the Arch of Concord, there were bands of musicians – fifes and drums, more trumpeters and yet more bands of Waits – at key points along the route, until the procession reached the fourth arch, the Garden of Plenty, half way along Fleet Street. Twenty-one musicians, a mixture of drummers, trumpeters and Waits, manned this arch, which was intended to suggest that, with Charles's return, winter had given way to a time of growth and harvest. From the Garden of Plenty, the King and his entourage proceeded by slow stages to Whitehall, accompanied by music all the way.

The next morning, the King travelled by boat to Westminster Hall, where he robed – to the strains of an unidentified anthem – and then, accompanied by a full complement of the English nobility, processed to Westminster Abbey. The anthem *I was glad* was sung as he entered through the west door. For Charles, the symbolic aspects of the Coronation were extremely important. This was to be a restoration of the traditional order, so the same order of service was followed, the same psalms were sung, and same anthem texts were used as at the Coronation of his father in 1626 – though the music, except for the Litany, was newly composed. Even the crown of St Edward, which had been destroyed on the orders of Cromwell, was remade for the occasion. We have no complete record of the music performed during the ceremony, but we do know that Charles turned to three trusted figures who had served his father and remained loyal to him. William Child, recalled from life on the farm, presided at the organ and certainly wrote the anthems *The King shall rejoice* and *O Lord, grant the King a long life*. He may also have written the setting of *I was glad* to which Charles entered the Abbey, although there were two other contemporary settings, by Michael Wise and William Tucker. Henry Lawes, a favourite of Charles I, now in his sixties, wrote the setting of *Zadok the Priest* which was heard immediately prior to the act of placing the crown on the King's head. Most of the rest of the music – anthems (including *Behold, O Lord, our Defender*, an early example of a symphony anthem), settings of psalms and a particularly complex setting of the Nicene Creed – seems to have been the work of Captain Henry Cooke, though few of the pieces actually survive. Cooke, another proven loyalist, may also have sung during the service, for he was a noted bass. The diarist Samuel Pepys, a great lover of music, was present in the Abbey, but left because there was too much noise for him to hear it properly. The quality of the performance also left something to be desired. The two choirs that were brought together for the occasion – the Chapel Royal and that of Westminster Abbey – had been disbanded under the Commonwealth and, despite rapid rebuilding, were still reliant on older men singing falsetto to make up for the lack of trained boy singers. Nonetheless, Charles was duly crowned in a ceremony which mirrored his father's Coronation thirty-five years previously and marked the final act in the formal restoration of the monarchy.

The Coronation took place just eleven months after Charles had arrived in England from Holland, where he had maintained his court in exile. In that time, he had sought to re-establish the old order through a policy of reconciliation (except with those who had signed his father's death warrant). He rapidly reassembled the Royal Music, with its labyrinth of different and not always consistent titles. Nicholas Lanier returned from exile to resume his position as Master of the King's Musick. Henry Lawes was restored to his various positions in the Chapel Royal, but seems never to have recovered his creative energies; he died in October 1662. William

Child was restored to his duties at St George's, Windsor, and also made one of three organists of the Chapel Royal. He appears to have remained a solid, loyal supporter of the status quo, writing anthems and as many as twenty settings of the Service, until his death at the age of ninety in 1697. Christopher Gibbons, another Chapel Royal organist, went on to become an influential composer, teacher and high-profile figure during Charles II's reign. John Jenkins, a favourite of Charles I, was appointed Musician in Ordinary to the King, but, while a highly respected and still very active composer, he remained on the edge of musical life at court. This was largely because Charles II, a very different and more outgoing character than his father, saw Jenkins' reflective style, his fondness for the fantasia and his commitment to the viol, as belonging to an earlier era: Charles preferred dance music to reflective music, and the violin to the viol. Those composers and musicians who had favoured or been in favour under the Protectorate – John Wilson, Benjamin Rogers, Charles Coleman, Davis Mell – were reinstated in their pre-Civil War roles or given other employment within the King's gift. There seems to have been room for everyone. Even John Hingeston, who had very definitely been Cromwell's man, became a Gentleman of the Chapel Royal and was later given responsibility for maintaining the organs and wind instruments used by the King's Musick. The new King was clearly in a forgiving mood – or perhaps one senses an echo of Wolsey's verdict on Taverner.

The heaviest burden fell on Captain Henry Cooke, who had been a chorister at the Chapel Royal under Charles I. Now appointed Master of the Children of the Chapel Royal, he assumed the enormous responsibility of rebuilding the choir from scratch. Such was the importance that the King attached to the task that Cooke was allowed to travel the country with the power, if necessary, to act as a kind of musical press gang, compelling promising young choristers to join up. Both the great diarists of the period commented on Cooke: John Evelyn thought him the best Italian-style singer in the country; Pepys acknowledged his quality but thought him an arrogant, vain coxcomb. Cooke was clearly an assertive figure, but he seems also to have had a kinder side, petitioning the King for an increase in pay for all members of the Chapel, and making efforts to ensure that his young charges found employment when their voices broke and they could no longer sing with the choir. He continued in the job, and continued composing adequate but undistinguished choral music, largely anthems, until his death in 1672.

In Dublin, a ceremony to mark the Restoration involving both Christ Church and St Patrick's Cathedral was held in January 1661. Descriptions of the event make it clear that a choir was in place and able to sing both the *Te Deum*, a hymn, and an unidentified anthem. The organ, too, was apparently in full working order. The choir of eighteen, including four boy singers, was apparently shared by the two cathedrals at this time; as was the organist, John Hawkshaw, who occupied the role for ten years but seems not to have composed. Vicars-choral were recruited and teaching at the choir school resumed. Changes in practice affecting the Chapel Royal were gradually transmitted to Dublin, so that by the 1670s viols, bass viols and possibly other instruments were included in services on important occasions. Charles promised religious toleration; the Church of Ireland was restored and Ireland, devastated during the Civil Wars, seemed ready to establish some degree of normality. In the still dominant popular tradition, the harp was giving way to the fiddle or violin, to the flute and the fife, and to various precursors of the uilleann pipes. Dance forms were also changing, and something close to what we would recognise as modern Irish traditional music was emerging. One newly evolved dance form, the Irish jig, attracted the attention of the Archbishop of Dublin, Michael Boyle, in 1674 when he censured Friar Peter Walsh for spending too much time dancing in the Harp and Crown.

In Scotland, the Restoration was proclaimed in May 1660 to the sound of trumpets and drums. All the bells of Edinburgh rang. There were bonfires. There was dancing to the music of bagpipes and fiddles. But when Charles II attempted to impose his religious settlement, which included the reintroduction of bishops, it was resented and resisted, often with violence. The kind of church music that Charles would have wished to see introduced alongside an episcopal structure stood no chance at all in Scotland. Metrical psalms remained the sole form of religious music acceptable to the Church of Scotland and its congregations. Only in Aberdeen, the one place where the Song School remained active throughout the whole period (perhaps because of its relative isolation from the rest of the country), was there a core of continuing secular musical activity. And it was in Aberdeen that John Forbes established a music publishing business. In 1662, he published *Cantus: Songs and Fancies*. This was a somewhat backward-looking collection of sixty pieces, one third Scots and two-thirds English (thirteen Italian songs were added in a later edition), drawn from a variety of sources. Nonetheless, it was the first book of secular music ever to be published in Scotland, a striking demonstration of Aberdonian defiance and determination to carry on regardless.[1] Farther south in Angus, George Maule, the 2nd Earl of Panmure, was building Panmure House, the library of which would preserve the Commonplace Book of Robert Edward (also Edwards), minister in the nearby parish of Murroes. Edward's collection, a mixture of European and Scottish songs, music for cittern and keyboards, dates from the middle of the seventeenth century but again looks backward, as if trying to keep a musical tradition alive.

In England and Wales, away from London, the restoration of musical life began at a municipal level, with the Waits. Almost everywhere they were restored to their former numbers and their former functions. In Canterbury, where they had been disbanded in 1640, the Waits were allowed to reform in August 1660 and that October city records state that 'the waite Players of this Cittie shalbe permitted to playe upon their waites about this Cittie in the morneinges in the winter times as formerly they were accustomed to doe.'[2] In Sheffield, they again attended municipal banquets and played at the town fair. In Exeter, 'after many Years Sequestration' they were 'restored to their Places and their Pensions.'[3] Even in cities such as Oxford where the Waits had continued to function under the Commonwealth, the Restoration gave them a new lease of life. Partly, of course, this was due to the revival of previously forbidden celebrations. Sheffield city archives record money being spent on raising the maypole, on ringing bells for the King's birthday and on the anniversary of the Gunpowder Plot. No doubt, tavern singers and itinerant musicians found life easier after 1660, but in terms of cathedral and church music, the restoration of anything approaching normality was a slow process.

The Church of England was formally restored in 1660 and a new *Book of Common Prayer* issued in 1662, but the ravages of the Civil Wars and the Commonwealth could not be legislated away. The fabric of many churches had to be restored. Choirs had to be re-formed. Some former choristers were able to return to their old positions, but they were aging and there were no young singers to take their places. Choir schools had to be re-staffed and reopened; hymn books had to be replaced; music re-copied. Lack of money meant that many churches were not able to recruit good choirmasters or organists, and the quality of church music took many decades to recover. Organs were a particular problem. Huge numbers had been destroyed, and even the few that had survived needed attention after years of neglect. Robert Dallam, with his sons Ralph and George, returned from France shortly after the Restoration, leaving his third son, Thomas, in Brittany. They worked on organs in St George's Chapel, Windsor, Durham Cathedral and Norwich Cathedral, before moving on to New College, Oxford – where Robert died in 1665 – but the family never regained the dominant position it had enjoyed before the Civil Wars. Organ builders were in demand and were to remain so. Initially, there were a number of successful individuals, among them John Loosemore of Exeter and Thomas Thamar of Peterborough, but before long two families came to dominate organ-building in England, Wales and Ireland and would continue to do so into the early decades of the eighteenth century.

Thomas Harrison's father was an organ-builder and his mother was a member of the Dallam family. Like the Dallams, the Harrisons were Catholics and fled to France during the Civil Wars. When he returned after the Restoration, Harrison changed the family name to Harris. He was awarded a number of high profile contracts – Winchester College (1663), Gloucester Cathedral (1666), Worcester Cathedral (1668) – and he was soon joined, and later eclipsed, by his son Renatus. Working backwards from later documents, it seems that Renatus Harris was probably born about 1652. This would have made him old enough to start an apprenticeship with his father in 1665, and, as apprenticeships normally lasted seven years, he would have been able to strike out on his own by 1672. In fact, he did so in 1675, and from that time until his death in 1724, he completed at least fifty major organ projects in cathedrals, collegiate and parish churches across the country. And when he died, his foreman Thomas Swarbrick seems to have carried on the business.[4]

The Harrises' competitors were the Smiths, and the competition was intense. Bernard Smith (1630–1708) was born Schmidt in Germany, perhaps in Bremen, and seems to have served his apprenticeship there before moving to Holland, where he built organs for two churches in Edam and one at a private residence in Amsterdam. He probably arrived in London in 1666, bringing with him his two nephews, Gerard and Christian – although frequently referred to as 'Father' Smith, this seems to have been a question of respect rather than relationship. Smith had been educated in the long German tradition of organ-building and was accounted a fine craftsman. He certainly won a number of prestigious contracts, first in Durham Cathedral, then in Canterbury Cathedral, Christ Church Cathedral in Oxford and Christopher Wren's newly rebuilt St Paul's. It was the German-born Smith not the Harrises who received the commission to build a new organ for the Chapel Royal in Whitehall Palace and was later appointed Organ Maker to the King. Rivalry between the two families came to a head in 1684 over plans to build a new organ for the Temple Church in London, the old one having been destroyed by fire in 1679. However it came about, those responsible for the project managed to commission two organs – one from Renatus Harris and one from Father Smith. They then decided that there should be a competition: both organs would be erected and played to allow a judgement to be made on grounds of quality. Expensive additions and alterations were made; the best musicians in London engaged to play. Harris took on the composer and keyboard player Giovanni Baptista Draghi, who had been brought to London by Charles II as part of his attempt to establish Italian-style opera in the capital. On his side, Smith had John Blow and his good friend Henry Purcell. At this time Blow was organist at St Margaret's Westminster, while Purcell was organist in Westminster Abbey. Harris is reported to have attempted to sabotage Smith's bellows, but, if he did, the tactic did not work. Smith was declared the winner and paid a very generous £1,000. Harris later re-erected his instrument in Christ Church, Dublin.

32 The Violin, and Matthew Locke

The word 'Restoration' is misleading. The King had returned, but his political position was inevitably weaker than his father's. He was naturally unwilling to admit the fact and sought to disguise it, playing 'the Merry Monarch' and seeking prestige by maintaining – even when he could not afford it – a court that might stand comparison with those of kings and princes on the Continent. A parallel situation applied to music. Efforts were being made throughout the country to get musical life back on track, but not everything could be restored. Too much had changed in the interim. So while the restored court flourished, the old musical structures were revived but never truly restored. In fact, under Charles II, British music became more narrowly focussed on the court and the Chapel Royal than ever before; a circumstance that ushered in one last and glorious period of music sponsored by royalty – after which the musical influence of the monarch and the Chapel Royal began to wither slowly away.

The most significant musical figure in the early years of Charles II's reign was undoubtedly Matthew Locke. He was born in or around Exeter *c.*1622, sang in the Cathedral choir there, probably under Edward Gibbons, and then stayed on to study the organ after his voice broke. From the first, he was an extrovert, combative character. He scratched his name into the Cathedral stonework in 1638 and was in trouble for fighting a couple of years later. He took the King's side in the Civil Wars, but exactly what he did is not certain. He was certainly in the Netherlands, probably at Charles II's court-in-exile at the Hague, and may have served in Ireland on the Catholic and Royalist side. He also became a Catholic himself during this period, something about which he was characteristically defiant when he returned to England in the 1650s – marrying Mary Garnons from a Herefordshire Catholic family, dedicating his *Flat Consort for my Cousin Kemble* to another recusant family from the same area, and conducting heated public arguments about religion, which resulted in him being denounced to the authorities. Against this background, it is surprising – or perhaps a tribute to his obvious musical abilities – that Davenant should have agreed to involve him in attempts to stage public operatic performances, an enterprise which was already the object of official suspicion. In 1660, however, with the return of the King, any problems deriving from his Catholicism simply melted away and Locke's star was in the ascendant. He was immediately appointed Composer in Ordinary to the King, which, among other things, necessarily involved writing music for Charles's Twenty-Four Violins – a French import that was to have a significant impact on English music.

In 1646, the sixteen-year-old Charles had fled to France by way of the Channel Islands, and begun his period of exile at the court of his first cousin, Louis XIV (then aged only eight). There he heard and saw 'Les Vingt-Quatre Violins du Roy'. 'Les Vingt-Quatre', as they were often known, had been established under Louis XIII and rapidly became an integral part of court life. They were, in effect, the King's personal string orchestra. They played at ballets, operas, weddings, ceremonial functions, dinners, and when the King entered or left the city. They were a symbol of the modernity and sophistication of the Bourbon court; and as soon as he was restored to his throne, Charles II followed the French lead and established his own 'Twenty-Four Violins'. This was the group that played to him as he passed beneath the Arch of Concord on his progress to Westminster. Charles was not a man of particularly sophisticated tastes. He liked music. He wanted prestige. Violins were modern and reflected French and Italian taste. For him that was probably enough. But his attitude was also a stimulus for the kind of change which had, understandably enough, been slow to take place during the Commonwealth years.

The violin became popular because of its flexibility and the quality of the sound it produced. The first fully recognisable violins appeared in northern Italy in the early decades of the sixteenth century. They quickly spread to France – the first technical description of the instrument appeared in a French musical treatise published in Lyon in 1556,[1] and Louis IX actually placed an order for (naturally) twenty-four of them with the famous Amati family in 1560. By the middle of the seventeenth century, design and construction had reached unprecedented levels of sophistication, with the city of Cremona boasting three of the greatest families of violin-makers of all time: the Amati, the Guarneri and the Stradivari. The violin was not slow in spreading to the British Isles – a number of Waits seem to have been early users – but as late as 1656 Anthony Wood could claim that it was 'not … used in concert among gentlemen; only by common musicians who played but two parts.' Wood's Oxford companions 'esteemed the violin to be an instrument only belonging to a common fiddler, and could not endure that it should come among them.'[2]

Given such comments, some attempt should be made at this point to distinguish between the terms 'fiddle' and 'violin'. The fiddle of the seventeenth century had developed from the medieval box fiddle, which had itself evolved from the various families of early bowed instruments. It had long been the basic instrument of the popular music tradition, used to accompany ballads or other folk songs, and for dancing in inns and taverns or on popular occasions such as May Day. As such, it was often looked down upon by those who regarded such entertainments as beneath them. The violin had similar origins, but had been crafted into a much more sophisticated instrument with a far greater expressive capability and purity of tone and, as a consequence, associated with classical or art music. In practice, once violins became widely available, the distinction effectively disappeared and today the two words are used interchangeably – though, with a nod to its origins, 'fiddle' is sometimes used to denote a connection with the folk rather than the classical tradition.

Violins were not new even in court circles. There had been violins at the court of Henry VIII, and they had featured regularly in the bands that played music for court masques. William Lawes had included violins alongside other instruments in some of his fantasias, and we have seen that

Davis Mell was accounted a virtuoso during the reign of Charles I. But both the English and, later, the Scots seem to have been slow to grant full social recognition to the new instrument. John Evelyn's view was that the tone of the violin was 'better suiting a tavern or a playhouse than a church.'[3] Certainly the British Isles were slower than other parts of Europe to abandon the idea that the viol was necessarily a superior instrument. It was Charles II's advocacy which changed that. Even John Jenkins, the great champion of the viol, was convinced and in the 1670s, when well over seventy, he wrote a number of startlingly lively and entertaining three-part fantasias for two violins and bass viol. The same Scottish library that contains Robert Edward's Commonplace Book also contains the violin books of Henry Maule, one of the sons of Panmure House. Printed in England about 1680, they include a number of traditional Scottish tunes arranged for solo violin, suggesting that the violin was spreading north of the border and becoming integrated into local musical culture.

Locke's music kept pace with these changes in musical taste and direction. His *Consort of Fower Parts*, written in the last years of the Commonwealth, consisted of six fantasy suites – each beginning with a fantasy and followed by a courant and ayre and a saraband – and was among the last great works for consort of viols. In 1661 and 1662, Locke published two collections called *The Broken Consort* – a broken consort in Locke's case included violins alongside viol and wind players – which again comprised a series of fantasy suites, though distinctly more advanced in character and instrumentation than those he had written earlier. Roger North, the lawyer and writer, claimed that Charles detested the fantasy as a musical form, so it may be that these works were not well received at court. Or perhaps Locke was simply busy with other duties: he was regularly called upon to compose everything from dance suites to occasional pieces for the Twenty-Four Violins to play in the King's private apartments; and in 1662 he was also appointed private organist to Charles's Portuguese Queen, Catherine of Braganza, an appointment for which his own Catholicism made him particularly suitable. Whatever the case, he did not publish any more instrumental collections until *Melosthesia* in 1673, the first volume of keyboard pieces in England to give details of figured bass continuo playing, a technique that was important throughout the Baroque period. And only in 1677, the year of his death, did he return to writing for broken consort, contributing three suites, each consisting of an introduction and seven different dance tunes, to a publication entitled *Tripla Concordia*.

Fantasy suites were not new. William Lawes had written them in the years before the Commonwealth and Christopher Gibbons had picked up both the form and something of Lawes' eccentric style. Indeed, Gibbons went further than Lawes, leaving strange, unresolved dissonances and making huge tonal leaps. Locke's fantasy suites, however, go further than either. There are sudden angular jumps and shifts of melodic subject. There are melodic phrases of irregular length punctuated by unexpected harmonies. There are odd dramatic gestures. Yet whatever oddities may be thrown up in the course of one of his fantasies – or in his descriptive instrumental pieces for the theatre – they are held together by Locke's great sense of musical architecture. The music remains polyphonic but it is also brilliantly expressive and personal, finely balanced between the long-established English consort tradition and the homophonic textures which characterised Baroque orchestral and chamber music.

Locke's own position on so many issues was one of stubborn balance in the face of opposing pressures. The King liked violins: Locke composed for violins, but never completely gave up the viol. The King disliked fantasies: Locke continued to compose them, but in his own way, developing the form and including violins. The King was under the spell of French and Italian music: Locke's certainly reflected continental influences. He even published a collection of songs that he had made during his time in the Netherlands. But he was critical of Charles II's dependence on continental models and continental musicians. The King sent one of his violinists, John Banister, to study Les Vingt-Quatre (though he was later demoted for a disparaging remark about the quality of French musicianship); he sent the young Pelham Humfrey, whom we shall meet shortly, to France and Italy to study church music; he invited the Catalan-born, French composer and violinist Louis Grabu to become Master of the King's Musick on the death of Lanier; he gave employment to the harpsichordist and poet, Giovanni Baptista Draghi. Locke's verdict on all this was succinct: 'I never yet saw any Forain Instrumental (a few French Courants excepted) worthy of an English mans transcribing.'[4] Only when the Reverend Thomas Salmon published an *Essay to the Advancement of Musick*, proposing a radical overhaul of the system of clefs used in musical notation, did Locke leap to a passionate defence of the status quo. 'What will a man not do to be chronicled an inventor?' was one of his more polite comments. Salmon fought back. Locke was 'a frightful scarecrow stuffed with straw, furnished with an old hat and a muckinger'.[5] It was an unedifying correspondence.

This same tense balance is visible in his religious music. Although a Catholic, he wrote thirty-two anthems and two services for the Anglican Church. The best known is *Be Thou exalted, Lord,* written to celebrate a naval victory during Charles II's war with the Dutch. It is a full production number, a symphony anthem, immensely rich in texture and offering a leading role to the King's violinists, which Charles had introduced into Chapel Royal services in 1662. It demanded four soloists, a two-part choir, a four-part viol ensemble, a five-part string ensemble plus an organ. Certainly nothing like it had been heard before within the confines of the Chapel; it looks forward to the elaboration and complexities of the later Baroque period. Locke also wrote fifteen Latin anthems, often in a very Italianate style. These pose something of a problem. It is tempting to suggest that they were written for the Queen's private worship, but they are too complex to have been performed in her private chapel. The setting of Psalm 136, *Super flumina Babylonis,* for example, begins with a two-part instrumental 'sinfonia' and then moves rapidly through a number of different sections including recitative and dance rhythms before returning to the original theme. It is possible that this and at least some of the other Latin works were written in the academic atmosphere of Oxford in 1665 when Charles and his court, including Locke, fled there to escape the plague.

Locke's theatrical and operatic work seems to have fallen off in the immediate aftermath of the Restoration, probably because of the other demands on his time. However, it revived in the 1670s, when he was involved in three major projects, all different but all contributing in some way to the development of English opera – and all staged at the newly opened Dorset Garden Theatre. The first was a play, a tragedy, by Elkanah Settle, *The Empress of Morocco* (1673). Locke wrote a short self-contained masque that forms part of the plot of the play: a miniature, through-composed opera lasting only twelve minutes, based on the story of Orpheus and Euridice, with four clearly distinguished characters and a distinct recitative style. The second was an operatic version of *The Tempest* (1674), with a libretto by the poet, playwright – and later Poet Laureate – Thomas Shadwell. Shadwell's text is itself an adaptation of a version made by John Dryden and Davenant some years previously and thus a very long way from Shakespeare's, but with elaborate scenery and special effects the production was a huge success. Locke's contribution was most of the incidental music (the other bits were written by Pelham Humfrey and Draghi), including the impressive, short final piece, 'Curtain Tune.' These descriptive instrumental pieces, which were later turned into a suite, must be among his finest work. Locke quite simply used powerful variations of tempi and dynamics in a new way that expanded what music was capable of in such a context, opening up a whole range of new possibilities for descriptive music. The following year, Shadwell and Locke cooperated on *Psyche*, a semi-opera often supposed to have been written as a competitive response to the performance of a French opera, *Ariane, ou le Mariage de Bacchus,* with music by Louis Grabu, at the Covent Garden Theatre. This time, Locke wrote the vocal music, while Draghi wrote the instrumental sections. The plot is ludicrously complicated, the scenes complex and so full of the opportunities for special effects that the whole thing was mocked by its opponents. Nonetheless, Locke's music seems to have been a success, offering, by his own account, everything 'from ballad to a single air, counterpoint, recitative, fugue, canon and chromatic music, which variety (without vanity be it said) was never in court or theatre till now presented in this nation.'[6]

Percy Young has written that Locke's death 'effectively marks the division between the old and the new. Modern music had come into its own, and Locke was its chief architect.'[7] Certainly, the musical world that Locke left in 1677 was very different from the one he had entered in the 1630s. He was undoubtedly the key musical figure of the time, England's leading composer, an imaginative man who notched up an impressive number of musical firsts and innovations. Yet he was no visionary. To see him as chief architect of the new age is to give him the benefit of our knowledge of what happened next. His involvement with the different strands of the social and cultural turbulence of his age, coupled with his assertive, abrasive personality and highly idiosyncratic musical style, perhaps make him seem more revolutionary than he actually was. He may have earned the description 'the stormy petrel of the Restoration period',[8] but at heart, like so many great English composers, he was a believer in the middle way, in the existence and value of an evolving English musical tradition.

33 Humfrey, Wise, Blow, and Turner

If Locke, with his versatility, his innovations and his bad temper, can be said to have laid the foundations of the last, late flowering of court and

Chapel Royal music, it was Captain Cooke's children who brought that music to its peak. Cooke's brief was not just to rebuild the choir but to return the Chapel Royal to its status as a centre of national musical excellence – where the brightest musicians of one generation could serve their God and their King, before passing their knowledge on to the next. It was a huge task, but he succeeded brilliantly, recruiting what must surely have been one of the most talented groups of young musicians in the Chapel's history. If political and religious circumstances changed so that the role and size of the Chapel itself were formally diminished, that was hardly his fault. Pelham Humfrey (1647–74), Michael Wise (*c.*1646–87), John Blow (1649–1708) and William Turner (1651–1740) were among Cooke's early finds. And they were joined, a few years later, by the young Henry Purcell.

Pelham Humfrey was obviously a talented young man. By the age of sixteen, he had written a number of anthems by himself – as well as what was known as a 'club anthem', *I will always give thanks*, in collaboration with Blow and Wise. His talent and perhaps his looks – Samuel Pepys describes him as 'a pretty boy'[1] – caught the eye of Charles II, who sent him off to France and Italy for three years to study how religious music was composed on the Continent. In Paris, he studied under Lully, who was then approaching the height of his cultural influence at the court of Louis XIV, but it seems to have been Italy, and in particular the work of Giacomo Carissimi, which had the greater impact. Carissimi was taking the drama, pathos and recitative of opera and incorporating it into religious music, creating the oratorio, which was to become such a pervasive form in England from the eighteenth century onwards. Humfrey obviously learned a lot, but by the time he returned to England in 1667, success seems to have gone to his head – Pepys described him as 'an absolute monsieur … [who] disparages everybody's skill but his own.'[2] Arrogant or not, no one felt inclined to deny his ability. He was clearly established as a favourite of the King, and the accounts of the Lord Chamberlain's office show a series of posts coming his way. In 1668, he and Thomas Purcell were appointed composers within the King's Musick (replacing Locke and George Hudson). Later that same year, he was made lutenist in the King's private music (replacing Lanier). In 1672, on the death of Cooke, he became Master of the Children of the Chapel Royal, where one of his charges was Henry Purcell. But his rapid ascent was suddenly cut short. He must have known he was ill, for in April 1674 he made a will. He died less than three months later, aged just twenty-six.

Humfrey left a modest body of work: nineteen anthems, thirty songs to secular texts, a few court odes, a setting of the Anglican Service and some incidental music for the masque sequences in Shadwell's 1674 opera based on *The Tempest*. Many of the anthems are, in effect, symphony anthems. This was a variant of the verse-anthem form that became popular in the years after the Restoration; it included lengthy instrumental or organ passages as well as solo vocal and chorus passages which expanded the scale of the work. It was a form that would be taken up and developed by both Blow and Purcell. Anthems such as *Lift up your heads* and *O Give thanks unto the Lord* are genuinely expressive and full of life with French textures in the string writing. *Hear, O Heav'ns* is particularly Italian in style, with its dramatic opening and operatic textures. Humfrey's work has charm and smoothness and great melodic qualities: *A Hymn to God the Father* has an impressively haunting tune; and some of his secular songs, such as 'A Lover I'm Born and a Lover I'll Be', are positively catchy. In the end, however, his music is imitative. It lacks a personal voice. Humfrey was young, talented and very pleased with himself. One can only speculate whether, had he lived, he would have absorbed the French and Italian influences more completely and developed a deeper emotional engagement with his work. What is not in doubt, however, is that in its time his music would have been seen as forward-looking and exciting, just the sort of thing to catch the interest of a young student like Henry Purcell.

Michael Wise was an entirely different proposition. Another highly talented youngster, he too was recruited to the Chapel Royal, attracted the attention of Charles II, and seemed destined for a glittering career. In 1663, he was appointed lay clerk at St George's in Windsor, and in 1668, when he can have been no more than twenty-two, he took up the post of Organist and Master of Choristers at Salisbury. But Wise had the kind of mercurial talent which is often associated with trouble. In his case, the root cause appears to have been drink – which led to other forms of bad behaviour, such as swearing and ranting in public against the Dean and Chapter, for which he was forced to issue a grovelling, written apology. He seems to have got away with quite a lot, while managing to retain the favour of the King. Indeed, on account of his outstanding skills as an organist, Charles even granted him the right to play the organ in any church which received a visit from the monarch. On the face of it, the accession of James II, a decidedly less outgoing and tolerant character than his elder brother, did not promise well for Wise; yet somehow he found favour with the new

King as well and, in 1687, even received a royal recommendation for the post of Almoner and Master of Choristers at the rebuilt St. Paul's Cathedral. Things were looking up. Then one night, while still in Salisbury, Wise got drunk, had a flaming row with his wife and ran out into the street. One version has it that he had said he was going to kill the first person he met. Unfortunately, this turned out to be a member of the city watch, who resisted Wise's assault, hit him on the head and fractured his skull, with fatal results. The story has a strange pathos about it and, in 1987, became the subject of a short theatrical piece written by the composer Francis Potts. It was called, predictably, *Wise after the Event.*

These days, Wise's best-known composition appears to be 'A Catch upon the Midnight Cats', which features as a YouTube video. Otherwise, he is largely forgotten. In his lifetime, however, his church music was copied more frequently than that of Blow or Purcell and was circulated to cathedrals and churches throughout the country. The catches, which also include the bawdy 'Counsel for Married Folks', and Wise's one surviving drinking song, 'Old Chiron thus Preach'd' are, naturally enough, extrovert, lively pieces, but his church music shows a much more serious, even formal character. He was not a prolific composer and appears to have composed less as he grew older, though he was only about forty when he died. He left several settings of the Anglican Service and a number of anthems. The anthems, in particular, show a fondness for duets between bass and treble voices – a technique that he used to great effect in *The ways of Zion do mourn,* often regarded as his best work. *Prepare ye the way of the Lord* and *Awake, put on thy strength* both deserve to be heard more often; and *How Are the Mighty Fallen* (which, confusingly, is sometimes called *Thy beauty, O Israel*) is another very fine anthem, deeply emotional in its appeal, but made more effective by the sense that the emotion is never let loose. This is characteristic. Much more than Humfrey, Wise has his own style. The scale is modest, but that is deceptive and belies Wise's achievement. The music – perhaps surprisingly given his life story – maintains a balance, or perhaps a tension, between his ability to create melody and phrasing and a sense of restraint. It has a curiously disciplined, English feel – as if the composer has deliberately chosen to rein himself in, to contain his talents within the accepted musical forms of his age.

Humfrey and Wise died young. John Blow and William Turner lived longer – long enough to see the huge changes which overtook British music in the last decades of the seventeenth century and the early years of the eighteenth. Blow came from the village of Collingham in Nottinghamshire and seems to have been one of those promising boys scooped up by Captain Cooke during his regional hunts for talent. Turner came from Oxford, where his father was a cook at Pembroke College, and had already begun his singing career at Christ Church when he was recruited for the Chapel Royal. Blow was undoubtedly the more gifted of the two, but both enjoyed successful careers and led lives which, at least when compared with Wise, appear models of respectability. Sir John Hawkins (1719–17), whose *General History of the Science and Practice of Music* was published at the same time as Burney's great work, describes Blow as 'a very handsome man in his person, and remarkable for a gravity and decency in his deportment.... He was a man of blameless morals and a benevolent temper.'[3]

Blow, like so many Restoration composers, began composing early. He had certainly written a number of anthems before leaving the Chapel Royal to become Organist and Master of Choristers at Westminster Abbey in 1668, a position he held until 1679, when he was replaced by Purcell. In fact, he had two periods at the Abbey, for he was recalled in 1696 after Purcell's death. Blow seems to have made a habit of stepping into the shoes of his deceased friends. In 1684, he replaced Pelham Humfrey as Master of Children of the Chapel Royal and then, three years later, he stepped into the vacancy created by Wise's death to become Almoner and Master of Choristers at St. Paul's. He was the first to receive a doctorate of music as a so-called Lambeth Degree (conferred by the Archbishop of Canterbury and named after the Archbishop's London residence). In 1699, he was also appointed to the newly created post of First Composer to the Chapel Royal. This was no doubt welcome, but, as we shall see, by that stage the Chapel Royal had ceased to be the influential force in English music it had been for the preceding three centuries or more.

Blow was a prolific church composer. He left ten settings of the Service – of which the Service in G major is undoubtedly the best known and the most frequently sung – one hundred and fifteen anthems, and nine Latin motets. Many of his best anthems are occasional pieces – *O Lord, I have sinned* was written for the funeral of the Duke of Albemarle (previously General Monck, the man who made the Restoration possible); *Awake, awake, utter a song* was composed to celebrate Marlborough's victory at the Battle of Blenheim in 1704; and there were numerous anthems for royal occasions, particularly for the Coronation of James II. He seems to have relished the opportunity for big, choral melodies coupled with strong supporting orchestral passages. Pieces like *I beheld, and lo! a great multitude* and the Eastertide anthem (sometimes referred to as a motet) *Salvator Mundi* are still heard today. Blow's achievements tend to be overshadowed by those of Purcell, who was – it has to be admitted – a far greater composer, yet it would be misleading to suggest that Blow's music was wholly conventional. In his *General History of Music*, Burney, writing some eighty years after Blow's death, is highly critical of what he sees as Blow's crudities of style. And it is true that some of his anthems – *Jesus seeing the multitudes* would be a case in point – contain difficult harmonic progressions of the kind one would never find in Purcell, though nowadays such moments are more often interpreted as praiseworthy attempts to break new ground rather than stylistic awkwardness. Three hundred years on, the quality of Blow's melodic invention was recognised when Sir Arthur Bliss took Blow's setting of Psalm 23 as the basis for what is possibly his finest orchestral work, *Meditations on a Theme by John Blow*.

Blow was equally prolific as a secular composer. He wrote over a hundred songs, a large number of pieces for harpsichord – his preferred instrument – some chamber works, and thirty-seven odes, including one *On the Death of Mr Henry Purcell*. The ode as a musical form emerged during the reign of Charles II. The restoration of the monarchy had been a success, but it had done nothing to allay anti-Catholic sentiment among the mass of the population. Previously, the royal year had been organised around religious festivals that were the occasion for the composition and performance of an anthem. Fearing that this might be interpreted as evidence of Catholic sympathies, Charles took steps to reorganise the year around secular events in the court calendar – New Year's Day, his birthday, his return to London after the summer break in Windsor, royal marriages or births – which could be celebrated by the commissioning of an ode. Other dates were added later – notably, from 1683 onwards, St Cecilia's Day – and odes were also commissioned to mark important political events, such as military and naval victories. In reality, of course, they were simply secular anthems, settings of texts written by a court poet, and they were often performed in the Chapel Royal, but – being secular – they offered composers a little more flexibility in form and treatment. Blow and Purcell were the first notable exponents.

Turner was less successful and less prolific than Blow, but still not a negligible figure. When his voice broke in 1666, he left the Chapel Royal and went to Lincoln, singing as a counter-tenor. Some sources suggest he was Master of Choristers there, but as he would have been no more than sixteen this seems unlikely. In any event, he soon returned to London, became a Gentleman of the Chapel Royal in 1669, and remained one for the next seventy-one years. He also became a vicar-choral at St Paul's Cathedral in 1687, a lay vicar at Westminster Abbey in 1699, and was awarded an honorary doctorate by Cambridge University in 1696.

Like the others of his Chapel Royal generation, Turner's positions put him at the heart of London's musical life. He wrote two anthems for the Coronation of James II in 1685, and was invited to compose the St Cecilia's Day Ode that year to words by Nahum Tate, the Irish poet who was later to become Poet Laureate – though the music was not printed, which may suggest that it was not considered a success. He is certainly recorded as being among the singers on several St Cecilia's Day celebrations, and in 1697 wrote an anthem – *The King shall rejoice* – to start that year's celebrations which were held in St Bride's Church on Fleet Street. The following year he wrote a birthday ode for Princess Anne and in 1702 an anthem – *The Queen shall rejoice* – for her Coronation. All in all, he wrote over forty anthems and odes, at least two complete services, some hymns, well over a hundred secular songs and catches, and some dramatic music for one of Shadwell's plays, *The Libertine.* He died in 1740, aged eighty-nine, at his house in Westminster, just four days after his wife, Elizabeth, to whom he had been married for nearly seventy years.

34 Purcell, and King James II

Locke, Humfrey, Wise, Blow, Turner – these were the background to Henry Purcell. Growing up, as he did, in a musical family – both his father and his uncle were Chapel Royal musicians – these were the men he would have heard talked about. They were the composers whose anthems and services he would have sung when he himself became a chorister at the Chapel Royal. They were the composers whose manuscripts he later copied, who influenced his early compositions and who, in turn, were influenced by him. Locke knew the Purcell family and extended the hand of friendship to Henry when he was only seventeen. Humfrey was his teacher at the Chapel Royal; Blow his teacher at Westminster Abbey; and it is possible that he may have taken keyboard lessons from Christopher Gibbons.

Purcell is often referred to as the greatest English composer. Whether or not such judgements are helpful, it is certainly true that he rose with incredible rapidity to a position where he was acknowledged by those around him as the dominant figure in English music. His background gave him many advantages; nonetheless, others who have achieved a similar dominance – Tallis, Byrd or, in later times, Elgar and Vaughan Williams – took much longer to get there. Byrd was about thirty-five when he published his first major work, *Cantiones Sacrae*, jointly with Tallis. At the same age, Elgar was still slowly building his reputation, writing choral works for festivals in the English Midlands; and Vaughan Williams had yet to complete his first symphonic work. At the age of thirty-six, Purcell was dead.

Given the position and the reputation that he enjoyed during his lifetime, it is remarkable how little biographical information we have about Purcell and how little sense we get of his character. He seems, to use a phrase from a later age, to have risen without trace. He was probably born in 1659 just off Old Pye Street, Westminster, three minutes' walk from Westminster Abbey where his father, Henry Purcell senior, sometimes played the organ. Henry senior was a noted singer and lutenist, who may have given Henry junior his first lessons, but he died when the boy was only five, and the young Purcell seems to have passed to the care of his Uncle Edward. At the age of eight, he was already writing music and contributed a short, three-part song, apparently addressed to the King, *Sweet Tyranness, I Now Resign* to an edition of Playford's *Catch that Catch Can*. At the age of nine, he joined the Chapel Royal. At the age of eleven, he wrote a now lost piece which was *An Address of the Children of the Chapel Royal to the King, and Their Master, Captain Cooke*. As far as one can tell, he was a model choir-boy. For many young choristers, the day that their voice broke marked the beginning of a difficult transitional phase in their musical career. Not for Purcell. When that day came, in 1673, he was immediately given the post of assistant to John Hingeston, who was responsible for maintaining all the wind instruments of the King's Musick.[1] Moreover, his voice soon settled, so that he could sing either as a counter-tenor (or male alto) or a bass, and he was accounted an excellent singer. Pluralism was a fact of life among court musicians, but it has to be said that Purcell turned it into an art. In addition to his position with Hingeston, he soon became both tuner of the organ at Westminster Abbey and copyist for the organist – who was John Blow. And the positions kept on coming. In 1677, on Locke's death, he became Composer in Ordinary for the Violin; in 1679, he took over from

Blow at Westminster Abbey; in 1682, he became Organist at the Chapel Royal; in 1683, when Hingeston died, he took over full responsibility for wind instruments; and in 1685, James II appointed him Royal Harpsichordist. And yet, at no stage in this rapid ascent do we catch any whisper of jealousy, of resentment, of anything but admiration for this young phenomenon.

The succession of positions and promotions reflects the reputation that Purcell's compositions were earning him. It is not always easy to date particular works, at least in the early stages of Purcell's career, but we do know that by 1679 some of his verse anthems were already in regular use in both the Chapel Royal and Westminster Abbey and probably had been for some time.[2] One of these was probably *My Beloved Spake* (1678), a symphony anthem with a complex structure and some highly effective word painting, an astonishing achievement for a teenager. At the same time, Purcell was composing instrumental works including fantasies, *In Nomines* and pavans. Some of these were probably required by his appointment as Composer in Ordinary, but, given Charles' distaste for intellectual music, some may have been composed for his own amusement and satisfaction. He was also working on a series of Italian-style trio sonatas for violin which he collected and later published. It was in the context of these pieces that the term 'movement' was first used in England to indicate a section or division of a longer musical work; and it was also at this time – reflecting the Italian influence which Charles so encouraged and Humfrey in particular had been so keen to promote – that the terms 'Cantata' and 'Sonata' began to be used. At this stage, they were used mainly to distinguish a sung piece from an instrumental one; the strictly defined 'sonata form', which was to play such an important part in Romantic and post-Romantic music, was still a long way in the future. Purcell's sonatas were written for two violins and a bass and have a lot in common with dance suites. They follow what may be loosely defined as the Baroque sonata model: a slow introduction, an allegro, a slow movement and a broadly dance-like finale. By 1679, Purcell had also begun his friendship with Playford, whose *Second Book of Choice Ayres and Songs to Sing to the Theorbo-lute or Bass Viol* contains five of his songs. These vary in mood quite incredibly, from a moving elegy for Matthew Locke, 'What hope remains for us now he is gone', to a boisterous, light-hearted song written from the point of view of a man who is fed up with women, 'Since the Pox, or the Plague'.

Yet it was the ode and his development and expansion of the possibilities the genre offered that really showed the King and the wider musical public what Purcell could do. In 1680, he was given the opportunity to write an ode to celebrate the King's return to the capital. The text of *Welcome Vicegerent of the Mighty King* was (and is) execrable, featuring couplets such as 'Then all that have voices, let 'em cheerfully sing / While those that have none may say "God save the King!"', but Purcell was to prove as adept as Tallis at overcoming an unhelpful text. He combined rich orchestral passages and full-blooded choral singing with sensitive solo and duet writing to create a complex and effective musical structure. The ode expressed joy at the King's return without in any sense undermining royal dignity, and Purcell employed the full forces of the King's Musick and the Chapel Royal to perform it. He was just twenty-one. The following year came *Swifter Isis, swifter flow*, written to mark the King's return from a visit to Newmarket. This time, he added flutes and oboes to an ensemble which already included strings, trumpets, a harpsichord and, when necessary, drums. He was writing for something very like an orchestra and proving that he could write in a way which balanced the differing sounds.

In 1683 came the Rye House Plot. Charles was suspected, with justice, of harbouring Catholic sympathies while his brother, the Duke of York, made no secret of his Catholicism. The plan was to assassinate them both and put Charles's illegitimate but Protestant son, the Duke of Monmouth, on the throne – but the plot miscarried and Charles was able to execute or imprison a large number of his political opponents. John Blow celebrated the royal escape with a large symphony anthem, *Hear my voice, O God*, while Purcell was more explicit with his autumn ode, *Fly bold rebellion*. More odes followed – for the marriage of Princess Anne to Prince George of Denmark (*From hardy climes*) and, of course, for St Cecilia's Day.

As time went on, Purcell increased his mastery of both ode and anthem. The chorus and the orchestra began to interact more closely, moving towards the kind of sound world which we think of as defining the Baroque – and which reached its apogee, at least in the British Isles, with Handel's great oratorios. This process was assisted, inadvertently, when James II streamlined the various differing consorts based on families of instruments into one body, known as the Private Musick, which became, in effect, a small Baroque orchestra. The narrow distinction between ode and anthem is illustrated by the aftermath of a yachting trip in the early 1680s when Charles II and the Duke of York were caught in a sudden, violent storm off the North Foreland and narrowly escaped shipwreck. One of those on board was John Gostling, a Gentleman of the Chapel Royal and a celebrated bass. When they returned to London, Gostling made a selection of lines from the Psalms which describe the dangers of life at sea and presented the assembled text to Purcell who wrote the now celebrated, *They that go down to the sea in ships.* The whole event, the King's dramatic escape from shipwreck, is a natural subject for an ode, but because Gostling's text was taken from scripture, Purcell's work, which is musically extremely challenging and bears witness to Gostling's great vocal range, is officially an anthem.

Then, in February 1685, at the age of fifty-five and quite unexpectedly, Charles II died. Even if he had wanted to, he could never have hoped to match the absolutist monarchy of his cousin, Louis XIV – he was too constrained by Parliament – but he had sought to imitate Louis in other ways. During his twenty-five years on the throne, and despite a chronic shortage of cash, he expanded the musical resources of the court and concentrated them to an unprecedented degree on himself as monarch. For those whose livelihood depended on the King, the future suddenly seemed uncertain – not least because Charles's younger brother, now James II, was a Catholic.

As it happened, London and the country as a whole took James's accession calmly and he planned an early coronation to capitalise on the nation's goodwill. It took place in April 1685 and was a spectacular affair, the high point not only of his reign, but also of the court-based musical culture that had grown up under the Stuart kings. The full choirs of the Chapel Royal and Westminster Abbey combined with thirty-six musicians and a company of royal trumpeters and drummers to provide the music. William Child's *O Lord, grant the King a long life*, which had been written for Charles II's Coronation, was revived at the start of the ceremony. Purcell's *I was glad* came next, followed by Blow's *Let Thy hand be strengthened.* The sung litany was probably by Tallis; and this was followed by four more anthems: William Turner's *Come, Holy Ghost, our souls inspire*; a revival of Henry Lawes' *Zadok the Priest*; Blow's *Behold, O God our defender*; and Turner's *The King shall rejoice.* Child's *Te Deum* induced a calmer, more religious frame of mind; then came the actual crowning of James and his Queen, Mary of Modena. This took place to the accompaniment of two massive anthems. Blow's forthright, almost aggressive, *God spake sometime in visions*, is a clear statement of the principles of divine right: God has appointed the King and will protect him from his enemies. Purcell's *My heart is inditing*, which accompanied the crowning of the Queen, deploys equally large forces (eight soloists, an eight-part choir and a full consort of instruments), but is far less warlike. It does not ignore the King's enemies, but it also contains references to the grace and beauty of women; and the shifting textures of Purcell's music throughout this long piece both illustrate the text and create an additional level of rejoicing which reaches its climax in the series of 'Alleluias' with which the piece ends. The magnificence and the uplifting nature of these two anthems – which, together, would have lasted nearly half-an-hour – was intended to obscure the fact that new King and Queen would not receive Anglican Communion following the act of Coronation. This was a potentially damaging, even provocative, departure from tradition, but their Catholic principles would not allow it; and, in the event, the tactic seems to have worked: the sheer, overwhelming splendour of the music and the occasion allayed any hostility, at least for the moment.

All might have been well had James had the tact of his elder brother. Charles had long been suspected of harbouring Catholic sympathies, and actually did convert to Catholicism on his deathbed, but during his reign he did nothing to challenge the position of the Church of England. He understood that any open espousal of the Catholic cause would arouse opposition from both people and Parliament. James, by contrast, believed that it was his duty to return the country to Catholicism and quickly antagonised everyone, from Parliament to his own court musicians. He ordered Sir Christopher Wren to create an elaborate, Baroque chapel for Catholic worship within the confines of Whitehall Palace, the monarch's main residence. This new Catholic Chapel Royal was staffed mainly by Italian, and therefore Catholic, musicians. Giovanni Draghi and Bartolomeo Albrici, both already resident in London, became its organists and may have composed music for worship there; Innocenzo Fede came from Italy to become choirmaster; and the Queen's father, the Duke of Modena, sent the famous castrato Giovanni Francesco Grossi to sing in the correct Italian manner. North of the border, James was, if possible, even less tactful, establishing a Jesuit seminary in Holyrood Palace and turning the Abbey Church into a Catholic Chapel Royal for Scotland.

All this created understandable resentment and anger among the musicians of the official Anglican Chapel Royal. They did not suddenly cease to carry out their various duties, for Princess Anne, James's daughter and a

Protestant, continued to make the Chapel the focus of her worship. Nonetheless, without the presence of the King, there was an inevitable lack of focus and direction, and standards began to slip. Despite the tensions, Purcell composed some remarkable odes, including *Ye Tuneful Muses* (1686) – which breaks new ground by incorporating a folk tune, 'Hey then, and up we go', from that year's edition of Playford's *Dancing Master* – and *Sound the trumpet, beat the drum* (1687), written for King James's birthday. Another anthem, *Thy way O God is holy*, also composed in 1687, shortly after the completion of the Catholic Chapel, is such a powerful piece, with such spectacular interplay between the vocal parts, that it has been interpreted as a deliberate attempt to confront, match and outshine the elaborate theatricality of the papal chapel across the road.

In 1688, James issued his second Declaration of Indulgence. It promised universal religious toleration and effectively lifted the ban on Catholics holding public office. It also appeared to assert the King's authority over Parliament. James ordered that it should be read out to congregations in churches throughout the country. The Archbishop of Canterbury and six other bishops declared the Declaration illegal. They were arrested and charged with seditious libel. During their trial, the choir of the Anglican Chapel Royal sang in public a new anthem by Blow – *O God, Thou art my God* – the text of which could only be construed as an attack on Catholics and the alternative Catholic Chapel ('He shall bring down the noise of strangers: the branch of the terrible ones shall be brought low'). Purcell followed with his *O Sing unto the Lord* which contains a series of not-terribly veiled references to both Catholicism and the trial ('The gods of the heathen, they are but idols.... He shall judge the people righteously'). James had succeeded in doing something that even Charles I had failed to do: he had turned his own court musicians against him.

Yet it was not only in the Chapel Royal that music was used to give expression to the widespread and growing opposition to James. In the period between the acquittal of the bishops in June 1688 and James's flight to France that December, a new song took the country by storm. A Scottish origin, in the form of a tune called 'Joan's Placket is Torn',[3] has been suggested. It has also been credited to Purcell – and he certainly published a version of it under the title 'new Irish tune' in the 1689 edition of *Musick's Handmaid*. The most likely scenario, however, is that Purcell simply adapted a current Irish tune and produced a version under his own name. This was not unusual at the time: it would have been regarded as no different, in fact, from Vaughan Williams producing his own version of a folk song. The tune in question was, of course, 'Lilliburlero', which attained a sudden and devastating popularity when sung to words written by Thomas Warton, one of the leaders of the parliamentary opposition to James. The lyrics satirise the character and abilities of Richard Talbot, 1st Earl of Tyrconnell, a Catholic and Royalist die-hard whom James had appointed as Lord Deputy of Ireland and who was busily appointing Catholics to all the senior positions in the Dublin administration.

There was an old prophecy found in a bog
Lillibullero bullen a la
The country'd be ruled by an ass and a dog
Lillibullero bullen a la
Now this prophecy is all come to pass
Lillibullero bullen a la
For Talbot's the dog and Tyrconnell's the ass
Lillibullero bullen a la

As lyrics go, they are neither profound nor particularly witty, but they were sufficiently subversive, and the tune sufficiently catchy, to act as a rallying cry among those opposed to James and his plans to reintroduce Catholicism. The song became, in effect, the theme tune of what is now known as 'The Glorious Revolution'. Ireland certainly had a history of music being used for political and cultural ends, but it is doubtful whether in Ireland or in Great Britain a single song ever had such a major political impact.

The song's subsequent history is equally impressive. Uncle Toby, in Laurence Sterne's *Tristram Shandy,* is supposed to have served in King William's armies, and he famously whistles it when faced with an embarrassing or contrary opinion. In Sir Walter Scott's *Waverley*, it is sung – somewhat oddly – by the clan chieftain Fergus Mac-Ivor, a staunch supporter of Bonnie Prince Charlie. It was adopted and given new words by the Union side in the American Civil War. It crops up in *Treasure Island*. It became the official regimental march of the Royal Electrical and Mechanical Engineers. The tune is still current in Northern Ireland under the name 'Protestant Boys'. And, of course, it is heard daily throughout the world as the signature tune of the BBC World Service. Few songs and few tunes can have had such wide currency.

35 William of Orange, Purcell, and the First Concerts

William of Orange, Stadtholder of most of the Dutch provinces and husband of James II's elder daughter, Mary, landed his army at Brixham in Devon in November 1688. James fled to France in December. The English Parliament offered the crown to William and Mary jointly in February 1689; and the Convention of the Estates of Scotland followed suit in May. Bloodshed was limited. The attendants and staff of the Catholic Chapel Royal in Whitehall simply melted away, and the chapel itself was left empty and unused; in Scotland Holyrood Abbey was sacked, leaving the ruin that we see today. The Protestant identity of both kingdoms was maintained but, like all revolutions, it had consequences.

William was a Protestant, but he was not an English Protestant. He was a strict Calvinist, and he was also a soldier, two factors which together determined his strong aversion to elaborate ceremonial, whether in church or at court. The Coronation took place quickly, on 11 April 1689. He and Queen Mary had Parliament's backing, but he knew that a coronation would go a long way toward legitimising the new regime in the eyes of the people. Yet it was not a coronation to match that of James II just four years previously. It was reduced in scale and in splendour, appropriate for a King of austere tastes, who associated religious music with popery; for a constitutional monarch who had no pretensions to divine right; and for a Queen who, by and large, shared her husband's views. Purcell's *I was glad* was once again played as the royal procession filed into Westminster Abbey, but the choir was significantly reduced – only twelve Gentlemen of the Chapel Royal received payment for taking part. Instrumental accompaniment was provided by the Private Music as reformed and streamlined under James II. Four new anthems were sung during the service – one by Purcell, *Praise the Lord, O Jerusalem* (which cleverly takes a verse from Isaiah and uses it to praise the joint nature of the reign); and three by Blow, *Behold, O God our defender; The Lord God is a sun and shield*; and *Let my prayer come up* – but they were shorter, more restrained, and scored for more modest resources than in 1685. The last of Blow's anthems was sung during Holy Communion, which had been reintroduced into the ceremony to emphasise the Protestant credentials of the new monarchs – although as it happened neither monarch approved of Communion and both are said to have been shocked during the ceremony by the emphasis on pomp and ritual rather than on prayer and spirituality.

In the streets, where no one noticed such subtleties, there was a wave of popular enthusiasm which expressed itself in the printing of new broadsheets, such as 'The Court of England, or, The Preparation for the Happy Coronation of King William and Queen Mary'; and 'The Protestant's Joy', which chose to emphasise the religious complexion of the new reign.

> Let Protestants freely allow
> Their spirits a happy good cheer,
> Th' eleventh of April now,
> Has prov'd the best day in the year.
>
> Brave boys, let us merrily sing
> While smiling full bumpers go round
> Hear joyful good tidings I bring
> King William and Mary are crown'd.

It was clear, however, that the neither the Chapel Royal nor the Private Musick were going to share this enthusiasm. Within days of coming to the throne, the King and Queen had given orders that music for services in the Chapel Royal should be strictly choral. No instruments were to be allowed. This austerity was soon extended beyond the religious sphere. Queen Mary's birthday fell on 30 April, less than three weeks after the Coronation. Purcell composed a birthday ode, *Arise My Muse*, to a text by the poet Thomas d'Urfey. It is a spectacular piece, which uses the full resources of the Private Musick. Purcell was clearly trying to appeal to his new patrons. He opens with an impressive, almost military, fanfare; following it with an immensely skilful orchestration of d'Urfey's text, which first hails Queen Mary as the new Gloriana, and then declares William – who was on the point of leaving to fight in Ireland – to be the new Caesar. William was apparently proof against such flattery: even before his departure for Ireland, he gave orders to cut the Private Musick by a third and to cut a number of the (admittedly numerous and confusing) court musical appointments which, to him, were unnecessary. These included Purcell's position as Royal Harpsichordist.

Purcell would continue to write birthday odes for Queen Mary, of whom he became quite genuinely fond. Some of these are among his finest works. They vary greatly in scale and approach – from the tuneful exuberance of *Welcome, Welcome Glorious Morn* (1691) and the smaller scale, more intimate but richly harmonised *Love's goddess sure was blind* (1692), to the massive *Come Ye Sons of Art* (1694), with its extended overture, nine-movement structure and elegant, often dance-like rhythms. Glorious as they are, these are the last flowerings of the Restoration ode, and they already show the influence of Purcell's work for the theatre. Similarly, after the accession of William and Mary, he wrote only one more of the great symphony anthems that had been such a feature of English royal music in the years since the Restoration: *My song shall be always of the loving kindness of the Lord.* And there was one last religious masterpiece – the *Te Deum and Jubilate* in D, written for the St Cecilia's Day celebration in 1694, the first work of its kind to be scored for orchestra. But the Chapel Royal, reduced in size and restricted in function, no longer had the resources to do justice to such works. Nor could it train and nurture the English musical talent of the future as it had done in the past. And the King's Private Musick suffered a similar fate. Only its wind players were now required for court functions such as balls and dinners; and only on full state occasions did it perform together with the Chapel Royal choir. The great days of court music in England were over.

Radical, even shocking, as these changes may appear, they were in one sense only a manifestation at the highest level of society of trends which had been developing more widely since the time of the Commonwealth. The courts of Charles II and James II were based on the French model: everything was focussed on the role of the monarch. The result in musical terms was glorious – an undisputed high point in British musical history – but it did mean that music and musical structures in and around the court were increasingly distinct from those in the rest of society. William and Mary's decision to scale down the size and importance of the Chapel Royal and the Private Musick was based on personal preference and religious conviction, but it can also be seen as an appropriate response to a society where patronage, based on money, was beginning to move away from the court and the aristocracy towards the mercantile classes and the bourgeoisie.

Samuel Pepys was in many ways representative of the new middle class of the second half of the seventeenth century. He was not only a talented amateur musician himself – he sang, played the theorbo (or bass lute), the flute, the viol and the violin – he also taught his wife music and observed the musical interests of those around him. His diaries reveal how much music was played at the time – in private houses, in churches, in taverns, at dinners and other public functions, even on board naval ships – and what an important role it played in daily life. In his description of the Great Fire of London in 1666, he even notes the large number of virginals to be seen among the rescued household goods floating down the river on barges. Pepys had a considerable musical acquaintance: he knew Captain Cooke, Locke, Purcell's father, and also John Banister, the violinist whom Charles II had dismissed from the King's Musick for making derogatory comments about French musicianship.

Banister was a professional musician, but he understood the mercantile temper of his age. On 30 December 1672, he placed a notice in the *London Gazette* 'to give notice that at Mr John Banister's House (now called the Music School) over against the George Tavern in Whyte Fryers, this present Monday, will be musick performed by excellent masters, beginning at four of the clock in the afternoon.' There had been music clubs of varying kinds before, but this was the first instance of members of the public paying to be admitted to a strictly musical performance. The idea caught on. Banister continued his concerts on a regular basis until his death in 1679, and his idea was copied by Thomas Britton, a charcoal merchant in Clerkenwell who fitted out the loft of his coal house as a concert room where he staged weekly concerts.

Britton's story is a curious one. He was largely self-educated and his job involved carrying sacks of charcoal around the streets of London. Yet his commitment to music seems to have allowed him, in a very class-conscious age, to mix with all levels of society and become respected for his knowledge, conversation and good taste. He also amassed a huge library. One of Britton's early supporters was Roger L'Estrange, the controversial writer and Royalist politician, whose family had sheltered John Jenkins during the Civil Wars. He played the viol at Britton's first concert. Once he was sure that he had an audience, Britton charged an annual subscription of ten shillings and offered coffee at one penny a cup. The loft was small and accessible only via an outside staircase, but the concerts were a great success and continued for thirty-six years until his death in 1714. They attracted some of the leading musicians of the period – including John Banister (who does not seem to have minded Britton copying his idea); the German composer Dr Johann Pepusch; the Irish composer and violinist, Matthew Dubourg; and even, soon after his arrival in England, Handel himself.

Concerts quickly became an increasingly popular form of entertainment for the middle classes. They were held in the music rooms of taverns, in the large halls of dancing schools, and even in the halls belonging to the City of London's livery companies. In 1683, a group of musicians founded the London Musical Society and instituted annual celebrations in honour of St Cecilia, the patron goddess of music. They commissioned odes by Blow, William Turner and Draghi, all of which were performed in Stationers' Hall in Milk Street – an example of a musical genre which originated at court transferring to a public stage. The best known of the St Cecilia's Day odes is, of course, Purcell's *Hail! Bright Cecilia*. His grandest ode by far, it demonstrates his ability not only to write and orchestrate memorable tunes, but to sustain both invention and variety across thirteen movements and some fifty minutes. Purcell himself sang alto in the first performance at Stationer's Hall in 1692. It was repeated the following year in York Buildings in Villiers Street, which had been adapted as a venue for concerts by a group of musicians in 1685, and soon became a recognised gathering place for London's professional musical community. Other similar venues sprang up: at Charles Street in Covent Garden, at the Two Golden Balls in Bow Street, and at Freeman's Yard in Cornhill. It was probably in 1696 that concerts first moved south of the Thames, to Lambeth Wells, where entry to the 'Great Room' was priced at threepence. Concert rooms were established at Richmond, which was eight miles (thirteen kilometres) from London; and we begin to hear of the first provincial concerts, at Nottingham, to coincide with race meetings. This activity in the public sphere was paralleled by a growth in the number of private concerts given by aristocratic families, usually in their London houses, for the benefit of their own social circle.

Music, in economic terms, was becoming 'a good', something that could be bought or traded to satisfy the requirements of individuals or groups, and this has remained the socio-economic basis of our society's relationship with music to this day. For instrumentalists, a number of whom had been affected by the reduction in the number of musical jobs at court, these changes opened up a new marketplace in which they could hire themselves out for a fee to play at individual events or in regular concert seasons. Such a market had previously only really existed in the world of the theatre, and even there musicians had often been employed as part of the company. As a commercial marketplace for music opened up, so performing musicians, and to a lesser extent composers, became less dependent on patronage – whether royal, aristocratic or religious –

although this was a long and slow process; and patronage, of course, still exists today, principally in the form of commercial or corporate sponsorship. Strangely, the idea of paying for admission to a concert was slow to transfer to the Continent. One or two attempts were made, but it was not until the establishment of *Le Concert Spirituel* in Paris in 1725 that the practice really took off.

36 Purcell, the Theatre, and *Dido and Aeneas*

Purcell was one of the first to see which way the wind was blowing and adapt to the new situation. His official status at court had not changed, so it was natural that, when Queen Mary died of smallpox in 1694, at the age of just thirty-two, the King should turn to him for funeral music. Purcell's *Music for the Funeral of Queen Mary* is simple and dignified. The March is military in character, almost certainly reflecting the musical preferences of the King, but deeply moving and instantly recognisable. Over two hundred and fifty years later, it was adapted for synthesiser and used to great effect in Stanley Kubrick's film, *A Clockwork Orange*. The Canzona is restrained and restricted to trumpets. The anthem *Thou knowest, Lord, the secrets of our hearts*, which comes in two settings, has an almost hymn-like directness; and the later anthem, *I'm sick of life*, is a brilliant miniature, again restrained and direct in what appears to be a personal expression of grief. His response to the death of the Queen was heartfelt, but there is no doubt that, during the years she was on the throne, Purcell was (as we would say today) moving into the private sector.

He took a number of private commissions for odes – from the London Musical Society, from a school in Westminster run by the Reverend Louis Maidwell, from the Society of Yorkshiremen in London, and from Trinity College, Dublin, which was celebrating its centenary – but it was the theatre that absorbed much of his attention. In 1680, he provided incidental music and some songs for a tragedy called *Theodosius, or The Force of Love* by the playwright Nathaniel Lee. The play was a success and one or two offers of similar work came Purcell's way, so that by 1688 he had been involved with half-a-dozen London productions. In the next eight years – from the accession of William and Mary until his own death in 1695 – he composed music for another thirty-seven, a quite astonishing level of activity, which undoubtedly made him financially independent of his court and Chapel Royal positions. In one sense, this was hack work: the play was the thing, and the overtures, incidental music and songs had to fit in with it. There was little scope for formal innovation, but Purcell does not seem to have minded: he used his imagination and his music to enhance the drama within the framework offered to him. And there is no doubt his music proved extremely popular with both the producers of plays and the London public. Once again, he seems to have risen to the top without arousing criticism or hostility.

The masque which Purcell composed for the end of Act II of the 1694 production of *Timon of Athens* – a surprisingly cheerful piece given the play – is still sometimes performed, largely because it has the advantage of a defined, thirteen-section structure. Much of the rest of his theatre music, though lively, melodic, even inspired, can suffer when removed from the specific context for which it was composed. The Rondeau from the 1695 revival of Aphra Behn's *Abdelazer, or The Moor's Revenge,* was popular as a dance tune in its day, and is known now because it was chosen by Benjamin Britten as the theme for his *Young Person's Guide to the Orchestra* (1946). More often, it is the songs from the plays that are heard: the famous 'Nymphs and Shepherds' from Shadwell's *Libertine*; 'Music for a While' from *Oedipus*, a collaboration between Dryden and Nathaniel Lee; 'I'll sail upon the Dog-Star' from *A Fool's Preferment*; or the appealing dialogue of 'Fair Iris and her swain' from *Amphitryon*. In terms of the development of music in the British Isles, however, it is Purcell's involvement with opera rather than stage drama which left the more important legacy.

Opera in Britain was lagging behind. The form itself was neither fully understood nor accepted. There were several reasons for this: the rich tradition of music in stage drama; the equally rich tradition of the masque (which Purcell was busily exploiting); the lack of royal patronage of the kind offered to opera by Louis XIV in France or by Władysław IV in Poland-Lithuania; and purely commercial considerations. Both *The Siege of Rhodes* and *The History of Sir Francis Drake* had been successful, but during the twenty years that followed the emphasis had been on semi-operas (also known as 'dramatic' operas, or 'English' operas), where songs, dances and incidental music were combined with spoken dialogue. The number of genuine operas had been very small, and those that were produced did not yield financial rewards. In 1682, John Blow composed *Venus and Adonis* to a libretto by an unknown hand. It is described in the original manuscript as 'A Masque for the Entertainment of the King', but, though very short and lacking developed characters, it has a number of features which can legitimately be considered operatic: it is through-composed, the music is continuous, and it uses recitative to move the plot forward. In 1685, Dryden collaborated with Louis Grabu, the former Master of the King's Musick, on a genuine, full-scale opera called *Albion and Albianus*. A heavy-handed allegorical tale equating life under the Stuart dynasty with the England of King Arthur, it was full of 'machines', as they were known, to create special effects, notably a chariot drawn by peacocks, which was so expensive to build that it had to be reused in subsequent productions. The project was hugely ambitious – and it flopped. To some extent, this was bad luck. The first night was delayed some months by the death of Charles II, and then when the piece was eventually performed, it managed to coincide with the Duke of Monmouth's rebellion. More significant, however, was the fact that both Dryden's libretto and Grabu's music were essentially dull. The next year, an imported French opera by Lully – *Cadmus et Hermione* – was performed at the Dorset Garden Theatre without apparently arousing much public enthusiasm.

Purcell watched what was going on and took note. We do not know the precise genesis of *Dido and Aeneas*. We know that Nahum Tate wrote the libretto specially, and we know that in the spring or summer of 1689 the opera was performed at a boarding school for young gentlewomen run by one Josias Priest. Priest was a former dancing master who had opened a school in what is now Leicester Square in 1675. Five years later, he had moved to the charming, riverside village of Chelsea, where he and his school occupied a large Tudor mansion that had once belonged to Sir Arthur Gorges, a poet and naval captain who had fought against the Spanish Armada with Raleigh and Drake. Blow's *Venus and Adonis* received its second performance at Priest's school, having initially been played before the court. What we do not know is whether *Dido and Aeneas* was also given its first performance at court. Perhaps it was intended for the court but then dropped after the Glorious Revolution – it seems unlikely that William and Mary would have been interested; but then it seems equally unlikely that such a work should have been written for a girls' school on the outskirts of London.

Dido and Aeneas, like many of Purcell's odes, is a thorough mixture of influences. Lully and French opera are detectable in some of the music; but elsewhere his models seem to have been Italian. The sense of a single unifying concept for the whole work is more Italian than French. It is also clear that Purcell had learned from Blow's *Venus and Adonis*. But the whole is much greater than the sum of its influences. It is regularly described as a masterpiece or even the greatest ever English opera, but it is not easy to decide what makes it a masterpiece. All its components were already familiar – overture, arias, arioso, recitative, chorus, dances, instrumental passages – and, in fact, the structure is slightly unbalanced because the tenor and male lead, Aeneas, is comparatively unrealised. He has some strong recitative and arioso passages, but, unlike Dido, he is not given a major aria to establish his character. The fact that it is a short opera – performance time is about an hour – with a small cast and a simple plot that demands no complicated special effects, may well have helped Purcell: elaboration and complexity were simply not possible. As it is, the directness of the narrative is echoed by economy and directness in the musical characterisation. The recitative dialogue is vivid and focussed; so, too, is the choral writing. However, the real uniqueness of *Dido and Aeneas* lies in Purcell's ability to set an English text; not just to set the words, but to convey the semantic and emotional implications through fresh, uncomplicated melodies in a way that makes an old story mean something special. Dido's 'When I am laid in earth' is often described, for very good reasons, as the greatest English aria.

The quality of *Dido and Aeneas* was recognised immediately by Thomas Betterton (1635–1710), the son of a cook who had become an actor and had emerged as London's leading theatrical manager and director following the death of Davenant in 1668. He immediately signed up Purcell and Priest for a full-scale, five-act semi-opera based on Fletcher's *Prophetess, or, The History of Dioclesian,* and adapted by Betterton himself. *The Prophetess* suffered, as did most dramatic operas, from the fact that the music was shoe-horned artificially into the action and the songs were not actually sung by the characters. Nonetheless, both Purcell's music and the work as a whole were an immediate success. It was praised as the greatest opera yet produced in England. Queen Mary and the Czar of Russia, Peter the Great, both attended performances,[1] and it continued to be performed into the first decade of the eighteenth century. It was also the first opera ever to be seen outside London when it was produced in Norwich in January 1700. Purcell's music is barely remembered now – only the air, 'What shall I do to show how much I love her?' is still heard – but it was sufficiently popular at the time for him to publish a subscription volume at a price of ten shillings.

The Prophetess was first produced at Dorset Garden in the summer of

1690. Soon afterwards, Purcell began to work with John Dryden. Initially, they collaborated on Dryden's play *Amphitryon*, for which Purcell wrote three songs. Then Dryden resurrected the idea of an opera based on King Arthur – for which *Albion and Albianus* had originally been intended as a prologue, before becoming a vastly inflated semi-opera in its own right. *King Arthur* is another five-act semi-opera, but it is a step closer to full opera: this time two of the main characters sing (the good and bad spirits, Philidel and Grimbald), and the music is better integrated into the plot. King Arthur is pitted against his arch-enemy, the Saxon King Oswald, who is supported by the magician, Osmond. The beautiful Emmeline, with whom Arthur is in love, falls into Oswald's clutches, but Arthur frees her by defeating him in single combat. It has been noticed that some of the ideas and images in Dryden's text – Arthur's journey to the forest lair of an evil spirit, a sword which can release enchantment, the idea of a wall of fire, welcoming birdsong, naked sirens in the river seeking to entice him to join them – seem eerily to anticipate Wagner's *Ring*.[2]

This may be the case, but Dryden's essential opposition between Briton and Saxon, Christians and pagans, is not Wagnerian in scale or intent. It was widely held at the time to reflect the political opposition between Tories and Whigs. Responding to all this, Purcell wrote some stunning music, showing off his ability to express a range of different moods – though the long, at times rambling, narrative does not lend itself to the kind of coherence we would expect from a modern opera. The incidental music is full of lyrical passages; the dances (choreographed by Josias Priest) are lively; the choruses help focus the plot; the famous Frost Scene in Act III shows both Purcell's ability to set words with real understanding and a sense of humour; and the masque which ends Act V contains some of his most uplifting and patriotic pieces, including 'Fairest Isle, all isles excelling' and 'Saint George, the Patron of Our Isle'. The Frost Scene music subsequently proved an influence on Michael Nyman in the 1980s: echoes can be heard in both 'Memorial' from the score to *The Cook, The Thief, His Wife & Her Lover* and 'Chasing Sheep is Best Left to Shepherds' from *The Draughtsman's Contract*.

King Arthur was first given at Dorset Garden in 1691 and proved not only an artistic success, but also a financial one. Purcell and Priest immediately moved on to their next project – a version of *A Midsummer Night's Dream*, again promoted and produced by Betterton, and retitled *The Fairy Queen*. Purcell composed what were essentially short masques for each of the five acts, but there was little of the interaction between plot and music that had been so successful in *King Arthur*. He set none of Shakespeare's text and none of the characters sang. In terms of the development of opera, this was something of a retrograde step, but again there is expressive music for a range for differing moods and some fine individual pieces: the stuttering, drunken poet in Act I; the elegant dance for swans and the comic one for monkeys; the simplicity of 'If love's a sweet passion'; the cycle of seasonal songs in Act IV. The problem with *The Fairy Queen* was that costs spiralled out of control – despite expedients such as reusing the peacock chariot from *Albion and Albianus* – reaching some £3,000. Purcell sought to cover his costs by publishing a selection of the songs, but the opera does not seem to have been performed after 1693 until it was revived at Cambridge in 1920.

During 1693 and 94, theatrical and operatic life in London was disrupted by a combination of debt – Alexander Davenant, Sir William Davenant's son and the man in control at Dorset Garden, fled to the Canary Islands – discontent among the actors and actresses who were either paid a pittance or not paid at all, and the death of Queen Mary. During this period and in the months that remained to him before his death in November 1695, Purcell worked on two or three more semi-operas. The main point about *The Tempest*, adapted by Dryden and William Davenant and produced at Drury Lane Theatre in 1695,[3] is that recent scholarship has concluded that Purcell probably did not write the music so long attributed to him. It seems that it was written by the competent if at times old-fashioned John Weldon, who had been one of Purcell's pupils. This, of course, involves a change of attribution for the famous songs 'Full Fathom Five', 'Come unto these yellow sands' and 'Halcyon Days', which has caused some distress among traditionalists. *Bonduca*, which followed, was another adaptation of a Fletcher play. It, too, was produced at Drury Lane, but does not seem to have been a great success. Purcell's main contribution was music for a tribal sacrifice in Act III; and 'Britons, strike home!' – sung by the Chief Druid – is worth mentioning to show that he did not consider himself above popular sentiment. A patriotic crowd-pleaser in 1695 at a time of war with France, it was revived with new words during the Napoleonic invasion scare of 1805. Purcell's last operatic work was *The Indian Queen*, based on a play written some years previously by Dryden and his brother-in-law, Sir Robert Howard. The play, set in South America in the period before the Spanish conquest, was then turned into an opera by Betterton, but it is not known precisely when it was produced. Purcell wrote most of the music, but the masque in Act V was written by his younger brother, or possible cousin, Daniel Purcell (1663–1717), suggesting either that Purcell died before the opera was complete or that the Act V masque was added later. *The Indian Queen* score shows no falling off in Purcell's abilities – there are some moving moments, particularly in the Act III – but the opera as a whole lacks the coherence of *The Prophetess* or *King Arthur* and has never become popular.

Dido and Aeneas pointed the way forward for English opera, but the signpost was largely ignored. The opera was inserted as a masque into Shakespeare's *Measure for Measure* in 1700, but was then lost to sight until revived at the Royal College of Music by Charles Villiers Stanford in 1895. It was Purcell's only through-composed opera and remains stranded, 'a fragile masterpiece' without issue.[4] All the rest were semi-operas to which the music, though an essential component, could not provide the thematic unity that it does in *Dido and Aeneas.* Betterton was a business man. The theatre- and opera-going public wanted productions full of spectacle and drama – they were often called 'Restoration spectaculars' – and that is what he gave them. Purcell obeyed the spirit of the times. Indeed, his versatility and his ability to match music and dramatic mood may well have extended the lifespan of what was always essentially a hybrid genre. Semi-operas continued to be produced after Purcell's death, stimulated in part by intense rivalry between George Powell's company at Drury Lane and Betterton's company at Lincoln's Inn Fields. But the market and public taste were both changing, as was the Lord Chamberlain's regime for licensing theatres, and ten years after Purcell's death, the genre was effectively dead.

37 After Purcell

In November 1695, Purcell was living in Dean's Yard Westminster in the shadow of Westminster Abbey. One story goes that he caught a fatal chill when he came home drunk, having spent too long in the Hole in the Wall, and was locked out of the house by his wife. Another theory suggests that he had tuberculosis. A third possibility is that he was among those unfortunate Londoners who around that time died from eating contaminated chocolate. In his will, he states that he is ill in body but clear in mind and leaves everything to his wife, Frances. He died on 21 November. Five days later he was buried in Westminster Abbey to the sound of the music he had composed for Queen Mary's funeral less than a year earlier.

The tributes flooded in. There were musical elegies. Blow set words by Dryden, 'Mark how the lark and linnet sing'. Henry Hall (*c.*1630–1707), the organist at Hereford Cathedral, who had been a contemporary of Purcell's at the Chapel Royal under Humfrey and Blow, set a pastoral dialogue between a shepherd and a shepherdess, *Yes, My Aminta, 'Tis Too True*. Jeremiah Clarke (*c.*1674–1707), an organist at the Chapel Royal who later shot himself because of a hopeless passion for a woman of vastly superior social rank, wrote, *Come, come along for a dance and a song*, an elegy in several movements, conceived on the scale of some of Purcell's own odes and scored for full Baroque orchestra. Thomas Morgan (dates uncertain), an Irish organist from Dublin who had come to England to improve his playing, produced 'Mr Henry Purcell's Farewell Tune'. Gottlieb (or Godfrey) Finger (*c.*1656–1730), a Moravian composer who had worked with Purcell at the court of James II, organised London's professional musicians to give a memorial concert in York Buildings which included his own, now lost, *Mr Purcell's Farewell*.

There were literary tributes. Dryden wrote his *Ode on the Death of Mr Henry Purcell*. Henry Hall was moved to verse as well as music:

> Sometimes a HERO in an Age appears
> But scarce a PURCELL in a Thousand Years

In 1698, Henry Playford, son of the publisher on whose death Purcell had written a lament, published a memorial volume of Purcell's songs with the title *Orpheus Britannicus*. In the prologue, he draws attention to Purcell's 'peculiar genius to express the energy of English words, whereby he mov'd the passions of all his auditors'. A second volume followed in 1702. Thomas Betterton wrote that 'Mr Henry Purcell, whose Music supported a Company of young raw Actors … penetrates the Heart, makes the Blood dance through your veins, and thrill with the agreeable Violence offer'd by his Heavenly Harmony'.[1]

The death of Purcell left a gap that was both musical and psychological. He had been the greatest composer in England, yet on the Continent he was scarcely known. His music had been open to French and Italian influences, yet it remained resolutely English, working in genres – the anthem, the ode, the semi-opera – that were almost unknown abroad. As a composer he had been untheoretical: his revision of Playford's *Introduction to the Skill of Musick* shows his ideas about tonality to be essentially practical and based on the reality of composition. Similarly, what are often seen as daring harmonies or dissonances can also be interpreted as stemming from the logical movement of the parts. As a musician and composer, he had not stood on his dignity, but accepted that he was living in a changing world and taken work where he found it – at court, in the Church, or in the theatre.

This undogmatic, essentially pragmatic approach, made Purcell difficult to follow or to learn from. Nor was the situation helped by the fact that his early death meant that he left very few pupils who had studied under him – and this at a time when the traditional role of the Chapel Royal in bringing on the next generation of musicians had been disrupted. Then, in January 1698, there came a disastrous fire, which destroyed almost all the old Whitehall Palace, including the Chapel Royal, giving physical expression to the changes in the musical world.

In the theatre, Daniel Purcell stepped into the breach, writing incidental music for a large number of plays, and also contributing to seven semi-operas. In the case of two of these, *Cinthia and Endimion* (1696) and *The World in the Moon* (1697), he borrowed and adapted some of Henry's music. Daniel Purcell was also chosen to write an operatic version of *Orlando Furioso* for the opening of Sir John Vanbrugh's Queen's Theatre, which was to play such an important part in Handel's London career. This certainly suggests that he was well regarded, even though the opening of the theatre was delayed and the piece, if finished, was never produced. Daniel had also had a Chapel Royal education and before coming to London in 1695, presumably to take care of the affairs of his elder brother (or cousin), had been organist at Magdalen College, Oxford. He was a highly capable composer, able to take over the writing of odes for public occasions, such as St Cecilia's Day, King William's return to England after the 1697 Treaty of Ryswick that ended nine years of war with France, and the birthday of Princess Anne in 1700. He wrote verse anthems and settings of the Anglican Service, as well as chamber works and a number of light, entertaining songs, but neither his ability nor his fame was ever going to rival that of Henry.

Of the younger composers who came to the fore in this period, probably the most interesting is William Croft (1678–1727). His was a steady career, rising to prominence through the old channels. Born in Warwickshire, he was a chorister at the Chapel Royal under Blow; obtained an organist's post at St Anne's in Soho; became one of the Chapel Royal organists (1707) on the suicide of Jeremiah Clarke; and then Master of the Children at the Chapel Royal and organist at Westminster Abbey (1708) on the death of Blow. By the age of thirty, he was the senior composer of the Chapel Royal and called upon to write music for great state occasions. Perhaps his most impressive work is his *Te Deum and Jubilate*, probably written to celebrate the Duke of Marlborough's famous victory over the French and the Bavarians at the Battle of Malplaquet in 1709; in a revised version, it remained popular for many years. Croft was on friendly terms with Thomas Bisse, Chancellor of Hereford Cathedral and one of the early driving forces behind the Three Choirs Festival. The Three Choirs, which rotates on a three-year cycle between Hereford, Worcester and Gloucester Cathedrals, claims to be the oldest classical-music festival in the world and celebrated its three hundredth anniversary in 2015. We know that Croft's *Te Deum* was performed at Gloucester in 1721 and it may have been played regularly during the Festival's early years. Croft wrote a large number of anthems, thirty of which were published in a two-volume collection called *Musica Sacra* (1724 and 1725). Not all are of the highest quality – his *Ode for the Peace of Utrecht* (1713) suffers badly by comparison with Handel's composition for the same occasion – but the best are magnificent. *The Lord is a sun and a shield*, written for George I's Coronation in 1714, and *Give the King Thy judgements, O Lord*, a big eight-movement piece, both have a wonderfully full, Baroque sound to them. Croft is best known today for three pieces of music. The first, the *Funeral Sentences*, was also published in *Musica Sacra*. Perhaps written for the funeral of Queen Anne in 1714 – and including one line by Purcell ('Thou knowest, Lord, the secrets of our hearts') because Croft did not believe it could be improved upon – this music has been heard at every British state funeral from the beginning of the eighteenth century to the present day. The second and third are the hymn tunes *Hanover* and *St Anne* to which in the Church of England 'O Worship the King' and 'O God, Our Help in Ages Past' are traditionally sung.

Croft and his generation of composers were lucky in that, unlike William and Mary, Queen Anne was genuinely interested in music. Although the Chapel Royal's traditional home no longer existed, she made sure that it was maintained as an institution, and she made extensive use of St Paul's Cathedral to stage services of thanksgiving with uplifting music to celebrate the great events of her reign. Composers such as Jeremiah Clarke, John Weldon (1676–1736), and Ralph Courteville (1676–1772) received employment within the orbit of royal patronage. Clarke, in addition to writing his elegy for Purcell, wrote a number of anthems and odes. These include *Praise the Lord* for Queen Anne's Coronation, and his *Ode on the Assumption*, which is sufficiently dramatic in its approach to sound more like a cantata than an ode. He wrote church music, and also the famous *Prince of Denmark's March*, which under its popular name, 'The Trumpet Voluntary', was for many years attributed to Purcell. Weldon, already noted as the composer of music for *The Tempest* previously attributed to Purcell, seems to have been a serious character who made a brief excursion into opera before concentrating on his duties at the Chapel Royal and writing songs, chamber music and a number of anthems, none of which are particularly memorable. Courteville was educated at the Chapel Royal, after which he spent most of his life as organist at St James's Piccadilly – a position received as a gift from Queen Mary and maintained under Queen Anne – while writing chamber music and songs. Thomas Tudway (*c.*1656–1726) was a chorister at the Chapel Royal in the 1660s and became Cambridge University's second Professor of Music in 1705 – his predecessor, Nicholas Staggins (?–1700), a somewhat mediocre Master of the King's Music, having died five years previously. Tudway also petitioned the Queen for an appointment at court and may have received some kind of informal title or position, but in 1707 he was stripped of all his appointments following a remark held to be critical of the Queen and her administration. He was noted for his addiction to puns and this may have led him to overstep the mark, but he was also something of a Tory malcontent: either could have got him into trouble. A public recantation and apology saw him reinstated and he went on to compose a number of anthems – including *I will sing of Thy great mercies*, to celebrate Marlborough's victory at the Battle of Blenheim. His real claim to fame, however, is as a musicologist. On behalf of the Earl of Oxford, Robert Harley (though in reality at the suggestion of the librarian and antiquarian, Humfrey Wanley), Tudway made a collection of Anglican church music from the Reformation to the Restoration which runs to six volumes and 3,000 pages.

Croft, Clarke, Weldon and Courteville were also involved, to a greater or lesser extent, in the theatre, particularly in the early stages of their careers. So, too, were Nicholas Staggins; John Eccles (1668–1735), a prolific and extremely popular songwriter; and Richard Leveridge (1670–1758), known today (if at all) for his songs 'Black-eyed Susan' and 'The Roast Beef of England'. They were all musically competent, but none of them really offered anything new. Nor did Tudway. Nor, despite their many qualities, did John Blow and William Turner, who were by this time the elder statesmen of English music.

Two events show the lack of direction in the London musical world. Arguably the greatest political event of Queen Anne's reign was the passing of the Acts of Union in 1707, which formally united England and Scotland as a single nation with a single Parliament. Guns were to be fired to salute the Queen in St James's Park and at the Tower of London. A ceremony of thanksgiving was to be held at St Paul's. It was a major constitutional landmark and the occasion cried out for a suitable musical monument. The Queen seems to have thought so, for she asked Blow, Croft, and Clarke to collaborate on an anthem. Unfortunately, *Behold how good and joyful* appears (only part of the score survives) to have been a lacklustre setting of a thoroughly limp text. In the theatre, it was a similar situation. Lord Halifax and the members of the Tory Kit-Cat Club sponsored a competition to promote all-sung, through-composed operas in English. The libretto, entitled *The Judgement of Paris*, was written by the playwright William Congreve and operas by four composers were selected for the final round of judging at Dorset Garden in the summer of 1703. The first prize of one hundred guineas went to John Weldon. John Eccles came second; Daniel Purcell third, and Gottlieb Finger fourth. None of the entries were of sufficient quality to have an impact on future opera-writing in English. Indeed, both Eccles and Purcell gave up writing for the stage soon afterwards. And none of the operas was revived until 1989 when the BBC Proms staged a re-run of the competition (without Finger's contribution which had been lost). The Proms' audience judged Eccles the winner.

As it was, two other, very different events would combine and, over the course of just a few years, reinvigorate British music, setting it off on an entirely new course. The first, in 1705, was the opening of Vanbrugh's Queen's Theatre with a production of an Italian opera, *Gli amori di Ergasto*, by the German composer, Jakob Greber. The second, at the end of 1710, was the arrival in London of George Frederick Handel.

38 Scotland and Ireland in the Early Eighteenth Century

It took Scotland some time to respond to musical and social changes south of the border, and to shake off the tendency to look backwards that had established itself with the departure of James VI. During the 1670s and 1680s, children at the Aberdeen Song School were still to be found singing four-part songs with words by Alexander Scott dating from before the Reformation[1] – and this despite the presence of Louis de France, a French music master who had studied under the singing teacher and renowned composer of airs and chamber music, Michel Lambert.[2] Vocal collections from the period – one by Louis de France, another by John Squyers – combine aspects of old court culture with folk songs. Instrumental collections made before and after the turn of the eighteenth century emphasise Scotland's rich heritage of folk tunes. One made in the 1690s by the Glaswegian musician Andrew Adam, and known as the Leyden Lyra Viol Manuscript after a later owner,[3] contains simple arrangements of eighty-one Scottish airs, but without the words. The Balcarres Lute Book contains two hundred and fifty-two arrangements for lute, mixing Scottish airs with English and French tunes. Among them is a tune called 'Old Long-Syne', which probably refers to the poem with that title written by Sir Robert Ayton (or Aytoun; 1570–1638). 'Auld Lang Syne' as we know it today was Burns' reworking of this earlier text. He also set it to a different tune.

These were private manuscript collections, but interest in the Scottish folk tradition was growing in the public sphere, too. In 1724, the Lanarkshire poet Allan Ramsay published his *Tea-Table Miscellany*, giving the words to a collection of old Scottish songs but no tunes. Ramsay, it should be noted, had originally moved to Edinburgh to study wig-making, but by this stage was making a living as a bookseller and the proprietor of Britain's first circulating library. The violinist Adam Craig, seeing an opportunity, produced *Musick for Allan Ramsay's Collection of Scots Tunes* (*c.*1726), which was a collection of tunes without the words. In 1725, William Thompson published *Orpheus Caledonius*, a collection of fifty songs, in arrangements which were not always of the highest quality. A musically improved second edition, in two volumes and with twice the number of songs, was published in 1733.

Some of these collections may have been published with an eye on demand from London where interest in Scottish music was also growing. This seems to have begun in the 1680s when Queen Mary expressed a liking for Scottish tunes. Henry Purcell made a keyboard arrangement of 'Peggy, I must love thee' which appeared in *Musick's Handmaid* in 1689; he built the tune 'Cold and Raw' into the texture of his 1692 birthday ode; and he wrote a number of jigs based on the syncopated, Scotch-snap rhythm.[4]

Daniel Purcell also made some arrangements of Scottish songs. In 1701, Henry Playford published a volume entitled *Original Scotch-Tunes*. The Acts of Union in 1707 may have played a part in stimulating interest, but probably more influential was the new celebrity culture that was developing as a result of England's emerging enthusiasm for opera. Singers such as Mrs Jane Barbier, Mrs Anne Turner, Alexander Gordon and John Abell were all noted for their renditions of arrangements of Scottish traditional songs at London concerts. John Walsh, a competitor of Playford's, published a *Collection of Original Scottish Songs* (*c.*1720). What began as a trickle of interest became a flood. Scottish traditional music was now a London fashion. Although what London audiences heard was often arranged, reworked, even sanitised in a way that diluted its essential character, the Scottish folk tradition had nonetheless made a breakthrough in terms of recognition and popularity.

Once William and Mary came to the throne in 1688, any attempt to impose any kind of religious music in Scotland ceased. And once music had ceased to be a matter of controversy, it became possible for the Scots to develop, or re-establish, a tradition of classical or art music. An important contributor to this process was Sir John Clerk of Penicuik (1676–1755), the son of a rich and successful Scottish politician who had been awarded a baronetcy by Charles II. Clerk studied law in Glasgow and then in Leyden in the Netherlands, before spending two years taking the Grand Tour. Italy impressed him more than anywhere else. In Rome, he pursued archaeological and antiquarian interests under the guidance of Giovanni Ciampini. He also studied music under both Arcangelo Corelli (1653–1713), whose violin and trio sonatas had made him perhaps the most popular foreign composer in England, and Bernado Pasquini, who was organist at Santa Maria Maggiore. While in Italy, Clerk wrote no less than five cantatas – including one to celebrate the wedding of the Duke of Bedford and another, called *Leo Scotiae Irritatus*, about Scotland's abortive attempt to set up a colony in Central America. He seems to have been a talented composer, but, returning home in 1700, gave up composition to concentrate on his career as an MP and judge. He did, however, become one of Scotland's leading patrons of the arts – painting, poetry and music all benefitted from his attention – and he was a good friend of Allan Ramsay's. His cosmopolitan outlook is characteristic of the changes in social attitudes that made the expansion of Scottish musical life possible.

The first public concerts in Edinburgh took place in 1695 in a small chapel in the centre of the city. They were put on by singer John Steill, violinist Adam Craig, and harpsichordist Henry Crumden, and were so successful that they developed into a series of recitals that continued for some twenty years. In 1705, John Abell, who was born in Aberdeen, made what appears to have been his only return to his native Scotland. By then a celebrated countertenor, composer and lute player, he had travelled across Europe – the King of Poland apparently threatened to throw him to the bears unless he agreed to sing – written a coronation song for Queen Anne (*Aloud proclaim the cheerful sound*) and sung in Daniel Purcell's version of *The Judgement of Paris*. His return to Scotland and the recitals he gave are poorly documented, but they would certainly have shown a new generation of Scottish musicians what could be achieved. Two years later, Ralph Agutter, a successful London music publisher, moved to Edinburgh and set himself up as an instrument maker, advertising all kinds of violins and *violas da gamba,* lutes and trumpets, which suggests that there must have been sufficient interest in making music among the prosperous middle classes for him to make a living.

In 1720, another series of concerts began. The man behind these was an Aberdonian called Alexander Gordon, one of whose patrons was Sir John Clerk. Gordon had studied singing in Naples and returned to Scotland together with an elusive Italian called Lorenzo Bocchi, who was probably the first person ever to play what the *Edinburgh Evening Courant* referred to as the 'Violin Chello' north of the border. How long these concerts continued is not known, but it does not seem to have been more than two or three years, for Gordon was soon off doing a variety of other things, including trying to drive a canal between the Forth and the Clyde.

Then, in 1728, the Edinburgh Musical Society was founded. For some time, a group of musicians had met more or less regularly in a tavern called the Cross Keys, run by John Steill. This informal grouping now became a formal society – with Sir John Clerk, as one might expect, among its leading members – the foundation of which marks the beginning of a continuity of musical life in the city that has never been interrupted. William McGibbon (*c.*1695–1756) was an early (possibly the first) leader of the orchestra. He is known to have been a composer of Italian-influenced sonatas and concertos, although little of his work survives. From the first, Italian influence (which, of course, includes Handel) was dominant; and in 1735, the Society recruited its own Italian leader, the composer and flautist, Francesco Barsanti (1690–1770), whose initial salary was £50 a year. The fashion for all things Italian had London musical society in its grip, and Edinburgh was determined not to be left behind.

The native Scottish musical tradition had achieved a new level of recognition, but it remained largely separate from imported classical models and the imported classical tradition. There were instances (some of which have already been described) of what we would now call crossover, but it would take a long time for significant interplay between the two traditions to develop. A partial exception is James Oswald (1710–69), Scotland's most successful eighteenth-century composer. Born in the ancient fishing village of Crail in Fife in 1710, Oswald seems to have begun his professional life as a dancing master in Dunfermline before moving to Edinburgh in his mid-twenties. In 1736, he published *A Collection of Minuets* and, in 1740, *A Curious Collection of Scots Tunes*, demonstrating his ability to work effectively in both traditions. One of his most interesting works, however, is his *Sonata on Scots Tunes*, also published in 1740 and originally written as a trio for 'two instruments and a continuo.' Trio sonatas had been made popular by Francesco Geminiani (1687–1762), whose influence as a teacher and disseminator of the influence of Scarlatti and Corelli is something to which we shall return, but, by rooting his work in the Scottish folk tradition, Oswald was making a genuine, and still entertaining, experiment in bringing art music and folk music together.

He left Edinburgh in 1741, an event publicly lamented by Allan Ramsay, for London, where he carved out a highly successful career. His *Caledonian Pocket Companion*, consisting of simple, one-line arrangements of Scottish tunes suitable for the violin, flute or recorder, was undoubtedly designed to cash in on the vogue for Scottish music. It did so most effectively and eventually ran to twelve volumes. It was to *The Caledonian Pocket Companion* that Burns turned when he wanted tunes for his many songs. Oswald was probably music tutor to at least some of George II's nine children, and when George III came to the throne in 1761, he was appointed Chamber Composer to the King. He continued to write in a classical vein, while drawing on his Scottish heritage. *Airs for the Four Seasons* (1755) is an example of the kind of light, attractive and tuneful music for which he became known.

In Ireland during this period, the dominant figure in the native Irish musical tradition was Turlough Carolan (sometimes O'Carolan; 1670–1738). Born in Nobber in County Meath, Carolan and his family moved to Ballyfarnon in Roscommon when he was about fourteen. His father, who was either a farmer or an iron founder, took work with an old-established landowning family called MacDermott Roe. Carolan was educated together with the MacDermott Roe children, but became blind after a bout of smallpox at the age of eighteen. The MacDermott Roes arranged for him to spend three years learning the harp and so, at the age of twenty-one – or so the story goes – he set off with a harp, a horse, and a servant to guide him to become a travelling, professional musician in the time-honoured Irish manner.

There are many stories about Carolan, and no doubt some of them are true, but it is not easy to distinguish the man from the myth. He is revered in Ireland as the last of the great bards, although by all accounts he was not a great harpist, having started playing too late to achieve the level of skill required. His strength was his talent for composing tunes and then for finding words to fit them. Over two hundred Carolan tunes survive. A few were published in his lifetime – in Dublin, by the influential father-and-son partnership of John and William Neale; and some appeared later in unlikely places, such as a 1749 Wesleyan Hymn Book; but for the most part his tunes passed down through the playing of Irish harpists, fiddlers and singers, until collected by Donal O'Sullivan in the 1950s. Carolan's tunes and songs have had a wide currency in Ireland for three hundred years, and they began to reach a wider audience during the folk revival of the 1960s and 70s with the music of groups such as The Dubliners, Planxty, The Wolfe Tones, but particularly through the playing of the harpist Derek Bell with The Chieftains.

Although he married and had seven children, much of Carolan's life was spent wandering, moving between the great houses of Ireland, enjoying the hospitality and patronage of Ireland's great families: most of his tunes are 'planxties', songs composed at the end of a visit to honour, to thank, and sometimes to tease, the host and his family. This was a wholly traditional manner of proceeding. Where Carolan differs, and where he marks the end of an era, is that he did not confine his visits to the old Catholic families, but included English incomers and members of the Protestant ascendancy. As a result, neither he nor his music took on the assertive political or religious character which would have been normal in previous generations. He also differed from his predecessors by showing an awareness of the classical tradition and by introducing an Italian flavour into some of his tunes. There are echoes of Vivaldi and Corelli, and also of Geminiani, whom he probably met in Dublin. One story has it that the well-known *Carolan's*

Concerto – which has been used as a slow march by the British Foot Guards – came about as a result of a competition during which Geminiani tried to trick Carolan, but Carolan, ever the Irish hero, proved too wily for him.

Carolan could live and write as he did because of changes in the political situation in Ireland. The Treaty of Limerick in 1691 cannot be said to have solved Ireland's problems, but it marked the end of active Jacobite resistance to William and Mary's rule. The wars would not be forgotten but, for a while at least, Ireland enjoyed a period of comparative peace and stability during which Dublin developed into a cultural centre of sufficient repute to attract musicians of the calibre of Handel and Arne.

The beginnings were small and pre-dated William III's Irish wars, though, of course, Dublin had never been a completely unmusical town. In the winter of 1679–80, a number of vicars-choral from the city's two cathedrals – Christ Church and St Patrick's – began singing together in local taverns and went on to form the Hibernian Catch Club. Catches had a long history as part of the lighter side of the classical tradition, appearing in the publications of Ravenscroft and Playford, and featuring in court masques; they were written by many seventeenth-century composers, from Gibbons to Wise and Purcell. But they were, of course, secular, and while they could be musically skilful, they could also be bawdy. The existence of a club of professional cathedral singers (though vicars-choral were not actually in holy orders) dedicated to such music marked a breaking down of boundaries and no doubt caused concern to the cathedral authorities, but the Hibernian Catch Club served as a model for the singing clubs and glee clubs that sprang up in London and throughout the British Isles in the eighteenth century. It still exists, and claims to be the oldest surviving musical society in Europe.

As elsewhere, the beginning of music publishing was an important factor in the growth of musical life outside church circles. In Dublin, it seems to have begun in Skinners' Row, the centre of the city's bookselling and publishing trade, with Robert Thornton. In 1686, Thornton, whose premises were 'At The Sign of the Leather Bottle', advertised 'The Choicest New Songs, with Musical Notes, either for voice or instrument, fairly engraven or copper plated, will be constantly printed, and sold at Two-pence a Song.' Most of the earlier publishing – by Thornton and others – seems to have been of pirated editions of works that had already appeared in England or elsewhere: laws of copyright did not at that stage extend to Ireland. Little interest appears to have been taken in Irish music until the

1720s when the father-and-son team of John and William Neale published *Carolan's Tunes* (1721) and *A Collection of the Most Celebrated Irish Tunes* (1723). The latter, containing forty-nine tunes, about half of which may well also be by Carolan, was the beginning of a series that went on to include volumes of Scottish and English music, advertised in the *Dublin Courant* at 'a British Half Crown each'.

Public and subscription concerts were slower to catch on in Dublin than in London or Edinburgh, probably because there was a well-established tradition of playing classical music informally in the city's taverns – notably the George and the Bull's Head in Fishamble Street. In 1723, John Neale led the way in organising more formal, public concerts in the much larger premises of the Bear in Christ Church Yard. The venue was referred to in the *Dublin Courant* as 'Mr Neal's Musick Room'. Even these gatherings attracted the condemnation of the Dean of St Patrick's, Jonathan Swift: he forbade any of his vicars-choral to attend what he referred to as a 'Club of Fiddlers'. The Great Hall in Dublin Castle began to be used as a concert venue, so too did the City Hall, known as the Tholsel. The Neales remained central to Dublin's musical life as concert promoters throughout the period, but their supremacy was threatened when, in 1731, the first large, purpose-built concert hall was opened: Johnston's Great Room in Crow Street. John Neale died in 1737, but William went on to build Neale's Musick Hall, which opened in October 1741. It was there, the following April, that Handel's *Messiah* was given its first performance. By that time, concert-going had become just as important a part of life in Dublin as in London.

By 1700, Dublin was the second city in the British Isles with a population of over 60,000. Edinburgh's status had diminished when the Scottish court moved south in 1603, but Dublin remained a capital city with vice-regal status and a vice-regal court to match. The court was based on Dublin Castle and maintained an orchestra to provide music for state occasions. The presence of this orchestra contributed greatly to the quality of music in Dublin in the early decades of the eighteenth century. One important figure was John (Johann) Sigismund Cousser (1660–1727), a successful German composer, mainly of operas, who had studied with Lully at Versailles. In 1704, at the age of forty-four, Cousser left Germany for London. In 1707, he moved on to Dublin, where he taught and then fulfilled some undefined position at Trinity College, eventually being appointed 'Chief Composer and Master of the Musick' to the vice-regal court in 1716.[5] His main compositions while in Ireland were a series of some twenty *serenatas*, extended celebratory pieces for two or more voices and orchestra, commissioned by the Lord Lieutenant for the birthdays of Queen Anne and, after 1714, George I.

After Cousser's death, the position of Chief Composer was given to Matthew Dubourg (1703–67), who is generally better known as a violin virtuoso. He had been something of a child prodigy, playing a Corelli solo at one of Thomas Britton's concerts when very young and giving his first solo concert at the age of twelve. He was only twenty-five when he took up the Dublin post, but retained it until his death at the age of sixty-four. Either he was less diligent than Cousser or fewer demands were made upon him. He certainly seems to have spent a lot of time in England, where, as music tutor to George II's sons, the Prince of Wales and the Duke of Cumberland, he was extremely well connected. He seems to have written what ceremonial works were required by his position, but none of them were published. Some of his other compositions are occasionally heard – his Violin Concerto in D major, for example, and his *Variations on Druid Tunes*, although the latter work, which takes simple Irish tunes and turns them into complex Baroque structures, is perhaps an acquired taste. Dubourg worked with Handel on a number of occasions in both London and Dublin, and, in this context, a famous anecdote is worth repeating. At one Dublin concert, Dubourg extemporised a solo part or cadenza of great length, during which he seemed to lose his musical sense of direction. When he eventually returned to the right key, Handel said, to much applause, 'You are welcome home, Mr Dubourg!'[6]

39 The Arrival of Handel

Music in the British Isles at the beginning of the eighteenth century was inextricably involved with social and political factors. The mercantile age had begun and the economy was growing. The middle class was expanding. So, too, were the professional classes. There was new money to be spent and, for some, leisure to spend it. The age of the Grand Tour had begun. Italy was the land of antiquity and culture; and, undeniably, it was in Italy that the great musical developments of recent times – the madrigal, the violin, opera, the Baroque – had begun. It was natural that the new consumers of music should look to Italy for the songs, tunes and dances they wished to enjoy in their leisure time. While the Chapel Royal had existed in a form capable of carrying forward the English tradition, and while composers of the calibre of Locke and Purcell had lived and worked in distinctly English forms such as the anthem and the ode, Italian influence could be acknowledged, contained and absorbed without becoming overwhelming. But they were dead – even Blow, though never an innovator of the same class, was dead by 1708 – and it was Italian music and Italian musical forms that filled the gap. Then there was the political context. Charles II had championed both French and Italian music, but was generally more sympathetic to things French because Louis XIV had supported him during his years of exile. By the turn of the century, however, all that was forgotten: France was once again the enemy, and now associated with the Jacobite cause, giving extra impetus to a preference for Italian over French cultural influences.

There is, of course, a tremendous irony in the fact that it was a German who ensured the triumph of Italian opera and Italian music in Britain. Hindsight gives us a picture of Handel's long years of musical dominance as something inevitable, but it was not. There was nothing new about foreign musicians and foreign composers coming to work in London. Grabu had been Master of the King's Musick under Charles II and had tried to establish his operas on the London stage. Draghi continued to work in London until his death in 1708. What was new was the open, competitive nature of London's musical world which encouraged composers from other parts of Europe to come and try their fortunes. Nicola Matteis (*c.*1670–*c.*1715) was an Italian violinist and composer, regarded, in his brief glory, as second only to Corelli. He eventually died in poverty in Norfolk. Nicola Haym (1678–1729) came from Italy to work as a cellist and composer, but is now best remembered for his work on Handel's librettos. Johann Galliard (1687–1747), the German-born son of a French wig-maker and a favourite of Queen Anne's husband, Prince George, wrote a number of operas. Johann Pepusch, as we shall see, achieved success with *The Beggar's Opera*. And there was also Francesco Geminiani. Arriving in London from Lucca in 1714, within two years he was playing the violin for George I with Handel as his accompanist. He published a set of violin sonatas and some arrangements of works by Corelli. He established himself in London society as a teacher, composer and performer, giving concerts in the houses of rich patrons and popularising the work of Corelli and Scarlatti. In 1728, Geminiani was offered the position of Chief Composer in Dublin. He refused (and it was then offered to Dubourg) presumably because he wished to build on his London reputation.[1] In 1731, he organised a series of twenty concerts at Hickford's Room close to fashionable Piccadilly to present his fine, new *Concerti Grossi,* which were published the following year. Then Geminiani's luck ran out. He was imprisoned for debt and only released when the Earl of Essex intervened. He decided to go to Dublin after all, where public concerts and the patronage of the Baron of Tullamore allowed him to open Geminiani's Great Room, but he was still obliged to shuttle back and forth to London in order to make a living. He supplemented his income by writing instructional treatises – on the violin, the guitar, and on the art of accompaniment – and by dealing in fine art, for which he had a passion. In the end, Geminiani cuts a rather sad figure, but one can imagine that, under other circumstances, he might have played an important role in shaping the development of British music.

Handel looms so large in the annals of English music that it is important to establish a sense of perspective. The man who arrived in London in the autumn of 1710, speaking heavily accented and imperfect English was Georg Friedrich Händel, a young German composer of great promise who had recently spent a few years studying in Italy. That, over the next fifty years, he became George Frederick (sometimes Frideric) Handel, master of operatic and choral writing, one of the greatest figures in the history of British music, a man who was buried in Westminster Abbey with 3,000 people in attendance and whose musical influence went unchallenged for almost a century, was due to a number of factors: talent, energy, opportunism and the social and political zeitgeist.

On the face of it, the decision to open the new Queen's Theatre in London's Haymarket in April 1705 with an Italian opera by a German composer might seem strange. Vanbrugh himself was closely associated with Whig interests and his natural preference would have been for an English work. However, as we have seen, Daniel Purcell's *Orlando Furioso* was not ready; nor was *Semele*, John Eccles's collaboration with Congreve. That an Italian piece was the next best choice was probably suggested by events at Drury Lane that January. Thomas Clayton (1673–1725), working together with Nicola Haym and a French composer, Charles Dieupart (1667–1740), had presented *Arsinoe, Queen of Cyprus*. Billed as 'an Opera, after the Italian Manner', it contained little that was new and much that appeared to have been cobbled together from existing Italian sources. However, with Mrs Catherine Tofts making her London debut in the title role, it played for fourteen nights in its first season and was given a special performance at St James's Palace for Queen Anne's fortieth birthday. So, in the expectation that there was money to be made by playing the Italian card, the Queen's Theatre opened with Greber's *Gli amori di Ergasto*. It was meant to be a grand occasion, but it was little short of disaster. Both the singing and the opera, a distinctly pastoral affair with lots of nymphs and shepherds but little plot, were roundly criticised. *Gli amori* lasted only five performances. The singers, who had been brought over specially, returned to Italy, and Greber returned to Germany. Nonetheless, it was the first all-sung, Italian opera to be heard in England.

Drury Lane followed the success of *Arsinoe* with *Camilla* (1706), an English version of the Italian *Il Trionfo di Camilla*, with music by Marcantonio Buononcini. *Camilla* attracted good audiences from the beginning, but its popularity was boosted during its second season when Valentini (Valentino Urbani), the first castrato to appear on the London stage, joined the cast. He sang in Italian, while Mrs Tofts, again in the title role, and the rest of the company sang in English. *Camilla* was revived regularly over a period of twenty years, and by 1726, had been performed well over a hundred times. By contrast, Drury Lane's next venture was a complete flop. This was Thomas Clayton's *Rosamund* (1707) with a libretto by the essayist and man of letters, Joseph Addison. Addison and his influential Whig friends in the Kit-Cat Club wanted the arts, including opera, to reflect the English national character, so the plot was intended to be patriotic. It centred on the story of Rosamund Clifford, lover of Henry II; it also managed to praise the Acts of Union and flatter the Duke of Marlborough; and it creaked badly. Worse, Addison's words proved difficult to set and impossible to sing; and Clayton's score lacked both direction and melody. Criticism was vitriolic. One grudgingly positive review appeared in the *Muses Mercury*,[2] but it was a lone voice. The opera lasted only three performances. Italian opera, it seemed, might succeed. English opera stood no chance.

And so it continued. In 1707, the Lord Chamberlain altered the licensing arrangements affecting London theatres, confining plays to Drury Lane and operas to the Queen's Theatre. The first opera to be produced after the change was *Love's Triumph* (1708), an English adaptation of an Italian original. The first night's receipts were an astonishing £240 6s 9d.[3] Scarlatti's *Pirro e Demetrio* followed – as *Pyrrhus and Demetrius* – and was a huge success, not least because it marked the London debut of Nicolini (Nicola

Grimaldi), another celebrated castrato. Again, he sang in Italian opposite Mrs Tofts who sang in English. Italian musicians, Italian singers, even Italian painters were now working in London: Marco Ricci and Giovanni Pellegrini were working on the scenery at the Queen's Theatre. Italian opera was triumphant.

Such was the situation in 1710 when Handel arrived. He had been born in 1685 in Saxony, in the ancient city of Halle not far from Leipzig. His musical talents had been obvious from an early age, but they had come into conflict with his father's wish that he should become a lawyer. For a while he studied both subjects: music under Friedrich Zachow (sometimes Zachau), organist at Halle's impressive sixteenth-century Marienkirche; law at school and even, for a brief period, at university. In the end, however, music triumphed. In 1702, at the age of just seventeen, he accepted the position of organist at the city's cathedral; but Handel was ambitious and stayed only until the end of his probationary year before setting out for Hamburg. The attraction of Hamburg was the Oper am Gänsemarkt, the only theatre in Germany staging opera of any quality. The director – and also *Kapellmeister* of St Mary's Cathedral – was Reinhard Keiser (1674–1739), a prolific composer who wrote over a hundred operas; and it is interesting to note that Keiser's *Claudius*, which was performed shortly after Handel's arrival in the city, was the first Hamburg opera to feature Italian arias. Handel was given a job as a back-desk violinist at the opera, but in the space of just a year rose to become harpsichordist-conductor. (In those days, the orchestra was usually directed from the harpsichord.) He also became friendly with the young composer and singer, Johann Mattheson (1681–1764), who took the tenor roles.

Two stories concerning Mattheson give an indication of Handel's character at this time. In the summer of 1703, the two of them visited the city of Lübeck where the organist and composer Dieterich Buxtehude was approaching retirement. Lübeck was a musical city and to succeed Buxtehude would be a huge boost to any young composer's reputation, but Lübeck had no opera, which was where both Handel and Mattheson saw their futures; and, worse, a condition of the appointment was marriage to Buxtehude's eldest daughter. The two young men returned to Hamburg. A year later, Mattheson's opera, *Cleopatra*, was performed, with Handel directing and playing the harpsichord continuo. Mattheson's stage role of Antonius finished half-an-hour before the final curtain and he tried to take over at the harpsichord. Handel refused to move. In the foyer afterwards, a duel ensued, during which – so the story goes – Handel was only saved from injury or even death by a large metal button on his coat.

Handel's first opera, *Almira*, produced in Hamburg in 1705, received twenty performances; it was immediately followed by his second, *Nero*, which ran for only three before the season ended. He was also teaching. One of his earliest pupils was the son of John Wych, the British Resident in Hamburg, and a man noted for his musical interests. It is possible that it was through the Wych household and its many visitors that Handel first began to establish a network of British connections. By 1706, however, he obviously felt it was time to move on. He travelled to Italy, the land where opera and so much else had begun, and stayed there until 1710. Unusually for a musician at that time, he had no patron. He travelled independently, using his own savings and money he had inherited from his father's estate. He spent time in Florence, Rome, Naples and Venice. He met Alessandro and Domenico Scarlatti, Francesco Gasparini, Antonio Lotti and Arcangelo Corelli (whom he apparently disliked). And he composed a lot of music – some fifty cantatas; a surprising amount of Latin church music; his first two oratorios (*Il trionfo del tempo* and *La ressurrezione*); and two operas, *Roderigo*, first performed in Florence in 1707, and *Agrippina*, first performed in Venice at the end of 1709. It was a successful period during which Handel learned a lot, but he had no intention of staying in Italy permanently.

While in Venice, Handel met the British Ambassador, the Earl of Manchester, who – in the way of ambassadors – seems to have invited him to visit England. This lodged in Handel's mind, although there is no evidence that the invitation was ever followed up on by the Ambassador. Handel's musical abilities, like Byrd's, were matched by a very practical business sense and when he left Venice early in 1710, his priority was to secure himself a well-paid job. He found it in Hanover, where the Elector, George Louis (later King George I), revived the post of *Kapellmeister* for him and gave him a salary of one thousand *thaler.* It may be that he took the post on the understanding that he might take leave to visit England at an early opportunity; whatever the case, once appointed Handel spent only three or four months establishing himself in his new role – and ingratiating himself with the Elector's son and his wife (the future King George II and Queen Caroline) – before setting off for London.

It was opera and the potential rewards of opera on the London stage that drew Handel to England. He was twenty-five and ambitious; he had an impressive reputation, and no doubt brought with him introductions and recommendations from influential connections he had made in Italy – which were useful, although no guarantee of success. He attended and possibly played at Thomas Britton's musical evenings. He made himself known among the vicars-choral at St Paul's Cathedral, and would drink and play with them in the nearby Queen's Arms. Soon after his arrival, he met the playwright, Aaron Hill, who in November 1710 took over the management of the Queen's Theatre. The result was *Rinaldo,* a three-act opera set during the First Crusade, with a libretto by Giacomo Rossi, based on a story by Hill. Handel apparently wrote the music in just two weeks. It was the first fully Italian opera written for the London stage – although in a dedicatory address to Queen Anne, Hill, somewhat oddly, suggests that it should be seen as an English opera. Tickets went on sale at White's Coffee House in St James's Street and *Rinaldo* had its premiere at the Queen's Theatre in February 1711. It was an immediate success and Handel's score was published by J. C. Walsh at nine shillings a copy. Despite some carping reviews, including one by Addison in *The Spectator*, there were fifteen performances before the end of the season.

Rinaldo is a remarkably assured opera for a young man. From the opening bars of the overture, there is a confidence and dynamism that carry the work along, and it is full of attractive melodies. In fact, a significant number of the arias in *Rinaldo* are based on tunes that Handel recycled or adapted from his earlier works. A version of the famous 'Lascia ch'io pangia', for example, had appeared in *Il triofo del tempo,* and something like it was heard as a dance in *Almira* (and it continues to be recycled: it was used as the basis for a song by the rock band Procol Harum in 2003). Such self-borrowings have attracted criticism from modern scholars, but they were less detectable in an age before recorded sound and were the accepted practice of the time. They certainly do not detract from the work as a whole. *Rinaldo* is far from perfect, but it offered London audiences a level of musical, if not dramatic, consistency that had not been heard in opera in England before.

Handel returned to Hanover in June 1711 and stayed for about a year, but he was back in London for the autumn season of 1712 with a new opera, the rather lacklustre *Il Pastor Fido.* When this proved less popular than *Rinaldo,* which was still in the repertoire, he came up with *Teseo,* his only five-act opera, which was premiered in January 1713. *Teseo,* based on a play by Philippe Quinault which Lully had also used as the basis for an opera, attracted good audiences, not least because it included a number of spectacular special effects, including a flying dragon and Minerva descending from the heavens as a *dea ex machina*. Drama onstage was matched by drama offstage. After the second performance, Owen Swiney, who had taken over from Hill as manager of the Queen's Theatre, stole the takings and headed for Europe where he remained for the next twenty years. He was quickly replaced by Johann Jacob Heidegger, a Swiss impresario and manager, who was to prove both a more reliable manager and a long-term collaborator with Handel.

Handel's talent and his success in London's fashionable operatic circles quickly brought him into contact with the court. By the end of 1712, he had been commissioned to write both a birthday ode for Queen Anne and a work to celebrate the widely anticipated Peace of Utrecht. Quite how this came about is uncertain – though it is possible that the Queen herself may have made the choice – but it was one of several occasions in Handel's career when music and politics collided. The Treaty of Utrecht, eventually signed in April 1713, brought an end to twelve years of war with France, but it also meant abandoning some of Britain's allies; among them the Elector of Hanover, who was still technically Handel's employer as well as Queen Anne's successor. Composing a birthday ode for the Queen and a work to celebrate the Peace would publicly align Handel with the British rather than the Hanoverian establishment. Characteristically, he seized what he saw as the main chance. The ode, *Eternal Source of Light Divine*, was probably performed in February 1713, although Queen Anne was ill at the time and is unlikely to have heard it. Written to a splendidly sycophantic lyric by the hack poet Ambrose Phillips, it demonstrates Handel's ability to grasp an essentially English form and apply Italian techniques, giving it increased dramatic force, and building through different musical textures over a period of twenty-five minutes to reach an impressive climax. The *Utrecht Te Deum and Jubilate* was given at a service of thanksgiving in St Paul's Cathedral that April, though Queen Anne was once again ill and not present. The *Te Deum and Jubilate*, like the ode, works by a gradual escalation of musical intensity. In particular, it points the way forward in terms of Handel's ability to use large choral forces to build and sustain dramatic tension. Handel was suddenly a musical force outside the confines of the opera house.

It was evident by now that Handel had no intention of returning to Hanover and that same summer he was dismissed from his position as

Kapellmeister. Handel's first biographer, John Mainwaring, seems to have been responsible for the idea that this was the result of resentment, even anger, on the part of the Elector, but this is not backed up by the evidence.[4] The Hanoverian diplomatic representative in London, Christoph Friedrich Kreyenberg, took great pains to make it clear to Handel that he was not in disgrace and would have nothing to fear when the Elector eventually arrived in London. And we know that Handel actively assisted Hanoverian interests by informing Kreyenberg of the state of Queen Anne's health – information that he received from the Queen's doctor, John Arbuthnot. Arbuthnot, who was also a writer and the creator of the original character of John Bull,[5] was close to both Joseph Addison and Richard Steele, joint founders of *The Spectator*; and together they represented an important link between Handel and London's literary world, an indication of just how quickly and effectively he had established a social position for himself. That December, Queen Anne granted him an annual pension of £200 which more than compensated for the loss of his income from Hanover.

The Queen died at the beginning of August 1714, and the Elector arrived in London as King George I that September. When the new King and his family attended their first services in the Chapel Royal in St James's Palace, it was Handel's music (probably the so-called *'Queen Caroline' Te Deum*) that greeted them – something which would surely not have happened had he been out of favour. Handel's music did not feature at King George's Coronation in October. This was understandable. Anxious to stress his credentials as a British monarch rather than a German incomer, the King favoured William Croft and John Eccles, which was both appropriate and expedient. But Handel's pension from Queen Anne was continued and, at the end of 1715, he even received some arrears of pay from his appointment in Hanover. His position in relation to the new regime was evidently secure.

Handel wrote his short opera, *Silla,* which was probably given privately at the Earl of Burlington's London residence, in 1713, before the Queen's death, and *Rinaldo* was also revived that year. It was not until 1715 that he produced a new opera for the public stage. This was *Amadigi di Gaula,* noted for its special effects and oddly muddled plot. By that time, both George I and his son, the Prince of Wales, were attending the opera regularly and the future looked bright. However, in 1717, the King and his son had a spectacular falling out. London was suddenly divided both socially and politically. Fewer people attended the opera; revenues dropped; and productions at the now renamed King's Theatre ground to a halt.

It was against this background, with the King and the Prince of Wales vying for the support of the nobility and the good opinion of the public with rival displays of wealth and spectacle, that Handel wrote his three *Water Music* suites. As the King's barge, surrounded by a flotilla of other craft and moving slowly with the tide, made its way up the Thames from Whitehall to Chelsea, Handel's music, played by some fifty musicians in an accompanying barge, drifted through the summer evening. The King was delighted and insisted on all three suites being repeated several times. It was, of course, a piece of royal public relations, but it was hugely successful and the *Water Music* remains Handel's best-known instrumental work – rivalled only by the *Music for the Royal Fireworks* from 1749. It is energetic and tuneful, and undoubtedly best played on period instruments in order to convey the clarity and distinctness that would have been essential for it to carry effectively across the water as originally intended.

The fact that there was no opera in London does not seem to have bothered Handel. By the summer of 1717, he had found a new patron in the person of James Brydges, recently created Earl of Carnarvon and shortly to become Duke of Chandos. Brydges had been Paymaster-General for the British armies abroad during the war with France and, as a consequence, had amassed a huge fortune, which enabled him to create Cannons, a great house with a spectacular thirty-hectare park in the district of Edgware to the north of London. Handel was closely associated with Brydges for about a year and may have lived at Cannons for some of that time. He would certainly have had access to Cannons' resident instrumental band and choir. It was a period notable for three major works – the *Chandos Anthems*, *Acis and Galatea* and the oratorio, *Esther* – all of which, in their differing ways, show Handel coming to grips with Englishness and English musical forms, as well as pointing in the direction his music would take later in his career. Handel's eleven settings of the psalms, known collectively as the *Chandos Anthems,* are a masterpiece, perhaps a slightly neglected one, and certainly his greatest contribution to church music. They were originally performed in the Church of St Lawrence, close to Cannons (where the private chapel had not yet been completed), which still houses an organ played by Handel. Each consisting of between six and eight short movements – and written without alto solos, because Brydges was apparently not fond of the alto voice – they mark a new high point in Handel's mastery of choral writing. Not only do they display his apparently inexhaustible ability to create melodic lines of great beauty and delicacy, they also show a new freedom and flexibility in his management of soloists and chorus, which alternate and contrast, intermingle and complement in an array of dynamic combinations.

Acis and Galatea, as performed at Cannons in the summer of 1718, was a one-act masque for five singers, with a pastoral but tragic theme. Handel later turned it into a five-act *serenata,* and it has been variously added to and adapted over the years. There is even a version by Mozart. It is usually seen as a pastoral opera – and often praised as one of the finest in the genre – although *Grove's Dictionary of Music and Musicians* has traditionally referred to it as an oratorio. What is important is that it was Handel's first extended, dramatic work in English. It is beautifully crafted: the lovers' pastoral dream is gradually undermined and seamlessly transformed into tragedy. The libretto, probably by John Gay with additions by Pope and the writer John Hughes, is concise, clever and witty, but also serious. As Handel's biographer says, the work 'shows what degree of drama could be achieved within the pastoral convention: there is no sillyness about these nymphs and shepherds.'[6] *Esther*, which followed *Acis and Galatea*, probably in the same year, is most definitely an oratorio, and is a much bigger work. Cannons' musical establishment would have required significant reinforcement in order to stage it. Perhaps because he was working at speed, Handel again resorts to self-borrowing; and he does not appear to have been satisfied, for he altered, expanded and tinkered with it on several occasions right up to the end of his life. The libretto, while probably by the same team that produced *Acis and Galatea,* has nothing of the subtlety that characterised the earlier work. Nonetheless, *Esther* was not only Handel's first English-language oratorio, it was *the* first English-language oratorio – and it was the oratorio, not opera or the symphony, that was to become the dominant musical form in British music throughout the nineteenth century. In their different ways, both *Acis and Galatea* and *Esther* broke new ground, but Handel did not follow up the lessons he had learned until the 1730s, mainly because opera – which was his reason for coming to Britain in the first place – staged a comeback.

40 Handel, the Royal Academy of Music, and Ballad Opera

Although incorporated by a royal charter dated July 1719, and having the Lord Chamberlain as its effective governor, the Royal Academy of Music was to be structured and operated like a joint stock company. It would have a list of subscribers – among them seven dukes, thirteen earls and three viscounts – who would pay £200 per share and vote on important issues in the manner of shareholders. The King promised a subsidy of £1,000 a year. The Academy's stated purpose was 'for Carrying on Operas and other Entertainments of Musick', but it was also intended to make a profit for its subscribers, payable in the form of an annual dividend. All this was perhaps appropriate in the era of coffee houses, Change Alley, and the South Sea Bubble (which would burst the following year). It certainly took the idea of music as a commodity to a new level.

Handel, who was not among the investors, was sent off abroad even before the charter was signed to recruit singers for the new company. Margherita Durastanti, the Italian soprano, received £1,500 for an eighteen-month contract. Senesino (Francesco Bernardi), the outstanding castrato of the age, and a thoroughly difficult character with whom Handel was to have numerous fallings out, eventually agreed to accept £2,000. The Academy was determined to do things properly. Two Italian composers, Giovanni Bononcini (1670–1747) and Attilio Ariosti (1666–1729), were also recruited, although it was understood from the beginning that Handel would be the Academy's mainstay.

The Academy was inaugurated in April 1720 with a production of *Numitore* by Giovanni Porta. Handel's new opera – his first for five years – was *Radamisto*, staged at the end of the month. It is one of his most impressive operas, consistent and balanced throughout, with some highly effective musical characterisation, and using an unusually large orchestra featuring horns as well as trumpets for the first time. Its first night was a great success, for political as well as musical reasons. In a set piece worthy of an opera, the King and the Prince of Wales attended the performance together, publicly marking their reconciliation. The third opera performed during this first season was Domenico Scarlatti's *Narciso*, in a version adapted and probably directed by Thomas Roseingrave (1690–1766).

Roseingrave merits a digression here as an example of a talented, if eccentric, musician who made a career at the same time as Handel but never quite reached the heights. His father, Daniel, had been one of Captain Cooke's Chapel Royal recruits, eventually becoming organist at both St Patrick's and Christ Church Cathedral in Dublin where he was chiefly distinguished for his uncontrollable temper – he once actually sliced off the ear of a former Christ Church organist during a service.

Thomas Roseingrave's talents were recognised at an early age and in 1709, when he was nineteen, the Dean and Chapter of St Patrick's helped to pay for him to study in Italy. In Venice, Roseingrave met Domenico Scarlatti with whom he formed a close relationship. Indeed, he became something of a disciple, following Scarlatti to Rome and Naples and studying with him for a number of years. In 1717, Roseingrave returned to London where he taught, composed – very much in the style of Blow and Purcell – and became known as one of the leading organists of his generation. He probably met Handel when he joined a public competition to become the first organist at St George's, Hanover Square. This was Handel's local church when he was in London and he provided the theme on which the aspiring candidates were required to improvise. Roseingrave won and remained organist there until 1737, but it was a far from untroubled tenure, for he was never a stable character and his psychological problems were exacerbated when he proposed to a fashionable young lady whom he had been teaching, and was rejected. Her father would not allow her to marry a musician. Roseingrave eventually retired to Dublin, where he worked on an opera, *Phaedra and Hippolitus,* which was performed in 1753. When he died in 1766, he left a large and varied body of work – compositions for organ and harpsichord; flute sonatas; some English songs; cantatas; an impressive large scale choral piece, almost an oratorio in miniature, called *Arise, shine, for thy light is come*; and, of course, his version of *Narciso.*

Life at the Royal Academy of Music was never exactly untroubled. The practical difficulties of mounting elaborate productions were no less stressful and the egos of highly paid stars no smaller than they are today. Yet despite the inevitable problems and jealousies, the Academy did ensure a high level of artistic achievement and success over the eight seasons of its existence. Handel wrote thirteen operas during these years, including some of his best and most popular works – the categories may overlap but are not necessarily the same – and over half the performances given by the Academy were of his works. In some of the early seasons, Bononcini rivalled Handel in popularity: in 1721–22, his *Crispo* and *Griselda* proved deservedly more popular than Handel's lacklustre *Floridante.* But one thing Handel had was staying power. In 1723, he fought back with *Ottone,* the immediate success of which was boosted by the debut of the new Italian prima donna, Francesca Cuzzoni. *Ottone* was followed the same year by *Flavio,* but *Flavio* is lighter in texture and less heroic in approach – there is irony, even self-mockery, in Handel's treatment of the story – and it did not catch the public imagination in the same way. Then came one of the most sustained periods of successful composition in his career. In the space of twelve months, faced with competition from Bononcini and from Ariosti too, he produced *Giulio Cesare* (1724), *Tamerlano* (1724) and *Rodelinda* (1725). There are, of course, huge differences between the three operas, but, taken together, they represent the peak of Handel's operatic career. Nicola Haym was librettist on all three, and working together they improved the narrative structure so that one scene leads more naturally into the next. Handel also stretched his melodic inventiveness and musical characterisation beyond the big arias to include passages of recitative and whole scenes. As a result, all three operas achieve a new level of dramatic and musical consistency.

The next three years saw six new operas from Handel: *Scipione, Alessandro, Admeto, Riccardo Primo, Siroe, Tolomeo.* All have their moments, but none reach the degree of artistic coherence and success of their immediate predecessors. *Admeto* (1727) was the most successful at the time, its popularity assisted by the fact that it featured another new prima donna, Faustina Bordoni, playing opposite the now established queen of the London stage, Cuzzoni. Rivalry between these two, both on and offstage, created fierce partisanship among some opera-goers. Supporters of Cuzzoni would hiss Bordoni and vice versa. Things escalated to the point where, on the last night of the 1727 season, during a performance of Bonacini's *Asianette* with the Princess of Wales in the audience, the two leading ladies had a stand-up fight on stage and had to be separated by members of the cast. Whether this actively contributed to the demise of the Academy or not, it certainly did the image of opera no good. In any case, the Academy was failing. Shareholders had received a dividend after the 1721–22 season, but otherwise it had run at a loss. Now, its capital was exhausted and, early in 1728, it was formally wound up.

Handel did a great deal better out of the Academy than its shareholders. He saved a massive amount of money – perhaps as much as £10,000. In the same period, he also managed to triple his income from royal sources. Under George I, the Chapel Royal had fallen to something of a low ebb. Apart from regular services, few demands were made upon it. William Croft made an effort to reintroduce orchestral accompaniment to church music, and he was supported by Maurice Greene (*c.*1695–1755). They wrote occasional pieces and *Te Deums* to mark the King's return from his trips to Hanover or from his summer holiday outside London. Handel joined in and was rewarded with an additional salary of £200 as one of the Chapel Royal's composers, alongside Croft and John Weldon, both of whom received less than half that amount. He received a further £195 a year for acting as music tutor to the Princesses Anne and Caroline, the two elder daughters of the Prince of Wales. Possibly because of concerns that such positions should not be held by a foreigner, Handel decided to become a British citizen. The naturalisation bill – the process required parliamentary approval in those days – was one of the last pieces of public business conducted by George I before his death in June 1727. William Croft, the chief Chapel Royal composer, died in August. This meant that the newly British Handel was perfectly placed to compose the music for George II's Coronation that October. In fact, George II specifically chose him, excluding Maurice Greene, who was Croft's natural successor among British-born composers.

Huge musical forces were assembled. The choir of the Chapel Royal was reinforced by soloists from the opera. The orchestra consisted of one hundred and sixty players. The ceremony itself, however, was marked by confusion, so that Purcell's *I Was Glad* was missed out and Handel's anthems consequently came at the wrong place in the service, but that did not affect their very positive reception. Since that day in 1727, *Zadok the Priest* has been heard at the coronation of every British monarch. With its simple rhythmic opening (surely known to Philip Glass) followed by great bursts of emphatic acclamatory phrases, it must be one of the best-known English anthems. *Let Thy hand be strengthened* is a complete contrast, more intricate and melodic, making its point without the assistance of brass or percussion. *The King shall rejoice* and *My heart is inditing* are both thoroughly Baroque in their musical language, with the orchestration of the former at times clearly echoing the *Water Music*. These are effortless works, written by a man who has complete confidence in his abilities and complete control over his music. They undoubtedly lack the measured intricacy and beauty of the *Chandos Anthems*, but that in itself is evidence of Handel's understanding of his new, public role: he is writing to inspire at the coronation of a king, not to assist at the devotions of a private patron.

Opera remained Handel's priority. When the Royal Academy failed, he continued at the King's Theatre, going into partnership with Heidegger. George II continued to pay the annual £1,000 subsidy agreed by his father. Handel went to Italy to recruit singers, with only partial success. A string of new operas followed – *Lotario, Partenope, Poro, Ezio, Sosarme, Orlando,*

Ariadne in Crete – but none of them hit the longed-for operatic jackpot and, by the end of 1733, Handel and Heidegger found themselves facing competition. A new company called The Opera of the Nobility had been formed, under the patronage of the new Prince of Wales (the future George III). Things went from bad to worse. Senesino defected to the new company. Then, in 1734, when the lease on the King's Theatre ran out, Heidegger withdrew from the partnership. He threw in his lot with The Opera of the Nobility, and, without consulting Handel, allowed them to lease the theatre. Handel still had an opera company, but he had no theatre.

There was competition of another, if less obviously direct kind as well. For almost thirty years now, Italian opera had been the leading musical genre on the London stage, yet the masque had never quite gone out of fashion and from 1715 it staged a revival with new works by Johann Pepusch, such as *Venus and Adonis* (1715) and *The Death of Dido* (1716). Johann Galliard followed suit with *Pan and Syrinx* (1718) and *Decius and Paulina* (1718). These were not Jacobean court masques; they were scaled-down, one-act pieces, not negligible in themselves but offering a less sophisticated level of entertainment than the operas at the King's Theatre. Most were produced by John Rich who had leased William Davenant's old theatre in Lincoln's Inn Fields. It was probably the success of these masques that lay behind James Brydges' commissioning Handel to write *Acis and Galatea*.

Some of these masques – such as Pepusch's *Apollo and Daphne* (1716) and Richard Leveridge's *Pyramus and Thisbe* (1718) – contained strongly comic elements that proved popular with audiences. This seems to have given Rich the idea to develop a new kind of comic dramatic opera, drawing on the *commedia dell'arte* tradition and closer to pantomime than anything else we would recognise today. *Amadis, or The Loves of Harlequin and Columbine*, for which Rich himself was largely responsible, was the first, produced in 1718; but it seems to have been *Jupiter and Europa* (1723) that really established the popularity of the new genre, and *The Necromancer*, later the same year, that confirmed that he had found a successful formula. These pantomimes consisted of short airs and short recitatives with simple tunes, interspersed with dances and mimes. The action was divided between an ostensibly serious, formal plot and a bucolic, comic sub-plot that included a slapstick element and was, of course, the more popular of the two. Flats slid in and out from the wings along wooden grooves greased with soap, allowing for rapid scene changes.

Across the back of the stage, a dragon or a chariot, clouds or the sun might 'fly' to add to the spectacle. The whole piece would end with a rousing chorus and a dance.

From this background and this milieu emerged *The Beggar's Opera*. The original idea, arising out of correspondence between Dean Swift and Alexander Pope in 1716, had been for what Swift described as 'Pastoral Ridicule' or 'Newgate Pastoral' set among thieves and whores. (Newgate, the location of London's most notorious prison, was a synonym for criminal behaviour.) John Gay picked up the idea, gave it a comic and satirical twist, and created a new and original form, the ballad opera. (It is worth noting that in the early years of their popularity such works were simply termed *operas*; the term *ballad opera* was only applied later.) Of the music, only the overture, by Pepusch, was original. Otherwise, the piece consisted of sixty-nine airs to already existing tunes, the vast majority of which were taken from English, Irish, Scottish and French folk songs. The remainder were borrowed from a list of composers which included Purcell, Jeremiah Clarke, Handel, John Eccles, Bononcini, Geminiani and Pepusch himself.[1] Gay wrote new words for all but five of the tunes as well as the dialogue that links them into a narrative. There is no recitative; and, unlike other English dramatic operas, *The Beggar's Opera* demanded that all the main characters should be able to sing.

The first performance took place at Lincoln's Inn Fields in January 1728, just at the time when the Royal Academy was teetering towards financial collapse. The anti-hero is Macheath, a thief and serial seducer. The plot seems to lead inexorably towards his execution and the moral that only the rich can escape punishment, but at the last moment the Beggar, who acts as the narrator, is persuaded that the audience will want a happy ending. He invents a reprieve for Macheath and invites everyone to dance in celebration. The whole is a satire on the Italian operas which had so obsessed London's fashionable world, on political corruption, and on the morals of a society where only money and influence count. It was a stunning success, although attracting grumpy criticism from those who thought that its low-life setting and lack of a traditional moral message would actually encourage crime and immorality. It received sixty-two performances in its first season and over forty in its second. Gay's earnings on the first two seasons were in the order of £750, while Rich's profits, as producer, were in excess of £7,000.

Within two months of its London premiere, *The Beggar's Opera* was being performed at the Smock Alley Theatre in Dublin. There were forty performances in the city before the end of the year. Within three months, it was being given in Norwich. By May that year, it was in Bath, where there were over forty performances. May also saw its first performance in Newcastle-upon-Tyne. It was given fifty times in Bristol. It was taken into the West Country and Wales by touring theatre companies. The first performance in Edinburgh was in August, after which it moved on to Haddington. There is a story that the pupils of Haddington Grammar School, seeking a Scottish equivalent, persuaded Allan Ramsay to turn his pastoral comedy *The Gentle Shepherd* into a ballad opera by the simple expedient of including songs from his *Tea-Table Miscellany*.[2] This version of events has been challenged, but there is no doubt that the ballad opera version of *The Gentle Shepherd*, which was given an amateur performance in January 1729, perhaps by the pupils of Haddington school, was inspired by Gay's work.[3] There was even a performance of *The Beggar's Opera* on the island of Minorca, which had been a British possession since the Peace of Utrecht. Ballad opera proved capable of inspiring a much larger and much wider audience than Italian opera. And it showed clearly that that audience liked to hear things sung in English. Did Handel see *The Beggar's Opera*? He must have been aware of what was going on, but whether he read the lessons directly is an open question.

Gay, Pepusch and Rich sought to follow up the success of *The Beggar's Opera* with a continuation of the story, *Polly*, but it was suppressed by the Lord Chamberlain, apparently because the satire came too close for the comfort of Sir Robert Walpole, the Prime Minister. Nonetheless, the ballad opera genre was launched. Over a hundred such works were published during the next twenty years and, like *The Beggar's Opera*, many of them were given not only in London, but in cities and towns throughout the British Isles. One of the most successful was *The Devil to Pay, or, The Wives Metamorphos'd* (1731), originally billed as a 'ballad farce'. Based on a play by the obscure seventeenth-century playwright, Thomas Jevon, it was adapted by Charles Coffey (described as 'an itinerant Dramatist'[4]) and another playwright, John Mottley; it achieved success not only in Britain but also in translation in Germany. It then progressed through operatic versions in Austria, France and Italy, before returning home in 1852 as *The Devil's In It*, 'an entirely new and original comic opera' by the Irish composer, Michael William Balfe. Among those involved in writing ballad operas at this time were Henry Fielding, later to become one of the greatest

English novelists, and Henry Carey (1687–1743), the poet, dramatist, singer and musician. Fielding's gift for satire led to *The Welsh Opera* (1731), *The Mock Doctor* (1732) and *An Old Man Taught Wisdom* (1735), which, though they left little trace musically, were savage enough in tone to attract the notice of the government. Carey achieved success with his short, one-act ballad farces *The Honest Yorkshireman* (1736) and *The Dragon of Wantley* (1737), which contain some of his own very tuneful compositions. But in 1737, the government passed a new Stage Licensing Act. This gave it new powers to censor the content of stage performances, effectively depriving new ballad operas of most of their bite and much of their interest. Fielding turned to novels, where his satire could remain uncensored; Carey turned to burlesque operas in which the satirical content was much dimmed.

The ballad opera did not actually die; rather it blended with other musical narrative forms. Certain aspects resurfaced strongly in the burlesques that were popular in nineteenth-century theatre; while the satirical element is clearly evident, however greatly adapted to different times, in the comic operas of Gilbert and Sullivan. Vaughan Williams' opera *Hugh the Drover* (1924) is heavily based on folk songs, but is more a pastoral than a ballad opera. Ewan MacColl and Peggy Seeger's famous radio ballads from the 1950s and 60s clearly owe something to the ballad opera in the way they create a narrative from folk song and its imitation; while a more direct attempt to recreate the genre in both sound and narrative structure was made in 1977 by Peter Bellamy with his ballad opera, *The Transports*. Nor, of course, should it be forgotten that it was *The Beggar's Opera* that was the inspiration for Brecht and Weill's *Dreigroschenoper* in 1928.

In 1734, as his difficulties multiplied, Handel was not tempted to write a ballad opera, but he did turn to John Rich, who had rapidly become a powerful figure in the world of the theatre. The capital he had amassed from *The Beggar's Opera* had allowed him to build a new theatre in Covent Garden, and it was here that Handel agreed to base his homeless opera company. He wrote and produced six operas in three years – *Ariodante*, *Alcina*, *Atalanta*, *Arminio*, *Giustino*, *Berenice* – but the competition was fierce. Handel had his reputation, a new theatre, and a fine singer in the soprano Marie Sallé. The Opera of the Nobility had better singers: Cuzzoni; the bass, Domenico Montagnana; Senesino; and a possibly even greater *castrato* in Farinelli. They also benefitted from the fact there was a growing resentment at the way Handel had dominated London's musical life for over twenty years. Operas by composers such as Francesco Veracini

(1690–1768) and Johann Hasse (1699–1783) offered an alternative. And the craze for ballad opera sapped support from both. It was a hard fight in which music played only a walk-on part. Technically, the honours of war were Handel's in that the Opera of the Nobility closed its doors four days before he was forced to admit that his own company could no longer carry on. In reality, Handel was the loser. He had taken sole and personal responsibility for his company and was now on the edge of bankruptcy. Worse, the combination of workload and stress had taken its toll. In April, 1737, he had what appears to have been a stroke, resulting in partial paralysis of his right arm.

Even now, he would not give up. He went to Aix-la-Chapelle for an intensive cure. Astonishingly, he was back in London by November, composing a new opera, *Faramondo*, and apparently capable of playing the organ and the harpsichord as well as ever. That same month, Queen Caroline died and Handel had less than two weeks to compose her funeral anthem. *The ways of Zion do mourn* is a full anthem, without solo parts, and scored for strings, woodwind and percussion only. It lasts forty-five minutes and was performed by huge musical forces in Westminster Abbey on the day of the funeral, but its dominant characteristic is restraint. In Hanover, Handel had written duets and keyboard pieces for the young Caroline of Ansbach. In London, as Queen Caroline, she had been a faithful champion of his music. *The Ways of Zion* is public music, but has more depth than the coronation anthems of ten years previously. As with Purcell's *Music for the Funeral of Queen Mary*, which it echoes at times, the public composer is here joining his personal grief with that of the King and the public.

The remnants of the two opera companies which had fought so bitterly were now cobbled together into a single company at the King's Theatre – later shifting to Lincoln's Inn Fields. Heidegger, with whom Handel was now reconciled, had trouble raising the subscription. There was no longer the appetite to sponsor opera that there had been even five years earlier. Nor was public enthusiasm as great. Five new operas by Handel were produced between 1738 and 1741 – *Faramondo*, *Alessandro Severo* (a pasticcio, consisting of music assembled from other works), *Serse*, *Imeneo*, *Deidamia*. Together, they mustered only twenty-four performances. The third performance of *Deidamia* in February 1741 was the last of an Italian opera by Handel in London during his lifetime.

In a sense, he had failed. He had tried for thirty years to educate the

London public into Italian opera. There had been moments when they had seemed to follow him, but now their enthusiasm had definitely waned. It was not that opera, or even Italian opera, would cease to be performed on the London stage once Handel stopped composing it. It was rather that the experiment, or perhaps flirtation, which had seen the wholesale adoption of Italian forms and styles, was over. By the end of the seventeenth century, Locke, Blow and Purcell had established an English approach to opera – with others such as Clarke, Eccles, Weldon and Daniel Purcell following on behind. It was an approach too fragile to be called a tradition, and Handel had all but swept it aside with the great certainties of Italian opera. That moment had passed. An English tradition would quietly reassert itself. It would continue to be fragile and uncertain, and to have a pastoral bias; it would be open to foreign influence; it would often be hopelessly parochial; and it would not produce an opera of international significance until the twentieth century. For the next hundred years and more, opera in Britain would simply be less important than the alternative vocal tradition – what has been termed the cult of the oratorio – for the emergence of which Handel was principally responsible.

41 Handel and the Oratorio

In the spring of 1732, at the King's command, Handel was preparing a much-revised version of *Esther* for performance at the King's Theatre. He seems to have intended to stage it as an opera, but William Gibson, Bishop of London and Dean of the Chapel Royal, intervened. The bishop was not prepared to sanction a sacred, biblical story being acted out on a public stage. The alternative, which Handel adopted, was the oratorio solution: a concert performance with soloists and a static choir – and the businessman in him no doubt appreciated that this dramatically reduced the production costs. Oratorios, it seemed, were in the air. Towards the end of 1732, Maurice Greene produced his *Song of Deborah and Barak*, and at the beginning of 1733 came *Judith*, a collaboration between the Dutch-born composer Willem de Fesch and William Higgins. There was nothing in these works that could be seen as in any sense a challenge to Handel. Nonetheless, his competitive instincts were aroused. He responded with two oratorios in six months: his own version of *Deborah*, and *Athalia*, both of which achieved a measure of success and were revived on several occasions during the 1730s. Of the two, *Athalia*, which was premiered at Oxford's Sheldonian Theatre, is the better structured – perhaps because it was based on a play by Racine. The important point, however, is that Handel came to oratorio from opera; and his early oratorios were essentially operas without acting or stage sets. In his manuscripts, they are divided into acts, not parts, and the three-act structure he demanded from his librettists was essentially the same as for an opera – with the crucial difference that the words should be in English.

Operas kept Handel busy until 1739, when he composed *Saul*. First performed at the King's Theatre in the presence of George II, *Saul* is a big work, in every sense. It is full of powerful arias, big choruses, and grand orchestral effects. It also features the famously massive 'Dead March'. Handel augmented the orchestra for the occasion, bringing in trombones for the first time, as well as kettledrums and a large organ which he played himself. *Saul* is the first of Handel's great oratorios. It was popular from the beginning and went on to be one of the most frequently played oratorios at choral festivals during the nineteenth century. *Saul* was also the first collaboration between Handel and Charles Jennens, who assembled the libretto. Jennens was a rich landowner and patron of the arts from Leicestershire. He was also a non-juror (someone who refused to recognise the legality of the deposition of James II and could thus not swear allegiance to the Hanoverians), a stance which excluded him from any form of public office. At the same time, as a staunch Protestant, he scorned the Jacobite cause as an essentially Catholic movement. As these views indicate, Jennens was not always logical. He had a stubborn, even cantankerous, streak. He would often be vocal in his criticism of Handel – and Handel himself was given to explosions of temper – but somehow the two remained friends right up until Handel's death. Jennens provided the libretto for *Israel in Egypt*, which Handel wrote immediately after *Saul*, though it proved far less successful, perhaps because it contains some overlong choral passages. Jennens also worked on *L'Allegro, il Penseroso ed il Moderato* which followed in 1740. This represents a change of direction, although whether the finished piece is an oratorio or a pastoral ode – it has been called both – is open to question. The libretto is an attempt to create a classic eighteenth-century balance: two poems by Milton (*L'Allegro* and *Il Penseroso*) depicting contrasting human temperaments, are interwoven and then supplemented by a third written by Jennens himself, proposing a middle way. Handel responded to the strong pastoral element in Milton's poems with some wonderfully lyrical music: some of the earlier airs (significantly, not arias) come as close as he ever got to the cadences of English folk music. The structure is an attempt to create drama without characters, relying instead on the musically intensified juxtaposition of sections which express contrasting ideas. If it did not quite come off on this occasion, Jennens was to reuse and develop the idea to much greater effect in his next collaboration with Handel.

Handel had told Jennens, among others, that, for the first time since he had arrived in London thirty years previously, he would not be actively involved in the 1741–42 London opera season: the Lord Lieutenant of Ireland, the Duke of Devonshire, had invited him to visit Dublin. The invitation was confirmed in October 1741 and he seems to have been keen to get away. He travelled to Chester, where the young Charles Burney was among those who met him, and then on to Parkgate on the Wirral, where he took the packet boat to Dublin. Audiences in the Irish capital were already familiar with some of Handel's music: *Acis and Galatea* had been given at Johnston's Great Room in Crow Street in 1734, but, naturally enough given the available resources, it was his anthems and his church music that were better known. He took lodgings in Abbey Street and organised a series of six subscription concerts, which began at the end of December. The works played included *L'Allegro, il Penseroso ed il Moderato*; *Esther; Acis and Galatea; Ode for St Cecilia's Day*; and a number of organ concertos and *Concerti Grossi*. Handel does not seem to have known what to expect from the Dublin audience, but his presence was a huge draw and the concerts were a great success. The Duke of Devonshire attended all six of them and was among those who pressed for a second series. He even wrote to the King asking for Handel to be given leave to stay in Dublin longer than originally planned. The second series ran from February to the beginning of April 1742, and, among other works, featured concert performances of the opera *Imeneo* and the masque, *Alexander's Feast*. Again, the series was extremely successful, although the appeal of Handel and his music may well have been increased by the presence of the beautiful soprano, Susannah Maria Cibber, sister of Thomas Arne, who had (or so the rumour went) been involved in a *ménage à trois* before running off and having a child by her lover. It was only during this second series of concerts that Handel seems to have taken the decision to give *Messiah* as a kind of postscript or encore to his period in Dublin. He appears to have written it in a three-and-a-half week burst of creative activity the previous summer, but was either uncertain about the work itself or about how it would fit in with his other concerts.

The first public performance of *Messiah* began at midday on 13 April 1742 at Neale's Music Hall in Fishamble Street. The organisers, expecting a crush, had asked gentlemen to come without swords and ladies without hoops in their dresses. Tickets cost half-a-guinea and included admission to the rehearsal on 9 April. It was a charity performance, at a time when Ireland still suffering from the aftermath of the 1740–41 famine. The proceeds went 'for the Relief of the Prisoners in several [debtors'] gaols, and for the Support of Mercer's Hospital in Stephen-street, and of the Charitable Infirmary on the Inn's Quay'.[1] The soprano soloists, Christina Maria Avoglio and Susannah Cibber, had been specially brought to Ireland to sing at Handel's concerts. The male soloists, William Lamb, Joseph Ward and John Mason, were Dublin-based. The choir, probably about twenty strong, was drawn mainly from St Patrick's and Christ Church Cathedrals (Dean Swift's objections to his choristers performing in such a den of iniquity having been overcome). The orchestra was made up of Dublin-based players led by Matthew Dubourg. It was equally modest in size, consisting of strings, two trumpets and timpani only, with Handel himself directing from the harpsichord. Seven hundred people attended and over £400 was raised for the nominated charities. Even after the rehearsal, *Faulkner's Journal* was reporting that Handel's new work 'was allowed by the greatest Judges to be the finest Composition of Musick that ever was heard.' After the first, full performance, the adjectives mounted ever higher: 'exquisite', 'sublime', 'grand', 'tender', 'elevated', 'majestic', 'moving'.[2]

Jennens' libretto is a three-part meditation – part analysis, part celebration – on Christ's role in the Christian religion. Part I moves from the prophecies of Isaiah to the Nativity; Part II centres on the Crucifixion and the Resurrection; Part III deals with the resurrection of the dead, the Day of Judgement and the triumph of the Christian religion. It is a remarkably sensitive and intelligent synthesis of texts drawn from the King James Bible and the Book of Common Prayer (and as such is doctrinally solidly Anglican). All the same, it is not the obvious basis for one of the most popular pieces of classical music ever written and one which runs for about two-and-a-half hours. Unlike all Handel's other oratorios (with the exception of *L'Allegro, il Penseroso ed il Moderato* noted above), *Messiah* has no actual plot. There are no characters and, as a consequence, no dialogue. It draws on rather than tells the story of Jesus Christ, and would be incomprehensible to anyone not already familiar with it. Jennens left it to Handel to create the drama and the tension, which he did by responding musically to an underlying understanding of the spiritual rather than narrative highlights – an understanding his audience would, of course, have shared.

Messiah has three parts or acts, sixteen scenes and fifty-three movements.[3] The big choruses, such as 'For unto us a child is born', 'Hallelujah', 'Lift up your heads, O ye gates' and 'Worthy is the Lamb', play a major part in the oratorio's enduring popularity; but these choruses – and also later orchestrations of the work, including that by Mozart – can obscure the fact that *Messiah* is not, at heart, an assertive work. The Nativity, the Resurrection and the triumph of God are its climactic points, but much of the rest of the work is characterised by expressions of hope for mankind at the coming of Christ or melancholy at mankind's failure to respond. An aria such as 'I know that my Redeemer liveth' could be presented as statement of triumph, but Handel is more subtle than that. He allows doubt and melancholy to pervade the aria. It is these human moods that bring out Handel's melodic genius and make the work the masterpiece it is.

Messiah, like Handel himself, looms large in the history of British music. Originally performed at Easter and intended for modest musical forces, it is now firmly associated with Christmas and frequently performed by huge choirs and orchestras. The work's popularity grew during the 1750s and it became the centrepiece of the great nineteenth-century oratorio cult, given everywhere from cathedrals to village halls. The Great Handel Festival, held at London's Crystal Palace in 1857, featured a choir of 2000 and an orchestra of eight hundred and fifty. Even now, *Messiah* remains the single most popular choral work for amateur performance. Among professional musicians, as the twentieth century progressed, the tendency was to favour smaller choral and orchestral forces in an attempt to replicate as far as possible the kind of sound Handel might have heard, but, even so, large-scale performances remain popular. Every year for over forty years, the Royal Albert Hall has hosted '*Messiah* from Scratch', where 3,000 people spend a day rehearsing under professional guidance before singing the oratorio in the evening.

It would be tempting to see the premiere of *Messiah* as a watershed moment, the beginning of the oratorio cult, the moment when the British people awoke to the oratorio and its possibilities. Unfortunately, history is not so neat or accommodating. Handel returned to London in August 1742, having stayed in Dublin long enough to see Thomas Arne and his wife, the great soprano Cecilia Young, arrive in the city and begin their own concert series. He turned his attention to *Samson*, which he had begun the previous year before leaving for Dublin, but it was not played until March 1743 when it was the central work in a series of six successful subscription concerts at John Rich's Covent Garden theatre. A second six-concert series followed with three more performances of *Samson*, one of *L'Allegro ed il Penseroso* (but substituting *Ode for St Cecilia's Day* for the *il Moderato* section), and two of *Messiah* – fully eleven months after its Dublin premiere. *Samson* was the public's favourite. With nine performances in its first season, it proved the most immediately popular of all Handel's oratorios and, like *Saul*, became a favourite at choral festivals throughout the nineteenth century. Based on Milton's *Samson Agonistes*, it has a strong, tragic narrative and a number of rich character parts. It also reuses the device of having a funeral march as a dramatic set piece, in this case as the tragic finale.

Messiah's London premiere, by contrast, was something of disappointment. It certainly did not match Dublin. In part, this may have been because Handel was the subject of an attack in a newspaper article for allowing ordinary singers to present sacred material in a public theatre. Whether this was a serious objection or inspired by Handel's enemies and competitors is not clear. His English-language oratorios, sung by English singers, were, after all, in direct – and apparently successful – competition with a reconstituted Opera of the Nobility at the King's Theatre directed by the Earl of Middlesex. Whatever the case, interest gradually picked up and, even if it did not quite match the popularity of *Samson*, *Messiah* was given four times before the end of March.

Handel's new direction was clear, and over the next nine years he composed no less than thirteen full-length oratorios, but it was not an untroubled progress. Soon after the London premiere of *Messiah*, he suffered a recurrence of the paralysis in his right arm which had afflicted him a few years earlier. As soon as he recovered, he was under pressure to write a new opera for the now financially troubled Opera of the Nobility. His refusal annoyed not only Middlesex and the Opera's aristocratic backers, but also the Prince of Wales. However, he did agree to compose the so-called *Dettingen Te Deum* and a *Dettingen Anthem* to go with it. These were played at St James's Palace in November 1743 to celebrate the return of George II from the Continent and his victory at the Battle of Dettingen in June that year. They are full of martial vigour and perfectly appropriate to the occasion, but they were just that, occasional pieces, and one does not have impression that he poured his soul into them.

Semele, an oratorio based on the libretto written by Congreve for John Eccles's 1707 opera of the same name, was performed in February 1744. The story, which centres on the love affair between the mortal Semele and the immortal Jupiter, was regarded by some as profane, and Handel again found his work under attack on moral grounds. The piece itself was a moderate success, but was dropped after its first season and seems not to have been performed again until 1959. *Joseph and His Brethren*, which followed in the same season, marked a return to biblical stories. Handel clearly liked the work and revived it on a number of occasions during his lifetime, but it has not often been performed since. The same pattern was repeated in 1745, with the mythological *Hercules*, which was not popular despite being an impressively dramatic piece, followed by the biblical *Belshazzar*, which had a libretto by Jennens. It was disappointing season, disrupted by illness, changing theatres and endless administrative problems, and in the end Handel may have lost money. That autumn saw a recurrence of his illness, but he recovered sufficiently to put together the *Occasional Oratorio* at the beginning of 1746. This was written to celebrate the deliverance of the country from the 1745 Jacobite Rebellion. It is something of a pasticcio, making use of material drawn from other works, but with its strong martial feeling, an impressive march as part of the overture, and heavy use of trumpets, it suited the occasion perfectly and the public responded.

Handel was over sixty now. He continued to live in the house in Brook Street into which he had moved in 1723. He had never married. As a young man in Rome he had had an affair with a much-older Italian soprano, Vittoria Tarquini, but apart from that there are no records of any other relationships in his life. There has been speculation that he was homosexual, based partly on the texts of his cantatas and partly on the people with whom he associated, but it seems unlikely and the evidence is at best circumstantial. We know that he ate too much, drank too much and collected engravings; otherwise, he seems to have been devoted to his music. Given the pressure he put himself under – and it is worth remembering that many of his oratorios contain between two-and-a-half and three hours of music – one wonders how much time he would have found for a personal life.

Judas Maccabaeus, which appeared in 1747, was another big work. Again, it had political overtones, appearing to compliment the Duke of Cumberland on his victory at the Battle of Culloden. There is little drama in *Judas*. There are only three characters and the battles and other narrative actions all take place offstage. Yet it works, and has remained popular because, in some respects like *Messiah*, it is an outpouring of collective emotion. It also contains some fine choral writing, notably 'See, the Conqu'ring Hero Comes', which Beethoven turned into a set of variations, and the Swiss pastor Edmond Louis Budry turned into a hymn in 1904. Translated into English by Richard Hoyle in the 1920s as 'Thine Be the Glory', it is frequently heard at services involving the Royal Family, and – whether direct from the oratorio or via the hymn – the tune has also become a regular fixture at the Last Night of the Proms.

Joshua and *Alexander Balus* followed in 1748, biblical in subject, but still on the theme of the Hanoverian victory over the Jacobites. In 1749 came *Susanna*, a more delicate piece with a pastoral setting; and then *Solomon*, witty and well structured with a score that is heavily reliant on woodwind and brass. *Theodora*, in 1750, was unpopular and neglected at the time, but Handel thought it one of his best works and was particularly fond of the aria 'He Saw the Lovely Youth' at the end of Act II. Nowadays it is regarded as one of his greatest works and usually performed as an opera. These new oratorios were, of course, given alongside revivals of works which had been successful in previous years. *Jeptha* was intended for the 1751 season, but it took longer than usual to compose because the sight in his left eye was failing. As a result, the only new work that year was *The Choice of Hercules*, which was billed as a additional act to his much-earlier masque, *Alexander's Feast*, and ran for less than an hour. *Jeptha* was produced the following year, and it was Handel's last original work. (*The Triumph of Time and Truth*, a revised, English-language version of his very first oratorio, appeared in 1757, but Handel had no more than a supervisory role in putting the score together.) *Jeptha* is a deep and troubling work. Jeptha himself, leading the Israelites into battle against the Ammonites, swears that if he is victorious he will make a burnt offering of the first living thing he encounters on his return. That first living thing is his daughter, Iphis. Jeptha is caught between his vow to God and his love for his child, and the oratorio explores his dilemma in its social, personal and a philosophical context. The mood moves from the Israelites' celebration of the freedom which God-given military victory has brought them to Jeptha's soul-searching anguish and Iphis' almost visionary resignation to her fate. It is left to the chorus to try and draw some kind of meaning from the story when, at the end of Act II, they sing 'How dark, O Lord, are Thy decrees!'

Those words must have had meaning for Handel, too, for he was now effectively blind. William Bromfield, the Prince of Wales's surgeon, operated on him in November 1752, but the operation did nothing to improve the situation. He continued to direct and conduct and he could play certain pieces on the organ or harpsichord from memory, but from now until his death he was to rely heavily on the help of John Christopher Smith (1712–95), who acted as secretary and amanuensis. It was Smith who was responsible for the practical organisation of the annual oratorio seasons at Covent Garden and who, under Handel's direction, made the necessary amendments and additions to the scores. Smith was born Johann Christoph Schmidt. His father, confusingly also Johann Christoph Schmidt, had known Handel in Halle and come to London in 1716 to act as copyist to the great man. The younger Schmidt, now Smith, had studied with Thomas Roseingrave and, by the time he began working closely with Handel in the 1750s, had written at least eight operas and two oratorios of his own. One of these, *The Seasons*, based on the long poem by the Scottish poet, James Thomson, is an interesting and neglected work. Although composed in 1740 and written in the idiom of the time, it shows clear signs of looking beyond the Baroque towards early classical styles, and the representations of birdsong, storms, and peasants in the fields contain pre-echoes of both Haydn's oratorio of the same name and Beethoven's *Pastoral Symphony*.

Handel had been in England for forty years, but it was only in the last decade of his life that the English really took him to heart. London had been his battleground, but now the London public appeared finally to have been won over, with the oratorio season attracting consistent audiences, and the Handel cult was spreading to the provinces. Salisbury took the lead, putting on *Acis* in 1748 and 1749, then *Samson*, then *Judas*, then a string of other oratorios through the 1750s. *Judas* was played in Bath; *Messiah* in Bristol and Devizes. The Edinburgh Musical Society wrote to ask for the music so that they, too, could put on *Messiah*. The Three Choirs Festival, which had adopted Purcell, and which was to do so much to recognise and encourage English music right up to the twentieth century, now adopted Handel. One of his *Te Deums* had been given at Gloucester as early as 1736, but after 1751, when *Alexander's Feast* and *L'Allegro ed Il Penseroso* were given, again at Gloucester, Handel became central to the Festival's programmes. In 1752 at Worcester, *Samson* was given; at Hereford the next year, *Samson* again; at Gloucester in 1754, *L'Allegro* and *Judas*. Fashionable London was one thing; the prestigious but restricted circles around the court another; he had now achieved a level of recognition beyond either. He was a national figure.

Handel usually took time off in the summer to visit a spa town. In the summer of 1758, he visited Tunbridge Wells in Kent. There he met an oculist called John Taylor, who had operated on Johann Sebastian Bach's eyes some years previously. That operation had not only been unsuccessful but may even have led to the composer's death.[4] Taylor operated on Handel, but again without success. Handel returned to London for the winter where he and Smith made preparations for the next year's oratorio season. He was noticeably weaker now, but he would not stop working. During March and early April 1759, he conducted *Solomon, Samson, Susanna* and several performances of *Messiah*. After the last of these, a performance given in aid of the Foundling Hospital for which he had helped to raise large sums over the previous ten years, he took to his bed. He died on 14 April and was buried in Westminster Abbey a few days later. Three thousand people attended the funeral.

That Handel had business acumen as well as musical talent had always been evident, and his will showed just how successfully he had bounced back from near bankruptcy in the 1730s: his estate was worth some £20,000.[5] Other aspects of his character are less obvious from the bare facts of his life and career. Despite a volatile temperament and a volcanic temper, he was known as a generous man. He was a practising Christian, not given perhaps to parading or to analysing his beliefs – we have surprisingly little information about what he thought on any given subject – but certainly a man who acted on them. In his will, he left generous legacies to charities such as the Foundling Hospital and the Fund for the Support of Decayed Musicians and their Families, to his German relatives, to his servants and friends, to musicians and librettists he had worked with, to the widows of musicians he had known. He also left a musical legacy which was to prove both complex and long-lasting.

Handel was hugely prolific. There were not only operas and oratorios, masques, cantatas, odes and anthems; there were organ concertos, *Concerti Grossi*, and a range of orchestral works; there were English songs and Italian arias; there were sonatas for the flute, the oboe and the violin; there were trio sonatas, wind ensemble pieces and a large number of keyboard works. We remember Handel principally as a composer, but he was, of course, also a keyboard virtuoso, violinist and oboist. Most of his work was written in England for English audiences and has been absorbed into the English canon, yet it did not arise from the English tradition. That tradition had developed over some three centuries – from the time of Dunstable in the mid-fifteenth century, through the succession of great Tudor composers, and the vicissitudes of the Civil Wars, the Commonwealth and the Restoration. It had shown itself capable of accepting, adapting or absorbing foreign influences. It had benefitted from the freedom to invent the musical forms appropriate to sustain the newly established Church of England in the wake of the Reformation – with the result that the Anglican Service, the anthem and subsequently the ode all became central to its development. Too diffuse to be called a style, it was essentially a collection of broad national characteristics: a preference for melody over formal structure; a tendency towards control and understatement rather than flamboyance or virtuosity; a lyricism often based on a response to words; and – hard to define but undoubtedly present in the works of many English and British composers up to that time and since – an underlying sense of yearning, spiritual rather than erotic, which suggests an awareness of the transcendental. And it is equally characteristic that this awareness of the transcendental can co-exist, as in the case of men such as Wise or Purcell, with the ability to write and revel in ephemeral catches with bawdy lyrics.

As we have seen, by 1700, after the death of Purcell and the changes at court and in society that followed the accession of William and Mary, the English musical tradition was without a champion and had rather lost its way. Handel stepped into the breach, offering a new focus and new ideas, but while he was prepared to take British nationality, Handel could never become an English or a British composer. His musical origins and education were German, and his orientation predominantly Italian. He certainly attempted to understand and come to terms with the English tradition – notably with the *Chandos Anthems* and, to a lesser extent, in *L'Allegro ed Il Penseroso* – and he certainly had the ability to write tunes which British audiences appreciated. In the end, however, Handel's success stemmed from the fact that his music was underpinned by characteristics and values that were not English. English music had been subject to foreign influences in the past, absorbed them and come up with an English solution. The emergence of English oratorio from Italian opera represents the same process in action once again, but Handel's impact was of a different order. His direct, stylistic influence was limited: he did not become the model of choice for young British composers. It was rather that forty years of musical dominance had given him an almost heroic status. A generation of musicians and – which was now equally important – a generation of opera- and concert-goers, had grown up in the knowledge that Handel was the unchallenged master of British music. As a result, his popularity did not decline after his death as is normally the case with composers or with artists in any discipline. On the contrary, it grew. He rapidly became the subject of unprecedented veneration, and his work not only became central to the English musical mainstream, but achieved an iconic status unapproachable by later composers. This created a distortion which was to affect the way the British looked at their own musical history for very many years to come – in some cases even into the twentieth century. As late as 1912, Ernest Ford could speak of 'the fatal temptation to try and write on the lines of such a colossal genius as Handel.'[6]

42 The Pleasure Gardens, and the Folk Tradition

When Queen Anne wished to celebrate the Treaty of Utrecht and the end of the war of the Spanish Succession, she asked Handel to write a *Te Deum* for a service in St Paul's Cathedral. When George II wished to celebrate the Treaty of Aix-la-Chapelle and the end of the war of Austrian Succession, he asked Handel asked to write a suite of dance music for a gigantic fireworks display. On the morning of 21 April 1749, the Thames was crowded with boats and London Bridge was gridlocked with carriages as some 12,000 people made their way to Vauxhall Pleasure Gardens on the south bank of the river. So great was the demand for tickets that Jonathan Tyers, the entrepreneur-owner of the Gardens felt able to raise the normal entrance price of one shilling to two shillings and sixpence. Handel's *Music for the Royal Fireworks* – scored for woodwind, brass and timpani only, because the King did not want strings – was given a robust performance and the whole affair was a bustling, noisy success. But this was just a rehearsal. The right to hold a public rehearsal at Vauxhall Gardens was the condition that Tyers had extracted for agreeing to help with the lighting effects and the organisation of the official performance, which took place six days later on a rather damp evening in London's Green Park. This was a much less democratic affair. The King himself was present. There were special enclosures reserved for the aristocracy, the military and the London gentry.

Those who could afford half-a-guinea could gain admission to the grandstand, while the rest of the public milled round the outside. The music was a success, but the accompanying fireworks were affected by the drizzle. A painter was killed falling from the fireworks gantry; a shoemaker was drowned after he fell into a pond; and the evening concluded in chaos when a large, mock-Palladian wooden pavilion constructed especially for the occasion caught fire and, despite the rain, burned to the ground.

The social context of music in the British Isles was changing. London, with its population of some 750,000 – more than eight times that of Dublin and thirteen times that of Edinburgh – naturally led the way, but there is no doubt that attitudes were changing everywhere. Music was increasingly seen as recreational, as something to be enjoyed in one's leisure time as a listener, or simply as a background to other activities. These attitudes found expression in the phenomenon of the pleasure garden. At various times during the eighteenth century, there were over sixty such gardens in and around London, but the best known were Vauxhall Pleasure Gardens south of the river, Ranelagh Gardens in Chelsea, and Marylebone Gardens. These were large areas – Vauxhall covered five hectares (twelve acres) – of formal gardens and parkland, walks and archways, prospects and pavilions, all designed to give city dwellers a vision of a romantic Arcadia. They were open to anyone who could pay the admission fee. Those who visited could walk up and down the avenues, seeing and being seen. They could admire the statues and artworks (which led Vauxhall to be considered one of the first public art galleries); they could eat and drink and dance; and, for those who were interested, there was also the prospect of an amorous encounter in the less populous parts of the garden. And, of course, there was music.

There were formal concerts and organ recitals which included works by a wide range of composers. Apart from Handel – whose statue in marble, by Louis François Roubiliac, was one of the first things visitors saw when they entered Vauxhall Gardens – there would be compositions by popular Italian composers such as Corelli and Scarlatti, and also by a long list of English composers, including Thomas Roseingrave, Thomas Arne, William Boyce, Capel Bond, John Stanley, James Hook and many others. Vauxhall, in particular, was noted for staging premieres of works by British composers. There were song recitals by many of the leading opera and oratorio singers. These would include popular favourites such as 'Nymphs and Shepherds', 'Black-Eyed Susan', 'Sally in Our Alley', 'The Dashing White Sergeant' and 'The Lass of Richmond Hill', as well as favourite arias from operas and oratorios.[1] Hook (1746–1823), who belongs to a slightly later generation, began his career at Marylebone Gardens before crossing the river to Vauxhall, and is reputed to have written some 2,000 songs for performance there between 1774 and 1820. Each garden would have a big hall or pavilion, such as the famous Rotunda at Ranelagh (the subject of a Canaletto painting), where bands of musicians played long into the night while couples danced minuets and rigadoons or more rustic measures, such as cotillions, strathspeys and reels. Elsewhere among the trees and the avenues, there would be groups of musicians hidden in discrete pavilions, or even in subterranean chambers, whose music was deliberately chosen to create and sustain a magical atmosphere. Was this perhaps the first muzak? And music was essential to spectacular events such as Ranelagh's Venetian Masquerade (staged the day before the official performance of the *Fireworks Music*) or the Ranelagh Regatta, when thousands of boats crammed the Thames. Provincial cities quickly began to develop pleasure gardens of their own: Norwich, Bath, Dublin, Edinburgh, and Newcastle-upon-Tyne were among the first to do so. What this meant in terms of total audience numbers is almost impossible to estimate – although we know that concerts at Vauxhall Gardens alone attracted over 100,000 people a year – but, taken together, the crowds who attended all Britain's pleasure gardens during the middle- and later-eighteenth century represented a paying mass audience of a kind and size that British music had never known before.

The pleasure gardens were an important piece in the jigsaw of British music, but it is worth remembering that an even larger – although completely different – mass audience engaged with folk music. There are no statistics, so we have to build up a picture from letters, diaries, early newspaper reports and other documents, but it is undoubtedly the case that folk music – Scottish, Irish, Welsh, Northumbrian, or from another region – was the type of music most often heard by ordinary people. It was played at fairs and markets, in taverns, at dances, at harvest suppers, at wedding parties and even after funerals. At a time when the majority of the population went to church regularly, the only other music that might have approached folk music in terms of the size of its audience would have been that played or sung during services.

Folk-dancing changed comparatively little over the generations and most of the dances common in the eighteenth century would have been found, in one form or another, in Playford's collections in the 1650s. The mixture of jigs, reels, strathspeys and country dances, such as 'Strip the

Willow' or the 'Virginia Reel', would have varied from one part of the United Kingdom to another, but most of them would have been familiar to those attending pleasure gardens up and down the land. With folk song, however, it was different. At least until its closing decades, the eighteenth century was the last pre-industrial period in British history. Folk songs dating from the period were, therefore, untroubled by the social issues surrounding industrialisation and urbanisation which, as we shall see in Volume Two (Chapter 65), began to enter the folk tradition after 1800. Many of the English folk-song collectors of the late-nineteenth and early-twentieth centuries, seeking to justify their view that folk song in some way contained the essence of English music, appear to have taken an idealised view of eighteenth-century rural life as a time when happy peasants made music in the fields. Even the Marxist A.L. Lloyd in his *Folk Music in England* (1967) contrives to imply that folk music sprang from a somehow better or purer agrarian society. Such contentions are, of course, unjustified. Folk song evolved up to, and continued to evolve after the eighteenth century, its concerns and subject matter a partial – but only a partial – reflection of the concerns of the people who wrote and sang it.

Many well-known folk songs appear to date from the late-seventeenth and eighteenth centuries. This is because more broadsides have survived than from previous centuries – although still surprisingly few given the number that were printed, suggesting that such songs were regarded as essentially ephemeral in nature. It is also because of the work of those scholars and antiquarians, like Samuel Pepys and Bishop Percy, who did not share the view that folk music was ephemeral and, as we have seen, began to collect ballads as items of cultural and historical interest. But a first reference or a surviving broadside is no evidence as to when a song was written. Sometimes it is possible to make an informed judgement. Our earliest knowledge of the ballad 'Johnnie O'Breadislee',[2] for example, comes from the end of the eighteenth century, but textual evidence suggests that it was probably written much earlier. More often, however, we are left guessing or have just to accept that the first written record we have of the song is a rough indication of when it was composed.

As noted above, it was not until the nineteenth century that folk ballads regularly began to express ideas of social and political protest. Nonetheless, numerous eighteenth-century songs show the beginning of that change, using folk song as an expression of something more than personal feelings or personal complaints. 'The Painful Plough', the first chapbook record of which dates from 1774, draws attention, in very measured tones, to the hardships of a ploughboy's life and the fundamental importance of his work to society. 'The Greenland Whale Fishery', already in print by 1725, records the sufferings and risks endured by whalers in the northern seas, making the point that they are driven to go because they are in debt. Then there is 'Hard Times of Old England', best known from the version collected from the Copper family of Rottingdean in Sussex after the Second World War, but in fact another eighteenth-century song. It is unusual in that it laments the state of society – tradesman have no business; there are no jobs; soldiers and sailors returned from the wars are starving – in an almost contemporary manner.

For the most part, however, the songs that have come down to us from the late-seventeenth and eighteenth centuries deal with people and stories, rather than ideas. Indeed, with hindsight, we can say that these songs actually established the range of what we now regard as normal subject matter for folk songs. Heroes were always popular, so broadsides celebrating national heroes – especially those who died in action – could be relied on to sell well. 'Bold General Wolfe', which tells the story of his victory over the French at Quebec, was probably written within a few years of his death in 1759, although no early broadsides have been found. Seafaring ballads, whether recounting the gallant exploits of sailors ('The Bold Princess Royal') or the agonies of separation from a sweetheart ('Nancy of Yarmouth'), reflected the fact that even landlubbers understood that Britain's well-being was dependent on its seafaring prowess. Poachers, and to a lesser extent smugglers and highwaymen, were also popular figures, their exploits usually framed in such a way as to suggest that the law was made to benefit the rich, not the poor. 'The Lincolnshire Poacher' – sometimes Gloucestershire, sometimes elsewhere – sums up the ethos succinctly:

> Success to every poacher that wants to sell a hare,
> Bad luck to every gamekeeper that will not sell his deer.

There were songs celebrating rural life, like 'All Jolly Fellows Who Follow the Plough,' 'The Waggoner's Song', and 'The Lark in the Morning'; there were drinking songs, like 'Fathom the Bowl' or the nonsensical 'Derby Ram'; and there were ballads of cruelty and death, like 'Lambkin' or 'Hugh of Lincoln', to some extent precursors of the murder ballads that were so popular in Victorian times. There are even some ballads which appear to have been imported from the Continent. Variants of 'The Outlandish

Knight', for example, have been found everywhere from Norway to the Balkans, but the version collected by Child, which can be dated to the second half of the eighteenth century, seems to be based on a Dutch text. However, as one would expect, the most popular subject for songs and ballads of the period is love.

It is not possible here to go into all the different varieties of love song – requited, unrequited, tricked, betrayed, bereaved – to be found in eighteenth century broadsides and collections, but it is worth noting the prevalence of certain distinct categories. In what have become known as 'returned lover ballads', a soldier or a sailor arrives home after years away, and meets his sweetheart, who fails to recognise him. He tests her fidelity before proving his identity, often by producing one half of the ring they divided between them before he left, and they fall, reunited, into each other's arms. There are German ballads with much the same narrative, and there are British antecedents in two apparently older ballads collected by Child – 'The New-Slain Knight' and 'The Kitchie Boy' – but this sub-genre seems to have enjoyed a new lease of life at the end of the eighteenth century and into the Napoleonic era, and particularly in southern England, quite possibly because of the increase in military and naval activity overseas at the time.

Such happy endings do not feature in those ballads which deal with honour killings. These seem to come from Scotland and the north of England more frequently than from the south. 'Lady Maisry' and its variants, 'The Burning' and 'Bonnie Susie Cleland', tell of a girl who is burned alive by her parents in order to prevent her marrying an Englishman. 'The Cruel Brother', first published in 1776, but apparently in circulation for some time before that, tells of a king's daughter who is murdered with a penknife by her brother because she forgot to ask his permission to marry. 'Bruton Town' (which exists in numerous variants, such as 'The Bramble Briar', 'The Jealous Brothers', 'The Merchant's Daughter', and 'The Murdered Servantman') tells of two brothers who kill a servant because he wants to marry their sister. The story is a version of one told by Boccaccio, and also by Hans Sachs and Keats, but the ballad as we have it appears to date from the first half of the eighteenth century – although modified in the oral tradition afterwards. The content of these ballads and others like them may perhaps owe something to the rise of the Gothic, but they, too, can certainly be seen as the precursors of the Victorian murder ballads.

A third sub-genre of folk songs concerned with love certainly flourished in the eighteenth century, but caused problems for the nineteenth- and early-twentieth-century collectors, who were reluctant to publish them because of their content. They deal with sex. They treat it wittily, light-heartedly and in a refreshingly non-sexist manner, with both parties presented as equally willing. Puns and extended metaphors are both crucial. A sportsman goes out with his gun to hunt the 'Bonny Black Hare'. A young woman tells him it is to be found under her apron. Matters take their course; she wants more of his 'old sporting gun'; but he is obliged to confess:

> Oh, my powder is wasted and my bullets all gone.
> My ramrod is limp, and I cannot fire on.

'The Cuckoo's Nest' is, unsurprisingly, found in the same location as the bonny black hare; while 'The Game of Cards' – also known as 'The Game of All Fours' – explores a similar situation with a somewhat more complex metaphorical structure, with the jack and the ace taking on quite specific meanings. Songs such as these have, of course, been sung through the ages, but the first record of many of them is in eighteenth-century broadsides or chapbooks.

As ever with ballads and folk songs, we have little information about the original tunes, beyond the occasional reference on a broadsheet. Tunes would have been passed on orally by the pedlars or chapmen who moved from market to market and village to village selling broadsides. Chapmen were also to be found in the towns, particularly in the later decades of the century as urban populations began to expand. We know that they were frequently found in the pleasure gardens – or outside the gates if they had been refused entry – selling their latest broadsides, and thus creating a link between popular music in the urban world and the still essentially rural folk tradition. This connection was to be of great importance in the nineteenth century. Initially, it would allow the content and the nature of the folk tradition to evolve, reflecting the increasing relevance of urban and industrial topics. In due course, however, as Britain became a predominantly urban and industrial society, it would lead to the folk tradition being pushed aside and eventually eclipsed by music hall.

In much of Continental Europe, aristocratic families could still offer patronage on a major scale, as the Esterházys did with Haydn for nearly fifty years. In Catholic Europe, too, the Church continued to play a much larger part in musical life than it did in Britain. Of course, there were still rich patrons around, and there was still a significant demand at all levels (from the Chapel Royal and the big cathedrals to country parish churches) for anthems and settings of the psalms and the Anglican Service. The demand for music in the British Isles had never been higher, but most of the new music being written was now secular and commercial. Across the country, there were more theatres than ever before, demanding operas and oratorios, as well as quantities of incidental music for new plays and for new productions of old ones. The pleasure gardens were not only staging concerts almost every evening, they were actively competing with each other to offer the newest music. There were other sources of demand, too. Music festivals are rightly regarded as a central feature of British musical life in the nineteenth century, but they began in the eighteenth. The Three Choirs was probably established in 1715. Salisbury launched its festival in 1744; Liverpool in 1766; Birmingham in 1768; Leeds in 1784. Concert halls were being built and subscription concerts organised. Music clubs and societies were springing up all across the country. These varied from formal organisations like that in Newcastle-upon-Tyne, founded in 1736 to run subscription concerts by professional players, to a few enthusiastic amateurs, gathered in the back room of an inn, who wanted something they could play themselves. The composers and musicians of the mid-eighteenth century thus had a broader range of customers than previous generations, which meant that they had a broader range of professional options and, indeed, of locations where they could pursue a musical career.

Maurice Greene was one of the last composers whose career took a distinctly traditional path. Born in 1695 to a London clergyman who had been Chaplain at the Chapel Royal, he was a boy chorister at St Paul's Cathedral and continued to train there after his voice broke. At seventeen, he gained his first appointment as organist, at St Dunstan-in-the-West. Three years later, in 1717, he became organist at St Andrew's, Holborn, and the next year, still aged only twenty-three, he became organist of St Paul's Cathedral. In 1727, on the death of William Croft, he became organist at the

Chapel Royal. A doctorate in music (for which he composed an *Ode to St Cecilia* to a text by Alexander Pope) and the Professorship of Music at Cambridge followed in 1730. Then, on the death of John Eccles in 1740, Greene became Master of the King's Musick. Although still not quite forty, all the top jobs in the musical establishment were his.

This sense of Greene as an establishment figure is reinforced by the fact that, at a time when opera and the pleasure gardens were booming, his best-known and most-praised works are anthems. *Forty Select Anthems* was published in 1743, although it is clearly a retrospective collection. *Lord let me know mine end* and *Lord, how long wilt thou be angry?* have both attracted praise (perhaps a touch back-handed) as 'the finest masterpieces produced by a native-born Englishman in the whole period … quite worthy to stand side by side with the great anthems of earlier times.'[1] In fact, his anthems, while tuneful and well constructed, are always just a little too controlled, a little too civilised, to rank with those of the great Elizabethans. Greene's *Six Overtures in 7 Parts*, published in 1745, shows him at his best. The terms *overture* (or *ouverture*) and *sinfonia* were both widely used at this time, more or less synonymously. The music so described was, of course, still some distance from symphonic form as it was later to emerge: it was in three movements, usually with a slow middle section and dance-like finale – though Greene varied this structure to suit his own preferences. The *Overtures* are not profound pieces, but they display a genuine lightness of touch, a feeling for balanced orchestration and an ability to charm. The same characteristics can be found in some of his songs, such as 'Go, Rose' and 'Orpheus with His Lute', which we know were performed at Vauxhall Gardens. Unfortunately, when he tried to work on a bigger scale, it did not come off. *Amoretti*, a kind of song cycle consisting of settings of twenty-five poems by Edmund Spenser, and dedicated to the Duchess of Newcastle, suffers from a dearth of variation and lacks the freshness of which he was capable elsewhere. The same criticism has been levelled at his two operas, *Florimel* (1734) and *Phoebe* (1747).

Greene was, however, typical of his age in that he was involved in a number of musical societies. In the 1720s, he was a founder member of the Castle Society which gave recitals every Wednesday to audiences of two hundred or more crammed into the Queen's Head, and later the Castle Tavern, in Paternoster Row, close by St Paul's Cathedral. The Society took itself very seriously and fined members of the audience half-a-crown if they made noises during the performance. He was involved with the

Madrigal Society, founded by John Immyns in 1741, and which – like the Hibernian Catch Club – claims to be the world's oldest still-functioning musical society. He was also a founder member of the Academy of Antient Music [*sic*] which met at the Crown and Anchor on the Strand, but resigned in 1731 after a dispute over the composition of a particular madrigal. Greene introduced it as being by Bononcini, and Bononcini claimed it was his, but other members of the society accused him of plagiarising a work by Antonio Lotti. Bononcini and Greene resigned, and Greene went off to start his own society, the Apollo Academy, based at the Devil Tavern in Fleet Street, where he collaborated with Michael Christian Festing, a well-known violinist. The Apollos put on odes, masques, and even oratorios, but Greene's act of loyalty, resigning in support of Bononcini, cost him the friendship of Handel, who disliked Bononcini and would have nothing to do with those who supported him.

Greene's final project, and one that again shows his interest in the music of earlier periods, was to collect, collate and edit anthems and settings of the Anglican Service going back over the centuries so that contemporary composers could be more aware of their Anglican heritage. It was a huge task. John Alcock, organist of Lichfield Cathedral – and former chorister at St Paul's where he had known Greene – had already begun just such a collection, which he selflessly handed over to help Greene. In the early 1750s, when his health was beginning to fail, Greene was lucky enough to inherit the estate of Bois Hall in Essex. The income of £700 a year was enough to enable him to retire from public life and devote himself to his great project. Unfortunately, he died in 1755 with the work still a long way from completion. He bequeathed his collection and a moral, if not a formal responsibility for completing the task to his former pupil – and successor as Master of the King's Musick – William Boyce (1711–79).

Like Greene, Boyce began his career in a conventional manner. The son of a London cabinet maker, he became a chorister at St Paul's at the age of twelve and, when his voice broke, he stayed on to study under Greene. In his early twenties, he studied with Pepusch and became organist first at the Oxford Chapel in Cavendish Square and then at St Michael's Cornhill. In 1736, at the age of twenty-five, he became composer to the Chapel Royal and his career was launched. That same year saw the composition of his first major work, an oratorio called *David's Lamentation over Saul and Jonathan*, which was premiered at Greene's Apollo Academy and later, in 1744, given a performance in Dublin. In 1737, Boyce was appointed conductor of the Three Choirs Festival, a connection he maintained for many years, and, in 1739, following the precedent of Purcell and Handel as well as his teachers Greene and Pepusch, he composed his own *Ode to St Cecilia*. It enjoyed both a London and a Dublin performance and was well received by audiences in both cities.

Boyce's duties at the Chapel Royal kept him busy. He composed over thirty anthems as well as a number of *Te Deums and Jubilates*. These have been damned with faint praise as 'solid, dignified work, thoroughly sincere and clean,'[2] and it is true that Boyce approaches these works from a conservative standpoint. Nonetheless, there are one or two, such as *Wherewithal shall a young man*, with its unaccompanied polyphonic opening section, and the delicate, almost intimate, *By the waters of Babylon*, which stand out as exceptional pieces. From around 1740, Boyce's career began to broaden out. He wrote *Peleus and Thetis*, variously described as a masque or a short opera, to a text by Lord Lansdowne. We have no idea when, where, or even if, it was performed, but Boyce's music is sharp, cleanly orchestrated and effortlessly catchy. This marks his first real excursion into the theatrical world to which he would devote much of his later career. In 1749, he struck up a friendship with David Garrick, the most famous actor and impresario of the day, which led to a series of commissions for incidental music. Boyce's music for Moses Mendez' *The Chaplet* was immediately popular, and he followed it up with a score for *Romeo and Juliet*. This was written in 1750, when Garrick's Drury Lane Theatre and Christopher Rich's Covent Garden were effectively at war and both putting on the same play at the same time. Boyce's score was better received than Thomas Arne's music for Covent Garden and thus gave Garrick the advantage in the fight. Boyce and Garrick also collaborated on a masque, *The Shepherd's Lottery*, produced in 1751, and a pantomime, *Harlequin's Invasion*, designed to whip up patriotic feeling against the French. This contains what is probably Boyce's best-known song, 'Hearts of Oak'. As happened with almost all the theatre composers of the period, many of Boyce's songs were immediately extracted from his theatrical scores and played at Vauxhall, Ranelagh or Marylebone Gardens, something which impresarios like Garrick no doubt welcomed since they served to advertise their productions.

Although involved with the theatre, Boyce continued to compose on a smaller scale as well. His collection of trio sonatas (for two violins with cello or harpsichord), published in 1747, was a huge success, selling more than six times the normal number for a musical subscription publication, reviving interest in the trio as a form, and massively boosting his reputation. Once again, these were pieces that were soon heard in the pleasure gardens of London and elsewhere. Then, in 1755, Greene died and Boyce replaced him as master of the King's Musick. This meant a minimum of two odes a year – for New Year's Day and for the King's birthday. None of the odes he composed for these occasions are particularly memorable in themselves, but he took the instrumental introductions to them and reworked them into his *Eight Symphonies,* published in 1760. These are symphonies in the English Baroque, and not the classical, sense. They are, for the most part, three-movement pieces, with no attempt at extended musical argument. They are driven by melody, not by rhythmic patterns or by the kind of virtuosic ornamentation so common at the time; and the emphasis is on bright tunes, crisp orchestration and simple, satisfying musical structures, which at times take off in unexpected directions. Taken in these terms, Boyce's *Eight Symphonies* represent one of the high points of British music in the second half of the eighteenth century. And they were so successful that he repeated the idea with *Twelve Overtures* in 1770 – again we see the terms *symphony* and *overture* being used interchangeably. Boyce applied the same approach and principles to these overtures as to his symphonies, but one has to say that, perhaps because he was by this time increasingly deaf, the magic is not there. They are enjoyable, but they do not sparkle in the same way. Boyce's orchestral music was largely forgotten until Constant Lambert rediscovered and produced an edition of the symphonies in 1928. Lambert then went on to use Boyce's music in his ballet, *The Prospect Before Us,* in 1940. Gerald Finzi followed Lambert's lead and published an edition of the overtures in 1957.

Deafness blighted Boyce's last twenty years. He gradually retired from public life and devoted himself to extending and editing the huge collection of Anglican church music he had inherited from Greene. This was eventually published in three volumes as *Cathedral Music* (1760, 1768, 1773), the biggest collection of its kind and the first to be published in score. Consequently, it became an invaluable source for later scholars and musicians and, until the rediscovery of Boyce's music in the twentieth century, was the main reason his name was remembered. He died in 1779, apparently of gout, and was buried in St Paul's Cathedral to the sound of his own music. His wife, Hannah, published two volumes of his anthems and *Te Deums and Jubilates* after his death.

If the careers of Greene and Boyce were versions of the path long trodden by English composers, with Boyce following Purcell by branching out into the theatre during the second half of his working life, those of Charles Avison (1709–70) and Thomas Arne (1710–78) were based on career choices which had not been available to previous musical generations. Avison was born to a large, musical, but far from prosperous family in Newcastle-upon-Tyne, where his father was a member of the Town Waits and his mother was organist at one of the city's churches (making her the first professional female musician to appear in these pages). We know very little about Avison's early life. His parents were presumably responsible for his early musical education – although his father died when Charles was only eleven.

Avison dedicated his first published work, *Six Sonatas for Two Violins and a Bass* (1737), to Ralph Jenison, who was an MP, a local patron of the arts, and owner of the grand Elswick Hall on what was then the edge of Newcastle; this may imply that Jenison was an early supporter or benefactor. He dedicated his second work, *Six Concertos in 7 Parts* (1740), to Sir John Blaithwaite (or Blathwayt), who was connected with the Royal Academy of Music and its operatic programme, again suggesting the possibility of patronage. Did Jenison or Blaithwaite pay for Avison to travel to Italy? Charles Burney says that he visited Italy at some time in his youth, although there is no other evidence to support the idea. If he did, it would have to have been in the early 1730s, for Avison was definitely in London by 1733, and probably studying under Geminiani. We know also that he was given a benefit concert at Hickford's Room in 1734. Then, in late 1735, he was offered, and accepted, the post of organist at the Church of St John the Baptist in his native Newcastle at a salary of £20 a year.

Avison stayed at St John's for just a few months before accepting a similar position, at twice the salary, at the larger church of St Nicholas (which later became the city's cathedral). He never returned to London. Both before his departure from the capital and in the years which followed, he was offered a series of far more prestigious and lucrative posts – organist at both of Dublin's cathedrals, at York Minster, at Charterhouse London, a teaching post in Edinburgh. Geminiani seems to have been responsible for most of these offers, but Avison was not to be tempted. He remained rooted in his native city. Soon after his return, he became involved with the newly formed Newcastle Musical Society, organising and playing at its subscription concerts, and in 1738 was elected its president. The Newcastle Society was soon one of the most influential of the many regional societies that were formed at this time. Apart from Avison's own works, it introduced music by Purcell, Scarlatti, Jean-Philippe Rameau, C. P. E. Bach, the madrigalist Carlo Clari, almost certainly Geminiani (although, oddly, his name does not survive in the society's archives) and, of course, Handel. Often these composers would be heard in Avison's own arrangements because, while the society's concerts were popular – two-and-sixpence would admit one gentleman or two ladies for the whole series – it was not always easy to find enough musicians. One regular player at Avison's concerts was the Durham-based cellist and composer, John Garth (1721–1810), who composed a fine set of cello concertos and also published, with help from Avison, a massive eight-volume edition of psalm settings by the Italian composer Benedetto Marcello. It seems that for some years Avison's concerts in Newcastle and Garth's in Durham were scheduled so as to allow the two men to participate in each other's events. This would be wholly characteristic. Although a well-regarded composer, in his own region Avison was also a recognised educator and promoter of music – a role which saw him working with local theatres and with New Spring Gardens, Newcastle's answer to Vauxhall.

Avison wrote an oratorio, *Ruth*, in collaboration with a wandering Italian musician called Felice Giardini, but otherwise, and unusually for the age, his focus was almost wholly on instrumental music. He wrote over forty concertos and *Concerti Grossi* – including the first solo keyboard concerto by an English composer. Most of these works are in the Italian style, of which he was a passionate advocate, and frequently draw their inspiration from the works of composers such as Scarlatti and Geminiani. His *Twelve Concerti Grossi after Scarlatti* (1744) are deservedly well known for the way in which they exploit the possibilities of the string ensemble, moving skilfully between dance-like liveliness and, in the slower movements, a sense of emotional depth. Avison's decision to remain in Newcastle did not mean that he was out of touch with developments on the Continent. Indeed, he was clearly in advance of most other British composers in appreciating the possibilities of the fully-fledged sonata form that was being pioneered by C. P. E. Bach and Haydn. The later numbers of his *Twelve Concertos in Seven Parts* (1758) show him consciously moving away from the through-composed Baroque concerto towards the new formal sonata-form structure. The same progress is also evident in his later collections, particularly *Six Sonatas* (1764), where theme, development, recapitulation, and coda sections are clearly discernible, and one can sense

Avison's musical ideas becoming integrated with the structure of the piece. This was new territory, though his example was not immediately followed.

Avison was one of the first composers to exercise a significant influence on the musical life of the country while remaining at a distance from London. His concertos attracted widespread attention, but so, too, did his book, *An Essay on Musical Expression* (1752), the first serious attempt to establish a framework for musical criticism in English. The work remains interesting because Avison's views are so clearly those of a practical and practising musician, with chapter titles like 'On Musical Expression, so far as it relates to the Composer'; 'On Musical Expression as it relates to the Performer'; and 'On the expressive Performance of Music in general'. He distinguishes between music which is inspiring and sublime, and music which is graceful and elegant but essentially entertaining. In the process, he criticises Handel for writing too much and too quickly. Given Handel's public status at the time, this was almost blasphemy; it aroused a storm of counter-criticism and publicity.

44 Thomas Arne

Thomas Arne was even more of an outsider than Avison. His family certainly had their ups and downs. His grandfather died in London's notorious Marshalsea debtors' prison. His father made enough money from upholstery and undertaking to rent a big house in Covent Garden and send young Thomas to Eton, but then lost it all. From childhood, Arne was passionate about music, but his father, by all accounts a wholly mercenary individual, wanted him apprenticed as a lawyer. As ever in such cases, there are stories of the young musician's secret defiance. Arne is supposed to have smuggled a spinet into his room and dampened the strings with a handkerchief while practising at night. He is also supposed to have disguised himself as a liveryman carrying a message to his employer in order to get into the opera. This may have been how he came to meet the well-known composer and violinist Michael Festing (1705–52), who was playing in the orchestra at the King's Theatre at the time. Festing was part of the London musical community, well regarded as a composer – his *Twelve Sonatas in Three Parts* (1731) was much played at the time – and also known for his compassionate nature. He was one of the main instigators of the Fund for the Support of Decayed Musicians and their Families that

Handel did so much for. It was Festing who gave Arne violin lessons, and who introduced him to London's musical society – in particular to the kind of musical evenings that took place at York Buildings, where Festing played regularly, and elsewhere. At one such evening, Arne was apparently discovered by his father, who was subsequently persuaded (perhaps by Festing) to release his son from the law and allow him to pursue a musical career.

Arne's lessons with Festing were the only formal tuition he ever received: he was otherwise self-taught. He was also a Roman Catholic, which debarred him from becoming a church organist or from being appointed to any Chapel Royal or court position. This deprived him of the kind of financial foundation that supported the careers of Handel, Greene and Boyce, and also significantly reduced his chances of obtaining aristocratic patronage. But Arne never wanted confidence, or the ability to write an appealing melody. On liberation from his legal apprenticeship, he taught both his sister, Susanna, and his brother, Richard, to sing, and the three of them performed in Handel's *Acis and Galatea* at the King's Theatre in 1732. Arne pushed himself forward and his first major work, his opera *Rosamund*, written to Addison's old libretto, was put on at Lincoln's Inn Fields the following year. This was at a time when Handel's company and the Opera of the Nobility were both producing operas in London and the vogue for ballad opera was still in full swing. Despite the competition, *Rosamund* was considered a success. Little of the music survives, but we know that it again featured Susanna and Richard and was repeated ten times. Arne was launched.

Between 1733 and his death in March 1778, Arne composed full scores or incidental music for over a hundred theatrical productions (*opera seria*, comic opera, burlesques, masques, pantomimes, plays, even a ballet);[1] somewhere approaching two hundred songs; five collections of instrumental music; and a few religious pieces, including two settings of the Mass and two oratorios. From 1734, partly through family connections, Arne became the leading composer at Drury Lane, which was then under the control of Charles Fleetwood.[2] It was for Drury Lane that he composed the music for a version of Milton's masque *Comus* (1738), and for a second masque, Congreve's *Judgement of Paris* (1742). And it was Drury Lane's production of *As You Like It* in 1740 that first led him to set Shakespeare's lyrics. *Twelfth Night*, *The Merchant of Venice*, *The Tempest*, and *Love's Labour's Lost* all followed at various times during the 1740s and resulted in songs such as 'Under the greenwood tree', 'Blow, blow, thou winter wind', 'When daisies pied', 'When icicles hang by the wall' and 'Tell me where is fancy bred?' which are among his best known pieces. But Arne's most famous composition comes from another masque, *Alfred*, which was produced in 1740 at the country home of the Prince of Wales, Cliveden in Buckinghamshire. The plot, which sought to equate the Prince of Wales with King Alfred the Great, is deeply unremarkable, but the finale, with words by the Scottish poet, James Thomson, is 'Rule, Britannia'. Although not played in London until 1745, when it became associated with George II's victory over the Jacobite rebellion, 'Rule, Britannia' rapidly went on to achieve an independent existence. Handel quoted it in his *Occasional Oratorio*; Beethoven wrote a set of variations on it; Wagner wrote a concert overture based on it; Johann Strauss quoted it; Sir Arthur Sullivan quoted it; Sir Edward Elgar quoted it; Noel Coward quoted it in 'Mad Dogs and Englishmen'; and since 1906, as the concluding part of Sir Henry Wood's *Fantasia on British Sea Songs*, it has been an essential component of the Last Night of the Proms.

Arne is also closely associated with another British institution: 'God Save the King'. He did not write the tune, the origins of which are still debated – plainchant, the Scottish carol 'Remember O Thou Man', and an instrumental piece by John Bull, have all been suggested – but it was Arne who, as Jacobite forces under Charles Edward Stewart swept southwards in 1745, defeating Sir John Cope's army at the Battle of Prestonpans, arranged and promoted it as a patriotic anthem. It was delivered by three singers in front of the curtain at the end of the evening performance at Drury Lane. It was a patriotic gesture – and almost certainly a deliberate attempt to gain royal favour – and a successful one. The idea caught on. The gesture was repeated. A choir was added to the soloists. The audience joined in, and 'God Save the King' soon gained both national recognition and iconic importance. The story also says something about Arne, who was an inspired adaptor and developer, as well as something of a showman, but not really an originator.

In 1742, no doubt encouraged by the example of Handel, Arne and his wife, the soprano Cecilia Young, went to Dublin. They stayed two years, running several successful concert series. The programmes, which were designed to show off his wife's voice, naturally concentrated on Arne's own music – including his oratorio, *The Death of Abel*, which was premiered in 1744 – although, being a good businessman and wanting to attract a good audience, he also made sure that Handel's work featured prominently. The Arnes returned to London at the beginning of 1745. Arne returned to his position directing the orchestra at Drury Lane, and, at the same time, was appointed as a kind of composer-in-residence at Vauxhall Gardens. He displayed an immediate understanding of the Vauxhall audience and rapidly produced *Colin and Phoebe*, a pastoral dialogue, 'Consisting of Eighteen entire new Ballads'. These simple and tuneful pieces were instantly popular and together with his many other songs, some folk-influenced, some with a Scottish flavour, established him as a long-term favourite with the public who continued to throng London's pleasure gardens. In 1750, Arne fell out with Garrick, who had taken over the management of Drury Lane in 1747, but even this could not dent his success. He was snapped up by the rival Royal Opera House in Covent Garden, an association which was to last for the next fifteen years.

Arne's marriage eventually broke down following another trip to Ireland in 1755. His wife stayed in Ireland while Arne himself returned to London with his student and mistress, Charlotte Brent, another highly gifted soprano. The marriage had not been a happy one: Arne had long had a reputation as a sexual predator and made little secret that he was a regular frequenter of the prostitutes who plied their trade in and around Covent Garden. In the 1740s, Charles Burney, then a young man newly arrived in London, spent four years as Arne's apprentice. He appreciated his master's musicianship, but was critical of his character, particularly his morals – a view shared by Arne's biographer, William Cummings.[3] Dr Johnson apparently called him a fop and a rake.[4] The public Arne, however, remained a bankable proposition and a respected musician – he received a doctorate in music from Cambridge in 1759. It was only in his later years that his poor treatment of his wife and his low moral character began to have an impact on his career.

It was for Covent Garden in 1762 that Arne composed his opera, *Artaxerxes*. This was a calculated move. With Handel dead, there was a revival of interest in Italian-style opera which Arne moved to satisfy – and he succeeded, producing the first English *opera seria*: a story of love, death and intrigue in ancient Persia. It was based on a libretto by the Italian poet, Metastasio, and generally well plotted, but from the parts of the score that have come down to us, it seems to have lacked musical coherence. It was, however, well received by the London public, largely because it contained a series of highly tuneful arias – 'Water parted from the sea', 'O too lovely, too unkind', 'Fair Aurora', and above all 'The soldier, tir'd of war's alarms' – most of which soon took on independent life in the pleasure gardens and concert halls. In Dublin, *Artaxerxes* was performed nearly fifty times in three years. Mozart attended a performance in London in 1765; Haydn is said to have praised it; and it was revived regularly until more romantic musical styles became fashionable in the nineteenth century.

As if to demonstrate his versatility, Arne moved immediately from *opera seria* to a ballad opera, *Love in a Village*, produced at Covent Garden in 1762. He wrote five new songs and reworked a number of others from previous compositions, but most of the forty-two songs in the three-act piece were by other composers, among them both Boyce and Geminiani, while the overture was written by the London-based German composer, Carl Friedrich Abel. A tale of love and misunderstanding with a happy ending, and a thoroughly lightweight piece by comparison with *Artaxerxes*, *Love in a Village* is characteristically tuneful and received forty performances in its first season alone. It also started a fashion for operas cobbled together from the works of different composers (known as 'pastiche' or 'pasticcio' operas) which, like *Artaxerxes*, remained popular into the nineteenth century. Arne's continued success over so many years in so many different genres was truly remarkable.

In 1767, he published *Four New Overtures or Symphonies in 8 and 10 Parts*. He was slower to realise the implications and importance of sonata form than Avison, and his exploration of its possibilities was somewhat perfunctory. The symphonies themselves are not particularly impressive or incisive, but the decision to compose symphonies at all is both surprising and revealing. Unlike most of Arne's music, which was written for the theatre, they appear to have been intended as concert pieces. Perhaps he saw a business opportunity – he certainly knew his marketplace – but issues of reputation almost certainly played a part. It is indicative of his tough, competitive nature that, even after thirty-five years of success, he was still willing to expend considerable effort to keep up, and be seen to keep up, with the latest musical forms and fashions.

By 1768, now in his late fifties, Arne was back at Drury Lane producing a revival of *Artaxerxes*. Competition between the two main theatres was as fierce as ever, so Covent Garden decided to stage a rival production of the same work featuring Charlotte Brent in the role of Mandane, which had originally been written for her. Brent had left Arne two years earlier, having fallen in love with the distinguished violinist and composer, Thomas Pinto (1728–83), and now performed under her married name. Arne, needless to say, never forgave what he saw as her betrayal and was mortified when the

Covent Garden production with her in the lead role proved far more popular and profitable than his own. The events of that year seem to have marked a turning point. It was not that he went into rapid decline – he continued to compose and enjoy moments of recognition and popularity, as with his masque *The Fairy Prince* (1771) – but he seems never to have regained the same level of commitment and interest. He died in 1778, having been reunited with his wife, Cecilia, the previous year.

By any standards, Arne enjoyed a successful career. His Catholicism prevented him from obtaining any of the traditional establishment posts that a composer of his eminence might normally expect, but that did not in any way hinder his work from being the toast of the pleasure gardens and of London's theatres. In his day, his music was more genuinely popular than Handel's. And, even more than Handel, Arne regarded music as a business. Perhaps because he remembered the vicissitudes of his father's business career, he concentrated on music that would earn him financial reward. As a consequence, he wrote more songs, incidental music and ephemeral pieces and fewer of those status works – operas, odes, oratorios – by which composers of the period were usually judged and remembered. This reflected his natural orientation in that his musical gift was essentially a light and lyric one, but it may also explain why in a later age, which looks for bigger, more serious achievements on the part of its classical musicians, Arne's reputation does not loom large. Another reason may well be his moral reputation. He was not personally popular among his colleagues. He was not lamented in the way that Purcell or Handel were lamented. Nor did he leave a network of devoted former students to praise his work and his character – Burney claimed that Arne gave him plenty of work, but little actual instruction. Nonetheless, he was the outstanding English composer of the period and an influential figure in the development of British music: he and Handel would have been the reference points for any young composer growing to maturity from the 1740s onward.

45 Continental Music, and Carl Abel

On the Continent of Europe, the second half of the seventeenth century was a period of radical change in music. From the ornate orthodoxies of the Baroque emerged forms and structures which would become fundamental to the organisation of classical composition right up until the second half of the twentieth century; structures which are still recognised and employed by many composers today. In the hands of C. P. E. Bach and Josef Haydn, the loose, through-composed Baroque sonata evolved into the more defined structure which we still call sonata form. Haydn and Mozart, building on the work of the Mannheim composer, Johann Stamitz (1717–57), and Vienna's Georg Monn (1717–50), took the new sonata form and developed it into something more subtle and flexible, so that it became the basis of the four-movement symphonic form as we still understand it. And Haydn, an absolutely pivotal figure, took these developments off in a different direction to define what we now call the string quartet. The Baroque era thus gradually gave way to the Classical.

In Britain, the transition was painfully slow, complicated by the long, posthumous shadow cast by Handel and by the complex character of British society at the time. The British composers who spanned the middle years of the eighteenth century were talented, professional musicians, working in an environment where music was more widely heard and appreciated than ever before. In fact, the musical life of the British Isles was probably busier and more diverse, involving more people in performance and appreciation, than that of any other European country. However, the very complexity and busyness of their environment seems to have reduced the willingness, or perhaps the capacity, of British composers to experiment. Some of them may have been too young to feel the full force of the musical changes taking place on the Continent; others clearly were not. Yet, faced with a demanding market on their doorstep, they do not seem to have taken the long view of the music on which their creativity and their professional lives were based. And almost all of them were in one way or another in thrall to Handel, whose reputation, most unusually, continued to grow after his death, to the point where it effectively discouraged innovation. Handel never adopted sonata form or wrote symphonies, so the argument might run, and Handel's reputation with the public was unassailable. In which case, what incentive was there for others to experiment?

It was not a question of talent. Boyce, as we have seen, was an immensely gifted composer, but his creativity and his innovation operated within the accepted Baroque framework. The same might be said of Richard Mudge (1718–63), another composer whose works were rescued from oblivion by Gerald Finzi in the 1950s. Born in Devon, a graduate of Pembroke College, Oxford, and a clergyman first in Birmingham and then in Bedworth in Warwickshire, Mudge never rose high in the church hierarchy and never joined London's musical elite, but he was certainly talented. His concertos for strings are both ambitious and imaginative, while clearly following closely the models provided by Handel and Corelli. William Felton (1715–69) was educated at Manchester Grammar School and St John's College, Cambridge, before moving to Hereford Cathedral, where he naturally became involved with the already well-established Three Choirs Festival. Felton achieved a degree of fame with five sets of organ concertos and a series of lessons for the harpsichord – all popular but, again, all strongly influenced by Handel. Samuel Howard (1710–82) started his musical life as a Chapel Royal chorister before becoming a songwriter for Drury Lane pantomimes and for London's pleasure gardens – though he did also assist Boyce in the preparation of *Cathedral Music*. Allatson Burgh, an early-nineteenth-century writer on music, said of Howard that 'this honest, true Englishman ... preferred the style of his own country to that of any other so much, that he never staggered his belief of its being the best in the world, by listening to foreign artists or their productions.'[1] No one could doubt the determination or the ability of John Stanley (1712–86). He overcame blindness, caused by an accident at the age of two, to become a skilful harpsichord, organ and violin player, as well as a composer of everything from hymns and anthems to concerti grossi, oratorios and odes. Yet, once again, Stanley never strayed outside the limits of the accepted style of the day. James Nares (1715–83) had a thoroughly conventional career path – chorister at the Chapel Royal, organist at York Minister, organist at the Chapel Royal (in succession to Greene) – and his output consisted mainly of choral religious music, together with a number of pieces and lessons for harpsichord, which probably represent his most interesting work. His Service in F, written while he was at York, and his anthem, *The souls of the righteous*, are still heard occasionally in the Church of England today, but they look backwards towards the sound and style of William Croft, who was one of his early tutors. Together, these composers formed a generation in which something – imagination, ambition, or a sense of adventure; or even just a simple refusal to conform – seems to have been lacking.

Of course, there were exceptions. As we have seen, Avison was particularly taken with the new musical forms that were emerging from Germany and Austria; and he also committed the heresy of criticising Handel. Then there was the case of Thomas Erskine (1732–81), one of a number of talented Scottish composers active at the time. Among the others were Hugh Montgomerie, 12th Earl of Eglinton, now remembered principally for the song, 'Ayrshire Lasses'; David Foulis, an Edinburgh doctor, who wrote a handful of attractive violin sonatas in the Italian manner; and, of course, James Oswald, whose work we looked at earlier. It was Erskine who, at the age of nineteen, took himself off to Mannheim to study with Johann Stamitz. He stayed there four years, returning only in 1756 on his father's death, when he succeeded to the title of the 6th Earl of Kellie, henceforth writing and publishing under that name. He brought with him an awareness and a knowledge of what was happening on the Continent that is reflected particularly in his *Six Overtures in 8 Parts* (1761), and in his overture for the pasticcio opera, *The Maid of the Mill* (1765). Kellie, as he had become, was a busy and versatile composer, who also wrote minuets and songs that were popular at Ranelagh and Vauxhall. He was a performer, too. A violin virtuoso – having learned his musicianship as a very young man with the Edinburgh Musical Society – he played on his Scottishness and attracted the nickname 'Fiddler Tam'. During his London years, he was noted for his appreciation of all the other good things, besides music, that the pleasure gardens had to offer. Returning to Scotland and to the Edinburgh Musical Society whose concerts he directed, a fondness for drink seems to have hastened his demise. His posthumous reputation was boosted as recently as 1989 by the discovery in Kilravock Castle of a manuscript containing, among other things, nine string quartets, making him probably the first British composer to experiment with the new genre.

In the end, it was left to another Scot and three Germans to take the lead in exposing the British public to sonata form and the music of the Mannheim school – even though their successes and occasional moments of glory have to be seen against the background of overwhelming conservatism and inertia that constituted British musical taste in the post-Handel period. The Scot was Robert Bremner, who, in 1754, established a publishing business in Edinburgh. The business did well and it was Bremner who, in 1761, published Kellie's innovative *Six Overtures*. The following year, he moved himself and his business south to London and rapidly developed what was, for the time, a large list. Italian names dominated and Kellie featured prominently, but Bremner obviously had a genuine understanding of music and was acute enough to begin publishing symphonies by Haydn (who had written about thirty by this stage), works by Stamitz, and works by other experimenters in sonata and symphonic form, such as Karl Ditters von Dittersdorf (1739–99) and Josef Mysliveček (1737–81). Although not a composer or a performer himself, Bremner's dissemination of new musical ideas at a time when they were not generally accepted – or even, in some quarters, welcomed – was of long-term relevance.

Of the three Germans, two were London based. For a period in the 1760s and 1770s, Johann Christian Bach (1735–82) – often referred to as the English Bach, or the London Bach – was the most popular composer in London and also a highly influential concert promoter. Much of his success, however, was achieved in partnership with Carl Friedrich Abel (1723–87), and it was Abel who arrived in London first. Abel's father was a noted musician who, in the year of young Abel's birth, had taken over from Johann Sebastian Bach as *Kapellmeister* to Prince Leopold of Anhalt-Köthen. Bach moved on to Leipzig as musical director of the city's Thomasschule. The two musicians remained in contact and, some ten years later, young Abel was sent to Leipzig to join the Bach household as both pupil and lodger. In the course of time, he developed into a gifted *viola da gamba* player and, in 1743, when he was twenty, Bach recommended him for an appointment with the court orchestra of the Elector of Saxony in Dresden. Abel stayed in Dresden for fifteen years and gave every appearance of being settled, when, suddenly, he set off for London, attracted – we can only assume – by London's reputation as a city where musicians had the opportunity of making money. He gave his first concert in April 1759, at the Great Room in Dean Street, Soho. The programme consisted entirely of his own compositions, performed on the *viola da gamba,* the harpsichord and an odd, newly invented instrument called the pentachord – in effect, a five-stringed cello – invented by Sir Edward Walpole. From there, he never looked back. Queen Charlotte, consort of King George III and herself a skilled harpsichord player, appointed him as a member of her private chamber orchestra at a generous salary of £200 a year; and, apart from a return visit to his native Germany in the 1780s, he spent the rest of his life in London, organising concerts, playing the *viola da gamba* and cello and, of course, composing. His royal appointment naturally gave him the opportunity to make influential friends, such as the Countess of Pembroke, Queen Charlotte's Lady of the Bedchamber. He became a good friend of the Earl of Kellie; he knew the author Laurence Sterne; and he had his portrait painted twice by Gainsborough.

When he died, in 1787, Abel left a substantial body of work that was widely heard and played – Charles Burney admired both his compositions and his playing – but there is a crucial distinction to be made between Abel's public music and the works for *viola da gamba* that he wrote for his own private purposes. The public music – the symphonies, overtures, concertos, quartets and trios, much of which was published by Bremner – was clearly in advance of what was being produced by British composers. Structurally, it showed an awareness of sonata form, while stylistically it leaned towards the *galant*, a style that flourished across all the arts in the mid-eighteenth century as a reaction against the excesses of Baroque ornamentation. In retrospect, the *galant* appears as an intermediate stage in the evolution of the classical style. It was marked by a preference for melody-driven pieces that featured comparatively simple harmonisation; and, as a consequence, it tended to place a greater musical distance between the solo voice or the solo instrument and its accompaniment. Abel's public music was clearly written to meet public demand and contractual obligations. It was bright and accessible, often suited to amateur performance, and, above all, popular. The symphonies, in particular, had a discernible influence on Mozart when, as an eight-year-old prodigy, he visited London from 1764 to 65. Mozart actually copied one of them – the Symphony in E flat which appears in Abel's *Six Symphonies*, opus 7 (1767) – in order to study it. Many years later, long after both men were dead, musicologists rediscovered the manuscript and, because it was in full score and in Mozart's handwriting, assumed that the symphony was his and not Abel's.[2]

Abel's private music, which survives in two manuscripts which were once the property of the Countess of Pembroke, was neglected for many years. This is not altogether surprising. It was never intended for publication and consists solely of works for the *viola da gamba,* which, although always Abel's preferred instrument – he was one of the last great virtuoso players – was at the time was rapidly losing out to the cello. These works show a very different Abel. They are not in the *galant* style. They show a man working out musical ideas on a plane that is emotional, at times intense, but also highly disciplined. And they show far more clearly than his public offerings what Abel had learned from Johann Sebastian Bach – although it is worth noting that, at the time, to be known as Bach's pupil or to emulate his style would not have been a particular recommendation. Bach did not enjoy anything like the reputation he does today, either in Germany or elsewhere. Indeed, Johann Sebastian's second son, Carl Philip Emmanuel, was far better known; and Charles Burney, who travelled in Germany at the beginning of the 1770s collecting material for his *History of Music,* thought of Johann Sebastian as principally an organist and composer for the organ.

Johann Christian Bach, Johann Sebastian's youngest surviving son, arrived in London in 1762, three years after Abel. He had been born and brought up in Leipzig, but at the age of fifteen, following the death of his father, had moved to Berlin where his half-brother Carl Philip Emmanuel was already a respected musician at the court of Frederick the Great. He lived with and studied under his distinguished (and much older) half-brother until 1756. At the age of twenty, and by now an accomplished keyboard player, Johann Christian was ready to strike out on his own. He travelled to Milan to become resident musician in the household of the rich and influential Count Agostino Litta. He seems to have fallen on his feet in so far that Litta was sufficiently impressed – and sufficiently generous – to send him to Bologna to study composition under Giambattista Martini. At this point, influenced by his exposure to Italy and Italian culture, and perhaps also by considerations of employment, Johann Christian converted to Roman Catholicism. His solidly Lutheran family was outraged and ostracised him, but the conversion, coupled no doubt with Martini's influence, made it possible for him to be appointed organist at the Duomo in Milan in 1760. The duties do not appear to have been exacting. During the two years he was there, he managed to compose not only the handful of liturgical works required by his position, but also three full-scale operas – *Artaserse*, premiered in Turin in 1760; *Catone in Utica*, Naples, 1761; and *Alessandro nell'Indie*, also in Naples, 1762. It was on the strength of these that Johann Christian received the offer of a contract to compose two operas for the King's Theatre in London. The Milan cathedral authorities gave him leave of absence for a year – and he never returned.

Johann Christian Bach's first two London operas were *Orione* and *Zanaida*, both produced for the 1762–63 season and both sufficiently popular for the theatre management to ask for more. Five more – and a masque – followed during the 1760s and 1770s, all composed for the King's Theatre. The most successful was probably *Carattaco* (1767), based on a dramatic retelling of the story of Caractacus by the now almost forgotten poet and gardener, William Mason. Bach also wrote operas for Mannheim and for Paris; but, perhaps because he sought to avoid the financial risk and the endless infighting that surrounded Italian opera, particularly in London, he never demonstrated the single-minded commitment to opera that Handel displayed during his operatic years – which is not to say that he did not leave his mark. A large number of Italian operas were produced in London during the Baroque period, often with very little to distinguish one from another. Most arias in operas and oratorios alike were based on what is known as the da capo principle: a self-contained first section; a second section which offered a contrast in both mood and musical texture; followed by a da capo, a return to the beginning, and a repetition of the opening section, varied only by improvisation and ornamentation on the part of the soloist. Bach's innovation was to loosen this structure, to provide contrast and manipulate dramatic tension through the use of orchestral colour, which was one of his strong points. He was also, in *Orione*, the first man to integrate the clarinet – which had previously been regarded as little more than a novelty – into the orchestra and orchestral textures.

Arriving in London, Bach lodged in the house of the popular Italian soprano, Signora Columba Mattei, who was managing the King's Theatre, but he soon made contact with Abel, whom he had known as a child in Leipzig, and by early 1764 the two of them were sharing a house and working in partnership. Success came rapidly. Bach's obvious musical talent was matched by an attractive, outgoing personality – and Abel's already established social and musical connections no doubt helped. Less than a year after his arrival in London, Bach was appointed music master to Queen Charlotte, a post he retained until his death; and by 1764, he and Abel were acting jointly and successfully as concert promoters, first at Vauxhall Gardens and then at Carlisle House in Soho.

Carlisle House had been bought in 1760 by a beautiful and charismatic Venetian singer, who went by the name of Theresa Cornelys, though she had used several others in the course of an adventurous career.[1] She began a series of exclusive subscription concerts – subscribers were known as 'The Society' – the organisation and management of which passed to Bach and Abel in 1765. The Bach-Abel concerts, as they are now called, rapidly became the most fashionable ticket in town and were attended at various times by members of the Royal Family and even the King of Denmark. They continued at Carlisle House for ten years, by which time the two promoters felt they needed a purpose-built concert hall. This was a mistake. By the mid-1770s, fashions were changing and costs were rising. The new hall in Hanover Square was the epitome of Georgian elegance, and concerts would continue to be staged there up to and after Bach's death in 1782, but the project left them both seriously in debt.

The concert programmes, which naturally included a generous selection of works by both Bach and Abel, broke new ground. They gave fashionable London audiences the opportunity to hear symphonies and concertos in the *galant* style; to hear works by new foreign composers; and, for the more knowledgeable, to become familiar with the principles of sonata form. Here were works based on thematic contrast and the use of contrasting keys, creating tensions which were then resolved to create a musical whole. The programming would seem immensely tame to us, but to an audience schooled in Handel and Arne, Corelli and Scarlatti, music by Haydn, Stamitz, Dittersdorf, Filtz, Holzbaur, and Mysliveček must have seemed new and exciting. The Bach-Abel concerts even gained an international reputation; but, in Britain, it was only in London that they were able to exert any real influence. Elsewhere, in the provinces, particularly in the north of England, but also in Scotland and Ireland, a more conservative, Handel-dominated musical outlook continued to reign. The only significant exception, as we shall see, was where provincial music came under the influence of a third German.

Like Handel, Bach rapidly adapted to English conditions and adopted an English personality. His position as the Queen's music teacher naturally gave him access to court circles, and, like Abel, he came to know many of London's artistic elite: Gainsborough (with whom he was once robbed by a pair of highwaymen), Sir Joshua Reynolds, John Zoffany, Sheridan, and, of course, Charles Burney, who was a great supporter. As a composer, Bach was versatile enough to please almost any audience. Apart from his operas, he wrote incidental music and songs for a number of pasticcios, including *Maid of the Mill* and *The Flitch of Bacon*, as well as numerous songs for Vauxhall Gardens; and his gift for finding a good tune on such occasions recalls Arne's. He was a prolific composer of instrumental music, leaving over forty symphonies, more than fifty concertos and concertante pieces,[2] and a large number of keyboard and chamber works. Bach was certainly an effective exponent of sonata form, yet his music, in the main, is elegant rather than innovative. It is the product of its time, written for and suited to Georgian London's equally elegant drawing rooms and concert halls. Where he offers something new, it is usually in his ability to exploit orchestral colour for pleasing effects. Just occasionally, however, he gives us something more. The C minor piano sonata, no. 6 of his opus 5 set, is one in which Bach appears to write more personally and emotionally than usual. The G minor symphony, no. 6 of the opus 6 set, written in the late 1760s, is even more revealing. A gradual build up of emotional tension in the long, slow movement gives way to an explosive finale which, quite remarkably, leaves both musical and emotional tensions unresolved. These pieces, in which normally hidden emotions are expressed and German *Sturm und Drang* breaks through, are glimpses of what perhaps might have been if Bach had been writing in a different social context. Interestingly, Sir John Hawkins, in his *Memoirs of Dr William Boyce*, criticises both Abel and Bach for having 'two styles of composition, the one for their own private delight, the other for the gratification of the many'.[3] Hawkins' judgement is sometimes suspect – he was one of those who deified Handel, believing that music would never again attain the same level of excellence – but he is right to identify a dual approach, almost a split personality, in the way composers were beginning to approach their music. It was an attitude that was to have an important and long-term impact.

Bach's duties as organist in Milan had involved the production of a few sacred and liturgical pieces, but otherwise he wrote hardly any choral music. In the end, this was his undoing. London had welcomed him with open arms, but London was fickle. By the late 1770s, the Bach-Abel concerts were no longer so exciting and Bach's music had fallen out of fashion. Outside London, where the English choral tradition was building in strength, his reputation was not great enough to challenge or even stand alongside that of Handel. By the time he died, on New Year's Day 1782, at the age of just forty-seven, Bach was long past the height of his fame. He was also badly in debt, partly because of Hanover Square, and partly because his steward had stolen £1,000, a very significant sum at the time. After his death, Queen Charlotte stepped in personally, assisting Bach's widow, the Italian soprano, Cecilia Grassi, to pay off some of his debts and helping her to return to her native Italy.

Johann Christian Bach has one other claim to historical fame in terms of British music. The first pianos, in a form that we would recognise today, were built by Bartolomeo Cristofori in Italy at the beginning of the eighteenth century. They were not an immediate success, but by the 1730s Gottfried Silbermann was building them in Germany. Johann Sebastian Bach tried out a piano in 1736 and was not impressed, only changing his mind when he heard an improved version ten years later. These early pianos – known as 'fortepianos', to distinguish them from the more modern 'pianoforte', which has a metal frame and a different tone based on higher string tensions and leather- rather than cork-covered hammers – gradually spread across the Continent. They were particularly slow to reach Britain, and, once again, it was a German who took the initiative. In the mid–1760s, Johannes Zumpe, who had been one of Silbermann's apprentices, began producing his own design of simple, square pianos in his workshop in Princes Street, close by Hanover Square. It was Johann Christian Bach, then at the height of his popularity, who championed the new instrument. In 1766, his opus 5 set of keyboard sonatas was the first music published in Britain to state explicitly that it could be played on the piano as well as the harpsichord. He did not give the first public performance on the piano in London. That honour seems to have gone to the songwriter and singer, Charles Dibdin. The playbill for the performance of *The Beggar's Opera* at Covent Garden on 16 May 1767 states: 'End of Act I. Miss Brickler will sing a favourite song from "Judith" accompanied by Mr Dibdin on a new instrument, call'd Piano Forte.'[4] But it was Bach who, just a few weeks later on 2 June, gave the first solo concert performance on the instrument at the Thatched House Tavern in St James's Street. And from that time, the piano's success never looked back. Zumpe's pianos proved popular, not least because they were comparatively inexpensive. The Burney household had one by 1768 and, quite possibly, two by the early 1770s.[5] Americus Backers produced the first English grand piano in 1771; and two years later John Broadwood, who as a young man had walked from Scotland to London in search of work, established the piano company that would make his fortune and perpetuate his name.

The third German actively promoting new music in Britain in the years following the death of Handel is today a lesser-known figure – at least as a musician – and his musical career was confined to the English provinces. Nonetheless, his achievements have to be considered alongside those of Bach and Abel. Frederick William Herschel (1738–1822) was born in Hanover, the son of an oboist in the band of the Hanoverian Guards. He too trained as an oboist and joined up, visiting England with the regimental band in 1756, at the age of eighteen. He was immediately struck by the opportunities to earn money available to musicians in English society and resolved to return. He did so the following year – an action which resulted in his being accused of desertion, though he was later pardoned by George III – and found work in London copying music. Before long, he was appointed to head what was called a military band in Richmond, Yorkshire, although in fact the band consisted of just two oboes and two French horns. Undaunted, Herschel stuck to his task, composed music, raised the standard of playing, and by 1760 he was in charge of the band of the Durham Militia, living in Sunderland, and composing his Eighth Symphony. It was in Sunderland that he came into contact with Charles Avison, who was then experimenting with the ideas of the Mannheim school with which Herschel would probably already have been familiar from his musical education in Hanover.

Avison recruited Herschel to play as first violin and soloist with his Newcastle-upon-Tyne orchestra. Their collaboration lasted only one season, after which Herschel was head-hunted by a Mr Crompton who was running a series of subscription concerts in Leeds. The city had been staging concerts since 1726 and had an active musical community, but wanted things run on a more professional basis. Would Herschel be interested? Herschel dropped his military connections, left Avison's orchestra, and moved to Yorkshire. He spent the next four years, from 1762 to 1766, managing the city's concerts and acquiring the reputation of a pioneer in terms of the music he programmed. He was not, as we shall see, in any way opposed to Handel's music, but the music heard at his concerts was much closer to that which featured in Bach and Abel's London concerts – with the notable addition of pieces arranged for wind bands of various configurations, of which he was particularly fond.

After four years in Leeds, Herschel moved to Halifax to be organist at St John the Baptist, the town's largest church, but he stayed only four months. From Halifax, in 1767, he moved to Bath as organist at the city's Octagon Chapel and Director of Concerts at the Pump Room, positions he retained for the next fifteen years. Bath, of course, was a fashionable spa town and Herschel shared a house in New King Street with his sister, Caroline, who often sang soprano at his concerts. His new role offered great opportunities to promote the music that interested him, and under his direction new names began to appear on the programmes of the Pump Room concerts. As things turned out, however, music gradually became less important in his life. It was during his time in Bath that Herschel developed the interest in mathematics, lenses and astronomy for which he is now remembered. He built his first large telescope in 1774 and from then on, ably assisted by Caroline, spent much of his time surveying the night sky, cataloguing nebulae and double star systems. In the course of these investigations, he discovered the planet Uranus and, in 1782, was appointed Astronomer

Royal by George III. This effectively ended his musical career, but it led to a series of impressive scientific discoveries – among them infrared radiation, the moons of Saturn and Uranus, and the movement through space of the solar system – a knighthood, and worldwide recognition as a pioneer of modern astronomy.

Only for the first half of his life, then, was Herschel a professional musician. He was a skilled performer on the oboe, violin, and harpsichord, and also a more than competent composer, who left twenty-four symphonies; a number of concertos for oboe, violin, and viola; and some harpsichord sonatas. Of these, the earlier compositions are the more interesting, showing evidence of a musical potential that was, in the end, not fully realised. The oboe concertos from the beginning of his career are well constructed and, as one might expect, display a great understanding of the instrument; but the F major Viola Concerto, dating from 1759, also early in his career, shortly after his arrival in England, is an altogether more intense and impressive piece. It is a young man's work, marked by odd contrasts and strong emotions, but still controlled and constructed in a way that looks forward to the world of the classical concerto of the early 1800s. Yet only two years later Herschel, still only twenty-three, was writing his Violin Concerto in G in a very different style. It was much more tuneful and probably, with its *galant* elegance, much more to public taste at the time than the Viola Concerto, but it was also less demanding, less inventive and less interesting. The contrast recalls the dual approach identified by Hawkins in the work of Bach and Abel, and leads one to reflect again on the impact on composers and musicians of Britain's highly developed market for music. Herschel was undoubtedly a 'modern' composer in that his German musical upbringing had given him an understanding of the developments of the Mannheim school and sonata form that is reflected in his work, but as time went by and his scientific interests deepened, he naturally wrote less and wrote with less conviction. His later works have been described as conventional and superficial[6] and, although he lived for forty years after his appointment as Astronomer Royal in 1782, he wrote no more music.

One odd footnote to Herschel's story is that it was his passionate interest in astronomy as much as his work in music that cemented his friendship with Charles Burney. Burney was also a keen amateur astronomer: he had published an essay on comets and lived for some years in the London house that had once belonged to Sir Isaac Newton.

47 The Cult of Handel

For all the efforts of men like Avison, Kellie, Bremner, Bach, Abel, Herschel, and even Crompton, to diversify British music, to move it forward to embrace new styles and structures, the dominant single factor throughout the second half of the eighteenth century remained the cult of Handel. Overseas, despite the loss of its American colonies, Britain was going through a period of commercial expansion, while at home, particularly in the north, the first stages of the Industrial Revolution were beginning to transform the economy. These were significant changes, yet they took place within a conservative social framework. The Hanoverian dynasty, though intermittently troubled, was essentially secure, and the political situation comparatively stable. The newly wealthy and the upwardly mobile sought to imitate or join the aristocracy, not replace them. Handel, like the Hanoverians, was German but had become British. Handel's music had been publicly endorsed by both George I and George II. He was the composer to whom they had turned when they wanted to commission something special. He had become a kind of symbol of the age, so that, on one level, the Handel cult became an expression of loyalty, a patriotic gesture.

It also expressed a powerful and complex social phenomenon. It would be wrong to exaggerate the degree of social mobility that was possible in Georgian England, except to say that it was greater than in any previous age, and was particularly noticeable in the context of the arts. Sir John Vanbrugh, architect of the King's Theatre, came from comparatively humble origins; Thomas Gainsborough was the son of a weaver; and Charles Burney was probably the first professional musician to be accepted in society as a gentleman. Handel's own life story – the son of a German barber-surgeon who became a rich, popular and respected composer, favoured by kings – was an example of what was possible. Few, if any, of those who sang *Messiah* or *Saul* in the Handel festivals which sprang up in towns and cities across the country would have cited such examples or seen their participation as a step on the road to riches or a title. Nonetheless, such events did reflect the aspirations of the participants. They did raise levels of culture, musicianship and education, and they did contribute to social change.

In this context, it is not surprising that the Midlands and the North of

England, where manufacturing, industrialisation and consequent social change were just beginning to gather speed, should have played a significant part in the development of the Handel cult. The cult centred on the great choral works, particularly *Messiah*. The ability to stage *Messiah* came to be seen as a badge of cultural progress and a matter for civic pride. It was performed in Birmingham, Coventry and Wolverhampton in 1760, with Coventry repeating the oratorio in 1761 and 1763. Manchester staged performances in 1763 and 1764. Sheffield followed in 1769. Chester joined in with a four-day festival in 1772 that included *Judas Maccabaeus* and *Samson* as well as *Messiah*. This was followed in 1783 with a five-day festival that added *Acis and Galatea*. In Halifax, a town which had doubled its population in the twenty years between 1744 and 1764, the parish choir actually set up a '*Messiah* Club', the members of which were predominantly working men, in the expectation that they might stage the first Yorkshire performance – which they did in August 1766, a date chosen because it marked the completion of a magnificent new organ for the parish church. Herschel's move from Leeds to Halifax was connected with the city's musical ambitions; his failure to stay more than a few months was due to the local infighting that accompanied them. Then, in 1767, on Christmas Day, *Messiah* was given in the chapel of the small village of Holbeck on the southern edge of Leeds. *Messiah* was not, at that time, associated with any particular time of year. The Holbeck performance seems to have marked the beginning of its now traditional association with the celebration of Christmas. The performance also marked the start of a *Messiah* craze in Yorkshire. Beginning in September 1768, the Leeds Assembly Rooms staged a series of no less than eighteen fortnightly performances of the oratorio. And the following year saw a two-day Handel festival, featuring *Messiah* and *Judas Maccabaeus*, in the small town of Holmfirth – a festival that drew performers from all over Yorkshire and as far away as Lichfield and Manchester.

The Handel cult was not, of course, confined to the north. Salisbury, Bath, Bristol, and the Three Choirs venues – Hereford, Worcester and Gloucester – were also among the towns and cities that contributed to a rising tide of enthusiasm. This culminated in the great Handel Commemoration of 1784, marking the twenty-fifth anniversary of the composer's death. The Commemoration was a musical event on an unprecedented scale. It was sponsored by the Earl of Sandwich (inventor of the food item which bears his name) and by the alliterative Sir Watkins

Williams Wynn, a veteran of Chester's Handel festivals; it was blessed with the formal patronage of George III; and it was chronicled extensively by Charles Burney in two volumes which not only tell the full story of the Commemoration and its evolution, but also give precise details of the musical forces deployed – no less than two hundred and seventy-two instrumentalists and two hundred and fifty singers – down to a diagrammatic representation of how they were placed physically in the two chosen venues. Joah Bates, who had directed the Halifax *Messiah* eighteen years previously, acted as musical director, but also as organist. Incredibly, he had to control his vast orchestra and chorus from his seat at the organ with a nod and a frown in the direction of those musicians and singers who could actually see him – and there were many who could not. Nevertheless, all went well. Three concerts were originally planned. Two were to be in Westminster Abbey, which accommodated an audience of some 4,500, and the third in the Pantheon. This was London's largest assembly rooms, built in 1772 on the south side of Oxford Street; it probably allowed for a slightly larger audience than the Abbey. (The branch of Marks and Spencer's currently occupying the site is named 'The Pantheon'.) The first concert included anthems such as *Zadok the Priest* and parts of the *Dettingham* and *Utrecht Te Deums*; the second mixed favourite extracts from Handel's operas and oratorios (mixing secular and sacred music in this manner was considered very daring); while the third was devoted – inevitably – to *Messiah*. Such was the level of demand that the first and third concerts were repeated in Westminster Abbey a few days later. And the whole event so gripped both the public and the official imagination that it was repeated every year for the next three years and again in 1791.

The significance of the Handel Commemoration would be hard to overestimate. It pushed the cult of Handel into the next generation. It gave Handel's popularity yet another huge boost, and it strengthened the identification of the man and his music with the social and political establishment. Both, in turn, further encouraged the participation of people who might otherwise have had neither the wish nor the opportunity to become involved in music, and thus further stimulated the development of the British choral tradition. What had been a phenomenon became an institution, and the impact on British music was immense, not least because it led to a hardening of attitudes. Because of Handel, oratorios were now seen as the pinnacle of musical achievement. This was only partly a musical judgement: the fact that they dealt with religious subject matter was a significant factor; as was the additional moral dimension: oratorio performances were frequently in aid of charitable causes. Handel may not have been the first to use this means of fundraising, but, as we have seen, he certainly adopted and popularised the idea. The oratorio had become 'serious' music, the yardstick by which a composer's status could be judged – an attitude which would persist throughout most of the nineteenth century. Unsurprisingly, few British composers were willing to invite comparison with the master.

In the years following Handel's death, a number of new oratorios had appeared. John Christopher Smith's *Paradise Lost* (1760), based on Milton's poem, and Arne's *Judith* (1761), were perhaps the least feeble. But it was Handel and Handel's music that the public wanted. Smith had probably been closer to Handel than anyone else during the last decade of his life, and had actually worked with him on his oratorio scores. During the 1760s, he reworked bits of Handel's music to construct a series of Handel pasticcios on Old Testament themes – *Nabal, Tobin, Gideon*. In 1765, a London musician named Edward Toms borrowed the idea, cobbling together a pasticcio called *Israel in Babylon*. Ostensibly a companion piece to Handel's *Israel in Egypt*, it has survived and even been recorded. Another method of oratorio construction was to follow the example of *Messiah* and construct a non-dramatic oratorio with a libretto consisting of biblical quotations. Samuel Arnold (1740–1802) – who somehow managed to combine the duties of musical director at Marylebone Gardens and manager of the Lyceum Theatre with those of organist at the Chapel Royal and at Westminster Abbey – adopted this technique for *The Resurrection*, which received four performances at Covent Garden in the spring of 1770. James Hook, better known for the many popular songs he composed for Vauxhall Gardens, did the same with *The Ascension* which was premiered in 1776. And so, too, did Philip Hayes (1738–97), a notably cantankerous and corpulent Oxford Professor of Music, whose oratorio *Prophecy* was heard in Oxford at the end of 1778 and again in London the following year.

Samuel Arnold was undoubtedly the most persistent of these composers where oratorios were concerned, but he was not Handel. His *Abimelech* (1768), to a libretto by the poet Christopher Smart, was given only two performances – one in 1768 and one after heavy revision in 1772. *Prodigal Son* (1773) fared somewhat better both with the public and with the musical establishment: it was highly praised by the university authorities when Arnold received his doctorate from Oxford, yet given the temper of the times any oratorio was likely to be seen as derivative. Following the Handel

Commemoration and the great boost it gave to both Handel's reputation and the status of his oratorios, the number of new works in the genre was reduced to a trickle, and the number of any quality all but dried up. Arnold, who had been one of the assistant musical directors of the Commemoration, produced one more Handel pasticcio – *Redemption* in 1786, which was a modest success – but after that he preferred to direct oratorios at Covent Garden rather than write them. He also embarked on the mammoth task of compiling and editing a first edition of Handel's collected works. During his lifetime, Handel had transformed the oratorio as a genre. Now, however, the immense popularity of his works and the weight of his posthumous reputation was stifling it, at least for the present.

48 John Wesley, and West Gallery Music

If the writing of oratorios was in decline, so, too, was writing for the great tradition of English church music, although the reasons were very different. For the first hundred and fifty years of its existence, the Church of England had been under more or less constant threat, from 'reactionary' Catholicism on the one hand and 'radical' Puritanism on the other. From the time of Henry VIII right up until the departure of James II in 1688, the fate of the Church had been closely bound up with that of the monarch. The arrival of William of Orange and the subsequent 1701 Act of Settlement, which formally required the monarch to maintain the established Church, ushered in a period of greater stability. Religious controversies continued to arise, but they no longer threatened the Church or the monarchy in the same way. As a consequence, the importance of religious music in boosting and maintaining the royal image gradually diminished; and the Chapel Royal gradually ceased to act as a focal point for English musicians and English music as a whole.

Although he could never be described as a major figure, Maurice Greene did maintain a certain standard, particularly in his anthems, and can at least be seen as being part of the great tradition of English composers of church music, but Greene died in 1755. Thereafter, for the rest of the century, English church music remained resolutely in the doldrums. Despite the fact that his style harked back to the beginning of the century and beyond, James Nares is probably the most noteworthy of those who followed Greene. The name of Jonathan Battishill (1738–1801) is remembered for his anthem *O Lord, look down from Heaven*. Otherwise, the church music of the period has little to recommend it. Figures such as James Kent (1700–76), organist at Winchester Cathedral; Benjamin Cooke (1734–93) organist at Westminster Abbey; and William Jackson of Exeter (1730–1803) are little more than footnotes to the great tradition – their works have been characterised as 'faded proprieties'.[1] In losing its sense of risk and danger, the Church of England had also lost its power to inspire.

Worse still, in some cases the Church seemed to have ceased to care about music. John Alcock (1715–1806) – whom we met previously giving his collection of Anglican church music to Maurice Greene – seemed destined for a distinguished career along traditional lines. A chorister at St Paul's at the same time as William Boyce, and a pupil of the blind organist John Stanley, he received a degree and then a doctorate in music from the University of Oxford. He went on to become organist at a number of prestigious churches, including the Temple Church and All Hallows in London, before being appointed organist and Master of Choristers at Lichfield Cathedral in 1750. Here, he found neglect. Not only was there no music – unless he bought it himself – but even when he provided it the choir was not able to sing it. Alcock abused the choir for their lack of ability. The choir complained to the Dean and Chapter. The Dean and Chapter did nothing beyond trying to paper over the cracks. In the end, Alcock resigned from his Cathedral positions, preferring to play in parish churches in the diocese. Then there was the case of John Jones (1728–96), organist at St Paul's Cathedral. He obviously had certain musical gifts: he composed a large number of single and double chants – settings of non-metrical texts, such as psalms and canticles, which form part of the choral liturgy. Indeed, one such setting so impressed Haydn when he heard it sung in unison by over 4,000 children in St Paul's in the 1790s that he was moved to tears. Jones also appears to have been an able player and composer for the harpsichord. His *Lessons for the Harpsichord* (1761) has been praised for its attempt to extend the range of the instrument and for its imaginative inclusion of melodic and harmonic elements drawn from Scottish and Welsh folk music. But as an organist, Jones was clearly not good enough for the position at St Paul's. Burney considered him mediocre at best; and his technical shortcomings attracted widespread criticism. Nonetheless, he remained organist at the Cathedral for forty-one years. These were not isolated instances.

Of course, there were musicians of talent and pockets of musical quality in various places across the country, but, taken overall, church music as written in, and for, the Church of England was in a depressed and directionless state. However, in the course of the middle decades of the eighteenth century, two new strains of music emerged, both at some distance from the central Church authorities, which did much to revitalise church music at a grass-roots level. The most obvious was the practice of evangelical hymn-singing.

John Wesley (1703–91) preached his first open-air sermon in Bristol in 1739, and opened his first London Meeting House later that same year. Wesley was an ordained Anglican minister who had originally intended to launch a movement to reform and revitalise the Church of England from within. However, his ideas rapidly developed both a mass appeal, particularly among populations in the new industrial centres and in poor rural districts, and an unstoppable momentum, so that by the last decade of the eighteenth century what had become known as Methodism effectively broke away from the Church of England and established itself as a separate Church. Both John Wesley and his brother Charles (1707–88) recognised the fundamental importance of singing in communicating and sharing their evangelical message. Hymns had been a feature of Church of England services ever since the sixteenth century, but they had never assumed the same level of importance that they enjoyed in, for example, German Protestant churches. Metrical psalms were still more commonly heard and sung. The Wesley brothers changed all that. They made hymns a central feature in Methodist worship.

In doing so, they built on ideas and trends that were already making themselves felt elsewhere in the nonconformist community. One crucial element in evangelical hymnody was first expressed by the hymn-writer and theologian, Isaac Watts (1674–1748). He stated that hymns should express the emotions of the people singing them rather than just repeating or paraphrasing biblical texts. This is reflected in some of his best-known hymns (he wrote over seven hundred and fifty), such as 'Joy to the World', 'O God, our help in ages past', and 'When I survey the wondrous cross'. It was something of a breakthrough for hymn-writers, opening up vast new areas of subject matter, and it had a huge influence on the two Wesleys.

As early as 1742, just three years after his Bristol sermon, John Wesley published the oddly titled *Collection of Tunes Set to music as they are commonly sung at the Foundery* (the Foundry in Moorfields being the location of the London Meeting House). Demand for hymns grew rapidly and further volumes followed in 1746, 1753 and 1761. Wesley translated many of the texts from German and wrote some of the tunes himself; in this he was aided by converts and friends, such as John Frederick Lampe (*c.*1703–51) and Thomas Butts (dates unknown). But the greatest hymn-writer of the period was his brother, Charles, who was responsible for some six thousand hymns, including many that are still frequently sung today, such as 'Amazing Grace', 'Soldiers of Christ, arise!', 'Love divine, all loves excelling', and 'Hark! The Herald Angels Sing'. They had words that were easily understood, and modern, accessible tunes – some based on folk songs, some based on melodies from Vauxhall Gardens, some even based on tunes borrowed from Handel and Arne. Methodist congregations responded with enthusiasm, partly because of the nature of the hymns themselves, and partly also because of the importance John Wesley placed on singing them correctly. On a number of occasions, he gave instructions about how he believed hymns should be sung during worship. These can be seen at their most concise in the preface to his 1761 volume, *Select Hymns with Tunes annext*. Members of Methodist congregations are urged to learn the tunes; to sing them exactly as printed; to join in together with the rest of the congregation; to sing 'lustily and with good courage'; to 'sing modestly' and not to bawl; to sing in time; and 'above all [to] sing spiritually.' This level of attention to the quality of the singing was new and stimulating. It made the congregation feel involved and valued.

In 1741, when William Knapp, Clerk to the Parish of Poole in Dorset, wrote that 'Church-Musick was never more in Vogue in this Nation than at present,' he was not talking about Methodist hymns.[2] He was referring to a new kind of musical practice which had appeared in some parts of the Church of England, and which, like Methodism, also sought to revitalise current forms of worship. He was also exaggerating, but this was perhaps understandable: he was a lowly clerk from a rural parish and his 1738 volume, *A Sett of New Psalm-Tunes and Anthems*, had just been reprinted in London. The music about which Knapp enthused has come to be known as West Gallery music. The name derives from the galleries that were constructed at the west end of many parish churches during the second half of the eighteenth century in order to accommodate the choir and, later, the musicians who played during services. Although its precise origins are uncertain, West Gallery music seems to have emerged during the second and third decades of the century. At the time, the Church of England was losing traction in the country as a whole, and there was a significant gap in both communication and practice between the higher echelons of the Church and the rural or more remote parishes. It may well be that priests in these areas simply sought to enliven their services by making use of whatever local musical talent was available, but it was in these parishes that this new approach to music in church during services first took hold.

When it first appeared, West Gallery music consisted of an unaccompanied male choir singing simple harmonies in three or four parts, with the tenor usually taking the lead – in effect, a church version of the way folk songs were often sung. As time passed, female voices were added, and then instruments introduced to support the singers, most of whom would have been villagers, labourers, farmers or tradesmen, with only limited musical education. There would have been fiddles, perhaps a cello or a bass viol, and certainly an oboe and a bassoon, both of which were very popular. Each instrumentalist would have been at the centre of the group of singers whose vocal line he or she followed. Thomas Webster's well-known painting, *The Village Choir*, which dates from the middle of the nineteenth century, is the probably best available representation of what a West Gallery ensemble might have looked like.

The first West Gallery choirs would have confined themselves to the psalms normally heard in Church of England services at the time, albeit probably in a more lively rendition than was usual. As the century progressed, as West Gallery practice spread, and as the impact of Methodism was felt throughout the country, they began to sing hymns as well. And by the nineteenth century, carols, glees and even folk songs with a religious burden were being included in the repertoire. Some West Gallery bands would even oblige with short instrumental interludes, confusingly called 'symphonies'. The arrangements would have been simple, lively, and frequently imbued with rhythms, styles and an improvisational approach drawn from the folk tradition; and performance, as far as we can gather, was marked by enthusiasm as much as accuracy. Nonetheless, it was a musical tradition and a mode of performance that gave a new and animated spirit to rural worship for a considerable length of time.

West Gallery Music died out during the middle years of the nineteenth century, a victim of shifts in both doctrine and economics. On the one hand, under the influence of the Oxford or Tractarian Movement, the Church of England was going through a period of revival and reform, and a new generation of clerics was calling for a return to simplicity and spirituality in worship, which was incompatible with the rustic liveliness of

West Gallery performance. On the other, West Gallery musicians came at a cost. Although the sums involved were paltry, singers had to be rewarded and instruments maintained. Economic changes meant that it was soon considered to be cheaper to install and maintain an organ. Moreover, an organ was felt to be more suitable to accompany the kind of congregational hymn-singing which, again as direct result of evangelical Methodism, was becoming ever more popular in the Church of England. This, of course, is the scenario brought to life so vividly by Thomas Hardy in *Under the Greenwood Tree*; and his 'Mellstock Quire' is a convincing picture of a West Gallery ensemble from the latter years of the tradition.

West Gallery Music was at heart a Church of England phenomenon. Although it did find its way into some non-conformist chapels, it was not really suited to the mood or the tone of evangelical worship. It failed to gain a significant foothold in Ireland: its English folk elements and essential informality would not have appealed to congregations in the Protestant Church of Ireland, while the majority Catholic population was suspicious of anything connected with Anglicanism. Nor was it calculated to appeal to the austere musical traditions of the Church of Scotland, dominated as they were by the chanting of metrical psalms to a limited number of approved tunes. Methodism, with hymn-singing as an integral component of its appeal, was an altogether more dramatic phenomenon. It swept into areas where Anglicanism had not kept pace with developments in society – the industrialising north of England, the mining towns of Cornwall – and its impact in Wales was nothing short of a social transformation. It, too, failed to find adherents in Ireland – beyond a few groups in the Protestant plantations and in the army garrisons – but in Scotland it did take root in the industrial towns of the central belt, and also in many fishing villages along the coast.

However, the transformation of Scottish church music that occurred in the mid-eighteenth century was only indirectly the result of Methodism. The prime mover was Sir Archibald Grant, a landowner in the parish of Monymusk, some twenty miles from Aberdeen. Expelled from Parliament for involvement in various frauds, he had decided to devote himself to the cause of agricultural improvement. He also loved the language of the psalms and decided to form a choir, drawn initially from the workers on his estate, to sing in the local kirk. In the early 1750s, there was still a substantial military presence in the area as a legacy of the 1745 rebellion. Grant persuaded a soldier by the name of Thomas Channon – a Methodist, who also clearly had some knowledge of West Gallery music – to train his choir. The aim was that they should sing the tune without excessive ornamentation, adding harmonies where they enhanced the grandeur and solemnity of the words and the meaning. It worked; the Monymusk choir was a great success; and Channon began to teach in other parishes as well as at Robert Gordon's Hospital in Aberdeen, a school for boys whose families had fallen on hard times. In 1755, he led a seventy-strong choir in a performance in Aberdeen's newly rebuilt Kirk of St Nicholas. The response was overwhelming. The Church of Scotland authorities disapproved strongly of singing in parts and of Channon's additions to the traditional repertoire, but their objections were swept aside by popular enthusiasm. Grant paid for Channon to be discharged from the army and to continue his work as a choirmaster, and when, in 1761, John Wesley visited Monymusk to hear the choir, his verdict was that they were as good as any cathedral choir in England. Within just a few years, there were choirs in Aberdeen, Edinburgh, Glasgow and elsewhere; singing teachers were being appointed; and Scottish publishers were finding that bringing out works such as Thomas Moore's *Psalm Singer's Pocket Companion* (1756) and *The Psalm Singer's Delightful Companion* (1761) was a profitable activity. In the space of a decade or even less, Scotland's choral tradition had been revitalised and set on a new course.

In the end, West Gallery Music was to prove a less influential and less enduring tradition than evangelical hymnody. For many years, it was all but forgotten, and, although today there is a well-organised West Gallery Music Association as well as a number of 'quires' that attempt to recreate the sound and the ambience, some even dressing up in period costume, it remains a minority interest. The influence of evangelical hymnody, by contrast, continued to develop and went far beyond the confines of the non-conformist movement. It provided the basis for the English and Welsh tradition of congregational hymn-singing which remained a powerful musical and religious force well into the twentieth century and, although diminished, is still alive today – reflected in the singing of hymns by Welsh rugby fans, and of the now ritualised performance of 'Abide with me' every year at the F.A. Cup Final. Nonetheless, these two musical strains developed in parallel for over a century and, like the cult of Handel – although in a more immediate and, for many, more accessible manner – they both encouraged the democratisation of music.

49 Hook, Dibdin, Shield, and the Historical Perspective

Dominated by the cult of Handel, appreciative of new Continental forms such as the symphony while at the same time continuing to regard them as essentially foreign, the second half of the eighteenth century was undeniably a conservative period in the history of British music. It was characterised by drift in the broad intellectual sense of the term. There were many talented musicians and composers pursuing their careers. None of them had the overwhelming genius of a Purcell, a Byrd or a Tallis, but they might have gone on to make a greater musical mark than they actually did, had they not been squeezed by the society in which they worked. When not venerating Handel, the society of the day placed its emphasis firmly on music as entertainment, as a consumable, leisure-time activity. Composers were in demand, especially if they had a talent for writing melodies with popular appeal; musicians and singers were in demand, for there was more music being performed than ever before; and there were rich rewards for the successful. Music as a business was growing, but, as a consequence, composers, musicians and singers alike were increasingly constrained by what audiences and promoters demanded.

James Hook's musical education was on traditional lines. He was a pupil of Thomas Garland, who was organist at Norwich Cathedral, and early in his career he composed a symphony-overture in the manner of the Mannheim school for a pantomime called *The Sacrifice of Iphigenia*. But it was his gift for songwriting and the 2,000 he songs composed for Marylebone and Vauxhall Gardens over the course of nearly fifty years that formed the basis of his successful and lucrative career. His name is hardly known at all today, but one of his songs – 'The Lass of Richmond Hill' – is still heard. Similarly, Charles Dibdin (1745–1834), whom we met at Covent Garden giving London its first hearing of the piano, began his career as a chorister at Winchester Cathedral. He gained much of his musical education from studying the works of Corelli, but once in London, where he stayed with his brother – the inspiration for 'Tom Bowling', the one song for which Dibdin is still remembered – he threw himself headlong into the world of popular music. His was a tumultuous career, rocked by scandals and marred by rows with theatre managers and singers alike. At one stage, he was Musical Director for Covent Garden at the impressive salary of £10 a week. At another, he was almost destitute and set off to try his luck in India – though he never got farther than Devon. He too had a gift for song-writing and produced some 1,000 songs. The most popular of these he incorporated into his 'entertainments', such as *The Whim of the Moment* and *Poor Jack*, which he toured to all parts of the British Isles. He also produced music for over a hundred plays, pantomimes and musical dramas of various sorts, so his music was regularly performed, not only in the pleasure gardens and concert halls, but also at Covent Garden, Drury Lane and Sadler's Wells. Both Hook and Dibdin came to London having lost their fathers at an early age and were forced to struggle, tuning harpsichords and copying music, to establish themselves in a competitive environment. Both also made a deliberate decision, evidently for financial reasons and without any apparent regret, to pursue freelance careers concentrating on the ephemeral, 'popular' end of the market.

A similar dynamic is evident in the career of Thomas Linley (1733–95). He trained as an organist at Bath Cathedral, married at nineteen and supported his wife and a rapidly growing family by teaching music. He soon became a recognised figure in Bath's active musical life, promoting concerts and oratorios, and eventually, in 1771, becoming Musical Director of the city's new Assembly Rooms. In 1767, his opera, *The Royal Merchant*, was performed at Covent Garden; his reputation grew steadily and in 1774 he was appointed joint director of the annual Lent oratorio season at Drury Lane. Linley had twelve children, seven of whom pursued a musical or theatrical career; and he shamelessly exploited their talents in order to make the money needed to support them and to further the family's social and professional ambitions. Given his character, however, it was always going to be the theatre with its promise of financial rewards that attracted him. In 1775, he wrote a number of songs for *The Duenna*, an opera with a libretto by the playwright Richard Brinsley Sheridan (who had eloped with Linley's daughter, the soprano Elizabeth Ann, in 1773). It ran for seventy-five consecutive performances in its first season and attracted effusive praise from Lord Byron. Linley was launched. By 1776, when he finally left Bath for London, he was wealthy enough to buy a quarter-share in the Theatre Royal in Drury Lane.

The story of William Shield (1748–1829) offers a different perspective. Shield was a complete outsider. He was born in Swalwell on the south bank of the River Tyne, just outside Gateshead. His father was a music teacher, but he, too, died young and nine-year-old William was apprenticed to a boat-builder. Fortunately, the boat-builder in question, Edward Davison of North Shields, was also a violinist who played in the Newcastle Musical Society's subscription concerts organised by Charles Avison. Davison recognised and encouraged Shield's talent. He introduced him to Avison, who gave him lessons in musical theory, and within a relatively short time, Shield was leading the Newcastle Musical Society orchestra and also playing at the city's pleasure gardens. Once he had served his apprenticeship, Shield gave up boat-building and went to Scarborough where he led the orchestra in the theatre and at local concerts. Over the next few years, he led orchestras in Durham, Stockton-on-Tees and Newcastle, gradually building a reputation as a talented and reliable player – the fact that there were orchestras in all these towns is itself an indication of how both the practice and the appreciation of what we would now call classical music had spread throughout the country. He was also developing a reputation as a composer. Some of his first compositions – settings of poems by his friend, the Irish writer and actor, John Cunningham, who had settled in Newcastle – were played at Scarborough; and in 1769, he was commissioned to write an anthem for the consecration of a new church, St John's, in Sunderland, which received enthusiastic notices throughout the region. Shield's opportunity came when he returned to Sunderland in 1772. Two London-based musicians – the violinist, Luigi Borghi, and the composer and oboist, Johann Christian Fischer – urged him to go to London and recommended him to Felice Giardini, who was in charge of the King's Theatre orchestra (and whom we have already met as a collaborator with Avison). He went, and was immediately taken on as a violinist. The following year, 1773, he was appointed principal viola, a position he retained for the next eighteen years.

Like Hook and Dibdin, Shield had a gift for melody. In his case, it may well have been derived from the folk songs that had been a part of his childhood – and for which, as we shall see, he retained an enthusiasm – but as a composer his real interest was in 'serious' music. His opus 1, published in 1775, three years after his arrival in London, was *Six duettos, five for two violins, one for two German flutes*. Inevitably, however, the theatre drew him in. In 1778, the King's Theatre staged a two-act comic opera, *The Flitch of Bacon*, for which he edited and arranged the music. It was a success. Covent Garden offered to employ him as a composer and over the next twenty years he produced music for over thirty dramatic works – English-style operas, pantomimes and even one or two ballets – with titles such as

The Poor Soldier, The Magic Cavern, The Midnight Wanderers, The Mysteries of the Castle, and *The Village Fête*. These were not demanding pieces; many were pasticcios, for Shield was adept at finding and integrating tunes and songs written by others – a talent that extended to his other works as well. Others were short 'afterpieces' designed to be played after the conclusion of the evening's serious, and usually Italian, main work. Shield's best-known operatic work, the comic, two-act *Rosina* (1783) – the only one of his theatre pieces to have survived in full score – comes into this category. It is light and witty, with a number of tuneful arias (sung memorably by Joan Sutherland in the 1970s) and an atmosphere that has been compared to that of latter-day musical comedy. Much of Shield's best music went into the overtures for his theatrical scores, which took the form of three movement English symphony-overtures. Those for *Rosina* and *The Woodman* (1791) are the most accessible today. Within the context of his theatre work, Shield could be very inventive, recreating medieval music for *Robin Hood* (1784) or using conch shells and strange percussion in an opera based on Captain Cook's voyage to the South Pacific, *Omai* (1785).

Shield had an ability – demonstrated in works such as *Robin Hood* and *Fontainbleau* (1784) – to write extended, high-range arias for his leading ladies. Such pieces were natural crowd pleasers, and even attracted the attention and admiration of Haydn who was in London in 1791 and attended one of the first performances of *The Woodman*. Haydn was critical of the behaviour of the audience and the attitude of the orchestra, but became friends with Shield. The two of them spent only four days in each other's company, but for Shield it was a revelation. He claimed that those four days taught him more about music than he had learned in the rest of his life. This may explain why, later that same year, he resigned from Covent Garden to spend time travelling and studying in France and Italy. On his return in 1792, he was immediately reinstated by Covent Garden and in the five years that followed composed no less than twelve scores. Nonetheless, the story points to a tension in Shield's creative life which one does not sense with Hook or Dibdin: he never quite gave up composing serious music. In the 1780s, he had published a series of duets for two violins and a number of quartets, including an oboe quartet, written for his friend William Parke. And on his return from Italy, he returned to composing chamber music: *Six trios for violin, tenor and violincello* was published in 1796.

Shield left Covent Garden for a second time in 1797. Although he did write two more dramatic scores, the last in 1807, he seems to have lost interest in the commercial world. He was appointed to what had become known as the King's Band; he wrote books – *An Introduction to Harmony* (1800) and *The Rudiments of Thoroughbass* (1815); and he continued to compose chamber music, such as *Three String Trios*, published in 1811. In 1817, he was appointed Master of the King's Musick, a slightly unexpected appointment perhaps, but one senses that Shield had always wanted to be a composer in the formal or traditional mode, and that circumstances rather than choice had led to his – undeniably successful – career as a composer for the theatre. His duty compositions as Master of the King's Musick have either not survived or not been recorded, but we do know that, following the death of King George III in 1820, it was decided that formal occasions at court should no longer be marked with a musical ode; so it was Shield who composed the last one, bringing to an end a tradition that had lasted over a century and a half. In 1823, he was appointed as one of the founding professors of the new Royal Academy of Music, a final indication that he had now achieved his ambition to be recognised as a serious musician – unless one counts the posthumous honour of burial in Westminster Abbey on his death in 1829.

Shield took a particular interest in folk song and constantly wove the tunes into the fabric of his scores. He also collaborated with antiquarian Joseph Ritson and others on several volumes of arrangements of Scottish and English songs – with a clear bias towards songs from County Durham and Northumberland, reflecting his Tyneside background. His affinity with folk songs has created some confusion to the extent that he has, at various times, been credited with writing the tunes to 'The Arethusa', 'Coming through the Rye', and even 'Auld Lang Syne', when what he did was to borrow and rework existing tunes. On the other hand, a song such as 'The Farmer', which appears in Britten's *Folk-Song Arrangements,* is not a traditional folk song at all, but Shield's own composition.

William Smethergell (1751–1836) was another talented composer who seems to have preferred the serious end of the musical spectrum, although he never quite made the impact he should have done. Apprenticed to a weaver, he found, like Shield, that his master was also a musician – in this case an organist. He kept up his association with weaving long enough to be admitted to London's Weavers' Company, but by the age of nineteen he was already organist at All Hallows, Barking. During the 1770s and 80s, he began building a reputation for himself, starting with a set of harpsichord lessons. This was followed by a set of six concertos for harpsichord or piano that attracted over a hundred subscribers, including the publisher Robert Bremner. In 1780, he published *Six Overtures in Eight Parts*, opus 2, followed by another set of six, opus 5, in 1784. These overtures are, of course, English symphony-overtures, but they are conceived with precision, and both well structured and well scored – and the second set was sufficiently popular to be reprinted ten years later. The melodic and flowing *Favourite Concerto for the Harpsichord or Pianoforte* was also published in 1784 – the same year that, incidentally, saw him playing among the second violins during the Handel Commemoration. His music was heard occasionally at Vauxhall Gardens where he enjoyed at least one 'hit' with a song entitled 'Moggy MacBride'.

It was the kind of base from which a solid musical career might have been launched, but his output and his profile suddenly slumped. His name barely appears in the records and directories of the period, although we know that he was expelled from the Society for the Support of Decayed Musicians for not paying his subscription. He remained organist at All Hallows until 1823, but he published nothing during the last thirty or more years of his life. Timothy Rishton succinctly sums up the man and the age in which he lived:

> William Smethergell is a curious, but not untypical, case of promise unfulfilled. While some of his works – the keyboard concertos in particular – display an imagination and musicianship far above that of most of his English contemporaries, he was perfectly capable of writing lifeless and insipid music. Perhaps it was the realisation that the latter was as much in demand as the former in the torpid musical environment of early 19th-century England that prompted Smethergell to give up composition and retire into an obscurity from which he has never returned.[1]

The distinction between popular and serious music is an awkward and, in some senses, an artificial one. To some extent, of course, it had always existed in, for example, attitudes to tavern music and to church music; but in the latter part of the eighteenth century it was being increasingly applied to the works of professional composers. On one level, the sense that popular song and theatre music were ephemeral and in some way of limited value sprang from the beginnings of a demand-led, consumer culture in which music had become effectively a disposable good. On another, it arose from a more complex realisation that began to see music in a new, longer-term, historical perspective.

Previously, composers had been able, within limits, to develop their art secure in the patronage of the Church, the court or a noble family – a system which still obtained on the Continent to a far greater extent than it did in mercantilist Britain. Composers wrote for their patrons, not for posterity: if their music was played regularly, or if it became a fixture in church services or coronations, that constituted success. The whole idea of collecting and studying the music of the past, let alone the works of a single composer, was a new one. Tallis and Byrd were distant figures in the age of Handel and Arne, their music all but forgotten. The idea of a composer gaining immortality through his collected *œuvre*, a central tenet of the late classical and romantic eras, was something that only gradually achieved currency, and – in Britain at least – was yet another area where reverence for Handel played a part. Manuscript collections from previous centuries such as the Eton Choirbook and the Carver MS were made with a view to performance, not study. The impulse was practical, not academic. The Dunkeld Music Book was probably put together to prevent music being lost in the heat of the Scottish Reformation. The impulse behind Boyce's *Cathedral Music* was quite different. It sought to record, to be comprehensive, to impose order. In the same way, though written from very different perspectives, Hawkins's *General History of the Science and Practice of Music* and Burney's *General History of Music* are innovative precisely because they see music in a historical context and (Burney's many digressions notwithstanding) present the subject as worthy of and capable of repaying academic study. Once awakened, interest in the music of the past began to gather momentum. Joseph Ritson, an antiquarian whose principal interest was poetry rather than music, published some forty historical studies of various kinds, among them several works on music with heavily historical titles, such as *Ancient Songs and Ballads from the Reign of King Henry the Second to the Revolution* (1792) and *A Select Collection of English Songs, with Their Original Airs: and a Historical Essay on the Origin and Progress of National Song* (1813). However, the high point of this first wave of historical interest in the music of the past came in 1812 with the publication of John Stafford Smith's *Musica Antiqua*. Smith, who had been a pupil of Boyce, sought to be comprehensive in a different way. He collected one hundred and ninety pieces, some of them dating back as far as the twelfth century. He did not limit himself to English composers, nor did he concentrate on choral and vocal music (unlike other early musical historians). He certainly included motets and madrigals and anthems, but he also included folk songs, dance tunes, harpsichord and organ music, pieces from Jacobean masques, even metrical chants, thus broadening the scope of past music that was available for study or performance.

In performing terms, the Academy of Antient Music, founded as long ago as 1710, had sung and played motets and madrigals from the sixteenth century, but theirs was very much a minority interest. The new attitude was reflected by the establishment in 1776, under heavy aristocratic patronage, of the Concerts of Antient Music – which from 1785, when George III began to take an interest, were also known as The King's Concerts. The stated objective was to perform music which was at least twenty years old and written by composers who were no longer living. Originally, there were twelve concerts a year, but the King insisted that there be a thirteenth to allow for a performance of – naturally – *Messiah*. Today, of course, we expect concert programmes to consist principally of music which is considerably older than twenty years, but in the late eighteenth century that was simply not the case: the audience expected what we would term contemporary music – the main exception being, as ever, the works of Handel. The Concerts of Antient Music continued for many years, remaining an essentially aristocratic organisation – Prince Albert was one of its last directors – and remaining dedicated to a limited number of works and composers, particularly Handel, until 1848. By that time the world had changed, but the Concerts had not and it was wound up, having quite simply failed to evolve.

In the context of these changes, it was natural that both musicians and the musical public should come to have a much stronger sense that certain music and the music of certain composers had a value beyond the accepted norms of its own or their own age; that it was worthy of preservation. It thus became increasingly common to place a given composition or a given composer's musical output on a spectrum that ran from the popular, meaning ephemeral and likely to appeal to the masses, to the serious, which meant elevated in purpose and aimed at a more educated and exclusive audience. Such categorisation is, of course, crude and perhaps ultimately unsustainable, but over the years it has been used by critics, commentators and the public to indicate how they receive and understand a particular piece of music – and, in that sense, it has a certain broad validity. It also became important, as we shall see, in the Victorian era when composers began to be assessed by their moral intent as well as their musical abilities.

50 A Reverence for Foreigners, and Haydn

One curious aspect of British social and artistic conservatism at this time was a conviction that foreign composers and performers were necessarily superior to British ones. Other countries might trumpet the successes of their own, but not the British. Thomas Linley's son, Thomas the Younger (1756–78) was a child prodigy. He played a violin concerto at a public concert in Bath at the age of seven, was tutored for the next five years by Boyce and then, at the age of twelve, sent to study violin and composition in Florence. There, he met and became friends with the other prodigy of the age, Wolfgang Amadeus Mozart. They were exact contemporaries and continued to correspond after Linley returned to England in 1771. For the next seven years, Linley's life was a kaleidoscope of activity. He led orchestras in Bath and at Covent Garden. He played solo concerts. He wrote violin sonatas and violin concertos. He wrote a *Lyric Ode on the Fairies, Aerial Beings and Witches of Shakespeare* which, even as late as 1824, was being compared favourably with Purcell and Mozart. He wrote the overture to the immensely successful *Duenna*. Then in 1778, he was drowned in a boating accident at Grimsthorpe Castle in Lincolnshire, aged just twenty-two. His was a prodigious talent – Mozart remembered him as a genius – and one can only speculate what direction his career might have taken had he lived, or if he might have altered ideas about English music. Yet, even with a talent such as his, it was acknowledged by the *Morning Chronicle*, albeit tongue in cheek, that his being English was a 'misfortune'; and just four months before his death, the *Morning Post* suggested that the enthusiastic reception given to Linley's playing was proof that 'an English audience will give proper encouragement to true merit and genius, even though it is the production of their own country.'[1]

British audiences, and particularly London audiences, clearly equated foreign names and foreign styles with a level of musical imagination and sophistication they did not believe British musicians could match. Why should this have been the case? It was certainly true that in the hundred years since the death of Purcell, the British Isles had failed to produce a composer of international stature or even a composer who was capable of suggesting new musical directions. This would have impressed itself more strongly on the collective consciousness as a more historically-aware attitude to the music of the past evolved. And we have already seen how the figure of Handel dominated the more recent past, his reputation discouraging younger composers from trying to follow in his footsteps. Even the innovations of Bach and Abel may have played their part. Certainly, the open nature of the British musical world and the opportunities it offered for financial reward meant that there were proportionally more foreign musicians in Britain than in other countries. They came principally from Italy, the German states, and from France. An extended list of names would not be instructive, but one has only to look at accounts of Charles Burney's famous musical *soirées* to realise how completely foreign musicians had become integrated into London's musical fabric, whether as singers, instrumentalists, composers, opera directors or teachers. This may have encouraged the *nouveau riche* who were benefitting from Britain's new prosperity to demonstrate their cosmopolitan credentials by preferring concerts featuring foreign music and musicians, thereby avoiding any suggestion of provinciality. And, of course, once established, the idea that foreign music and musicians were, for whatever reason, preferable to the native variety began to influence what concert promoters were willing to programme and who they were willing to engage. A vicious circle was thus created. Things would get worse before they got better; and they would not get better for a very long time.

One of the best-established foreign musicians in London was the Mannheim-born violinist Wilhelm (later William) Cramer (1746–99). He arrived in 1772 and within less than ten years became the orchestra leader of choice. He led all four of the big Handel Commemorations; he led concerts before the King at Buckingham House[2] and at Windsor Castle; he led the orchestra at the Pantheon, at the Italian Opera at the King's Theatre, at the Concerts of Antient Music, and at the Three Choirs Festival. From 1783, he was also leader at the Professional Concert, the name by which the Bach-Abel Concerts became known after Bach's death in 1782. These concerts were now financed by Willoughby Bertie, 4th Earl of Abingdon, himself a talented flautist and composer. His support – reputed to amount to £1,600 in just eight years – ensured that they remained the most prestigious, if not the most profitable, concerts in London, and that they could maintain the policy of promoting new, Continental styles of music.

However, by the mid–1780s, the Professional Concert had begun to face competition from a new series organised by another German arrival in London: Johann Peter Salomon (1745–1815). He was a violinist and a formidable character who spoke German, French, Italian and English fluently. He had worked at the court of the Elector of Cologne. He had worked for Prince Heinrich Ludwig of Prussia. He had composed at least four operettas and an oratorio. He was a friend of the young Beethoven – they had, coincidentally, been born in the same house, though twenty-five years apart. His first performance in London, in 1781, was at Covent Garden where he was both soloist in one of his own compositions and orchestra leader. For a short while, he joined Cramer's orchestra at the Professional Concert, but the two quickly fell out and in 1786 he started his own series of concerts, which, given his background, naturally programmed Continental music, including Haydn.

Twenty years previously, the Bach-Abel concerts had been the first to promote Haydn in London, something they continued to do under their new name. In that time, awareness of Haydn's music had spread, not only across London, but elsewhere. It featured on concert programmes in Newcastle, Bath, Oxford, Edinburgh and Dublin, where his symphonies were regularly played alongside works by Handel. The first record of a performance of a Haydn string quartet in Britain was in 1769 at Manchester; followed by another in Oxford four years later. By the mid-1780s, popular enthusiasm for Haydn's music was little short of a public craze. In 1787, in order to cash in on his popularity and also to fight back against the competition, Cramer and Abingdon conceived the idea of inviting Haydn to London. Salomon got to hear of the initiative and, using different channels, made a better offer. In the event, nothing happened. Haydn may have been the most celebrated composer in Europe, but he was not – or did not consider himself to be – a free agent. Since 1761, he had been in the service of one of the richest and grandest of Hungarian noble families, the Esterházys. His main patron, Prince Nicholas (Miklós) Esterházy was generous, for the most part considerate, and a music lover, who had his own personal enthusiasms – such as playing the baryton – but also encouraged Haydn to pursue his. It was the patronage system and the support of Prince Nicholas Esterházy that allowed Haydn to develop as a composer, but the same system kept him in relative isolation in the Hungarian countryside at the new palace in Esterháza or tied to the Prince's court during visits to Vienna. Only when Prince Nicholas died in 1790 did things change. Prince Anton did not share his father's musical enthusiasms: he dismissed the court orchestra and closed the Esterháza opera house. Haydn retained his official position (at a reduced salary) and was given permission to travel.

Sensing an opportunity, Salomon chased off to Vienna to negotiate terms, so that when, in 1791, Haydn did appear in London, after a gruelling ten-day journey with bad food (and Haydn liked his food), it was under Salomon's auspices. It was a huge business coup, but one that had to be paid for. Haydn was to give twenty concerts, presiding at the harpsichord as was the custom of the day. He was to compose six new symphonies (nos. 93 to 98), an opera (*L'anima del filosofo*, which was not performed because of difficulties over the licence, although Haydn was paid for it), and twenty smaller works.[3] For all this, he was to be paid some £1,100. In addition, he would be entitled to the takings from a benefit concert – Salomon guaranteed £200, but in the event the receipts amounted to £350. Salomon initially struggled to put together a decent orchestra, and Haydn was unfamiliar with the individuality displayed by British musicians, but in the end the concerts in the Hanover Square Rooms were a staggering success; so much so that in order to try and win back an audience Cramer and Abingdon were driven to bring over a former pupil of Haydn's, Ignaz Pleyel, from Strasbourg, and to spread false rumours that Haydn's musical abilities were failing. Haydn found both London and the reception he received overwhelming. He was lionised wherever he went; everyone wanted to meet him. He attended the 1791 Handel Commemoration, a larger musical spectacle than he had ever previously witnessed, and is supposed to have wept with emotion at the 'Hallelujah Chorus'. He received a doctorate from the University of Oxford. He visited and enjoyed Vauxhall Gardens. He enjoyed the horse racing on Ascot Heath. He also had an affair with Rebecca Schroeter, the wealthy widow of a German music teacher, and later the dedicatee of his opus 73 Piano Trios. In the end, and to the annoyance of Prince Anton, Haydn stayed for a second season, not returning to Esterháza until June 1792. For a man who had never previously travelled more than a hundred and twenty kilometres from Vienna, the whole thing was a considerable triumph.

In January 1794, Haydn set off for London again, having signed another contract with Salomon. Despite the fact that there was less competition than previously – Abingdon had reached the limits of his generosity and the Professional Concert had disbanded – the terms were once again generous. Haydn wrote six more symphonies (nos. 99 to 104) as well as a number of other works. This time the orchestral concerts were given at the King's Theatre, while his oratorios were performed at Covent Garden and Drury Lane. He became the first living composer to have his music played by the Antient Concerts. He met George III and Queen Charlotte and played for them at Buckingham House. He was a frequent visitor to the Prince of Wales's London residence, Carlton House. The King and Queen apparently tried to persuade him to stay in England, but, while appreciating that London was the only place where he could earn a sum such as the £1,200 he took home with him, Haydn decided to return to Austria, where a new Prince – Nicholas II who, unlike Prince Anton, was a noted patron of the arts – was expecting him.

Between 1791 and 1795, Haydn spent a total of three years in England. They were years that changed how he was perceived in the rest of Europe. He had been well known and highly respected, but now, as if the adulation he received in London had been necessary in order to prove the point, his status as Europe's leading composer was in no doubt. Moreover, he would never have to worry about money again. Creatively, too, there was a legacy. During his first visit, Haydn had seen *Messiah*, *Esther* and *Saul*, but had been particularly impressed by *Israel in Egypt*. Unlike his British contemporaries, he was undaunted by Handel's reputation, and the experience caused him to reassess what was possible in the oratorio. Salomon encouraged him and, in 1795, just as Haydn was on the point of returning to Vienna, presented him with a possible libretto. The result, three years later, was *The Creation*, one of the great pieces of classical music. And *The Creation* was followed by *The Seasons*, based on the poem by James Thomson. Had Salomon not brought Haydn to London, neither of these masterpieces would have been written.

The reception given to Haydn and his music was certainly a further indication that the British musical world and the British musical public were the most open and receptive in Europe. Among composers, Haydn's influence is perhaps most obvious in the work of John Marsh (1752–1828), a lawyer and gentleman composer, who moved around the cathedral towns of southern England – Romsey, Salisbury, Canterbury – before settling in Chichester in 1787. Marsh wrote more than forty symphonies and a large number of other works, many of which show a capacity for orchestration beyond that of many of the professional composers of his day. Some of his later, 'Chichester' symphonies and a string quartet, an explicit imitation of Haydn, show that he was aware of what was happening in London. Thomas

Haigh (1769–1808) actually studied under Haydn while he was in London and wrote numerous works for violin and piano, but became better known as an arranger of works by Haydn and by other composers than as a composer himself. Yet these, and other equally obscure names that could be cited, only emphasise how limited Haydn's influence on British composers was. More significant was his impact on British orchestras. His twelve London symphonies were, naturally enough, scored for the kind of orchestra he was used to in Austria. This led to widespread changes, and a better balance, in the composition of orchestras up and down the country; they were accompanied by pressure from promoters and organisers for better discipline among orchestral players. But the real legacy of Haydn's time in Britain was to confirm the perceived superiority of foreign music and foreign musicians; not least because, during this period, his popularity rapidly extended beyond the sphere of public concerts into the home.

The music that Haydn wrote or premiered in London (some of it was naturally written in preparation for the visit) amounts to well over two hundred pieces. There was an opera, twelve symphonies and other orchestral works, but the vast majority of the compositions were for chamber ensembles, for individual instruments or for voice and accompaniment: there were string quartets, piano trios, piano sonatas, and a large number of songs, many of them – perhaps surprisingly given his limited grasp of the language – with English words. It seems to have been Mrs Anne Hunter, the wife of Haydn's London doctor, who, on his first visit, persuaded him to begin setting English texts. She received her reward with *VI Canzonettas* (1794), a setting of six of her own poems. Haydn's celebrity status meant there was great demand for all these works among music publishers and he shared his favours between John Bland (who also commissioned the famous portrait of Haydn by the artist Thomas Hardy), William Forster and William Napier. His music was thus able to reach, and become popular with, amateur musicians throughout the country, particularly with those – and the number was rapidly growing – who possessed a piano.

William Napier was a Scottish violinist and viola player who ran a music shop in the Strand. He had been ill with gout and was on the verge of bankruptcy when his plight was brought to Haydn's attention, probably by Anne Hunter. Haydn made arrangements of a hundred Scottish folk songs, mainly for piano, violin and cello, and often including instrumental preludes and postludes, which he allowed Napier to publish in 1792, apparently without payment – though quite what Haydn made of songs with titles such as 'My mither's ay glowran o'er me' and 'The mucking of Geordie's byer' is anyone's guess. This started Napier on a new career as a music publisher and, when the story became known, only added to Haydn's reputation. It seems to have been these arrangements which suggested to the Scottish music collector and publisher, George Thomson (1757–1851), the idea of commissioning other famous composers to make arrangements of Scottish songs.

For nearly sixty years, Thomson worked for an organisation called The Board of Trustees for the Encouragement of Arts and Manufactures in Scotland. He was a close friend of Robert Burns and was devoted to Scottish culture. Inspired by the music he heard at concerts given by the Edinburgh Musical Society in the 1780s, he began collecting and, later, publishing volumes of Scottish songs. And yet, for all his Scottish patriotism, Thomson evidently shared the general conviction that if music was to be taken seriously, it required foreign input to give it credibility and, to that end, he approached the top musical names in Europe. Between 1793 and 1841, he published six volumes in a series called *A Select Collection of Original Scottish Airs*. As well as straightforward Scottish material, the early volumes contain arrangements by Ignaz Pleyel (1757–1834) and the Bohemian composer, Leopold Koželuch (1747–1818). Haydn was persuaded to contribute to the third and fourth volumes; and the last two volumes feature both Johann Nepomuk Hummel (1778–1837) and Carl Maria von Weber (1786–1826). But it was Beethoven who responded most vigorously to Thomson's request. In the ten years between 1808 and 1818, he composed or arranged settings of some one hundred and fifty Scottish songs, most of them to traditional texts, but some to new ones commissioned by Thomson. For these, Beethoven was initially paid three ducats a song, a fee later raised to four. Thomson also published a comparable, though shorter, series of *Original Welsh Airs* and *Original Irish Airs*, featuring arrangements by the same composers.

Interesting though some of the settings are, it is clear that none of these composers really understood Scottishness, or, indeed, any of the other Celtic cultures. They did not understand Scottish music; nor did they understand the characteristic interplay of irony and tragedy in the lyrics. How could they? Haydn barely spoke a word of English before arriving in London and never went farther north than Hertfordshire; Beethoven and Hummel never set foot in Britain at all; and Weber arrived in London just in time to die. They were writing out of their own folk traditions, converting Scottish songs into German lieder, which confirmed the prejudices of the age, but missed the musical point. Nonetheless, Thomson's attempt to integrate folk song into the classical mainstream is interesting in view of what was to happen during the next rediscovery of folk music a hundred years later. The attitude of Vaughan Williams, Butterworth, Holst, Moeran, Grainger and others showed much greater sensitivity towards the origins of the songs and dances they arranged, seeking to draw out rather than modify or disguise their essential, national and regional characteristics.

51 The Glee

If foreign influences remained dominant in the concert hall, there was one area where British musical inventiveness was flourishing: in the clubs, the taverns and those private homes where groups of men gathered to sing glees. A glee is a homophonic, a cappella vocal composition in three or more parts, originally for male voices, though, by the end of the eighteenth century, female voices were sometimes included. The first use of the term as a musical descriptor was in Playford's *Catch that Catch Can* in 1652 and it seems to derive from the Anglo-Saxon *glēo*, meaning music or entertainment. As the derivation indicates, it was an essentially English form, despite the fact that its origins are probably to be found in the madrigal tradition. The first composition generally accepted as a glee, *Turn, Amaryllis, to thy Swain*, is attributed to the viol-player and composer of rounds and catches, Thomas Brewer, who died *c.*1660; and there are further examples from the latter part of the seventeenth and the early decades of the eighteenth century. It was not until the 1740s, however, that the glee took off in popularity. It is difficult to know why. The Chapel Royal organist, John Travers (1703–58) and the Oxford Professor of Music, William Hayes (1708–77), both enthusiastic writers of glees, are frequently credited with increasing interest in the form. No doubt they did, but the explosion in the popularity of glee singing, and the fact that it remained a significant feature in British musical life for the next century, requires a broader explanation.

The glee was a neat, small-scale form. To compose, it required a good understanding of harmony, an ability to set English words, and – because so many of the texts came from or were based on literature – some awareness of the English literary canon. Performers required little beyond a voice and the level of musical education that you might expect in a church choir. Above all, it was a social form of music: it had no intellectual pretensions, and was perfectly suited for an evening among friends in a coffee house or a public house, or, indeed, for after-dinner entertainment at home. As such, it appealed to the talents, tastes and lifestyle of the expanding middle classes – although, as we shall see, that was no bar to aristocratic participation. In the end, it was probably a musical form that suited the age.

During the second half of the eighteenth century, a number of high profile clubs were founded in London. The Noblemen and Gentlemen's Catch Club was established in 1761 and is still going, though the name is misleading. Catches, as we know, had been popular for many years, but the Catch Club, as it is generally known, sang just as many glees as catches; and, indeed, catches, which often tended to be bawdy, fell away in popularity as the century wore on and the company became more respectable. The Catch Club was well known for its distinguished members. The Prince of Wales (later George IV) was a member. Dukes, including the Duke of Clarence (later William IV), abounded; so, too did Earls, among them the Earl of Sandwich, later a patron of both the Concerts of Antient Music and the Handel Commemoration. In the early days at least, dinner and singing were of equal importance in the club's activities, but it was notable also for a well-funded and hotly contested annual competition to find the best new catch, canon and glee.

The Anacreontic Society was founded just five years later in 1766, but its membership was very different, consisting mainly of barristers, bankers and merchants who now formed the core of London's commercial life. It began life in a coffee house on Ludgate Hill before moving to more spacious premises at the Thatched House Tavern. It also differed from the Catch Club in that it included instrumental music in its programmes. Also essentially middle class in its membership, and perhaps more famous in its day, was the Glee Club. Beginning as an informal gathering at the home of a former St Paul's chorister, Robert Smith, where glees were sung after dinner, it became a fully constituted club in 1787, meeting first at the Newcastle Coffee House and then shuttling back and forward between the Freemason's Arms and the Crown and Anchor. The Glee Club took its music seriously and over the years was able to boast some distinguished guest performers, including Samuel Wesley, whom we shall meet again shortly; the Bohemian composer and pianist, Ignaz Moscheles; Haydn; and even Mendelssohn. And it continued to meet every other week until 1857 when it was formally dissolved and the library it had accumulated over the years was sold off.

There were other London clubs, too: a second Glee Club, formed in 1793, which met at the Garrick's Head Coffee House and counted William Shield among its members; and one called Concentores Sodales, established in 1798 by, among others, the organist and composer Benjamin Cooke, and another leading glee composer, John Wall Callcott. In one sense, these clubs were at the heart of the glee singing movement. Their membership, even when not aristocratic, was wealthy and socially influential, able to promote their activities and attract musical guests of the top rank. And the British musical world, for all its regional diffusion, was still strongly London-centred: London was where the composers were, and thus where the majority of glees were written. Yet to focus on London's various glee clubs is to miss the point.

Glee singing emerged as a musical force at the same time as the Handel cult and Wesleyan evangelical hymn singing; and, like them, it was a part of the democratisation of music that characterised the second half of the eighteenth century. From the 1770s onward, glee clubs or glee-and-catch clubs sprang up all over the country. Dedicated clubs tended to be confined to the main towns and cities, but where there was no dedicated glee club, glee singing was usually taken up as part of the activities of the local musical society. There were now over three hundred of these and they had spread well beyond the major centres of population and into rural areas. Take Norfolk as an example: Norwich naturally had an active society, but so, too, did much smaller centres such as Fakenham, Swaffham, Walsingham and Wymondham. There were societies as far north as Aberdeen, as far south as Truro, and as far away as Douglas, on the Isle of Man. By the early 1780s, there was even a club singing catches and glees in Calcutta. This network of musical associations meant that glee singing spread widely and rapidly; and it maintained its popularity well into the Victorian period.

Provincial clubs and societies were often very different in tone and atmosphere from those in London. John Marsh, whom we have met as an amateur symphonist and disciple of Haydn, was also a keen catch and glee singer. When he moved to Salisbury in 1776, he joined the local Catch Club, which met at the Spread Eagle, paying a quarterly subscription of seven shillings and sixpence, which covered the cost of food, drink and tobacco.

The Glee Club in London, by contrast, charged a thirty-guinea admission fee and an eight-guinea annual subscription. The Salisbury club, however, was often overcrowded and became sufficiently rowdy for Joseph Corfe (1740–1820), a glee composer who later joined the Chapel Royal as well as singing principal tenor in the Handel Commemoration, to set up a rival group. Remarkably, given that the town had a population of little more than 7,000, there was enough interest and enthusiasm to allow both clubs to prosper. Marsh later moved to Canterbury and left an account of the Catch and Glee Club there. Founded in 1779, it met once a week at the King's Head and charged a sixpenny entrance fee rather than a subscription. This made it accessible to local shopkeepers and tradesmen who sang enthusiastically into the early hours and smoked so much that the room was like a fog. Later still, when he settled in Chichester, Marsh set up his own club, attempting to give it a more genteel character than those he had experienced in the past, as well as making it more musically disciplined.[1] In this, he was adhering to the social dynamic of the age, for, as the eighteenth century gave way to the nineteenth, the middle classes became more concerned with public morality. He was also demonstrating a pattern, not uncommon in popular culture – and which we will see repeated with music hall and other popular forms during the nineteenth century – for what had begun in loose informality to assume a more disciplined and more institutional character once it became familiar and accepted.

In its heyday, glee singing was immensely popular. In the early 1800s, the Bristol Orpheus Glee Society – a purist club which stuck rigidly to a cappella performance – met regularly throughout the year but gave only one public concert, for which 1,200 tickets were sold. And as late as 1875, the Canterbury Club had a membership of five hundred. Demand was huge. It has been estimated that between 1750 and 1885, some 23,000 glees were published, and an unknown number, perhaps as many again, were written but not published. Certainly, in the first eighty or ninety years of that period, it is almost impossible to find a composer who did not at some stage write a glee or two.

It was Samuel Webbe (1740–1816) who defined the glee as it became understood in clubs and societies up and down the land. Webbe had no musical background and no musical training. Having lost both his parents by the age of thirteen, he was apprenticed to a cabinetmaker when, one day – or so the story goes – he was asked to mend a harpsichord. Fascinated by the instrument, he learned to play by ear, only later taking lessons with Charles (Carl) Barbandt, who was the organist at the chapel of the Bavarian Embassy in Soho. Barbandt was one of the earliest clarinet virtuosos in the country, as well as being the first man to publish Catholic music in Britain – *Sacred Hymns, Anthems and Versicles* (1766) – since William Byrd. He appears to have taken the young Webbe, who was also a Catholic, under his wing; and Webbe certainly learned enough from him to be appointed first as organist at the Sardinian Embassy Chapel and then at the Portuguese Embassy Chapel. The chapels of Catholic diplomatic missions were important in that they were places where Catholic Mass could be celebrated and music for the Catholic rite played. Several volumes of Webbe's church music were printed privately, and Catholic churches in Britain continued to draw on two of them in particular – *A Collection of Motetts and Antiphons* (*sic*; 1792) and *A Collection of Masses for Small Choirs* (1795) – well into the middle decades of the nineteenth century. As a result, Webbe's music, which is tuneful rather than complex or profound, has come to be seen as one of the starting points of the nineteenth-century revival of Catholic liturgical music in England. He also wrote the tune *Melcombe* for the popular Church of England hymn, 'New every morning is the love'.

Webbe relied on his work as an organist and on paid engagements as a bass – such as at the Handel Commemoration – to make a living, but his real interest and his real musical legacy was the glee. He published his first book of glees in 1764 at the age of twenty-four, and his ninth in 1798 at the age of sixty-six. He was a member of both the Catch and the Glee Club – Secretary of the former; Librarian of the latter – but it was for the Glee Club that he composed what became its anthem, and one of the most famous glees ever written: 'Glorious Apollo'. In total, he wrote well over three hundred glees, mainly for the two clubs, though some may have been written for Vauxhall Gardens, where his work was often heard and where he may also have performed. He won his first Catch Club medal in 1766 for a canon, 'O, That I had wings' and went on to win a further twenty-six for canons, catches and glees. It is the glees, however, that stand out. Compositions such as 'Discord, dire sister', 'Swiftly from the mountain's brow', 'When winds breathe soft', 'Thy voice, O harmony' and 'Would you know my Celia's charms' helped define the glee for other composers of the period and show his melodic gifts at their best. Webbe's status as a self-made and self-educated man – he taught himself to speak at least six languages – who became accepted and respected for his musical abilities somehow matches the position of the glee and what it represented in the society of the day. Webbe's eldest son, also Samuel (1768–1843), became an organist at the Roman Catholic chapel in Liverpool and continued the family tradition of composing glees.

John Wall Callcott (1766–1821) was another self-educated man who became a leading glee composer. His father was a builder in Kensington, but, encouraged by the organist at his local church, Callcott went regularly to the Chapel Royal and Westminster Abbey and managed to attract the attention of both Samuel Arnold and Benjamin Cooke, who helped him. In 1785, at the age of nineteen, he not only won three of the four medals on offer at the Catch Club's annual competition and but also took a degree in music at Oxford. He became a founder member of the Glee Club; he took lessons from Haydn during the first London visit; and became a careful and technically correct composer of catches and glees. However, he seems to have set great, even embarrassing, store on winning the Catch Club's annual competitions; so much so that one year he swamped the judges by submitting fully a hundred entries. Not unnaturally, this led to a change in the rules, limiting the number that could be submitted by any one individual. Callcott was also a good friend of Charles Burney and partisanship may explain the catch, popular at the time, 'Sir John Hawkins' History of Music' which holds Hawkins' work up to ridicule. Callcott's passion for self-education led to him to take a doctorate in music, to be asked to lecture at the Royal Institution on German music, and to start a massive dictionary of music (which he never finished); but, as with Webbe, it is his glees ('The Erl King', 'Farewell to Lochaber', 'Drink to me only with thine eyes') and one or two other choral works (such as the canon, 'Out of the deep') which are his legacy.

As noted earlier, almost all the composers of the period tried their hands at glees and catches at one time or another. Many of them held an organist's post and, no doubt, composing glees was a break from routine Church of England duties, as well as a contribution to their social life. It is impossible to give even a broadly representative account of all those who contributed to the form and its popularity. A few names that stand out will have to do duty for the multitude. John Stafford Smith (1750–1836), whom we have met as the compiler of *Musica Antiqua,* was a member of the Anacreontic Society and composed the glee, 'To Anacreon in Heaven' as the society's anthem. Today, however, the tune would be identified the world round as 'The Star-Spangled Banner'. William Horsley (1774–1858), who married

Callcott's daughter, published no less than five books of glees between 1801 and 1807, as well as writing many others. 'Come, gentle zephyr' and 'Now the storm begins to lower' are probably the best-known survivors, although Horsley is also remembered for the hymn tune *Horsley* used for 'There is a green hill far away'. R. J. S. Stevens (1757–1837), another member of the Anacreontic Society, wrote a much smaller number of glees, but has a much higher survival rate, mainly because he was particularly choosy with his texts. He seems to have been the first to make extensive use of Shakespeare, writing fifteen glees to Shakespeare's words, a number of which are still heard today – including 'Doubt that the stars', 'Ye spotted snakes', 'Sigh no more, ladies', and 'The cloud-capt towers'. As time went on and more and more composers were drawn to writing glees in order to meet the huge popular demand, so they rushed to their libraries and trawled the canon of English poetry for suitable texts: everyone from Philip Sidney to Robert Burns made an appearance at some point. It was to an anonymous lyric, however, that Reginald Spofforth (1769–1827) wrote 'Hail, Smiling Morn', which turned out to be the most popular glee of all time, and is still sung as a carol, particularly in Yorkshire.

The glee remained in fashion for much longer than the madrigal or the ayre, in part because it developed into a social as much as a musical phenomenon – analogous to setting out card tables after dinner in Victorian times or a pub quiz today. The advent of parts for female voices and, in some cases, simple instrumental accompaniment, marked a process of mild gentrification that reflected the increasing refinement of middle-class taste. But, although the glee adapted, it did not develop. There was nowhere for it to go. At its best, the glee was charming, light and melodic, but it was also insular. The insularity was inevitable, because the essential requirement was for a setting that matched the rhythms of an English – and often a classic English – text. At the same time, it is difficult to find a glee which goes beyond that rhythmic connection with the text to offer the kind of emotional interplay between words and music that one finds in the madrigals of Weelkes and Wilbye or the ayres of Dowland. It was a parlour game; it was fun; but it was essentially superficial. As such, it had little relevance to the broader development of music in the British Isles. If glee singing did offer any benefits, they are probably to be found in the stimulus it gave to basic musical education. Its most remarkable legacy, however, is to be found in the way it successfully crossed the Atlantic. A glee club was established at Harvard in 1858. Other colleges and universities followed suit and today clubs performing glees and other types of vocal music remain a feature of campus life in many parts of the United States.

52 The Vienna Four

Between 1784, the year of the Handel Commemoration, and 1787, the year the Glee Club was officially established, there was a small colony of British musicians resident in Vienna, seeking to learn and gain experience of the Continental styles and techniques that had become so saleable at home. Michael Kelly (1762–1826) was one of fourteen children born to an Irish Catholic family in Dublin, where his father juggled the unlikely combination of wine merchant, dancing master, and Master of Ceremonies at Dublin Castle. Dublin's status as the United Kingdom's second city meant that there was a pool of resident and passing musicians able to offer tuition to an obviously gifted young singer. Most of Kelly's early teachers were Italian, including the castrato Venanzio Rauzzini, although he did have at least one Irish teacher in Philip Cogan (1750–1833), who later became a well-known composer for the piano. Kelly benefitted from the attempt by a Portuguese impresario called Don Pedro Martini to set up an Italian opera in Dublin. He was invited to sing the role of the Marquis in Niccolò Piccinni's opera *La Buona Figliuola.* The Portuguese venture went bankrupt almost immediately, but not before Kelly had made his stage debut, and, despite his youth – he cannot have been more than sixteen – done well enough to be offered roles with other companies. By 1779, he had saved enough to take himself off to the Conservatorio in Naples to study. In Naples, he met Giuseppe Avrile, another leading castrato, and went with him to Palermo to study for two years. Avrile's endorsement meant that Kelly was suddenly in demand. He was offered engagements in Florence (where the Young Pretender was in the audience), Padua, Treviso, Verona and Venice; and it was in Venice that he received an invitation from the Austrian Ambassador to join a new opera company at the court of Emperor Joseph II in Vienna.

The father of Stephen Storace (1763–96) and his sister Nancy (1766–1817) was a double-bass player from Naples who became musical director of Vauxhall Gardens. Their mother was an Englishwoman from Bath, whose main claim to fame was making a particular kind of plum cake, which was sold at Marylebone Gardens where her father was the general manager.

Both children were brought up surrounded by musicians. Stephen became a proficient violinist, having learned from his father, and, when still very young, was sent to Naples to study harpsichord at the Conservatorio. Nancy, too, was precociously talented. She studied in London under the same Rauzzini who had taught Kelly in Dublin and sang in oratorios at Covent Garden; but she wanted to be an opera singer and went to study at the Conservatorio in Venice. By the age of eighteen, she was the toast of La Scala in Milan, where she sang Dorina in Giuseppe Sarti's *Fra i due litiganti il terzo gode,* a role which had been created especially for her. Stephen also had a hand in the opera, contributing some additional music. At one point in their travels, Stephen and Nancy found themselves in Leghorn where, by chance, they met Michael Kelly. A friendship was established, but did not develop until they met again in Vienna a year or two later. By that time, Nancy had also been recruited – at the almost unheard of salary of 4,000 florins (roughly £500) per season – to sing in the Emperor's new opera company; and Stephen, having returned to England for a few months to sort out family affairs following the death of their father, had come out to Austria to join her.

The fourth member of the English colony in Vienna was Thomas Attwood (1765–1838). His father, too, had had an odd combination of jobs: trumpeter, viola player and coal merchant. Attwood himself began his career in a more conventional manner: he was a Chapel Royal chorister by the age of nine, before going on to study organ and keyboards when his voice broke. At the age of fifteen, he was part of a chamber ensemble performing at Buckingham House when his playing caught the attention of the Prince of Wales, who offered to pay for him to study in Italy – which was itself unusual because, although highly knowledgeable about music, the Prince was immensely profligate and often too much in debt to be able to fulfil his promises. Attwood spent two years in Naples before moving north to Vienna, where it had been agreed that he would study under Mozart, arriving at much the same time as Kelly and the Storaces.

Musically, Vienna was the most exciting city in Europe – the home of Salieri, Gluck, von Dittersdorf and Vanhal. In large measure, this was due to the generous patronage of Joseph II. And where the Emperor led, the aristocracy followed, setting up their own orchestras and commissioning works which would eventually become the core of the classical repertoire. For the four young British musicians, the other major attraction was Mozart. At the time they arrived in Vienna, Mozart was in his late twenties.

His reputation stood high in Austria, and was growing elsewhere in Europe, but he was not yet appreciated in England. Burney, among others, regarded much of his instrumental music as a kind of experiment. (It was Haydn, deeply affected by news of the younger composer's death in 1791, who persuaded him of the value of Mozart's work.) Kelly, the Storaces and Attwood all became good friends with Mozart. No doubt, there was an element of self-interest in connecting themselves with the man whom they regarded as representing the future of music, but then, at the same time, Mozart almost certainly saw them as a means of getting himself invited to London and earning large amounts of money. The friendship appears to have been genuine.

Kelly took no time at all to establish himself in Vienna. He made a successful debut in Antonio Salieri's *La scuola dei gelosi*; and, possessed of at least his fair share of Irish charm, was in demand socially as well. At one dinner party, he met Mozart, and the two immediately established a rapport which, according to Kelly's *Reminiscences*, involved regular games of billiards which Mozart always won. From our perspective, the high point of Kelly's career in Vienna must be his creation of the roles of Don Curzio and Basilio in the premiere of *The Marriage of Figaro* in 1786. It would be interesting to know what Kelly felt. He was a busy operatic singer, rehearsing three new roles that season. Did he realise that he was participating in a seminal moment in operatic history?

Nancy Storace was also on stage that night as Mozart's first Susanna, but the progress of her Vienna years was rather more troubled than Kelly's. Everything began well. She was still very young; her voice was pure and unspoilt; she captivated her audience. Then, not long after arriving in Vienna, she married an English violinist called John Fisher. The marriage was disastrous and lasted only a matter of months. The Emperor, hearing that Fisher had been mistreating Nancy, expelled him from Vienna, but by that time she was pregnant. Unfortunately, stress and pregnancy led to a vocal and physical collapse. Even more unfortunately, it was in the middle of the premiere of her brother's opera, *Gli sposi malcontenti*, which was being given in the presence of the Emperor, his brother Archbishop Maximilian of Cologne, and the Duke of York. It was five months before she could sing again. Nevertheless, she did recover, and was able to work closely with Mozart on *The Marriage of Figaro*, making a great success as Susanna, one of the finest operatic roles of its kind.

The fact that Stephen Storace's *Gli sposi malcontenti* was performed at the Court Theatre – the Burgtheater – in Vienna says at least as much about his sister's influence with Joseph II as about his music. It was not that he was untalented – quite the reverse – but he was wholly inexperienced. Nonetheless, he clearly did not disgrace himself: the following year, 1786, a second opera, *Gli equivoci,* was performed. Based on Shakespeare's *Comedy of Errors*, with an ingenious libretto by Da Ponte and leading roles for both Kelly and Nancy Storace, it was a great success. This was what Stephen wanted. He had established his credibility in a very prestigious school. Now it was time for him and for his sister to return to England.

Early in 1787, the Storaces and their mother set off by coach from Vienna for London. Kelly travelled with them; and so, too, did Thomas Attwood. He had spent the previous four years studying under Mozart who, according to Kelly's memoirs, regarded him as a composer of great promise. During their time in Vienna, the four musicians had socialised together and supported each other. They had immersed themselves in Continental styles of music; they had worked with and learned from Mozart and the other leading Viennese composers. Now, surely, they could apply what they had learned and make successful, influential careers in Britain.

Kelly was engaged almost immediately by Drury Lane to sing in an opera entitled *Lionel and Clarissa* by Charles Dibdin, and became principal tenor at the theatre. He sang at the Concerts of Antient Music and was in demand for festivals such as the Handel Commemoration. In 1789, he wrote the music for two lightweight plays, *False Appearances* and *Fashionable Friends*, and over the next thirty years wrote incidental music – which usually meant no more than an overture and two or three songs – for over sixty more. It was undoubtedly something for which he had a talent, but it was essentially ephemeral music and even Kelly, to judge from his memoirs, does not seem to have valued it highly. Little has survived. In 1793, he and Storace jointly took over the management of the King's Theatre. Storace soon retired, but Kelly stayed on as stage manager. All this made for a busy life, but it was not quite the stardom that had seemed to beckon. As if to confirm the fact, in 1802 Kelly not only set up a music shop adjoining the King's Theatre, but also followed in his father's footsteps by starting to import wines. Sheridan, who was part owner of the rival Drury Lane, caused much amusement by suggesting that Kelly should describe himself as a 'Composer of Wines and Importer of Music', a not very oblique reference to the fact that Kelly was suspected of plundering continental sources for some his compositions. In fact, the wine business failed and Kelly was declared bankrupt in 1811. That same year, he crossed to Dublin to give his final public performances, singing *Cosi fan tutte* and his own composition, 'The Bard of Erin', in the city where he had begun his career over thirty years previously. He remained stage manager at the King's Theatre until 1820, and continued composing songs and incidental music until his death in 1826, the year that saw the publication of his lively, if sometimes suspect, *Reminiscences*.

Stephen Storace, with two operas of his own composition produced at Vienna's Court Theatre and experience of working with Mozart and Da Ponte, must have felt he was ready to take the London operatic world by storm. Within months of his return, his comic opera, *La Cameriera Astuta*, written partly as a vehicle for his sister, was produced by the Royal Italian Opera at the King's Theatre in 1788. It was certainly not a flop, but nor was it a huge success, though the music was well received. What it did, however, was provoke the opposition of the Italian clique who had monopolised the Italian opera for a considerable period of time and did not wish to see their comfortable position threatened by English upstarts. Storace expressed his resentment in a letter to Sir Robert Murray Keith, the British Envoy to the court of Joseph II, but, not being a man to repine, he immediately and successfully turned to Drury Lane and the English opera. He adapted a piece by von Dittersdorf, which, under the English title *The Doctor and the Apothecary* and billed as a 'musical entertainment', was given at Drury Lane before the end of the year and ran for thirty-six nights. This was followed by *The Haunted Tower* (1789) and *The Siege of Belgrade* (1791). These were popular successes, and Storace earned 1,500 guineas for the copyright to his music alone. At the same time, they represented a major change of direction, for they were English-style, pasticcio operas. Much of the music was by Storace, but the rest was cobbled together from the works of different composers, and any sense of musical continuity was interrupted by dialogue. It was profitable, but it was not what Storace wanted. He wanted to write coherent, dramatic operas in the Italian or Mozartian manner, with recitative as a means of reducing or even eliminating dialogue. The nearest he came was *No Song, No Supper* (1790). This is an hour-long operatic afterpiece, in which Storace goes a long way towards integrating the music with the drama it describes. It was undoubtedly his most popular work, played more than a hundred times at Drury Lane, quickly taken over to Dublin and up to Manchester, before spreading to other provincial centres. By 1792, it had even been played in Philadelphia.

Opera was going through a difficult time in London. The King's Theatre burned down in 1789. Drury Lane was closed for rebuilding the following year. An interim home for Italian opera was found at the Pantheon, but that, too, burned down in 1792. These difficulties were accompanied by squabbles over licences, including the one which prevented Haydn's *L'anima del filosofo* from being performed in London. Eventually, Storace's new work was produced by the Drury Lane company but at the rebuilt King's Theatre. This was *Dido, Queen of Carthage*, an attempt at a big, serious English opera, but it was still a pasticcio, featuring songs by Salieri and Sarti, as well as by Storace himself. Kelly took a leading role and the music was again well received by critics, but the whole thing was too long and (probably) too serious for English audiences. Storace continued to plough his furrow – the spectacular *Lodoiska* (1794); the exciting Wild West opera *The Cherokee* (1794); the more or less disastrous *Iron Chest* (1796) – but he died tragically young in 1796, just short of his thirty-fourth birthday. He was very definitely talented, very definitely a man of the theatre, and, as ever with a talented artist who dies young, it is tempting to ask 'What if?' in assessing his achievements. He left behind some very melodic operatic numbers – hardly any of which are ever heard today – but he certainly did not become the great composer of operas which must have been his aim when he left Vienna. Nor, despite the success of *No Song, No Supper*, did he succeed in influencing the London public in the direction of coherent, Mozartian-style opera.

Nancy Storace began by singing with the Italian opera at the King's Theatre, but finding herself squeezed out by the same clique who opposed her brother, she, too, transferred her attention to the English opera. Her performances in *The Haunted Tower* and *The Siege of Belgrade* were met with great applause, but there were suggestions that her voice did not have the quality required for serious operatic roles. Charles Burney, whose instinct was to be charitable when he could, gave her credit for liveliness and intelligence as an actress, but found a roughness in her voice in passages where sustained expression of emotion was required. Whether this was the legacy of her vocal collapse in Vienna, we can only speculate. She certainly never gave up 'serious' singing and continued to appear on the concert platform – she sang during the 1791 Handel Commemoration and was one of the leading soloists during Haydn's visit to London that same year – but it is equally true that her best performances seem to have been in lighter, often comic roles. She continued to sing professionally into her forties, often playing opposite or touring with the leading operatic tenor of the age, John Braham, with whom she had an affair that lasted over twenty years. She died in 1817, having amassed an impressive fortune, but without ever having reached the heights of operatic stardom that seemed within her reach when she sang Susanna in Vienna.

Attwood had come from a more institutional background than his colleagues in Vienna and, on his return, it reclaimed him. He became a deputy church organist and played in the Prince of Wales' small chamber orchestra. He obviously had some inclination towards the theatre for in 1792 he put together a score for a piece called *The Prisoner*. This was followed by *The Mariners* and *Caernarvon Castle* (both 1793). These were English-style pasticcios, and Attwood even went so far as to interpolate some of Mozart's tunes into the scores. Over the next twenty years, he worked on thirty such operas. He obviously found it easy work, and it was clearly a useful and lucrative sideline, but he did not let it interfere with the duties attached to the official positions which began now to accumulate: music teacher to the Duchess of York (1791), music teacher to the Princess of Wales (1795), organist at St Paul's Cathedral (1796), Composer to the Chapel Royal (1796), organist at George IV's chapel in Brighton (1821), Professor at the Royal Academy of Music (1823), and organist at the Chapel Royal (1836). Attwood was one of the many composers who wrote glees; but, as time went on, he concentrated on church music. Some of his anthems – *Come, Holy Ghost*; *Turn thy face from my sins*; *Music, all powerful* – are occasionally heard, and his *Evening Service in D minor* is still in use in the Church of England. Yet it is difficult to believe, listening to these pieces, that the man who wrote them was regarded by Mozart as a composer of promise. Just occasionally, in some the keyboard music, one catches a glimpse of something more, but overall his compositions are, at best, uninspired. Attwood did make a valuable contribution to British musical life, but as a founding member of the Philharmonic Society and a professor at the Royal Academy of Music, rather than as a composer. At the Philharmonic Society, he argued for the introduction of new and supposedly difficult music – which included Mozart's late symphonies and Beethoven's Symphony no. 5 – and he was also one of the first to make the case for Mendelssohn. The composer-that-might-have-been was squeezed almost out of existence by the demands of official and public life.

53 Commercial Pressures, Crotch, and Samuel Wesley

What do these stories tell us? They show just how difficult it was for even the most talented musicians to achieve artistic as opposed to commercial success. The Vienna four had talent, and they had ideas about the future of music and about the kind of music they wished to sing or write or promote. That was why they were in Vienna. Once back in London, however, the sheer busyness of life, the compelling need to maintain a public profile and earn money, inevitably led to compromise and pushed them into channels that were geared towards maintaining the status quo rather than exploring new directions. Such pressures, of course, are not unique to music, nor to the period we are considering. Nor, indeed, were the pressures themselves new. We have already seen how the replacement of patronage by a market-driven system put composers under pressure to deliver what the public wanted. And we have seen how the attitudes to music reflected in the Handel cult were allied to social changes – many of them related to commercial expansion and the Industrial Revolution – which took place within an essentially conservative social framework. By 1800, this combination of factors had had over forty years to embed itself into fabric of society. And the fact that George III had been on the throne for forty years did nothing to diminish conservative pressures. To change this situation, to introduce new ideas and new styles, to get them recognised or even heard, would have required not only the necessary musical talent, but also great reserves of self-confidence and self-belief and, quite probably, considerable financial support. Kelly, the Storaces, and Attwood had some of these things, but the British musical establishment, whether in its commercial manifestation (theatre managers, concert promoters and musical societies) or in its official guise (the court, the Chapel Royal and the Church of England) found ways to dampen or stifle change. They were not shut out: the establishment was not in the business of making martyrs or denying itself access to talent. All four were successful in financial terms, but they failed to make the kind of musical headway that they had hoped for, or, indeed, that might have been expected of them. They were either sucked down into the commercial whirlpool of London musical life or, in Attwood's case, promoted through busy official positions into musical obscurity.

And these were not isolated cases. William Crotch (1775–1847) was a child prodigy. At the age of three, he played the organ in public at Cambridge University. At four, he played before the King. He spent six or seven years being dragged round the country by his parents, while handbills, posters and newspaper reports trumpeted his unique musical gifts. Burney even prepared a paper about him for the Royal Society: 'An Account of an Infant Musician'. John Stanley, now in his seventies and widely regarded as something of a grand old man of English music, predicted a glorious future. By the age of eleven, Crotch was an assistant organist at both King's College and Trinity College, Cambridge. At fourteen, his oratorio, *The Captivity of Judah*, was performed. At fifteen, he switched universities, becoming organist at Christ Church, Oxford, and by the tender age of twenty-two he was appointed Professor of Music.

Did these early pressures damage him? It would hardly be surprising. As an adult, he became, if not a polymath, at least very talented in several disciplines. He was a more than competent artist, and gained the reputation for being extremely well read across a range of disciplines from art and astronomy to grammar and gunnery; examples from all of which he used to illustrated his lectures at the university and at the Royal Institution. At the same time, perhaps as a reaction to his youth, he became very much an establishment figure, known for his forceful conservative views: he disliked Mozart and thought the only way to write church music was to draw inspiration from what he saw as the sublime period of the sixteenth and seventeenth centuries. He was highly respected in official circles and was elected as the first Principal of the Royal Academy of Music when it was founded in 1822. Like Attwood, he was an enthusiastic reviver of unjustly neglected composers, including, in his case, J. S. Bach and Thomas Tallis. The one thing Crotch did not become was a great or even very interesting composer. As a man of his age, he necessarily composed glees. Otherwise, he also wrote a number of unremarkable Church of England anthems, some keyboard studies, and two oratorios.

The two sons of Charles Wesley, the brother of Methodism's founder, John, were also marked down for musical success at an early age. Charles junior (1757–1834) was a skilful harpsichord player when very young, and his father engaged Joseph Kelway – organist at the church of St Martin-in-the-Fields and an eccentric composer, as well as being Queen Charlotte's harpsichord teacher – to give him lessons. Samuel (1766–1837) was even more advanced, apparently able to play Handel, Scarlatti and Corelli at the age of six. He was given lessons by William Cramer, whom we have seen as the leader of the Professional Concert. Samuel was just eleven, but Cramer was sufficiently impressed and confident in his abilities to arrange for him to give an organ recital at one of the concerts, after which the young man received congratulations from Arne. The two boys had clearly taken on board the possibilities of making money from their talents and for a period of seven years, from 1778 to 1785, they organised and held subscription concerts in the family home in Chesterfield Street, in London's Mayfair, just north of Green Park. Their fame grew to the point where George III summoned them to Windsor. Unsurprisingly, he wanted them to play Handel. They also published their own compositions – Charles, six quartets and six organ concertos; Samuel, a total of eleven sonatas for harpsichord or piano.

Despite his own accomplishments as a hymn-writer, and those of his wife, Sarah, who had sung for George III and acquitted herself well as a soloist in Handel's arias, Charles Wesley senior objected to his sons becoming professional musicians. He only agreed on the condition that they should not accept court appointments, though quite why is not clear. As a consequence, Charles junior refused an offer to become organist at St George's Chapel, Windsor. Whether this was a major factor or not, his career never really took off. He held a series of appointments as organist in churches and chapels around London; he composed steadily throughout his life, but was in no sense prolific. He wrote keyboard and instrumental music, and both sacred and secular music – his brother called him an 'obstinate Handelian' – but nothing that fulfilled his early promise.

Samuel, by contrast, was a thoroughly prolific and much more adventurous composer. Unlike most of his musical generation, he wrote nothing for the theatre. Like everyone else, however, he did write glees. He also wrote a large number of works for the organ (including a concerto based on 'Rule, Britannia') and other keyboards, some string quartets, settings of the Mass, settings of the Church of England Service, motets, anthems – in fact, just about everything. Two of his motets stand out.[1] *Exultate Deo* is scored for a five-part chorus with an organ or orchestral accompaniment. It is based round two themes which are woven together with great freshness and energy. *In exitu Israel* is in eight parts without accompaniment. It begins with a stately exposition of the main theme which is suddenly thrown into tuneful and energetic relief when the higher voices burst in, creating a sense of excitement and momentum which is maintained right to the end. These are both major musical achievements, masterpieces of counterpoint, standing way above anything else that was being written at the time, and they should have been enough to guarantee Wesley recognition as a composer of real ability. Unfortunately, that did not happen. Only a few people recognised his brilliance as a composer and little of his work was published in his lifetime. He gained more recognition for his skills as an organist – as an interpreter of Bach and Handel, and as an improviser – but somehow, with the exception of 1811, when he was appointed conductor and solo organist at the Birmingham Festival, no major positions came his way.

In part, this was because Wesley himself was an unconventional, eccentric character. He became a Roman Catholic in 1784 – hence his settings of the Mass – a conversion which had the capacity to cause more ructions in the Wesley family than in most, though he later converted back to the Church of England. He held unconventional views on sex and marriage, and left his wife for a teenage domestic servant, by whom he had four illegitimate children. As a comparatively young man, he fell into a foundation trench for a new building. This resulted in a head injury that left him prey to recurrent bouts of depression and irritability for the rest of his life. Yet he was also capable of sustained and determined effort. From 1808 onwards, he set about mounting recitals and publishing editions of some of the works of J. S. Bach. It would be misleading to claim this as the beginning of the Bach revival because, in Britain, Bach had hardly been appreciated at all, but it was an initiative that was invaluable to later generations. Wesley communicated his passion to William Crotch, and to his son, S. S. Wesley, who would carry on his father's work; but to many others this enthusiasm for a dead German organist must have seemed further proof that Wesley just did not fit in.

However they manifested themselves in individual cases, there is no doubt that the social pressures we have examined were a significant force for conservatism in music; slowing, even preventing, the acceptance of new ideas; diffusing or diverting talent away from the potentially innovative towards the commercially successful. Did these pressures have a disproportionate effect on music as opposed to the other arts? Probably. At least in so far as music is more deeply embedded in social structures than literature or the graphic arts: it requires the organisation of a group of people – sometimes a large group – in order to perform it; it requires a building fitted out to allow the performance to take place; and the assembly of a large group of people in order to listen to and respond to the performance. Certainly, in a society which had an increasing regard for money and commercial success, the fact that money was made from collective ventures – a successful opera or the crowds at the pleasure gardens – meant that the collective would always exert pressure on, or in the last resort abandon, an individual who did not conform. On the other hand, a talented individual who worked within the now well-established framework of the music business could probably make him or herself a comfortable living.

The door was open to foreign musicians who were often – though certainly not always – able to make a successful career for themselves, while, as we have seen, there were cases of British musicians of at least equal talent finding it difficult to get a hearing. This was no doubt partly due to the attraction of the foreign or the exotic (the British love affair with Italy had already begun), but it was also a manifestation of the same complex of pressures. Foreign musicians who came to Britain did so explicitly in order to make money in a way that was not open to them in their own countries. By doing so, they were accepting the status quo, its rewards and its limitations. In the case of a visit by a major figure such as Haydn, musical change and innovation might follow, but that was acceptable. The drivers were commercial. Innovation was welcome as long as it was bankable.

Such a picture is necessarily painted with a broad brush. It would have been truer of London and the major provincial centres – Dublin, Edinburgh, Bristol, Norwich, Newcastle-upon-Tyne – than the more rural areas; and there would have been significant regional variations based on local conditions. Nonetheless, by the early years of the nineteenth century these attitudes and structures were established and, in some cases, entrenched; and they would play their part in shaping – and, in not a few instances, retarding – the development of British music over the next hundred years.

Notes

Ch 1 Very Early Music pp. 1-6

1 Margaret Gowen, '4000 year-old music', http://www.gaitadefoles.net/artigos/4000pipesenglish.htm. Consulted 1.12.2012.

2 Simon O'Dwyer, 'Four Voices of the Bronze Age Horns of Ireland', www.ancientmusicireland.com/files/contents/file/FourVoices.pdf. Consulted 01.11.2012.

3 J. Coles, 'Irish Bronze Age Horns and their Relations with Northern Europe', *Proceedings of the Prehistoric Society,* 1963, Vol. XXIX, pp.326–56.

4 The only Celtic writings that survive – some 400 inscriptions in a script called Ogham, which originated perhaps in Ireland and probably somewhere in the fourth century AD – are largely functional and tell us nothing about the nature and role of music.

5 Marcus Tullius Cicero, *Letters to Atticus,* 4.17.303.

6 Polybius, *Histories,* II, 29.

7 http://ancientmusicireland.com/files/contents/file/killyfaddy.pdf. Consulted 01.11.12.

8 http://homepage.eircom.net/~bronzeagehorns/printablePages/ironage.html. Consulted 01.11.2012.

9 http://www.gaitadefoles.net/artigos/4000pipesenglish.htm
http://ancientmusicireland.com/page/instruments-from-outside-of-ireland.html
http://ancientmusicireland.com/page/instruments-through-the-ages.html#stoneage
http://www.bbc.co.uk/news/uk-scotland-highlands-islands-17537147
Consulted 01.11.2012.

10 The term 'crwth' is also sometimes used to described the original, plucked Celtic lyre. It is reserved here for the Welsh bowed instrument simply to avoid confusion.

11 Diodorus Siculus, *Bibliotheca historia,* V, 31.

12 Ammianus Marcellinus, *The Roman History,* XV, 9.

Ch 2 Romans, Druids, and Bards pp.6-13

1 The period when the northern boundary of Roman occupation reached as far as the Antonine Wall was too brief to leave any lasting influence upon the native population.

2 Cassius Dio Cocceianus, *Roman History*, 62, 6.

3 Francis M. Collinson, *The Bagpipe: The History of a Musical Instrument.* Routledge, 1975, pp.55 & 60.

4 The term 'Celtic Church' is unpopular with scholars because it suggests a uniform and separate identity. It is used here simply as a convenient means of identifying a different but not homogenous tradition of Christianity which evolved in the Celtic parts of the British Isles.

5 http://images.is.ed.ac.uk/luna/servlet/detail/UoEwmm~1~1~34071~101678:Inchcolm-Antiphoner,-circa-1340,-f-. Consulted 10.04.13.

6 It is no accident that one of the poems contained in *Taliesin* manuscript, the '*Cad Goddeu*' or 'Battle of the Trees,' became the basis for Robert Graves' book about poetry and myth, *The White Goddess*. Graves' intriguing reconstructions may verge on fantasy but he does identify and explore the deep-seated connection between poetry, music and myth.

7 'Death Song of Uther Pendragon', *Book of Taliesin*, 48.

8 Norman Davies, *The Isles*. Macmillan, 1999, p.93.

Ch 3 Anglo-Saxons, Celts, and Harps pp.13-15

1 Percy M. Young, *A History of British Music*. Ernest Benn, 1967, p.4.

2 Norman Davies, *The Isles*, pp.195–6.

3 Widsith, ll.53–6 & 104–9.

4 Percy Young, *A History of British Music*, p.3.

5 One has to accept that similarities between the two instruments and inconsistencies in description mean that it is very difficult to establish anything like a reliable view of the process.

6 Sometimes identified as Catterick, although both the location and the date of the battle have been disputed.

Ch 4 Augustine, Plainsong, and Vikings pp.16-21

1 C. Linklater Thomson, *A Child's History of Great Britain*. Horace Marshall, [1910].

2 E. G. P. Wyatt, 'St Gregory and the Gregorian Music', *Plainsong and Mediæval Music Society*, 1904, p.7. This pamphlet also gives a summary of the evidence supporting the much-disputed idea that Pope Gregory was responsible for reforming church music.

3 St. Ambrose had approved four modes suitable for church use in the 4th century (Dorian, Phrygian, Lydian, Mixolydian). The 6th century reforms added four more (Hypodorian, Hypophrygian, Hypolydian, Hypomixolydian).

4 Plainsong began to be called Gregorian chant because the reforms that gave rise to it were thought to have been sponsored by Gregory the Great himself – although, in fact, the connection was not made until nearly three hundred years after his death when a biography was written by one

Johannes Hymonides (John the Deacon). There is no evidence to suggest he was personally involved.

5 Bede, *History of the English Church and People,* Book II, Chapter 20.

6 Bede, *History of the English Church and People,* Book IV, Chapter 2.

7 Percy Young, *A History of British Music,* p.7.

8 *Anglo-Saxon Chronicle,* year 793.

9 Brian Murdoch & Malcolm K. Read, *Early German Literature and Culture.* Boydell & Brewer, 2004, p.96.

Ch 5 Organum, Notation, and Organs pp.21-26

1 James Grier Ademar de Chabannes, 'Carolingian Musical Practices, and "Nota Romana"', *Journal of the American Musicological Society,* Vol. 56, no. 1 (Spring, 2003), pp.43–98.

2 A slightly curved wooden instrument with holes for fingering, not to be confused with the modern brass instrument.

3 Quoted in Betty Matthews, 'The Earliest English Organ-Builders', *British Institute of Organ Studies Reporter,* January 1982, Vol.1, VI, no. 1.

4 *The Organ: An Encyclopedia,* ed. Bush & Kassel. Routledge, 2006, p.644.

5 Percy Young, *A History of British Music,* p.14.

6 Cotton Tiberius, B 6.

Ch 6 Normans, Cathedrals, and Giraldus Cambrensis pp.26-31

1 *Anglo-Saxon Chronicle,* year 1137.

2 Gothic Voices, dir. Christopher Page, *The Earliest Songbook in England,* Helios CDH55297, based on Cambridge MS FF.I.17.

3 Quoted in Percy Young, *A History of British Music,* pp.22–4.

4 Giraldus Cambrensis, *Descriptio Cambriae,* Chapter XIII.

5 Giraldus Cambrensis, *Topographica Hibernica,* Chapter XI.

6 Giraldus Cambrensis, *Topographica Hibernica,* Chapter XII.

7 Giraldus Cambrensis, *Topographica Hibernica,* Chapter XI.

Ch 7 The Chapel Royal, Medieval Lyrics, and the Waits pp.31-37

1 Quoted in Percy Young, *A History of British Music,* p.25.

2 To the point of having inspired a famous parody by Ezra Pound, 'Winter is icumen in / Lhude sing Goddamm.'

3 Quoted in Henry Raynor, *A Social History of Music from the Middle Ages to Beethoven.* Barrie & Jenkins, 1972, pp. 36–7.

4 A dean, twelve secular canons, thirteen vicars-choral, four clerks, six choir-boys, two servitors, a verger and a keeper.

5 Robert Henry, *The History of Great Britain,* Vol. 4, 1789. p.451.

6 Charles Burney, *A General History of Music,* Vol. 4, 1789.

7 A 14th-century-traveller quoted in Meyer, *English Chamber Music,* p.51.

8 In 1377, the ten biggest towns in England were London, York, Bristol, Coventry, Norwich, Lincoln, Salisbury, King's Lynn and Colchester.

9 Meyer, *English Chamber Music,* p.36.

Ch 8 Minstrels, Troubadours, and Courtly Love pp.37-44

1 The name *ars antiqua* was a retrospective invention simply to distinguish between the two styles.

2 Julie Henigan, *Literacy and Orality in Eighteenth-Century Irish Song.* Routledge, 2015, pp.47–8.

3 Quoted in William Chappell, *Popular Music of the Olden Time.* Cramer, Beale, & Chappell, 1859, p.30.

4 The statement at the end of *Troilus and Criseyde* to the effect that English is so diverse a language that he hopes he is understood. Whether the poem is read or sung (all five books and 8219 lines of it) is probably no more than convention.

5 It is likely that only extant part of the *Romaunt de la Rose* was Chaucer's work, but that does not affect the argument relating to the presentation of musical forms.

6 Chaucer, *The House of Fame,* III, ll.1197–1200.

7 David Whitwell, *Essays on the Origins of Western Music,* no. 83, 'On the Ministrel,' pp.2–3. http://www.whitwellessays.com/. Consulted 11.01.2013.

8 Percy Young, *A History of British Music,* p.47.

9 Quoted in Anne Lingard Klinck & Ann Marie Rasmussen, *Medieval Woman's Song: Cross-Cultural Approaches.* U of Pennsylvania P, 2002, p.58.

10 Jane Bowers and Judith Tick, *Women Making Music: The Western Tradition, 1150–1950.* P of Illinois P, 1987, p.41.

11 Quoted in Meyer, *English Chamber Music,* pp.34–5.

Ch 9 The Morris, and the Ballad pp.44-50

1 Charles Burney, *A General History of Music,* Vol. 4, 1789.

2 John Playford's *English Dancing Master* (first published 1651) is a unique attempt to try and capture dance movements and tunes (as single line melodies).

3 A. L. Lloyd, *Folk Song in England.* Panther Arts, 1969, p.163.
4 Sir Philip Sidney, *An Apology for Poetry,* 1595.
5 British Library, Add. MS. 27879.
6 *Piers Plowman,* B Text, Passus v, l.402.

Ch 10 Music, Science, and Politics pp.50-53

1 Jeffrey Howard Denton, *English Royal Chapels 1100-1300.* Manchester U P, 1970, p.4.

Ch 11 Dunstable, and *la contenance angloise* pp.53-58

1 Percy M. Young, *A History of British Music,* p.56.
2 British Museum, Add. MS 57950.
3 Lambeth Palace, MS1.
4 Eton College MS. 178.
5 National Library of Scotland, MS Adv. 5.1.15.
6 Percy M. Young, *A History of British Music,* p.63.
7 Quoted in *Grove,* ed. Fuller Maitland, 1922, Vol. 1, p.744.
8 Clauditur hoc tumulo qui coelum pectore clausit
Dunstaple Joannes. Astrorum conscius ille
Indice novit Urania abscondita pandere coeli.
Hic vir erat tua laus, tua lux, tibi musica princeps
Quique tuas dulces per mundum sparserat artes.
Anno Mil. C. quarter semel L. tria jungito Christi
Pride natalem, sidus transmigrat ad astra.
Suscipiant proprium civem coeli sibi cives.
9 'Quo fit ut hac tempestate, facultas nostrae musices tam mirabile susceperit incrementum quod ars nova esse videatur, cujus, ut ita dicam, novae artis fons et origo, apud Anglicos quorum caput Dunstaple exstitit....' Tinctoris, *Proportionale musices,* dedicatory epistle to Ferdinand I. http://www.chmtl.indiana.edu/tml/15th/TINPRO_TEXT.html. Consulted 14.02.2013.
10 Eloy d'Amerval, *Le livre de la deablerie,* line 18844.
11 Eric Routley, *A Short History of English Church Music.* Mowbray, 1977, p.9.
12 Alexandra Buckle, *Power, Leonel, Lionel.* http://www.academia.edu/148886/Power_Leonel_Lionel. Consulted 12.04.2013.

Ch 12 The Eton Choirbook, and the Early Tudors pp.58-66

1 'Illi etenim in dies novos cantus novissime inveniunt, ac isti (quod miserrimi signum est ingenii) una semper et eadem compositione utuntur.' Tinctoris, *Proportionale musices,* dedicatory epistle to Ferdinand I, http://www.chmtl.indiana.edu/tml/15th/TINPRO_TEXT.html. Consulted 14.02.2013.

2 Percy Young, *A History of British Music,* p.77.

3 Other composers (including Dunstable) and other works are indexed, but these works have been lost.

4 Musica Antiqua of London, dir. Philip Thorby, *The Field of the Cloth of Gold.* Amon Ra, B000027PRQ, 1992.

5 Otto Carterllieri, *The Court of Burgundy.* Taylor & Francis, 1972, p.17.

6 Alison Weir, *The Six Wives of Henry VIII.* The Bodley Head, 1991, pp.91–2.

7 Fayrfax Ms., Ms. Add. 5465, British Museum.

8 Fayrfax Ms., Ms. Add. 5465, British Museum.

9 http://www.chmtl.indiana.edu/tme/16th/CORNPAR5_TEXT.html. Consulted 21.03.2013.

10 Stephen Hawes, *The Passetyme of Pleasure,* Chapter XVI, stanza 11.

11 R. App. 58, British Museum.

12 Henry V seems most likely. We can now say with some certainty that it was not Henry VI.

13 J. J. Scarisbrick, *Henry VIII.* Folio Society, 2004, pp.11–12.

14 I Fagiolini with the Forbury Consort, *Pastyme with Good Companye,* Griffin CRCD2365, 1992. The Isaak Ensemble Heidelberg have recorded a larger selection of Henry VIII's works interspersed with readings from his letters to Anne Boleyn: Isaak Ensemble Heidelberg, *Henry VIII: If Love Now Reigned.* Bayer B00000445F, 1992.

15 J. J. Scarisbrick, *Henry VIII,* p.12.

Ch 13 Pre-Reformation Ireland, Wales, and Scotland pp.66-70

1 William H. Grattan Flood, *A History of Irish Music,* Chapter X, http://www. libraryireland.com/IrishMusic/X.php. Consulted 23.03.2013. There are many occasions when Grattan Flood's assertions are questionable. Only those which are independently referenced are accepted here.

2 The Statutes of Kilkenny, Article XV, http://www.mesacc.edu/~thoqh49081/celtic/ KilkennyStatutes.html. Consulted 03.04.2013.

3 http://bodyliterature.com/2012/10/30/dafydd-ap-gwilym/. Consulted 06.04.2013.

4 Percy Young, *A History of British Music,* p.110.

5 The Sixteen, *Robert Carver,* CORO COR16051, 2006, notes by Isobel Preece, p.6.

6 The Sixteen, *Robert Carver,* notes by Isobel Preece, p.6.

Ch 14 Robert Carver, and the Scottish Reformation pp.70-75

1 The Sixteen, Robert Carver, notes by Isobel Preece, p.5.

2 http://www.bbc.co.uk/scotland/music/scotlandsmusic/pdfs/scotlandsmusic_15.pdf. Consulted 12.05.13.

3 https://alistairwarwick.com/content/wode-partbooks. Consulted 12.05.13.

Ch 15 The English Reformation, Merbecke, and Tye pp.75-82

1 http://www.nationalarchives.gov.uk/pathways/citizenship/rise_parliament/transcripts/henry_supremacy.htm. Consulted 20.05.2013.

2 John Bale, 'John Bale to the Reader', *The Laborious Journey and Search of John Leland for England's Antiquities,* http://sites.broadviewpress.com/16cpoetryprose/files/2011/09/2-16C-Anth-Online-BALE.pdf. Consulted 22.05.2013.

3 Quoted in William Smith, *The Reasonableness of Setting Forth the Most Worthy Praise of Almighty God.* T & J Swords, 1814, p.280.

4 Letter from Archbishop Cranmer to Henry VIII, 1544, http://www.adoremus.org/1199-Cranmer.html. Consulted 24.05.2013.

5 Quoted in Jason Smart, 'In Quires and Places where they Sing', http://www.plymouthorganists.org.uk/news_notes/2003-2_quires_and_places.pdf. Consulted 24.05.2013.

6 Stylistic evidence appears to contradict an alternative theory that it was written in 1545 for his doctorate.

7 Westminster Abbey Choir, *Tye: Missa Euge bone & Western Wynde Mass,* Hyperion CDA677928, 2012, notes by Jeremy Summerly.

8 *Psallite felices potecti culmine rose purpuree.*

Ch 16 John Taverner pp.82-87

1 No relation to Thomas Cromwell, Henry VIII's Chancellor.

2 Quoted in Colin Hand, *John Taverner: His Life and Music.* Eulenburg Books, 1978, pp.25–6.

3 Colin Hand, *John Taverner: His Life and Music,* pp.32–3.

4 Percy Young, *A History of British Music,* p.93.

5 Colin Hand, *John Taverner: His Life and Music,* p.53.

Ch 17 John Sheppard pp.87-91

1 John Sheppard, *Media Vita,* Stile Antico, Harmonia Mundi, HMU 807509, 2010, notes by Matthew O'Donovan.

2 Richard William Chivers, *The Hymns and Responds of John Sheppard.* MA thesis, U of Durham, 1997. http://etheses.dur.ac.uk/5034/1/5034_2487.PDF?UkUDh:CyT. Consulted 12.08.2013.

3 *John Sheppard (d. 1558/9), The Second Service 'in F fa ut': Magnificat and Nunc dimittis,* ed. Magnus Williamson. http://www.church-music.org.uk/commentaries/Sheppard-commentary.pdf. Consulted 18.08.2013.

4 John Sheppard, *Media Vita,* Stile Antico, Harmonia Mundi, HMU 807509, 2010, notes by Matthew O'Donovan.

Ch 18 Thomas Tallis pp.91-101

1 Professor Nicholas Sandon has argued that *c.*1510 is more likely. Notes to *Thomas Tallis, The Complete Works.* Chapelle du Roi with Alistair Dixon, Brilliant Classics, 93612, p.4.
2 Professor Nicholas Sandon, notes to *Thomas Tallis, The Complete Works.* Chapelle du Roi with Alistair Dixon, Brilliant Classics, 93612, p.3.
3 Donald Macleod, *Composer of the Week: Thomas Tallis,* Radio 3, 9 May 2011.
4 Isiah, 9:6.
5 Professor Nicholas Sandon, notes to *Thomas Tallis, The Complete Works.* Chapelle du Roi with Alistair Dixon, Brilliant Classics, 93612, p.19.
6 Quoted in Anna Whitelock, *Mary Tudor: England's First Queen.* Bloomsbury, 2009, p.259.
7 http://history.hanover.edu/texts/engref/er78.html. Consulted 02.11.2013.
1 http://web.archive.org/web/20090426001612/http://www.andante.com/article/ article.cfm?id=16297. Consulted 03.11.2013.
2 Professor Nicholas Sandon, notes to T*homas Tallis, The Complete Works,* p.58.

Ch 19 Early Byrd pp.101-108

1 John Harley, *The World of William Byrd: Musicians, Merchants and Magnates.* Ashgate, 2010, p.6.
2 The dedicatory verse in *Cantiones Sacrae,* written by Ferdinand Heybourne (who definitely was Tallis's student), seems to suggest it, but is capable of more than one interpretation. See John Harley, T*he World of William Byrd: Musicians, Merchants and Magnates,* p.46. And the only other evidence we have is a much-later statement by the seventeenth century writer and antiquarian, Thomas Wood, that Byrd was 'bred up to musick under Tho. Tallis.' Bodleian MS. 19 D. (4), no.106.
3 John Strype, *Historical and Biographical Works,* Vol. 24. Clarendon, 1821, p.14.
4 Davitt Moroney, notes to *William Byrd, the Complete Keyboard Music.* Hyperion, CDA66551/7, 1999, p.15.
5 For the full text of the Licence, see http://theoryofmusic.wordpress.com/2012/07/28/ licence-granted-to-thomas-tallis-and-william-byrd-in-1575-modern-english/. Consulted 01 December 2103.
6 Peter Warlock, *Thomas Whythorne: An Unknown Elizabethan Composer.* OUP, 1925.

7 Whythorne also published an autobiography, the manuscript of which was rediscovered in 1955 and later published by OUP.

8 Oxford Dictionary of National Biography http://www.oxforddnb.com/templates/article.jsp?articleid=4267&back=. Consulted 01 December 2013.

9 Quoted in Davitt Moroney, notes to *William Byrd, the Complete Keyboard Music*, p.23.

10 Andrew Carwood, notes to *Byrd: the Great Service*, The Choir of Westminster Abbey with James O'Donnell, Hyperion, CDA65573, 2005, p.4.

11 Edmund H. Fellowes, *English Cathedral Music*. Methuen, 1941, p.75.

Ch 20 Catholic Byrd pp.108-114

1 Davitt Moroney, notes to *William Byrd, the Complete Keyboard Music*, p.17.

2 The date is often given as 1593, but see *John Harley, The World of William Byrd: Musicians, Merchants and Magnates*, pp.153–4.

3 Andrew Carwood, notes to *William Byrd, Assumpta est Maria*. The Cardinall's Musick, Hyperion, CDA 67675, 2009, p.2.

Ch 21 Madrigals pp.114-24

1 The Hilliard Ensemble, sadly, ceased performing while this book was being written.

2 Quoted in Percy Young, *A History of British Music*, p.165.

3 Teresa Ann Murray, *Thomas Morley and the Business of Music in Elizabethan England*. Ph.D. thesis, U of Birmingham, 2010, p.57 http://etheses.bham.ac.uk/1247/1/Murray10PhD_A1b.pdf. Consulted 19.01.2014.

4 Despite the titles, Morley, like many others at the time, used the word 'madrigals' – and other musical terms – in a flexible manner.

5 *Canzonets to Three Voyces* (1593), *Madrigalls to Foure Voyces* (1594), and *Canzonets to Five and Sixe Voyces* (1597).

6 *The First Booke of Balletts to Five Voyces* (1595) and *The First Book of Canzonets to Two Voyces* (1595).

7 *Canzonets to Foure Voyces* (1597) and *Madrigals to Five Voices* (1598).

8 Robert Hollingworth, notes to *Thomas Tomkins: Music Divine*. I Fagiolini, Chandos, CHAN 0680, 2002, p.11.

Ch 22 The Waits, and the Theatre pp.124-30

1 Quoted in G. M. Stephens, 'The Waits of the City of Norwich', *Proceedings of the Norfolk and Norwich Archaeological Society*. Norwich, 1933.

2 Mark Cartwright Pilkinton, *Bristol*, Vol. 8. U of Toronto P, 1997, p.xli.

3 Quoted in Gustave Reese, *Music in the Renaissance*. Dent, 1954, p.878.

4 http://townwaits.org.uk/history_norwich.shtml. Consulted 26.12.2013.

5 Quoted in Bruce R. Smith, *The Acoustic World of Early Modern England.* U of Chicago P, 1999, p.221.

6 Quoted in Gustave Reese, *Music in the Renaissance,* p.881.

7 Thomas Heywood, *The English Traveller,* Prologue, ll.1–4; David Whitwell, *Essays on the Origins of Western Music,* No. 194, 'Music in the Jacobean Theater', p.8. http://www.whitwellessays.com/. Consulted 29.12.2013.

8 David Whitwell, *Essays on the Origins of Western Music,* No. 140, 'Music in the Elizabethan Theater', p.7. http://www.whitwellessays.com/. Consulted 29.12.2013.

9 *Twelfth Night,* Act II, scene iv, ll.19–20.

10 *Richard II,* Act I, scene iii.

11 John Marston, *What You Will,* Act II, scene I, ll.251–2.

12 John Lyly, *Mother Bombie,* Act III, scene iii, ll.1–14.

13 Beaumont & Fletcher, *The Queen of Corinth,* Act III, scene ii.

14 John Marston, *Antonio and Mellida,* Act V, scene i.

15 William Shakespeare, *As You Like It,* Act V, scene iv.

16 William Shakespeare, *The Tempest,* Act II, scene ii.

17 http://www.theguardian.com/culture/2011/aug/21/robert-johnson-tempest-william-shakespeare-composer. Consulted 04.01.2014.

Ch 23 Folk Music, Ravenscroft, and Ballads pp.130-36

1 Possibly *Cailin ó chois tSiúire mé,* 'I am a girl from beside the Suir', A. L. Lloyd, *Folk Song in England,* p.178.

2 Percy Young, *A History of British Music,* p.194.

3 Beaumont and Fletcher, *The Humourous Lieutenant,* Act II, scene ii, lines 113–15.

4 Also known as 'Johnnie o' Cocklesmuir' and 'Johnnie the Brine'.

Ch 24 The English Ayre, and Thomas Campion pp.136-43

1 Percy Young, *A History of British Music,* p.184.

2 Not to be connected or confused with the Catholic priest and martyr Edmund Campion (1540–81).

3 Thomas Campion, *A Book of Ayres,* 'To the Reader', 1601.

4 Thomas Campion, *Observations in the Art of English Poesie,* 1602, Chapter II.

5 Campion and Coprario, *Songs of Mourning: Bewailing the Untimely Death of Prince Henry,* 1613, title page.

Ch 25 John Dowland pp.143-53

1 Grattan Flood, 'New Facts about John Dowland', *The Gentleman's Magazine*, 1906, pp.287–91.

2 Diana Poulton, *John Dowland.* U of California P, 1982, pp.23–6.

3 Diana Poulton, *John Dowland*, pp.43–5.

4 Percy Young, *A History of British Music*, p.189.

5 Michael Praetorius, *Syntagma Musicum* III, 1619.

Ch 26 King James, King Charles, and the Masque pp.153-62

1 Donald Macleod, *Composer of the Week: Music at the Court of James I*, BBC Radio 3, 7 April 2008.

2 Percy Young, *A History of British Music*, p.199.

Ch 27 Orlando Gibbons pp.162-69

1 Quoted in Christopher Hogwood, notes to *Orlando Gibbons: Keyboard Music*, Decca Music Group, DSLO515, 1975.

2 Quoted in Christopher Hogwood, notes to *Orlando Gibbons: Keyboard Music.*

3 Interview with Geoffrey Payzant, quoted on http://www.orlandogibbons.com/works/. Consulted on 7 June 2014.

4 Daniel Ben Pienaar, 'Revisiting the Keyboard Music of Orlando Gibbons', http://danielbenpienaar.com/essays/Revisting%20The%20Keyboard%20Music%20Of%20Orlando%20Gibbons.htm. Consulted 8 June 2014.

5 The texts seem to have been chosen by Gibbons's patron and the dedicatee of the work, Sir Christopher Hatton.

6 Percy Young, *A History of British Music*, p.178.

Ch 28 Thomas Tomkins, and Church Music pp.169-78

1 It was used as the title of Anthony Boden's 2005 study of Tomkins and his work, but has been widely used both before and since.

2 http://www.allmusic.com/artist/thomas-tomkins-mn0001379727/biography. Consulted 2 July 2104.

3 Quoted in *Grove's Dictionary of Music and Musicians*, Vol. 1. Macmillan, 1922, p.417.

4 'Dr John Bull', www.alchemydiscussion.com/attachment.php?id=449. Consulted 28 September 2014.

5 J. Bunker Clark 'Adrian Batten and John Barnard: Colleagues and Collaborators', *Musica Disciplina*, Vol. 22, 1968, pp.207–29.

6 In 'Towards a Definitive Study of Pre-Restoration Anglican Service Music', *Musica Disciplina*, Vol. 14, 1960, pp.167–95, Dr Peter le Huray raises the possibility that the manuscript was not copied by Batten. With no conclusive evidence one way or the other, I have followed the traditional view.

Ch 29 King James, King Charles, and Archbishop Laud pp.178-87

1 Kenneth Elliott & Frederick Rimmer, *A History of Scottish Music*, BBC, 1973, p.41.
2 David Starkey & Katie Greening, *Music and Monarchy*. BBC, 2103, p.138.
3 David Starkey & Katie Greening, *Music and Monarchy*, p.147.

Ch 30 Civil War, Playford, and the Beginnings of Opera pp.187-97

1 Charles Burney, *A General History of Music*, Vol. 3.
2 David Starkey & Katie Greening, *Music and Monarchy*, p.159.
3 Charles Burney, *A General History of Music*, Vol. 3.
4 David Starkey & Katie Greening, *Music and Monarchy*, p.166.

Ch 31 The Return of the King pp.197-204

1 Anne Dhu McLucas, 'Forbes' *Cantus: Songs & Fancies* Revisited', *Defining Strains: The Musical Life of the Scots in the Seventeenth Century*, ed. James Porter. Peter Lang, 2007, p.297.
2 Quoted in James M. Gibson, *Kent: Diocese of Canterbury*, Vol. 3. U of Toronto P, 2002, p.1300.
3 John Hooker, *The Ancient History and Description of the City of Exeter*. Andrews and Trewman, 1765, p.123.
4 James Boeringer, *Organa Britannica: Organs in Great Britain, 1660–1860*. Bucknell U P, 1989, pp.99–102.

Ch 32 The Violin, and Matthew Locke pp.204-10

1 Jambe de Fer, *Epitome musical*, published in Lyon in 1556.
2 *The Critical Review*, ed. Smollett, Vol. 27, 1769, p.17.
3 John Evelyn, *Diary*, 21 December 1662.
4 Preface to *The Little Consort of 3 Parts for Viols or Violins*, quoted in A. K. Holland, *Henry Purcell*. Penguin, 1948, p.22.
5 Quoted in A. K. Holland, *Henry Purcell*, p.27.
6 Matthew Locke, Preface to *Psyche*, quoted in George Hogarth, *Memoirs of the Musical Drama*, Vol. I, Richard Bentley, 1838, p.124.
7 Percy Young, *A History of British Music*, p.239.
8 J. A. Westrup, *Purcell*. Dent, 1947, p.26.

Ch 33 Humfrey, Wise, Blow, and Turner pp.210-16

1 Samuel Pepys, *Diary,* 22 November 1663.
2 Samuel Pepys, *Diary,* 15 November 1667.
3 Sir John Hawkins, *A General History of the Science and Practice of Music,* Vol. 4. T. Payne and Sons, 1776, p.494.

Ch 34 Purcell, and King James II pp.216-23

1 Sources give this position so many different names, I have defined it by function rather than actual title.
2 Martin Adams, *Henry Purcell: The Origins and Development of his Musical Style.* CUP, 1995, pp.3–4.
3 Alternatively known as 'Jumping Joan', 'Jumping John' and 'Cock o' the North'.

Ch 36 Purcell, the Theatre, and *Dido and Aeneas* pp.229-35

1 Queen Mary attended in 1690; Peter the Great in 1698.
2 Eric Walter White, *A History of English Opera.* Faber and Faber, 1983, p.119.
3 This was a wholly different adaptation from the 1674 version by Shadwell with music by Locke.
4 Percy Young, *A History of British Music,* p.256.

Ch 37 After Purcell pp.235-40

1 Quoted in Eric Walter White, *A History of English Opera,* pp.133–4.

Ch 38 Scotland and Ireland in the Early 18th Century pp.240-48

1 Kenneth Elliott & Frederick Rimmer, *A History of Scottish Music,* p.45.
2 Michel Lambert was also the father-in-law of Jean-Baptiste Lully.
3 A lyra viol is a small bass viol.
4 A Scotch snap is where a short accented note is followed by a longer one. It is also known as the Scotch catch.
5 Cousser is often referred to as Chapel-Master at Trinity College but this is not supported by College records.
6 This anecdote has been much repeated and much embroidered. This version is taken from an anthology, *The Power of Music,* published by J. Harris, 1814, the earliest version of the tale I could find.

Ch 39 The Arrival of Handel pp.248-58

1 It has also been suggested that, as a Catholic, Geminiani did not wish to accept a post that would involve co-operation with the Anglican Church of Ireland.

2 James Anderson Winn, *Queen Anne, Patroness of the Arts*. OUP, 2014, p.443.
3 Eric Walter White, *A History of English Opera*, p.144.
4 John Mainwaring, *Memoirs of the Life of the Late George Frederic Handel: To which is Added a Catalogue of His Works and Observations Upon Them*. R. & J. Dodsley, 1760.
5 Donald Burrows, *Handel*. Oxford, 1994, pp.72–3.
6 Donald Burrows, *Handel*, p.97.

Ch 40 Handel, the Royal Academy of Music, & Ballad Opera pp.258-68

1 In the first few performances, all the airs were sung unaccompanied, but Rich insisted that proper accompaniment was necessary and Pepusch made the arrangements.
2 Eric Walter White, *A History of English Opera*, p.179.
3 Rachel Cowgill & Peter Holman, *Music in the British Provinces, 1690–1914*, p.77.
4 W.T. Moncrieff, 'Remarks', *The Devil to Pay*. Thomas Richardson, 1831, p.1.

Ch 41 Handel and the Oratorio pp.268-79

1 *Faulkner's Journal* (Dublin), 23 March 1742.
2 *Faulkner's Journal* (Dublin), 10 March and 14 April 1742.
3 The number of movements varies between 47 and 52, depending on the edition; this is from the 1959 Novello edition.
4 D.M. Jackson, 'Bach, Handel and the Chevalier Taylor', *Medical History*, Vol. 12, No. 4, October 1968, pp.385–93.
5 Approximately £3.4 million at 2015 values.
6 Ernest Ford, *A Short History of English Music*. McBride Nast & Co, New York, 1912.

Ch 42 The Pleasure Gardens, and the Folk Tradition pp.279-85

1 http://www.vauxhallgardens.com/vauxhall_gardens_briefhistory_page.html. Consulted 22 March 2015.
2 Also known as 'Johnnie o' Cocklesmuir' and 'Johnnie the Brine'.

Ch 43 Greene, Boyce, and Avison pp.286-93

1 Ernest Walker, *A History of Music in England*. Oxford, 1952, p.254.
2 Ernest Walker, *A History of Music in England*, p.255.

Ch 44 Thomas Arne pp.293-98

1 Unfortunately, only a fraction of his theatre music survives, many manuscripts having been destroyed in a disastrous fire in 1808.

2 Arne's sister, Susannah, married Theophilus Cibber, son of the poet and playwright Colley Cibber, whose company was in residence at Drury Lane.

3 William Hayman Cummings, *Dr Arne and Rule Britannia.* Novello & Company, 1912.

4 George Winchester Stone, *The Stage and the Page.* U of California P, 1981, p.130.

Ch 45 Continental Music, and Carl Abel pp.298-303

1 Allatson Burgh, *Anecdotes of Music.* Longman Hurst Rees Orme & Brown, 1814, p.418.

2 Breitkopf & Härtel, who published the first complete edition of Mozart's work between 1877 and 1883, catalogued this piece as Mozart's 3rd symphony.

Ch 46 The London Bach, and Frederick Herschel pp.304-10

1 Born Theresa Imer, she had married a singer named Pompeati, been the the mistress of an Italian senator and a German Margave. She sang sometimes as Pompeati and sometimes as Trenti, and appears to have borrowed the name Cornelys from a Dutchman.

2 Pieces which feature solo instruments, but not with the same prominence as a concerto, so that the solo patt or parts are retained within the orchestral mix.

3 First published as an introductory essay to the second edition of Boyce's *Cathedral Music* (1788).

4 http://www.ram.ac.uk/museum/item/20691. Consulted 12.06.2015.

5 Percy Scholes, *The Great Dr Burney,* Vol. 1, OUP, 1948, p.190.

6 Vincent Duckles, 'Sir William Herschel as a Composer', *Publications of the Astronomical Society of the Pacific,* Vol. 74, No. 436, 1961, p.55–9.

Ch 48 John Wesley, and West Gallery Music pp.315-21

1 Percy Young, *A History of British Music,* p.366.

2 Quoted in Sally Drage, 'Performance practice in 18th-century Georgian psalmody', http://www.gallerymusic.co.uk/articles/GP1/GP1-5-Drage.pdf. Consulted 20.09.2015. Georgian psalmody is an occasionally-used alternative name for West Gallery music, but as the music was not whole confined to the Georgian period and not wholly confined to psalms, the term West Gallery music is preferred here.

Ch 49 Hook, Dibdin, Shield, & the Historical Perspective pp.322-30

1 Timothy Rishton, 'William Smethergell, Organist', *Musical Times,* Vol. 124, No. 1684, June 1983, pp.381–3.

Ch 50 A Reverence for Foreigners, and Haydn pp.330-37

1 *Morning Chronicle,* 21 March 1776; *Morning Post,* 16 March 1778. Quoted in http://rslade.co.uk/18th-century-music/composers/thomas-linley-the-younger/. Consulted 1 October 2015.

2 It did not become a palace until the nineteenth century.

3 *L'anima del filosofo* was not premiered until 1951, and was not premiered in London until 1955.

Ch 51 The Glee pp.337-44

1 Brian Robbins, *The Catch Club in Eighteenth Century England.* http://artbourgogne.free.fr/catchandglee/. Consulted 26.10.2015.

2 Both works were originally listed as motets and Wesley seems to have referred to them as such. These days, they are sometimes referred to as Georgian anthems. It scarcely matters.

Printed Sources

Abraham, Gerald, *The Concise Oxford History of Music*. Reader's Union, 1979.

Adams, Martin, *Henry Purcell: The Origins and Development of his Musical Style*. CUP, 1995.

Anon, 'Shetland Notes and Queries'. *The Shetland Times*, 14 May 1887.

Anon, 'The Philharmonic Society'. *Quarterly Musical Magazine and Review*, Vol. 1, 1818.

Anon, 'The Present State of Music in England'. *Quarterly Musical Magazine and Review*, 1824, pp.281–292.

Anon, 'The Present State of Vocal Art in England', *Quarterly Musical Magazine and Review*, 1824, pp.1–17.

Anon, 'Walter Parratt, February 10, 1841 – March 27, 1924'. *Musical Times*, Vol. 65, No. 975, 1924, pp.401–403.

Archer, Jayne Elisabeth, Elizabeth Goldrin, and Sarah Knight, *The Progresses, Pageants, and Entertainments of Queen Elizabeth I*. OUP, 2009.

Auden, W. H., Kallman, Chester, and Nora Greenberg, eds., *An Elizabethan Song Book*. Faber & Faber, 1957.

Bacharach, A. L., *British Music in Our Time*. Pelican, 1946.

Bailey, Leslie, *The Gilbert and Sullivan Book*. Cassell, 1952.

Baker, Richard Anthony, *British Music Hall: An Illustrated History*. Pen and Sword, 2014.

Baldwin, David, *Royal Prayer: A Surprising History*. A & C Black, 2010.

Banfield, Stephen, *Gerald Finzi*. Faber & Faber, 1997.

Barlow, Michael, *Whom the Gods Love: the Life and Music of George Butterworth*. Toccata P, 1997.

Bathgate, Gordon, *Voices from the Ether*. Lulu.com, 2012.

Bax, Arnold, *Farewell, My Youth*. Longmans, 1943.

Bearman, C. J., 'Cecil Sharp in Somerset: Some Reflections on the Work of David Harker'. *Folklore*, No. 113, 2002, pp.11–34.

Beecham, Thomas, 'Dame Ethel Smyth'. *Musical Times*, Vol. 99, No. 1385, July 1958, pp.363–5.

Bicknell, Stephen, *The History of the English Organ*. CUP, 1996.

Bliss, Arthur, *et al.*, 'Arnold Bax 1883–1953'. *Music & Letters*, Vol. 35, No. 1, January 1954, pp.1–14.

Boden, Anthony, *Three Choirs: A History of the Festival*. Alan Sutton, 1992.

Boeringer, James, *Organa Britannica: Organs in Great Britain, 1660–1860.* Bucknell UP, 1989.

Bowen, Meirion ed., *Tippett on Music.* Clarendon, 1995.

Bowers, Jane & Tick, Judith, *Women Making Music: The Western Tradition, 1150–1950.* U of Illinois P, 1987.

Broadwood, John & Dusart, Geoffrey, *Old English Songs, as now sung by the Peasantry of Surrey and Sussex.* Betts, 1847.

Brown, Clive, *Louis Spohr: A Critical Biography.* CUP, 2006.

Budd, Vincent, *An Introduction to the Life and Work of Sir Granville Bantock.* Gnosis, 2000.

Burgh, Allatson, *Anecdotes of Music.* Longman, Hurst, Rees, Orme & Brown, 1814.

Burke, John, *Musical Landscapes.* Webb & Bower, 1983.

Burney, Charles, *A General History of Music,* 1789.

Burrows, Donald, *Handel.* Oxford, 1994.

Burton, Humphrey, *Menuhin.* Faber & Faber, 2000.

Bush, Douglas and Richard Kassel, eds. *The Organ: An Encyclopedia.* Routledge, 2006.

Buttall, Philip R., notes to *Frank Bridge, Cyril Scott, Piano Quintets.* NAXOS 8.571355, 2015.

Carley, Lionel, *Edvard Grieg in England.* Boydell, 2006.

Carley, Lionel, *Grieg and Delius.* Marion Boyars, 1993.

Carpenter, Humphrey, *Benjamin Britten.* Faber & Faber, 1993.

Carpenter, Humphrey, *The Envy of the World.* Weidenfeld & Nicolson, 1996.

Cartellieri, Otto, *The Court of Burgundy.* Taylor & Francis, 1972.

Carwood, Andrew, notes to *Byrd: the Great Service.* Hyperion, CDA65573, 2005.

Chappell, William, *Popular Music of the Olden Time.* Cramer, Beale, & Chappell, 1859.

Chivers, Richard William, *The Hymns and Responds of John Sheppard.* M.A. thesis, U of Durham, 1997.

Clark, Bunker, 'Adrian Batten and John Barnard: Colleagues and Collaborators'. *Musica Disciplina,* Vol. 22, 1968, pp.207–29.

Coles, John M., 'Irish Bronze-Age Horns and their Relations with Northern Europe'. *Proceedings of the Prehistoric Society,* 1963, Vol. XXIX, pp.326–56.

Collinson, Francis M., *The Bagpipe: The History of a Musical Instrument.* Routledge, 1975.

Collis, Louise, *Impetuous Heart: the Story of Ethel Smyth.* William Kimber, 1984.

Cooke, Mervyn, *A History of Film Music.* CUP, 2008.

Copper, Bob, *A Song for Every Season.* Heinemann, 1971.

Cowgill, Rachel & Peter Holman, eds. *Music in the British Provinces, 1690–1914*. Routledge, 2007.

Cowgill, Rachel & Julian Rushton, eds. *Europe, Empire and Spectacle in British Music*. Ashgate, 2006.

Cummings, William Hayman, *Dr Arne and Rule Britannia*. Novello, 1912.

Cunningham, John Patrick, *The Consort Music of William Lawes, 1602–1645*. Boydell & Brewer, 2010.

Davies, Norman, *The Isles*. Macmillan, 1999.

Davies, Walford *et al.*, 'Charles Villiers Stanford'. *Music & Letters*, Vol. V, No. 3, July 1924, pp. 193–207.

de Chabannes, James Grier Ademar, 'Carolingian Musical Practices and 'Nota Romana'. *Journal of the American Musicological Society*, Vol. 56, No. 1, Spring 2003.

de Sola Pinto, Vivian and A. E. Rodway, eds., *The Common Muse*. Penguin, 1965.

Denton, Jeffrey Howard, *English Royal Chapels 1100–1300*. Manchester U P, 1970.

Dobson, Collet, 'State of the Royal Academy of Music'. *The Musical World*, J. Alfred Novello, 1837, pp.18–21.

Downing, Sarah Jane, *The English Pleasure Garden*. Shire, 2009.

Drummond, Pippa, *The Provincial Music Festival in England 1784–1914*. Ashgate, 2013.

Duckles, Vincent, 'Sir William Herschel as a Composer'. *Publications of the Astronomical Society of the Pacific*, Vol. 74, No. 436, 1961, p.55–9.

Elliott, Kenneth & Frederick Rimmer, *A History of Scottish Music*. BBC, 1973.

Fawkes, Richard, *The Classical Music Map of Britain*. Elliot & Thompson, 2010.

Fellowes, Edmund H., *English Cathedral Music*. Methuen, 1941.

Fifield, Christopher, *The German Symphony between Beethoven and Brahms*. Ashgate, 2015.

Foreman, Lewis, *Bax*. Scholar, 1983.

Foreman, Lewis, *From Parry to Britten*. Batsford, 1987.

Foreman, Lewis, notes to *Dyson: The Canterbury Pilgrims*. Chandos, CHAN 9531(2), 1997.

Foreman, Lewis, 'The Canterbury Pilgrims'. *Three Choirs Festival Hereford 2012*, Three Choirs, 2012.

Frank, Alan, *Modern British Composers*. Denis Dobson, 1953.

Frogley, Alain & Aidan Thomson, eds., T*he Cambridge Companion to Vaughan Williams*. CUP, 2013.

Fry, Helen, *Music & Men*. History P, 2008.

Fuller Maitland, J. A., *English Music in the XIXth Century*. Grant Richards, 1902.

Fuller Maitland, J. A, ed. *Grove's Dictionary of Music and Musicians*. Macmillan, 1922.

Gant, Andrew, *O Sing unto the Lord*. Profile Books, 2015.

Gates, Eugene, 'Dame Ethel Smyth: Pioneer of English Opera'. *Kapralova Society Journal*, Vol. 11, No. 1, 2013, pp 1–9.

Gaul, Liam, *Masters of Irish Music*. Nonsuch, 1976.

Gibson, James M., *Kent: Diocese of Canterbury*, Vol. 3. U of Toronto P, 2002.

Gilbert, W. S., *The Savoy Operas*. Macmillan, 1926.

Gillespie, Don. C., *The Search for Thomas Ward, Teacher of Frederick Delius*. U of Florida P, 1996.

Gillies, Midge, *Marie Lloyd: the One and Only*. Gollancz, 1999.

Gollancz, Victor, *Journey Towards Music*. Gollancz, 1964.

Grattan Flood, W. H., 'New Facts about John Dowland'. *The Gentleman's Magazine*, 1906, pp.287–91.

Greenfield, Edward, 'Sullivan (The) Golden Legend'. *The Gramophone*, Awards Issue, 2001.

Gregory, E. David, *The Late Victorian Folksong Revival: The Persistence of English Melody, 1878–1903*. Scarecrow Press, 2010.

Hadow, W. H., *English Music*. Longmans, Green, 1931.

Hand, Colin, *John Taverner: His Life and Music*. Eulenburg, 1978.

Harker, David, *Fakesong*. Open UP, 1985.

Harley, John, *The World of William Byrd: Musicians, Merchants and Magnates*. Ashgate, 2010.

Harman, Alec, and Wilfred Mellers, *Man and his Music*. Barrie & Rockliff, 1962.

Haskell, Harry, *The Early Music Revival*. Thames & Hudson, 1988.

Haweis, H. R., *My Musical Life*. Longmans Green, 1898.

Headington, Christopher, *Peter Pears*. Faber & Faber, 1992.

Henigan, Julie, *Literacy and Orality in Eighteenth-Century Irish Song*. Routledge, 2015.

Hoare, Philip, *Noel Coward*. Sinclair-Stevenson, 1995.

Hogwood, Christopher, notes to *Orlando Gibbons: Keyboard Music*. Decca Music Group, DSLO515, 1975.

Hold, Trevor, *Parry to Finzi*. Boydell, 2002.

Holland, A. K., *Henry Purcell*. Penguin, 1948.

Hollingworth, Robert, notes to *Thomas Tomkins: Music Divine*. Chandos, CHAN 0680, 2002.

Holst, Imogen, *Gustav Holst: A Biography*. OUP, 1988.

Hooker, John, *The Ancient History and Description of the City of Exeter*. Andrews & Trewman, 1765.

Howes, Frank, *The English Musical Renaissance*. Secker & Warburg, 1966.

Hughes, Meirion & Robert Stradling, *The English Musical Renaissance 1840–1940*. Manchester U P, 2001.

Huntley, John, *British Film Music.* Skelton Robinson, 1947.
Hurd, Michael, notes to *Bantock.* Hyperion, CDA66450, 1991.
Jacobs, Arthur ed., *Choral Music.* Penguin, 1963.
Johansen, Claes, *Procul Harum: Beyond the Pale.* SAF, 2000.
Johnson, Stephen, 'Darkness and Light'. *BBC Proms Festival Guide 2017*, BBC, 2017, pp.46–49.
Johnston, Roy & Declan Plummer, *The Musical Life of Nineteenth-Century Belfast.* Ashgate, 2015.
Kassler, Michael, *The Music Trade in Georgian England.* Ashgate, 2011.
Keates, Jonathan, *Handel: the Man and his Music.* Gollancz, 1992.
Keates, Jonathan, *Purcell.* Chatto & Windus, 1995.
Kemp, Ian, *Tippett: The Composer and his Music.* Oxford, 1987.
Kennedy, Michael, Joyce Kennedy and Tim Rutherford-Johnson, eds, *The Oxford Dictionary of Music.* OUP, 5th ed., 2013.
Kennedy, Michael, *Portrait of Walton.* OUP, 1990.
Kennedy, Michael J., *Portrait of Elgar*, OUP, 1987.
Kildea, Paul, ed., *Britten on Music.* OUP, 2003.
Klinck, Anne Lingard & Anne Marie Rasmussen, *Medieval Woman's Song: Cross-Cultural Approaches.* U of Pennsylvania P, 2002.
Kynaston, David, *Family Britain.* Bloomsbury, 2009.
Lambert, Constant, 'Master of English Song'. *Radio Times,* 1 July 1938.
Lambert, Constant, *Music Ho!* Pelican, 1948.
Lang, Paul Henry, *Music in Western Civilization.* Dent, 1963.
Le Huray, Peter, 'Towards a Definitive Study of Pre-Restoration Anglican Service Music'. *Musica Disciplina*, Vol. 14, 1960, pp.167–95.
Lee-Brown, Martin, & Paul Guinery, *Delius and his Music.* Boydell, 2014.
Linklater Thomson, C., *A Child's History of Great Britain.* Horace Marshall, [1910].
Littlejohn, J. H., *The Scottish Music Hall 1880–1990.* G. C. Books (Wigtown), 1990.
Lloyd, A. L., *Folk Song in England.* Panther, 1969.
Lloyd, Stephen, *H.Balfour Gardiner.* CUP, 1984.
Macfarren, G. A., 'Barnett, John'. *The Imperial Dictionary of Universal Biography*, Vol. 1, William Mackenzie, 1863, p.389.
Macfarren, G. A., 'Jerusalem'. *Musical Times,* Vol. 5, No. 100, 1852, pp.51–54 & 59.
Mackerness, E. D., *A Social History of English Music.* Routledge & Kegan Paul, 1964.
Mainwaring, John, *Memoirs of the Life of the Late George Frederic Handel: To which is Added a Catalogue of His Works and Observations Upon Them.* Dodsley, 1760.

Marek, George, *Beethoven: Biography of a Genius.* Funk & Wagnalls, 1969.

Martin, Colin & Parker, Geoffrey, *The Spanish Armada.* Manchester U P, 1999.

Matthews, Betty 'The Earliest English Organ-Builders'. *British Institute of Organ Studies Reporter,* January 1982, Vol. 1, VI, No. 1.

McLucas, Anne Dhu, 'Forbes' *Cantus: Songs & Fancies* Revisited'. *Defining Strains: The Musical Life of the Scots in the Seventeenth Century*, Lang, 2007.

McVeagh, Diana, *Gerald Finzi.* Boydell, 2005.

McVeigh, Simon, *Concert Life in London from Mozart to Haydn.* CUP, 2006.

Mellers, Wilfrid, *Vaughan Williams and the Vision of Albion.* Barrie & Jenkins, 1989.

Meyer, Ernst H., *English Chamber Music.* Lawrence & Wishart, 1946.

Midgley, Samuel, *My 70 Year's Musical Memories.* Novello, 1934.

Mole, John, *The Sultan's Organ.* Fortune, 2012.

Moore, Frank Ledlie ed., *The Handbook of Gilbert and Sullivan.* Barker, 1962.

Moore, Jerrold Northrop, *Edward Elgar: A Creative Life.* OUP, 1984.

Morley, Sheridan, *A Talent to Amuse.* Penguin, 1974.

Moroney, Davitt, notes to *William Byrd, the Complete Keyboard Music.* Hyperion, CDA66551/7, 1999.

Morris, John, *Music and British Wartime Propaganda 1935–1945.* Ph.D. thesis, U of Exeter, 2011.

Motion, Andrew, *The Lamberts.* Chatto & Windus, 1986.

Murdoch, Brian & Malcolm K. Read, *Early German Literature and Culture.* Boydell & Brewer, 2004.

Murray, Teresa Ann, *Thomas Morley and the Business of Music in Elizabethan England.* Ph.D. thesis, U of Birmingham, 2010.

Norwich, John Julius, *Fifty Years of Glyndebourne.* Cape, 1985.

O'Donovan, Matthew, notes to *John Sheppard, Media Vita.* Harmonia Mundi, HMU 807509, 2010.

Palmer, Christopher, *George Dyson: man and music.* Thames, 1996.

Palmer, Russell, *British Music.* Skelton Robinson, 1947.

Palmer, William, 'Gibbons's Verse Anthems'. *Music & Letters,* Vol. 35, No. 2, April 1954, pp.107–113.

Parry, C. Hubert, *The Art of Music.* Routledge & Kegan Paul, 1950.

Pearsall, Ronald, *Victorian Popular Music.* David & Charles, 1973.

Pearson, Hesketh, *Gilbert and Sullivan.* Penguin, 1950.

Percy, Thomas, *Reliques of Ancient English Poetry.* Frederick Warne, 1887.

Pilkinton, Mark Cartwright, *Bristol*, Vol. 8. U of Toronto P, 1997.

Pirie, Peter J., *The English Musical Renaissance.* Gollancz, 1979.

Poulton, Diana, *John Dowland.* U of California P, 1982.

Pückler-Muskau, Hermann, *Tour in England, Ireland, and France in the Years 1828, 1829*. Trans. Sarah Austin. Carey & Lea, 1833.

Pulling, Christopher, *They Were Singing*. Harrap, 1952.

Pulver, Jeffrey, *A Dictionary of Old English Music and Musical Instruments*. Kegan Paul, Trench, Trubner, 1923.

Rayborn, Tim, *A New English Music: Composers and Folk Traditions in England's Musical Renaissance from the Late 19th to the Mid-20th Century*. McFarland, 2016.

Raynor, Henry, *A Social History of Music from the Middle Ages to Beethoven*. Barrie & Jenkins, 1972.

Reece, Isobel, notes to *Robert Carver*. CORO COR16051, 2006.

Rees, Terence, *Thespis – A Gilbert & Sullivan Enigma*. Dillon's U Bookshop, 1964.

Reese, Gustave, *Music in the Renaissance*. Dent, 1954.

Reid, Charles, *John Barbirolli*. Hamish Hamilton, 1971.

Reid, Charles, *Malcolm Sargent*. Hamish Hamilton, 1968.

Reid, Charles, *Thomas Beecham*. Gollancz, 1962.

Rigney, Anne, *The Afterlives of Walter Scott: Memory on the Move*. OUP, 2012.

Rishton, Timothy 'William Smethergell, Organist'. *Musical Times*, Vol. 124, No. 1684, June 1983, pp.381–3.

Routley, Eric, *A Short History of English Church Music*. Mowbray, 1977.

Russell, Dave, *Popular Music in England 1840–1914: A Social History*. Manchester U P, 1997.

Sandon, Nicholas, notes to *Thomas Tallis, The Complete Works*. Brilliant Classics, 93612.

Sant, John, *Albert Ketèlbey: From the Sanctuary of his Heart*. Manifold, 2001.

Scarisbrick, J. J., *Henry VIII*. Folio Society, 2004.

Schmitz, Oskar A. H., *Das Land ohne Musik: englische Gesellschaftsprobleme*. Georg Müller, Munich, 1914.

Scholes, Percy, *The Great Dr Burney*. OUP, 1948.

Scott, Derek B., *Sounds of the Metropolis: The 19th Century Popular Music Revolution in London, New York, Paris and Vienna*. OUP, 2008.

Scott-Sutherland, Colin, *Arnold Bax*. Dent, 1973.

Self, Geoffrey, *The Music of E. J. Moeran*. Toccata, 1986.

Shaw, George Bernard (Cornetto di Basso), '*Eden*'. *The Nation*, 14 October 1891.

Shead, Richard, *Constant Lambert*. Simon, 1973.

Simpson, Robert ed., *The Symphony 1: Haydn to Dvorak*. Pelican, 1966.

Simpson, Robert ed., *The Symphony 2: Elgar to the Present Day*. Pelican, 1966.

Smith, Bruce R., *The Acoustic World of Early Modern England*. U of Chicago P, 1999.

Smith, William, *The Reasonableness of Setting Forth the Most Worthy Praise of Almighty God.* T & J Swords, 1814.
Smither, Howard E., *A History of the Oratorio: The oratorio in the nineteenth and twentieth centuries.* UNC, 2000.
Sounes, Howard, *Down the Highway: the Life of Bob Dylan*. Black Swan, 2002.
Spencer, Charles, *The World of Sergei Diaghilev*. Penguin, 1979.
Spencer, Neil, 'Ewan MacColl: the godfather of folk who was adored – and feared'. *The Guardian*, 25 January 2015.
Spicer, Paul, *Herbert Howells*, Seren (Bridgend), 1998.
Spicer, Paul, *Sir George Dyson: His Life and Music.* Boydell & Brewer, 2014.
Stanford, Charles Villiers, *Interludes, Records and Reflections.* John Murray, 1922.
Stanley, Bob, 'Acker Bilk: the hitmaker who symbolised the generation gap'. *The Guardian*, 4 November 2014.
Starkey, David & Katie Greening, *Music and Monarchy.* BBC, 2103.
Stephens, G. M., 'The Waits of the City of Norwich'. *Proceedings of the Norfolk and Norwich Archaeological Society*, Norwich, 1933.
Sterndale Bennett, J. R., *The Life of William Sterndale Bennett*, CUP, 1907.
Stevens, Denis, *Tudor Church Music.* Faber & Faber, 1966.
Stoller, Tony, *Classical Music on UK Radio 1945–1995.* Ph.D thesis, U of Bournemouth, 2015.
Stone, George Winchester, *The Stage and the Page.* U of California P, 1981.
Strangways, A. H. Fox & Maud Karpeles, *Cecil Sharp.* OUP, 1955.
Strype, John, *Historical and Biographical Works*, Vol. 24. Clarendon, 1821.
Summerly, Jeremy, notes to *Tye: Missa Euge Bone & Western Wynde Mass.* Hyperion CDA677928, 2012.
Tame, David, *The Secret Power of Music.* Destiny, 1984.
Tarling, Nicholas, *Choral Masterpieces: Major and Minor.* Rowman & Littlefield, 2014.
Temperley, Nicholas, *Music and the Wesleys.*U of Illinois P, 2010.
The Annual Biography and Obituary. Longman, Rees, Orme, Brown, Green & Longman, 1832.
'The Musician About Town', *The Analyst*, Vol. 10. Simpkin & Marshall, 1840, pp.483–491.
Thompson, Wendy *et al*, 'A Sea Symphony'. *Three Choirs Festival Hereford 2012*, Three Choirs, 2012.
Tippett, Michael, '*The Mask of Time*: Work in Progress'. *Comparative Criticism, Volume 4: The Language of the Arts*, CUP, 1982, pp.19–29.
Tippett, Michael, *Those Twentieth Century Blues.* Pimlico, 1994.
Trend, Michael, *The Music Makers.* Macmillan, 1985.
Vaughan Williams, Ralph and A. L. Lloyd, *English Folk Songs.* Penguin, 1959.

Vaughan Williams, Ursula, *RVW.* OUP, 1988.
Walker, Ernest, *A History of Music in England.* Oxford, 1952.
Walton, Susanna, *William Walton: Behind the Façade*. OUP, 1988.
Warlock, Peter, *Thomas Whythorne: An Unknown Elizabethan Composer.* OUP, 1925.
Weibe, Heather, *Britten's Unquiet Pasts: Sound and Memory in Postwar Reconstruction.* CUP, 2012.
Weir, Alison, *The Six Wives of Henry VIII.* Bodley Head, 1991.
Weir, Christopher, *Village and Town Bands*. Shire Publications, 1981.
Westrup, J. A., *Purcell.* Dent, 1947.
White, Eric Walter, *A History of English Opera.* Faber & Faber, 1983.
Whitehouse, Edmund, *London Lights*. This England Books, 2005.
Williams, Ralph, 'Director's Report'. *Royal College of Music Magazine*, Vol. 40. No. 1, 1945.
Winn, James Anderson, *Queen Anne, Patroness of the Arts.* OUP, 2014.
Winnington, G. Peter, *Walter Fuller: The Man Who Had Ideas.* Letterworth, 2014.
Wood, Henry J., *My Life of Music*. Victor Gollancz, 1938.
Wyatt, E. G. P., *St Gregory and the Gregorian Music.* Plainsong and Mediæval Music Society, 1904.
Young, Percy M., *A History of British Music.* Ernest Benn, 1967.
Young, Percy M., *George Grove 1820–1900*. Macmillan, 1980.
Young, Percy M., *Sir Arthur Sullivan*. Dent, 1971.
Young, Percy M., *The Choral Tradition*. Hutchinson, 1962.
Young, Rob, *Electric Eden: In Search of England's Visionary Music.* Faber & Faber, 2011.

Internet Sources

Adoremus, Thomas Cranmer

httpps://adoremus.org/1999/11/15/quotMore-than-the-liberty-of-a-translatorquot/

Alchemydiscussion.com

httpp://www.alchemydiscussion.com/attachment.php?id=449

Allmusic.com

httpp://www.allmusic.com/artist/thomas-tomkins-mn0001379727/biography

Ancient Music Ireland

httpp://ancientmusicireland.com/page/instruments-through-the-ages.html#stoneage

Ancient Music Ireland.

httpp://ancientmusicireland.com/page/instruments-from-outside-of-ireland.html

Archive.org

httpp://web.archive.org/web/20090426001612/http:/www.andante.com/article/article.cfm?id=16297

Art Bourgone International

httpp://artbourgogne.free.fr/catchandglee/

BBC News

httpp://www.bbc.co.uk/news/uk-scotland-highlands-islands-17537147

BBC Scotland

httpp://www.bbc.co.uk/scotland/music/scotlandsmusic/pdfs/scotlandsmusic_15.pdf.

Body Literature

httpp://bodyliterature.com/2012/10/30/dafydd-ap-gwilym/

Broadview Press, John Bale

httpp://sites.broadviewpress.com/16cpoetryprose/files/2011/09/2-16C-Anth-Online-BALE.pdf

Buckle, Alexandra, 'Power, Leonel, Lionel'

httpps://www.academia.edu/148886/_Power_Leonel_Lionel_

Drage, Sally, 'Performance practice in 18th-century Georgian psalmody'

httpp://www.gallerymusic.co.uk/articles/GP1/GP1-5-Drage.pdf

Eighteenth Century English Music

http://rslade.co.uk/

httpp://rslade.co.uk/18th-century-music/composers/thomas-linley-the-younger/

Gowen, Margaret, '4000-year-old music'.

httpp://www.gaitadefoles.net/artigos/4000pipesenglish.htm

Grattan Floood, William, H., A History of Irish Music
httpp://www.libraryireland.com/IrishMusic/X.php

Hanover Historical Texts, Injunctions of 1559
httpp://history.hanover.edu/texts/engref/er78.html

Inchcolm Antiphoner
httpp://images.is.ed.ac.uk/luna/servlet/detail/UoEwmm~1~1~34071~101678:Inchcolm-Antiphoner,-circa-1340,-f-

Indiana U Bloomington
httpp://www.chmtl.indiana.edu/tml/15th/TINPRO_TEXT.html
httpp://www.chmtl.indiana.edu/tme/16th/CORNPAR5_TEXT.html

Iron Age Instruments.
httpp://homepage.eircom.net/~bronzeagehorns/printablePages/ironage.html

O'Dwyer, Simon, 'Four Voices of the Bronze Age Horns of Ireland'.
www.ancientmusicireland.com/files/contents/file/FourVoices.pdf

O'Dwyer, Simon, 'The Kilfaddy Four – Transition'
www.ancientmusicireland.com/files/contents/file/FourVoices.pdf

orlandogibbons.com
httpp://www.orlandogibbons.com/works/

Oxford Dictionary of National Biography
http://www.oxforddnb.com/

Oxford Music Online
http://www.oxfordmusiconline.com

Pienaar, Daniel Ben, 'Revisiting the Keyboard Music of Orlando Gibbons'
httpp://danielbenpienaar.com/essays/Revisting%20The%20Keyboard%20Music%20Of%20Orlando%20Gibbons.htm

Royal Academy of Music
httpp://www.ram.ac.uk/museum/item/20691

Smart, Jason, 'In Quires and Places where they Sing'
httpp://www.plymouthorganists.org.uk/news_notes/2003-2_quires_and_places.pdf

Statutes of Kilkenny, Article XV
httpp://www.mesacc.edu/~thoqh49081/celtic/KilkennyStatutes.html.

The Waits Website
httpp://townwaits.org.uk/history_norwich.shtml

Theory of Music
httpps://theoryofmusic.wordpress.com/2012/07/28/licence-granted-to-thomas-tallis-and-william-byrd-in-1575-modern-english/

Thorpe, Vanessa, 'Shakespeare's last masterpiece was really a musical'
httpps://www.theguardian.com/culture/2011/aug/21/robert-johnson-tempest-william-shakespeare-composer

UK National Archives, Act of Supremacy
httpp://www.nationalarchives.gov.uk/pathways/citizenship/rise_parliament/transcripts/henry_supremacy.htm

Vauxhallgardens.com
httpp://www.vauxhallgardens.com/vauxhall_gardens_briefhistory_page.html

War Music
httpp://www.ecwsa.org/entwarmusic.html

Warwick, Alistair
httpps://alistairwarwick.com/content/wode-partbooks

Whitwell, Essays on the Origins of Western Music
httpp://www.whitwellessays.com/

Index

I = Volume One; II = Volume Two

Main entry in **bold**

Lightning Source UK Ltd.
Milton Keynes UK
UKOW04n1412120118
316029UK00002B/39/P

9 782970 065463